Paved with Good Intentions

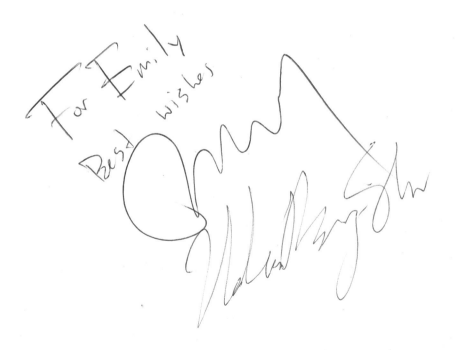

Paved with Good Intentions

Canada's development NGOs
from idealism to imperialism

Nikolas Barry-Shaw
Dru Oja Jay

with the collaboration of

Yves Engler

FERNWOOD PUBLISHING
Halifax & Winnipeg

Editing: Queequeg McVeigh
Book and cover design: Dru Oja Jay
Cover photo: Kim Ives
Printed and bound in Canada.

Published in Canada by Fernwood Publishing
32 Oceanvista Lane, Black Point, Nova Scotia, B0J 1B0
and 748 Broadway Avenue, Winnipeg, Manitoba, R3G 0X3
www.fernwoodpublishing.ca

Fernwood Publishing Company Limited gratefully acknowledges the financial support of the Government of Canada through the Canada Book Fund and the Canada Council for the Arts, the Nova Scotia Department of Communities, Culture and Heritage, the Manitoba Department of Culture, Heritage and Tourism under the Manitoba Publishers Marketing Assistance Program and the Province of Manitoba, through the Book Publishing Tax Credit, for our publishing program.

Library and Archives Canada Cataloguing in Publication

Barry-Shaw, Nikolas, 1982-
        Paved with good intentions : Canada's development NGOs from idealism to imperialism / Nikolas Barry-Shaw & Dru Oja Jay.

Includes bibliographical references.
ISBN 978-1-55266-399-8

        1. Non-governmental organizations--Canada. 2. Non-governmental organizations--Political activity--Canada. I. Jay, Dru Oja, 1980- II. Title.

HC60.B3147 2011   338.910971   C2011-903373-9

Contents

Acknowledgements

This book was made possible with the contributions of many people. It would not have come to be in its current form without Bianca Mugyenyi. Eric Schragge provided early guidance. Beverley Rach and Errol Sharpe of Fernwood Publishing have been patient with us and invaluable to the project. Gary Engler provided valuable publishing expertise. Thanks are also due to Martin Lukacs, who made available his considerable energies and editorial incisiveness. Dorothy Shaw, Stephen Barry and Aude Maltais-Landry gave much love, help and free food along the way. Thanks also to those who provided important encouragement, support and feedback: Jesse Freeston, Araceli Gonzalez, Diego Hausfather, Tom Jay, Sara Mall Johani, Isabel Macdonald, Claudia Masferrer-Leon, Amy Miller, Mabel Reyes and Maya Rolbin-Ghanie.

Many people read parts of the manuscript, made suggestions and caught typos and inconsistencies, including: Zinta Avens Auzins, Geneva Guerin, Al Hausfather, Nadia Hausfather, Dana Holtby, Steven Kaal, Tim McSorley, Linda Morrison, Julie Offerdal, Dawn Paley, Ted Rutland, Georgia Schurman, Chris Scott, Naava Smolash, Kevin Sutton, Lesley Thompson, and Angela Toharia.

We are also grateful to those who contributed to our analysis of NGOs, through conversations and e-mail exchanges. Among the many are: Roger Annis, Lisa Bornstein, Dominique Caouette, Bernard Cloutier, Aziz Choudry, Ben Dangl, John Dillon, Pascale Dufour, Shelley Feldman, Anthony Fenton, Rex Fyles, Todd Gordon, Guillaume Hebert, Tom Heinemann, Bill Hynd, Jeffrey Jackson, Lamia Karim, Jooneed Khan, David Lewis, Dave Markland, Annie McShiras, Pierre Minn, Brian K. Murphy, Adrienne Pine, Melanie Pinkert, Karen Rauh, Joan Roelofs, Kevin Skerrett, Macdonald Stainsby, Brian Tomlinson, and Dexter X.

We continue to be inspired by the work of our comrades in the Haiti solidarity movement. Some of those not already named include: Serge Bouchereau, Isabeau Doucet, Kim Ives, Stu Neatby, Justin Podur, Richard Sanders, Jean Saint-Vil, Mark Schuller, and Brendan Stone.

The list does not end there, and we regret the inevitable omissions. While the input of those listed above has been essential, all responsibility for the content of this work rests with us; any errors are ours alone.

Nikolas Barry-Shaw and Dru Oja Jay
Montreal, February 2012

For Lovinsky Pierre-Antoine and all those who give their lives for Haiti's liberation.

If I could fool myself, in a minute I'd fool you.
—Elvis Costello

Acronyms

APEC - Asia-Pacific Economic Co-operation
AQOCI - *Association québécoise des organismes de coopération internationale*
CARE - Cooperative for Assistance and Relief Everywhere
CBC - Canadian Broadcasting Corporation
CIDA - Canadian International Development Agency
CCIC - Canadian Council for International Cooperation
CECI - *Centre d'étude et de coopération internationale*
CLAC - *Convergence des luttes anticapitalistes*
CPH - *Concertation pour Haïti*
CSIS - Canadian Security Intelligence Service
CSR - Corporate Social Responsibility
CUSO - Canadian University Service Overseas
DFAIT - Department of Foreign Affairs and International Trade
DFID - Department for International Development (UK)
FFHC - Freedom From Hunger Campaign
FTAA - Free Trade Area of the Americas
FTQ - *Fédération des travailleurs et travailleuses du Québec*
GDP - Gross Domestic Product
HIPC - Heavily Indebted Poor Country
HNP - Haitian National Police
ICFID - Inter-Church Fund for International Development
IMF - International Monetary Fund
MAI - Multilateral Agreement on Investment
MINUSTAH - United Nations Stabilization Mission in Haiti
MSF - *Médecins sans frontières*
NAFTA - North American Free Trade Agreement
NATO - North Atlantic Treaty Organization
NCHR - National Coalition for Haitian Rights
NSP - National Solidarity Program
OAS - Organization of American States
OECD - Organisation for Economic Co-operation and Development
OPL - *Organisation politique Lavalas / Organisation du peuple en lutte*
PAMSCAD - Programme of Actions to Mitigate the Social Costs of Adjustment
PAPDA - *Plateforme haitienne de plaidoyer pour un développement alternatif*
PPP - Public Participation Program
PRSP - Poverty Reduction Strategy Papers
PRT - Provincial Reconstruction Team
RCMP - Royal Canadian Mounted Police
RQIC - *Réseau québécois sur l'intégration continentale*
SUCO - *Service universitaire canadien outre-mer*
USAID - United States Agency for International Development
WUSC - World University Service of Canada
WTO - World Trade Organization

Preface

Everybody's worried about stopping terrorism. Well, there's a really easy way: stop participating in it.
—Noam Chomsky [1]

One of the most striking things about the 2004 coup is the vigorously political role played by … NGOs, charities and human rights groups [which] so often disguise their political impact behind an ostensibly neutral and principled if not moral façade. If you can't trust a non-governmental charity then what can you trust?
—Peter Hallward [2]

This book was born in Haiti.

In the closing days of February 2004, Haiti's democratically-elected government was removed in a bloody coup d'état. U.S. Marines forced President Jean-Bertrand Aristide onto a State Department plane and exiled him to the Central African Republic. Elected officials at every level of government associated with Aristide's Fanmi Lavalas—Haiti's most popular political party—were removed from their posts. Over the next two years, a violent, unelected regime ruled Haiti. This episode saw thousands of Haitians killed, and thousands more imprisoned or forced into hiding.*

Haiti had burst onto the headlines in the months preceding the coup, but it disappeared from the media's attention shortly thereafter. U.S., French and Canadian troops were in control of the country as it descended into a nightmare of bloodshed and deepening poverty. But with hardly any questioning of U.S. claims that President Aristide had voluntarily resigned, foreign intervention was absolved of any responsibility for the situation. Journalists wearily described Haiti as experiencing yet another cycle of internecine violence and chaos and the news media quickly lost interest.

---

* For a detailed account of the events surrounding the February 2004 coup in Haiti, see Peter Hallward's *Damming the Flood: Haiti, Aristide and the Politics of Containment.*

In 2003, we knew little about Haiti. But as the coup unfolded, we began to dig deeper, trying to understand what was going on and how Canada was involved. Following events in Haiti during the 2004-2006 period served as a crash course in Haitian politics and introduced us to the dark side of Canadian foreign policy. What we discovered was probably Canada's worst foreign policy crime in the last 50 years. Even more shocking, though, was the role that Canadian development NGOs played in the sordid affair.

Canada's Participation in the Terror Campaign

The Canadian government was deeply involved in every aspect of the coup. Along with the U.S. and the European Union, Canada had cut off aid to the Fanmi Lavalas government while funding its opponents. Even worse, Canada participated in the planning and execution of the toppling of the government and the kidnapping of Aristide. On the night of the coup, 125 Canadian troops were on the ground in Port-au-Prince, securing the airport from which U.S. soldiers would fly Aristide into exile. Canada helped to install the new, unelected regime and provided it with hundreds of millions of aid dollars. Perhaps most shameful of all, Canadian troops and police officers dispatched to Haiti were actively supporting the repression.†

With full diplomatic and financial backing from Canada, the interim regime set about mercilessly persecuting those calling for the return of democracy. Supporters of the government, in particularly those in the strongly pro-Lavalas *quartiers populaires* of Port-au-Prince suffered massacres, summary executions, violent and indiscriminate raids on poor neighborhoods, and arbitrary mass arrests. Police attacked journalists and shot and killed peaceful demonstrators on numerous occasions.

Victims were overwhelmingly residents of the slums, whose votes had twice propelled Aristide to the Presidency. Aristide enjoyed strong support from Haiti's poor majority due to his moves to redistribute wealth, raise minimum wages and increase social spending, but these same policies had angered the country's light-skinned elite—and their foreign business partners, which included major Canadian multinationals. Thanks to its desperately poor population, Haiti was (and still is today) seen as an ideal export platform to the North American market, especially for labour-intensive industries like textiles and apparel manufacturing benefiting

---

† For a concise critique of Canada's role in the coup, see Yves Engler and Anthony Fenton's *Canada in Haiti*.

from its low-wage workforce. Aristide's mildly reformist agenda, however, frustrated the full implementation of what some Haiti scholars have called the "sweatshop model of development."[3]

Our Involvement

In the face of this Canada-backed repression, we felt we had to act. Our sentiment at the time was summed up by Noam Chomsky's formulation:

> Suppose you're living in a free, democratic society, with lots of privilege, enormous, incomparable freedoms, and the government carries out violent, brutal acts. Are you responsible for it? Yeah, a lot more responsible, because there's a lot that you can do about it. If you share responsibility in criminal acts, you are liable for the consequences.[4]

We became involved in a small but growing Haiti solidarity movement in Canada. In early 2005, we formed Haiti Action Montreal, to fight for the restoration of Haiti's democracy and to stir up opposition to the suffering inflicted by our government's foreign policy. We met up with members of Montreal's Haitian community opposed to the coup and began organizing demonstrations and pickets to draw attention to the situation. We hosted public film screenings, distributed leaflets at public events, and conducted a city-wide stickering campaign calling on the Canadian government to end its support for the regime. We linked up with other solidarity groups across the country and formed the Canada-Haiti Action Network to co-ordinate our efforts nationwide.

We lobbied and pressured politicians responsible for the Haiti dossier. We pressed them to publicly acknowledge what was going on, in an attempt to build up political pressure that might force them to reverse course. We met with then-Foreign Affairs Minister Pierre Pettigrew in February 2005 at his constituency office and presented him a human rights report from University of Miami Law School documenting the repression occurring in Haiti. When journalists later asked about human rights abuses in Haiti, Pettigrew scornfully dismissed the report–whose findings were corroborated by multiple sources–as "propaganda which is absolutely not interesting."[5]

We also began to develop links with those in Haiti resisting the coup, as members of our network traveled to Haiti, at times informally and at times as part of organized delegations. In December 2004, our colleague and Haiti Action Montreal co-founder Yves Engler visited Port-au-Prince and nearby cities. He traveled to the Petionville Women's Prison where, among others, he spoke with Annette "*So Ann*" Auguste, a folk singer and political activist jailed for her support of Fanmi Lavalas. During the coup, the prison system was packed with hundreds–if not thousands–of political prisoners like Auguste, including Lavalas presidential candidate Father Gerard Jean-Juste. Both were jailed for their political activities by the Canada-backed regime and subsequently named "prisoners of conscience" by Amnesty International.

While Auguste and other Haitians fighting for democracy languished in jail, Prime Minister Paul Martin flatly denied their existence, declaring during a November 2004 trip that there were no political prisoners in Haiti. Denis Coderre, Liberal MP and Special Advisor to the Prime Minister on Haiti, was particularly hypocritical on the matter of political prisoners, claiming that "Canada would not get involved in Haiti's justice system." In fact, Canada was already deeply involved in the functioning of Haiti's justice system. Deputy Justice Minister Philippe Vixamar, for instance, was a direct employee of the Canadian International Development Agency (CIDA), the Canadian government's official aid agency. Although officially a political appointee of the unelected regime, Vixamar told human rights investigators that he had been assigned to his position by the Agency, with his salary paid by Canadian tax dollars.[6]

Yves also met with Jeremy, a Haitian youth who had worked with a children's radio station set up by Fanmi Lavalas. Jeremy spoke of how his aunt was killed by police officers. His story was far from unique. Under the direction of the Canada-backed regime, police and paramilitary thugs had unleashed a wave of violence not seen since the dark days of the Duvalier dictatorship (1957-1986).[7] In one of the few detailed accounts to find its way into the corporate press, the *Miami Herald* wrote:

> The police carried assault rifles and wore black masks. The gang they accompanied had brand-new machetes. According to witnesses and UN investigators, they stormed into a soccer match during halftime, ordered everyone to lie on the ground and began shooting and hacking people to death in broad daylight as several thousand spectators fled for their lives. ... Some were handcuffed and shot in the head by police, witnesses said. Others were hacked to death.[8]

The officers carrying out these atrocities were likely trained by RCMP officers, who "monitored, mentored, trained and vetted" personnel for the regime's overhauled police force, one of the most significant perpetrators of violence in the post-coup period.[9]

NGOs Back the Coup

One of our main goals was to counter the media blackout and government denials by getting accurate information to the public. With Canada's complicity in Haiti's human rights cataclysm all but ignored by the corporate media, much of our time and energy went into researching, writing and publishing articles about Canada's negative role in the independent media. Following his trip to Haiti, Yves submitted an article about *So Ann* and Jeremy's stories to the *Journal d'Alternatives*, a widely-circulated monthly newspaper produced by Alternatives, a Montreal-based NGO. Yves' article was accepted, and even translated into French, but was never published. What Alternatives did publish was shocking.

In June 2005, Alternatives staff member François L'Écuyer wrote an article for the *Journal d'Alternatives* that did not once mention the political repression against Lavalas supporters. Instead, the article demonized the residents of impoverished neighbourhoods targeted for repression by the installed government. In particular, L'Écuyer denounced community activists Ronald St. Jean and Samba Boukman as "notorious criminals."[10] We had met Ronald St. Jean in March 2005 when he came to Montreal to speak at Concordia University. St. Jean was head of the *Comité de Défense du Peuple Haïtien* (CDPH–Committee for the Defense of the Rights of the Haitian People), which worked to defend the rights of political prisoners. Other members of the Canada-Haiti Action Network had met with Samba Boukman, a dedicated community activist from Bel-Air, one of the strongly pro-Lavalas neighborhoods of the capital victimized by the Haitian police. Both men were dedicated to non-violent resistance to the coup and were outspoken critics of the human rights violations that followed. Neither had a criminal record. At the time of L'Écuyer's writing, activists were regularly being killed and posthumously labeled "bandits." In the article, there was an unmistakable echo of the position of the Canadian government.

The article threw our assumptions about NGOs into question. Before the coup, we had expected Alternatives and other like-minded NGOs to be allies, given their involvement in the anti-globalization movement of the late 1990s. Alternatives described itself as working for "democratic rights and human dignity," and seeking to bring about a world where "solidarity, cooperation, respect for the environment, participatory democracy and peace are truly valued."[11] Alternatives had been endorsed by Noam Chomsky, a strong critic of the coup d'état in Haiti, as well as prominent Canadian and Québecois political and cultural figures, such as Margaret Atwood, Judy Rebick, Naomi Klein and Amir Khadir. Although Alternatives printed numerous articles about Haiti during the coup years, not once did these articles criticize Canada's role.

In August 2005, members of Haiti Action Montreal attended the Alternatives conference "Haiti: A democracy to construct," with the intent of raising the issue of Canada's role in the country. The invited panelists avoided almost any concrete references the political situation in Haiti, and did not mention the coup d'état or the ongoing bloodshed, never mind Canada's support for both. When we raised the issue of systemic political repression during question period, Alternatives Executive Director at the time Pierre Beaudet flatly denied that supporters of the government were being persecuted, dismissing examples given as exceptional cases. Another panelist sneered that we had been "intoxicated by propaganda." Again, the echo of the government's position was hard to miss.

We initiated a letter-writing campaign calling on Alternatives to acknowledge the well-documented campaign of repression. We were supported by a number of former Alternatives *stagiaires* (volunteers), as well as author and journalist Naomi Klein, who withdrew her support for Alternatives in protest of their position on Haiti. Throughout the grim years that followed the coup, however, Alternatives remained silent on the murders and human rights abuses committed by the unelected regime and its RCMP-trained police force.

The position of Alternatives was not idiosyncratic. All of the major Canadian NGOs working in Haiti were either silent on the situation or openly hostile to Haitians seeking the return of the democratic government. None criticized the interim regime's bloody war on the slums or the support given to this endeavour by Canada. Many positively cheered the toppling of a democratically elected government and the accompanying bloody repression. Our opponents in the struggle turned out to be the same organizations we had first looked to for support.

It was a shocking realization to make. How could so many groups support a coup against an elected government despite their stated commitments to democracy? Why did they deny or whitewash the serious human rights abuses committed by the interim government? Why did they totally ignore Canada's key role in orchestrating the coup and the violence that followed?

A glimmer of understanding came when we learned that CIDA had awarded Alternatives part of a $5 million contract for media work in Haiti. Once again, Alternatives was not alone; the overthrow of Haiti's government had produced a gusher of CIDA contracts for Canadian NGOs. Development NGOs working in Haiti received substantial funding from the Canadian government, and in the years leading up to the coup, many Canadian NGOs had served as conduits for channeling resources to opponents of the Aristide government. CIDA funding for NGO work increased substantially after the coup.

This raised a series of new, different questions: how common are these kinds of funding ties between government agencies like CIDA and development NGOs? And what impact do they have on what NGOs do abroad and say at home? Questions such as these led us to write this book.

1

Introduction

*In searching for alternative models of development ... North American
progressives need to question the assumption that NGOs are necessarily
allies in a common cause.*

–Laura Macdonald [1]

Few institutions epitomize Canada's foundational myth of international
benevolence like the non-governmental organization (NGO) devoted
to development abroad. "NGOs are as Canadian as hockey," a 1988
Parliamentary report declared.[2] Development NGOs are commonly
depicted as concrete expressions of a distinctly Canadian concern about
poverty and suffering in the Global South. Images of Canadian aid
workers caring for malnourished children, digging wells and building
schools in remote, impoverished villages are deeply embedded in public
consciousness. Volunteering with an NGO is a formative experience for
many young people, who come face-to-face with the daily realities of life
among the world's poor. Development NGOs form an indelible part of
Canada's national identity, akin to peacekeeping or indeed, hockey.

The popularity of development NGOs reflects a desire among Canadians
for a more equal, less violent and less ecologically destructive international
order. In a March 2006 poll conducted by Gallup International, Canadians
identified the global gap between rich and poor as the world's number one
problem by more than two to one over any other problem. And in January
2008, war and the environment were named as the most important issues
facing the world by Canadians in an Environics poll.[3] Canadians' views on
international issues are grounded in an ideal of "humane internationalism,"
which Canadian foreign policy scholar Cranford Pratt defines as "an
acceptance that the citizens and governments in the industrialized
countries have ethical responsibilities towards those beyond their borders
who are suffering and live in abject poverty."[4]

1

Many Canadians regard working with or supporting an NGO as a way of fulfilling their ethical responsibilities, a perception that development NGOs have tapped into very effectively.[5] Hundreds of thousands–perhaps even millions–of Canadians have donated money in support of NGO development initiatives, and tens of thousands have worked in the Global South as volunteers.[6] As non-profit or "voluntary sector" organizations, development NGOs depend to varying degrees on donations of time and money from the Canadian public for their work.

The voluntary character of development NGOs has generated great expectations about their capacity to combat poverty. Because they are ostensibly motivated by good intentions, many consider NGOs to be more effective vehicles for development than governments or corporations. "NGOs are idealized as organizations through which people help others for reasons other than profit or politics," writes anthropologist William Fisher.[7] NGOs are routinely described as more efficient, participatory and less bureaucratic than official aid agencies or Southern governments. Many commentators praise NGOs for working to correct the polarizing tendencies of the market and the deficiencies of government. Others claim that NGOs are part of a "global civil society" that empowers the poor in the Global South and engages lobbying or "advocacy" on their behalf in the North.

The trouble with such views is that NGOs are not quite as non-governmental as they seem. Over the years, NGOs' coffers have been filled by ever-increasing amounts of public funding, which has produced organizations that are professionalized, bureaucratic, and dependent on a continued flow of government money. With the typical development NGO now reliant on federal funding for over 50% of its annual budget, NGOs have steadily lost their institutional autonomy and are increasingly subject to the politics and priorities of the Canadian government. Contrary to their image as free-floating atoms of altruism, NGOs are actually tightly intertwined with the state. To understand development NGOs, an analysis of the power wielded by the government over these organizations is essential.

Government funding may be a ubiquitous fact of life for development NGOs, but it is seldom investigated in studies of these organizations. The problem is not a shortage of research on NGOs, which according to NGO scholar Alison Van Rooy has burgeoned into a "spectacular growth industry":

NGOs are a very popular topic of research these days. There are now dozens of courses on development NGOs offered in universities and training centres, compared with none a decade ago. There are thousands of articles and hundreds of books on NGO work currently available, an increase from a couple of dozen in the early 1980s.[8]

The voluminous intellectual output on the subject notwithstanding, the consequences of NGOs' dependence on government funding are rarely discussed. "There do not exist many coherent analyses," former NGO policy analyst Brian K. Murphy notes, "of the alienation and loss of vision and mission of voluntary agencies due to the difficulties associated with government funding."[9] Most studies of development NGOs dismiss the issue as irrelevant to understanding these organizations. "The power of the [governmental] donors is often mentioned, yet it is rarely central to the analysis of how development works," observe Tina Wallace and Lisa Bornstein in *The Aid Chain*, one of the few books to squarely address the issue. "Inequalities are acknowledged, then brushed aside or hidden through the use of language: the terms 'partner' and 'partnership' replace the concepts of donor-recipient or subcontractor."[10]

In public discourse, to the degree that the shadow of power cast by the Canadian government over development NGOs is discussed at all, it is treated as a very recent phenomenon. A phenomenon dating to November 30, 2009, to be precise.

The Conservative Defunding Drive

On November 30, 2009, the head office of KAIROS received a phone call from the Canadian International Development Agency (CIDA) notifying the church-based development NGO that its request for funding had been rejected. CIDA officials cryptically informed the organization that its $7.1 million in federal funding had been cut because its activities did not fit the Agency's development priorities. It rapidly became clear, however, that KAIROS had run afoul of Stephen Harper's foreign policy priorities, most notably his Conservative government's staunchly pro-Israel stance.[11] NGOs guilty of similar transgressions soon faced cuts as well. In December 2009, Alternatives–another NGO critical of Israel's occupation of Palestine–learned that its $2.1 million in CIDA funding would be cut. In April 2010, over a dozen groups concerned with women's rights, including development NGOs such as MATCH International and the International Planned Parenthood Foundation (IPPF), also suffered funding cuts. MATCH International ($400,000 in CIDA funding in 2009) and the IPPF ($6 million in 2009) had been critical of the Harper government's anti-abortion stance internationally.[12] For the targeted organizations, the loss of government funding meant between 40% and 75% of their annual budgets disappeared overnight. The cuts exacted a heavy toll: Overseas programs were shut down, offices closed, staff downsized and properties liquidated.

The spate of funding cuts was part of a broader effort to silence development NGOs. According to the Canadian Council for International Cooperation (CCIC), an umbrella group representing most of the major development NGOs in Canada, many NGOs received veiled warnings about taking positions that conflicted with Ottawa's on issues such as climate change, free trade with Colombia, or the Middle East. "NGOs are being positively invited to remain silent on key questions of public policy," explained CCIC President and CEO Gerry Barr. The wave of cuts, Barr said, was "a messaging operation to the entire sector which essentially says, in billboard fashion, 'Watch out what you say. You may pay a high price for it.'"[13]

Fear rippled through Canada's development NGO community. "In conversations that we have had with other NGOs it has of course created a chill," KAIROS's Executive Director Mary Corkery reported. "There is fear of being in support of Palestinian people and groups, who essentially are struggling for land and livelihood." When journalist Tim Groves asked Corkery which groups were feeling this pressure, she responded: "The chill is such that people don't want to be named."[14] Several NGO leaders anonymously told the *Globe and Mail* that they had received subtle warnings from officials that the government disliked their public stances, but were too frightened to speak out publicly.[15] Shortly after the CCIC publicly complained that the government had created a "chill" in the NGO community by adopting "the politics of punishment ... towards those whose public views run at cross purposes to the government," it too had its 3-year, $1.7 million CIDA grant cut.[16]

The KAIROS cuts and their aftermath revealed uncomfortable truths about the relationship between the Canadian government and development NGOs. With politicians holding the purse strings, development NGOs face serious limits on what they can do and say. The government possesses "unusual life and death power over many Canadian NGOs," former CBC journalist Brian Stewart remarked in the wake of the cuts. "In today's Ottawa, all NGOs know a simple fact of life: Displeasing the government means CIDA can turn off your NGO tap with ease. Either by simply eliminating the flow or diverting it to another group that the government favours."[17] Harper's cuts, however, did not provoke a sober reappraisal of the distortions and restrictions that accompany government funding. Instead, the cuts occasioned an attempt to breath new life into old fantasies about Canadian benevolence, development-as-humanitarianism and NGO independence.

Quiet Glories of a Pre-Harper Golden Age?

In their efforts to mobilize political opposition to the Conservative government's attacks, NGOs and their allies painted the defunding of KAIROS *et alia* as an unprecedented departure from longstanding Canadian traditions. Alternatives Executive Director Michel Lambert claimed the Harper government had disrupted the "symbiosis" between CIDA and development NGOs and pleaded for officials to recreate the "authentic partnerships" of the past, which had respected the independence of development NGOs.[18] Michael Casey, Executive Director of Development & Peace, worried that the defunding of KAIROS and Alternatives threatened to disturb the "healthy environment of critique" that once existed between NGOs and the government: "This has always been encouraged in an open spirit of dialogue between government and civil society over the last 40 odd years."[19] Political commentator Gerald Caplan argued that the "punishment politics" meted out against NGOs were a betrayal of quintessential Canadian values:

> The issue here is the reversal, by Stephen Harper, of a 60-year consensus shared by all previous governments about the central role of civil society in Canada. Every previous government has funded civil society groups and NGOs even when they espoused policies that contradicted the government's own. Governments might have done so grudgingly and not as generously as some of us hoped. But it has been one of the quiet glories of Canadian democracy that our governments have often backed groups that criticized them or had competing priorities.[20]

The accusations of his critics notwithstanding, Harper was breaking little new ground. If anything, his Conservative government's actions were in keeping with Canadian traditions. Liberal and Conservative governments alike have a long history of practicing the "politics of punishment" against dissident NGOs. In 1975, the CCIC faced funding cuts after it criticized Canada's position at the World Food Conference; in 1979, a radicalized Canadian University Service Overseas (CUSO), the most prominent Canadian development NGO at the time, had its funding shut off completely; in the 1980s, NGOs supporting liberation movements of Southern Africa and Central America were squeezed by CIDA; in 1991, the Inter-Church Fund for International Development (ICFID, a precursor organization to KAIROS) faced CIDA's wrath for its criticisms of structural adjustment; and in 1995, Canada's national network of development education centres was effectively destroyed when CIDA slashed 100% of its funding.

Neither the "60-year consensus" nor the "40 odd years" of government-NGO "dialogue" and "critique" ever took place. Ruling administrations of the past have disciplined NGOs that dared to contradict the government's international stance, often just as ruthlessly as the Harper government. The Harper cuts were merely the latest example of Canadian governments using their power over CIDA funding to narrow the political space available to development NGOs. What *was* surprising was just how little the victimized NGOs did to draw the ire of the government. The left-leaning advocacy of KAIROS and Alternatives was meek in comparison to the militant, confrontational approach of the radicalized NGOs targeted by CIDA in the 1970s and 1980s.

The historical amnesia of the NGO leaders and their allies is politically convenient. There is little doubt that they know the history of past funding cuts, even as they promote the myth of a 60- or 40-year consensus at CIDA respecting the independence of NGOs. Harkening back to a pre-Harper paradise lost allows the NGO leaders to maintain the pretense that their organizations were untainted by government influence until now. The decline of NGO independence may have accelerated under Harper, but the tendency has been playing out for decades. In Canada, as elsewhere, development NGOs have become increasingly integrated into the foreign policy apparatus. "While there was never was a golden age of NGOs," writes Tina Wallace, "they are now becoming increasingly tied to global agendas and uniform ways of working."[21]

Politics, Ideology and the Humanitarian Lens

Development is commonly viewed through a lens of humanitarianism. In this account, development is a matter of disinterested helping, driven by altruistic commitment. As such, development aid is described as a gift to the South, which demonstrates the generosity and concern for global poverty of the "donors." Because all of the parties involved–donors, governments, NGOs, the poor–share the same noble objective of fighting poverty, conflicts of interest over development do not arise.

The official aid agencies of Western governments (the biggest "donors") like to present their development aid spending in this sort of humanitarian light. This is particularly true in Canada, where our national identity has been strongly tied to our international reputation as a caring, disinterested "middle power." Prime Minister Lester B. Pearson (1963-1968), for instance, is best known for his support for UN peacekeeping and his call for industrialized countries to devote 0.7% of their GDP to development aid. It has been fashionable, historian Sean Maloney writes, for politicians "to present Canada to the world as an honest broker or linchpin between the West and the Third World."[22] Canada's aid program is frequently held up as the most visible symbol of our foreign policy's benign intent towards the South.

In the humanitarian view, poverty is a quantitative problem, not the product of social relations. Although development work seeks to attack the enduring, "root causes" of poverty, these causes are assumed to be primarily material. Poor people, the story goes, are poor because they lack various things: money, education, credit, agricultural inputs, decent housing, etc. The purpose of development is to transfer the resources, skills and technology necessary for the poor to live poverty-free in a "sustainable" way, i.e. without a continuous flow of outside resources. Hence the iconic catchphrase used by the UN Freedom From Hunger Campaign of the 1960s: "Give a man a fish and feed him for a day; teach him to fish and you feed him for a lifetime."[23] Overwhelmingly, NGOs share the development-as-humanitarianism outlook. In their study *Bridges of Hope?*, Tim Brodhead and Brent Herbert-Copley report that for most Canadian NGOs, development is a matter of "helping individuals, families and communities, not a matter of overarching structures or systems."[24]

The dominant humanitarian view of development is apolitical and functionalist. Good intentions are taken for granted; the only question is how best to put our benevolence into practice. Development is an objective, technical matter, about which the most important question is, "Does it work?" This question is usually followed by other related questions like whether the "it" at issue is cost-effective, sustainable, culturally appropriate, gender neutral and so on. Development research tends to focus on finding the "right" policies, applying the "right" model, or building the "right" institutions. Likewise, much of the literature on NGOs seeks to determine "best practices" by assessing which kinds of projects or approaches reduce poverty in the most efficient or sustainable way.

From this perspective, it follows that development should remain strictly separated from ideology and politics. These factors enter the picture only as unwanted intrusions that threaten to disrupt the smooth unfolding of the development process. Politics are conceived of as a source of corruption that can overwhelm development efforts, while ideology is seen as an impediment to rational planning. Interestingly, in the dominant discourse these irrational diseases frequently afflict the South, but hardly ever touch development actors from the North. Politics and ideology usually happen "over there," at times preventing "us" from realizing our sensible, well-meaning plans to help "them" better their conditions. In the humanitarian view of development, NGOs generate high hopes precisely because they are perceived to be insulated from politics and free of ideology.

When the KAIROS cuts occurred, NGO leaders attempted to defend their organizations by drawing on these widely-held ideas. In addition to violating a mythic tradition of NGO independence, the Harper government was accused of betraying our traditional international role as an even-handed diplomat and peacekeeper. Specifically, the NGOs claimed that by cutting off funding to their organizations, the government was engaging in a dangerous politicization of CIDA, which had historically managed development aid in a disinterested, un-ideological manner. "[I] f in fact the decision was a political one then that is very disturbing for the integrity of Canadian aid," KAIROS's Mary Corkery told journalists after losing funding.[25] Michel Lambert of Alternatives made a similar point, claiming the motives for the cuts were strictly "ideological" and had "nothing to do with development or humanitarian aid." "It's precisely to prevent humanitarian issues from becoming issues of foreign policy," Lambert wrote in response to losing funding for his organization, "that the Canadian government created CIDA in 1968."[26] Like the nostalgia for an age of NGO independence that never was, these arguments rest on myths and misconceptions about development and Canada's place in the world that hide a less flattering reality.

Development for Whom?

When we think about development, the most important question to ask is, "development for whom?" Who decides what shape development should take? Whose interests are served? Development, as Brodhead and Herbert-Copley note, "is about values, choices and allocation of resources, and hence inherently 'political'."[27] For this reason, development ideas are necessarily ideological. Different development paths imply different distributions of costs and benefits within society, and ideas about the "right" way to do development are unavoidably related to the underlying interests of various social groups. Theories of development become dominant not because they "work" in some abstract sense but because they work for *somebody*. Development cannot be understood independently of controversial issues related to the distribution of wealth and power in society.

For these reasons, development is somewhat more complicated than giving fishing lessons, as author and development consultant Maggie Black explains:

> The river might be polluted and the catch depleted. The trees from which boats were traditionally built had been cut down by loggers, or the right to fish on that waterway granted to others with powerful patrons and larger boats. Fishing families were forced to sell their catch to a marketing board, which depressed producer prices, so that they could no longer make a living. ... It became clear that interventions to support livelihoods not only had to fit economic and social realities, but also to contend with power structures. If they did not, vested interests might destroy them or co-opt every benefit to themselves.[28]

Power structures and vested interests that impinge on development are not restricted to the local or national level. In the South, the rich countries are not disinterested helpers, but rather powerful actors that possess substantial interests of their own. Modifying Black's development parable to include international dimensions can help to illustrate: Perhaps the river has been polluted by a nearby open-pit mine, operated with capital raised by financiers on stock exchanges in Toronto and New York; fish stocks may have depleted by owners of boats with powerful patrons, but it is large food processing conglomerates that buy the catch and put it on the shelves of Northern supermarkets; and although crooked local officials and loggers may have colluded to clearcut the forest, foreign pulp and paper corporations are the ones processing the tropical logs and pocketing the bulk of the profits. All too often, as corporations have gone global and capitalism has spread around the world, local elites exploiting the poor and despoiling the environment are partners with investors from the North.

Aid is presented as a form of generosity, but it is used to promote policies that have little to do with the interests of the recipients and everything to do with the self-interest of the givers. Historically, Western governments' development aid programs, as much as other aspects of their foreign policies, have been heavily influenced by calculations of economic gain and geopolitical advantage. Today, little has changed. Development aid remains a tool of the powerful, an inducement used to bring about changes in the attitudes and behaviours of the South. The aura of humanitarianism surrounding development has helped conceal these power relations.

Through their development aid programs, Northern countries have defined the dominant ideologies of development and put these ideas into practice in the impoverished countries of the South. As anthropologist Jeffrey Jackson points out, the self-interested motives of the donors are embodied in the very way development is conceived of and practiced. For the Northern donors, "'bringing development' is really something else. 'Development' is a euphemism for a multiplicity of agendas being promoted by donor countries to advance their own interests globally."[29] The dominant development ideas act as both a veil and a vehicle for the interests of industrialized countries.

Canada: Exception to the Rule?

Canadians tend to believe in a kind of "Canadian exceptionalism." Other Western countries might have self-interested foreign policies and aid programs, but Canada—and Canadian aid in particular—is somehow different. To win public opinion to their side, leaders of the defunded NGOs appealed to this shining, Pearsonian vision of Canadian foreign policy. Canada was a global good guy, disinterested and fair in its dealings with the South—at least until Harper came to power. But this vision of Canada was "never really accurate," political scientist Todd Gordon explains:

> Canada isn't some mere middle power riding the coattails of our superpower neighbour. … Canada has always had a self-interest to promote; Canadian capital has always had a controversial presence in the Third World, whether in banking in the Caribbean, manufacturing in apartheid South Africa or mining in General Suharto's Indonesia. But the neo-liberal era, with heightened competition among multinational corporations and the aggressive market liberalization imposed on the Third World by the North (including Canada) has seen an unprecedented international expansion of Canadian capital.[30]

Behind the mythology, Canada has economic and geopolitical interests it seeks to promote in the South, often at the expense of local populations. Canadian foreign policy is not exceptional, nor is Canada's development aid program insulated from less-than-benevolent motives. In one of the earliest studies on the subject, historian Keith Spicer described Canadian aid policies as designed "purely in the selfish interest of the state":

> Philanthropy is plainly no more than a fickle and confused policy stimulant, derived exclusively from the personal conscience. It is not an objective of government. Love for mankind is a virtue of the human heart, an emotion which can stir only individuals–never bureaucracies or institutions. ... Altruism as foreign policy is a misnomer, even if sometimes the fruits of policy are incidentally beneficial to foreigners.[31]

Despite 40 years of justifying development aid on humanitarian grounds, writes Cranford Pratt, "most scholarly commentators have concluded that humanitarian considerations have played little role within government in the shaping of those policies."[32] Reflecting the pro-empire orientation of Canada's foreign policy, Canadian aid spending has followed closely on the heels Western military interventions, from Vietnam to Haiti, from the former Yugoslavia to Iraq and Afghanistan. Much of Canada's development aid has also served to open up economic opportunities and to assure "stability," "predictability" and "transparency" for Canadian investors in the Global South, reflected in the flow of wealth from South to North which Canadian aid has generated. Although Canada gave out $4.35 billion in development aid in 2007, Canadian investors reaped $18 billion in profits annually from investments in the Global South.[33] Behind its humanitarian facade, Canada's aid program has been motivated by "quite different considerations" according to Pratt, from the "long-term interests of capitalism in Canada" and "immediate commercial gains," to "the dominant ideology among senior decision makers."[34]

Blind Spots

For years, aid critics have documented the ways in which CIDA has functioned to the benefit of Canadian multinationals while "perpetuating poverty" in the South.[35] The role of development NGOs in this process, however, has never been systematically investigated. Due to their dependence on CIDA funds, development NGOs have become entangled in the foreign policy of the Canadian government, which is neither benevolent nor disinterested in its dealings with the Global South. Without an understanding of Canada's foreign policy priorities and how development NGOs fit with these priorities, any analysis of these organizations is incomplete.

To understand the role of development NGOs in the world, it is also essential to move beyond the apolitical, humanitarian notion of development. One of the most dangerous ideological effects of development NGOs is that they lead us to think about development in an apolitical way. The humanitarian view of development can blind us to the fact that poverty and inequality cannot be addressed independently of wider social and political structures, as William Fisher argues:

> Just as the "development apparatus" has generally depoliticized the need for development through its practice of treating local conditions as "problems" that required technical and not structural or political solutions, it now defines problems that can be addressed via the mechanisms of NGOs rather than through political solutions.[36]

Even more dangerous is the political blindness development NGOs can transmit about Canada's actual relations with the Global South–and even more so about their own role within those relations. NGOs' own inability to perceive these issues severely affects how they function, as Brian K. Murphy explains:

> Ultimately, because they will be unable to make critical and politically aware choices, this limited vision will relegate the NGOs, at best, to a benign but marginal role in the world. At worst some will play a malignant role as agents of the very global social and economic forces that have created the conditions of poverty, deprivation, political repression, militarism, and environmental degradation experienced by billions throughout the world.[37]

This book aims to contribute to Canadians' ability to make "critical and politically aware choices" about development NGOs.

What are Development NGOs?

Before moving on to the arguments contained in the following chapters, it is important to clearly define the subject of this book, development

NGOs. This is not an easy task. The term "non-governmental organization" is notoriously vague; it defines organizations by what they are not, and its porous boundaries can cause much confusion. Save the Children and World Vision may be NGOs, but what about unions, chess clubs, political parties and professional associations? "Development" is also a slippery concept. Is development a process or an end point? Is it an aspiration or an activity? Judging by the wide scope of activities development NGOs undertake, "development" encompasses everything from planting trees to digging wells, from providing health care for the poor to forming microcredit organizations, from teaching peasants about their land rights to lobbying governments for policy changes. "When all is said and done," remarks Gilbert Rist in his book *The History of Development*, "every modern human activity can be undertaken in the name of 'development'."[38]

Given the bewildering diversity and sheer number of development NGOs, the subject seems to defy any broad assessments. There are hundreds of development NGOs in Canada, and they come in many different shapes, sizes and flavours: large or small, religious or secular, conservative or progressive, home-grown or imported. Some NGOs specialize in one type of development work (e.g. women, training, microcredit) while other NGOs take up all manner of projects. Some NGOs work only in a specific country or region, while others work on projects scattered across the globe. Consequently, many authors warn of "the dangers of over-generalizing in the NGO debate" and eschew critiques of development NGOs as a whole, since such critiques cannot possibly do justice to the "tremendous diversity" found in the NGO world.[39]

The imprecise nature of the term "NGOs"–and its equally ill-defined cousin, "civil society"–has a certain utility for development NGOs. The alleged diversity of development NGOs forms a crucial part of their appeal, since it allows observers from across the political spectrum to project their values, hopes and desires onto these organizations. As William Fisher remarks, "NGOs have been embraced and promoted ... by international development agencies like the World Bank as well as by radical critics of top-down development."[40] The fuzziness of the term means "NGOs" can be anything to anyone, a sort of Rorschach test for those concerned with development. Conversely, references to the unfathomable diversity of development NGOs can be used to deflect criticisms and steer debate away from uncomfortable commonalities in funding structure.

For the purposes of this book, development NGOs are professionalized, non-profit organizations that depend on CIDA for funding and whose primary aim is to permanently remedy poverty in the Third World. We have tried to avoid the risk of over-generalizing by laying emphasis on those relationships and characteristics that are common to virtually all development NGOs: their professionalized, bureaucratic structure and their dependence on government funding for maintaining that structure. This may seem like a contradictory way of defining development NGOs, given their supposedly *non*-governmental character. Yet the definition fits quite well with intuitive notions of what development NGOs are, since nearly all the major organizations commonly referred to as a "development NGOs" get substantial funding from the Canadian government. In what follows, the term "NGO" refers to development NGOs as defined above, unless otherwise qualified (e.g. humanitarian NGO, human rights NGO, etc.).

Looking at development NGOs as a whole is important for another reason. Taken on an individual basis, most NGO projects appear to be unquestionably positive. Who could oppose making small loans to poor women to help them start a micro-enterprise, or providing assistance to peasants eking out a living on marginal land? The trouble with examining NGOs on a case-by-case or project-by-project basis, which is characteristic of the bulk of NGO studies, is that it tends to preclude serious examination of the historical or political context. This approach also prevents understanding of the overarching structures within which NGOs operate. Development NGOs are best understood as an ensemble, as a constellation of organizations and activities in the Global South that exercises considerable social and political power–far more than any analysis of a single project or NGO might indicate. With such a narrow focus, most NGO studies miss the forest for the trees.

We consider development NGOs to be distinct from humanitarian agencies. Humanitarian action seeks to temporarily alleviate episodic instances of suffering, whereas development work seeks to address the root causes of poverty. Roger Riddell estimates that development NGOs devote approximately 65-75% of their resources to income generating and service provision projects in the Global South, 10-20% to "capacity building" and other initiatives in support of Southern organizations, and 15% to advocacy concerning development issues.[41] Although many development NGOs were originally founded as humanitarian groups, and many of the largest (e.g. Oxfam, CECI, World Vision) continue to deliver both humanitarian assistance and development projects, humanitarian action and development work in the Global South are sufficiently distinct that they are best dealt with separately.*

---

* For an excellent critique of humanitarian NGOs, see Alex de Waal's *Famine Crimes.*

Part I

Neoliberalism and the NGO boom

Grameen Bank founder Mohammed Yunus at the 2010 World Economic Forum.

2

A Spoonful of Sugar

Social funds and the bitter pill of neoliberalism

They're what botanists would call an indicator species. The greater the devastation caused by neoliberalism, the greater the outbreak of NGOs.

–Arundhati Roy [1]

Until the 1980s, development NGOs operated on the margins of the development world. Since then, a seemingly endless "NGO boom" has expanded both the number and reach of these organizations. All over the world, development NGOs have proliferated. In OECD countries, NGOs grew in number from 1,600 to 2,500 between 1980 and 1990. In Canada, the number of development NGOs rose from 107 in 1980 to 240 in 1990 and to over 500 in 2005. The blossoming of the NGO sector has been even more spectacular in the Global South. In Bolivia, the number of NGOs registered with the government increased from around 100 in 1980 to 530 in 1994; in Tanzania, 41 NGOs were registered in 1990 and more than 10,000 by 2000. In Kenya, the number of NGOs exploded from 511 in 1996 to 2,511 in 2003. According to a UN study, NGO development activities reached 100 million people worldwide in the early 1980s, rising to some 250 million by the early 1990s. In 2007, "probably well in excess of 600 million people in the developing world have some sort of direct contact with NGO projects and programmes." [2]

In the process, NGOs have become an integral part of the "development industry," and they are big business indeed. One study showed that by 2002 the NGO sector across 37 countries had an estimated operating expenditure of $1.6 trillion. [3] Other estimates are higher, with some studies showing an overall increase in the flow of funding through NGOs from $200 billion in 1970 to $2.6 trillion in 1997. Large NGOs have become important players on the global development stage. The Oxfam International network had a budget of $504 million in 1999 and worked in 117 countries, World Vision's budget was over $600 million and worked in 92 countries and Save the Children had revenues of $368 million and worked in 121 countries. The seven largest NGOs had a combined income of $2.5 billion in 1999.[4]

Many observers have hailed the NGO boom as a promising development, as a testament to the increasing vibrancy of "civil society" in both the North and South. For some, the growth of NGOs provides a welcome and necessary counterweight to both the state and the market. NGO professionals have been among the strongest proponents of this view, but it is common currency in wider progressive circles as well. The Council of Canadians founder and activist Maude Barlow, for instance, has praised the multitude of NGOs that sprang up in the neoliberal era. In her 2003 book *Global Showdown*, Barlow hailed the gap-filling role played by NGOs in the Third World as an inspiring alternative to the harsh, market-oriented development policies favoured by the powerful: "Unknown even to itself, a powerful 'third sector' of civil society was being created, largely unnoticed by the new global royalty of government and corporate elites."[5]

The "new global royalty" and their allied institutions–the International Monetary Fund (IMF) and the World Bank–were in fact the driving force behind the NGO boom. The growth of development NGOs was driven by the needs of the transnational corporate elite's ideological agenda: neoliberalism. As Western governments directed ever-larger shares of aid funding through non-governmental channels to deal with the "social costs of adjustment," NGOs expanded in the vacuum created by neoliberalism's relentless assaults on the social rights of the poor. The decision to put NGOs in charge of what was previously the responsibility of the state was promoted in pragmatic development terms, but its origins lay in the politics and ideology of neoliberalism. NGOs helped secure the continued implementation of "market reforms" by diverting the energies of the poor away from political protest and into ways of coping with deepened poverty that did not challenge its root causes. Far from constituting an alternative to the reigning development orthodoxy, NGOs have become an integral part of the neoliberal project.

The Debt Crisis and the Origins of Neoliberalism

The Third World debt crisis was the signal event that ushered in the age of neoliberalism. At the beginning of the 1980s, much of the Third World was weighed down by massive amounts of debt. Third World governments and businesses had borrowed from Western banks in the 1970s in order to finance investments and pay for imports, at a time when their economies were being squeezed by rising oil prices and falling commodity prices. In spite of mounting debt loads, Western banks continued to lend aggressively to the Third World, apparently unconcerned about the risk of default. Most Western bankers tended to assume that, in the words of Citibank's Walter Wriston, "countries don't go bankrupt." A sudden spike in U.S. interest rates in 1979 followed by a deep global economic downturn proved the optimistic bankers wrong.[6] The financial burden increased rapidly and by 1982, indebted countries throughout the South were teetering on the brink of default, threatening to bring down the world financial system.

The first priority of the wealthy capitalist countries was to prevent a major financial crisis and ensure that their banks were repaid. Beyond the immediate danger, however, political elites in the First World also saw in the debt crisis the prospect of pushing through major changes in development policy:

> [T]o the U.S. Treasury staff … the debt crisis afforded an unparalleled opportunity to achieve, in the debtor countries, the structural reforms favored by the Reagan administration. The core of these reforms was a commitment on the part of the debtor countries to reduce the role of the public sector as a vehicle for economic and social development and rely more on market forces and private enterprise, domestic and foreign.[7]

Prior to the debt crisis, many countries had used protectionist policies in an attempt to build up domestic industries and overcome the weak, dependent economic structure left behind by colonialism. Many post-colonial governments had also tried to address deep social inequalities by redistributing wealth and improving living standards of the poor. Nationalist governments imposed regulations on multinational investors, requiring them to serve the economic needs of the nation. Socialist regimes nationalized foreign businesses and enacted land reforms to break up large plantations and give land to peasants.

The debt crisis offered an opportunity to sweep aside these policies in favor of a more pro-business approach to development. With the U.S. government leading the charge, rich countries acted decisively to turn the precarious financial situation of the Third World to their advantage. The International Monetary Fund (IMF) and the World Bank were the principle vehicles for imposing this agenda. The two multilateral institutions, dominated by the U.S. Treasury and the Departments of Finance of other rich countries, offered to lend money to the debtor countries on the condition that they radically reform their economies along pro-corporate lines. Bilateral aid agencies, including the Canadian International Development Agency (CIDA), quickly aligned with the IMF and the World Bank, making aid conditional on the implementation of the new market-oriented agenda. The harsh, far-reaching changes were known as Structural Adjustment Policies (SAPs). These policies emphasized repaying debts, attracting foreign investment and producing for export markets. In the 1980s, much of the Third World was obliged to cede a substantial amount of their sovereignty over key economic decisions to the IMF and the World Bank, ushering in a new paradigm of development: neoliberalism.

Neoliberalism promoted a reorientation of development policies towards satisfying the needs of capital, especially foreign capital. Led by IMF and World Bank economists, neoliberals celebrated the "free market" as a powerful engine for economic growth, while denouncing government intervention as a developmental dead-end. Any effort by the state to promote domestic industries or redistribute wealth, neoliberals argued, inevitably generated inefficiencies and promoted corruption. Integration into the world market (later euphemistically called "globalization") was not only the best, but the *only* possible way out of poverty for the Global South. The rise of neoliberalism, political scientist Graham Harrison argues, led to a "narrowing of questions in international development discourse":

[N]o longer questions about the relative merits of market and non-market forms of economic organization, but how to make the expansion of the market work for the poor; no longer questions about the comparative benefits of public or private ownership, but how to make privatisation more efficient.[8]

The developmental role these functionaries desired for the state was to "enable" the market and create a "favorable investment climate" for the private sector, and especially for foreign multinational corporations. For the IMF and the World Bank, establishing such a climate meant doing away with policies and programs that reduced profitability or inhibited private sector investment. SAPs focused on weakening labour protections and keeping wages low, dismantling regulations, lowering taxes on the rich and businesses, and privatizing public enterprises. SAPs also imposed a massive rollback of social programs. In order to free up resources to promote export production and pay the debt, governments were required to slash social spending, end "price distorting" subsidies and lay off state employees. Often known as the "Washington Consensus," these policies were supposed to allow poor countries to pay off their debts while spurring economic growth, the benefits of which would then trickle down to the poor.

In practice, the embrace of "free market" principles involved a good bit of hypocrisy. SAPs required subsidies to domestic industries to be phased out and public enterprises sold off, in keeping with neoliberal hostility to government intervention in the economy. Conditions attached to subsidies for foreign corporations that aimed to benefit the local economy–local content rules, technology transfer requirements, job creation objectives, labour and environmental protections, or restrictions on profit remittances– were also eliminated. But as aid expert Judith Tendler notes, "anyone who has done field research in developing countries finds governments–despite the strong current anti-subsidy discourse–to be subsidizing industries in a variety of ways."

> One of the most conspicuous forms of this–though the details are not always made public–involves the subsidies provided to attract large transnational firms to locate in a particular country or state; in addition to the well-known tax exemptions and infrastructure investment, this includes significant credit at highly favorable terms and substantial discounts on public services such as telecommunications, electric power, and water supplies.[9]

In the neoliberal era, subsidies to foreign capital continued to be given out, only with fewer strings attached than in the past.

The outcome was lucrative for multinational business and Third World elites, but disastrous for the poor. As political scientist Timothy Mitchell argues, the actual result of neoliberal reforms was a massive transfer of public wealth into private hands:

The neoliberal program has not removed the state from the market or eliminated 'profligate' public subsidies. These achievements belong to the imagination. Its major impact has been to concentrate public funds into different, but fewer hands. The state has turned resources away from agriculture, industry and the underlying problems of training and employment. It now subsidizes financiers instead of factories, speculators instead of schools.[10]

The neoliberal solution to the debt crisis was a monumental injustice, as it effectively involved squeezing the poor to pay off debt incurred by political and economic elites. Though much of the debt had been used to finance luxury consumption, military spending or capital flight, the IMF demanded cuts to public programs that benefited the poor. As Noam Chomsky emphasizes, the debt was largely "odious" (i.e. possessing no legal or moral standing) since it had been "imposed upon people without their consent, often serving to repress them and enrich their masters."

The money was not borrowed by campesinos, assembly plant workers, or slum-dwellers. The mass of the population gained little from the borrowing, indeed often suffered grievously from its effects. But they are to bear the burdens of repayment, along with taxpayers in the West– not the banks who made bad loans or the economic and military elites who enriched themselves while transferring wealth abroad and taking over the resources of their own countries.[11]

For the poor majorities in countries following IMF strictures, structural adjustment was an assault on popular living standards that produced deep and enduring social and economic crises. The huge reductions in public investment, combined with anaemic private sector growth, sent much of the Third World into a deflationary crisis. Unemployment increased massively, capital flight accelerated and the productive base of many Third World countries crumbled. Rising import prices, falling wages, disappearing jobs and decaying social services expanded the ranks of the poor and worsened the grinding poverty of the poorest. Nutritional status, education, health and other social indicators declined in the wake of SAPs. For many Latin American and African countries the structural adjustment period was worse than the Great Depression. In post-Soviet Russia, the market reforms of the 1990s and the economic collapse that followed precipitated a drop in life expectancy greater than that caused by the Second World War.[12]

IMF Riots, Social Funds and NGOs

The imposition of neoliberalism did not pass uncontested. As poverty and unemployment worsened, Southern countries erupted in popular discontent. Hundreds of thousands of people throughout the Third World took part in often-violent protests against structural adjustment measures. According to social scientists John Walton and David Seddon, there were 146 "IMF riots" between 1976 and 1992, with protest activity peaking in the mid-1980s and continuing at a high level well into the 1990s. Demonstrators' demands ranged from the restoration of subsidies for basic goods to a repudiation of the foreign debt. In some places anti-IMF protests forced snap elections or toppled governments, while in others police or military repression was used to contain social unrest.[13] Whatever their ultimate outcome, the protests represented an angry and categorical rejection of the idea that the poor should pay for the debt crisis. The "IMF riots" put the political survival of regimes implementing SAPs into question.

The upheaval caused by SAPs brought the increased misery resulting from forced liberalization and debt repayment to the attention of the wealthy nations. They called these effects the "social costs of adjustment." Western governments, however, did not reconsider their drive to pry open the economies of the Third World because of the "social costs" borne by the poor. Their real concern was that unrest might cause Southern leaders to lose their nerve for pursuing deeper market-oriented reforms. Northern policy makers scrambled to find ways to maintain political momentum behind the neoliberal reforms. "Such widespread opposition resulted in some rethinking by official aid agencies and the multilaterals about how to present the same economic and social programmes with a more 'human face.'"[14] Aid dollars increasingly flowed to activities that promised to take the edge off of the worst impoverishment created by structural adjustment and dampen political opposition.

Increasingly, SAPs were accompanied by compensatory "social funds" into which donors pooled their aid. Social funds disbursed money for short-term employment-generating projects and other welfare measures intended to ease the pain caused by SAPs and defuse social unrest. Social funds provided leaders with a political cover while pursuing the rollback of the state's social welfare functions. According to economists Sanjay Reddy and Giovanni Cornia, using social funds to "make the bitter pill of adjustment easier to swallow" was a "central consideration" of

Northern policy makers, explicitly evoked in many early documents and discussions:

> It is well-known that the first [social fund], in Bolivia, was initiated in large part as a result of the forceful conviction of a World Bank consultant ... who argued that it was necessary to undertake "highly visible action" to mitigate the social costs of adjustment in order to make the latter more politically palatable.[15]

Spurred by the need to temporarily mitigate the "social costs of adjustment," social funds were a significant part of the funding increases that fueled the NGO boom. NGOs were identified as ideal vehicles for tackling "social costs" on the cheap. For those harmed by structural adjustment, non-governmental services and income-generating projects paid for by social funds would take the place of publicly-provided "social safety net" programs. Since NGOs worked at the grassroots level, policy makers expected financing them would help maintain the social peace during the rollout of neoliberal reforms. According to World Bank estimates, NGOs implemented 15-20% of social fund projects.

Canada was at the leading edge of the shift among Western donors. Canadian NGOs were among the primary beneficiaries of the new aid paradigm. Increasing shares of CIDA's budget were allocated to "poverty alleviation," rising from 7.2% for 1983-87 to 30.7% for the years 1988-92.[16] CIDA took pride in having promoted "adjustment with a human face" and Canadian NGOs rallied to the call for supplemental funds to blunt the impact of structural adjustment. According to political scientist Jean-Philippe Thérien, Canada "was one of the first to point out the potential of NGOs for lowering the social costs of adjustment."[17] Canadian aid funding to NGOs climbed relentlessly from just under $90 million in 1980 to $662 million in 1992.[18] CIDA financed a small NGO fact-finding mission to Guyana in early 1989 to investigate ways of dealing with the expected social hardships of a Canada-backed SAP.[19]

Though their effectiveness at addressing the misery caused by SAPs proved to be greatly exaggerated overall, NGOs helped to contain the political costs of adjustment. The "poverty alleviation" projects of NGOs gave "reforming" governments in the Third World a veneer of social legitimacy and an ability to neutralize opposition that was not otherwise available to them, as Kenyan activist Firoze Manji explains:

The aim of such programmes was to act as palliatives that might minimise the more glaring inequalities that their policies had perpetuated. Funds were made available to ensure that social services for the 'vulnerable' would be provided–but this time not by the state (which had after all been forced to 'retrench' away from the social sector) but by the ever willing NGO sector. The availability of such funds for the NGO sector was to have a profound impact on the very nature of that sector.[20]

NGOs were not only beneficiaries of the rise of neoliberalism; they also played a central role in securing the popular consent necessary for its implementation.

Ghana and PAMSCAD

In the early 1980s Ghana was seen as one of the only IMF/World Bank "success stories" in sub-Saharan Africa. Elsewhere on the continent, adjustment policies immediately exacerbated economic difficulties. But in Ghana, after a military coup brought Lt. Jerry Rawlings to power, the government adopted IMF reforms in 1983 and the economy appeared to turn around. As the 1980s wore on, however, opposition to the SAP intensified. Trade unions, students and left-wing intellectuals organized large strikes and demonstrations against layoffs of public sector workers and the imposition of user fees for public services. They denounced the military government's acceptance of IMF conditions as a betrayal of the Ghanaian state's historic commitment to equality and anti-imperialism.

The growing popular opposition caused donor countries to worry that the government might back off from implementing further reforms. Concerned that their star pupil could get off track, CIDA President Margaret Catley-Carlson promised Ghana's leaders that Canada would increase aid in order to "help you out over this very difficult period." "We know that if you take on this [IMF] program of reform it will cost you. Your food prices are going to shoot up, and in the urban areas that is going to be very destabilizing."[21]

The centerpiece of this effort was the Programme of Actions to Mitigate the Social Costs of Adjustment (PAMSCAD), an $85.7 million social fund designed to help Ghana's military leaders maintain political momentum for further neoliberal reforms while lessening their impact on the poor. CIDA was a key player in setting up PAMSCAD and contributed $8.4 million to the fund.[22] Created in 1987 as criticism of adjustment in Ghana was mounting, PAMSCAD funded five categories of projects:

employment generation, community initiative projects, help for laid-off civil service workers, basic needs for vulnerable groups, and education. PAMSCAD funds fueled a rapid proliferation of NGOs in Ghana. "The placing of NGOs on the aid agenda led to a flurry of formation of NGOs in Ghana. ... International NGOs flocked to open branches in Ghana."[23] The Ghana Association of Private Voluntary Organizations in Development, the national umbrella association of NGOs, had only 17 member organizations in 1987, but by the early 1990s had grown to 120 member organizations. (The umbrella group currently represents nearly 400 member organizations.)

Prior to the influx of funding to NGOs, Ghana's small development NGO community was dominated by the church and church-affiliated organizations. These organizations formed a centre of political opposition and were held in suspicion by the military regime. Shortly after the Rawlings dictatorship came to power in 1981, several Ghanaian NGO activists were jailed and many others–including critics of structural adjustment and "many of the brightest young development activists"–were forced to flee the country.[24]

The advent of PAMSCAD, in contrast, resulted in the growth of regime-friendly NGOs. "The government realized it needed to enlist NGOs in the hope of 'cushioning the blow' of adjustment."[25] PAMSCAD funds were used as part of a campaign to silence critical voices, while rewarding those willing to be co-opted. CIDA and other donors agreed to direct their funding through the Ministry of Finance and Economic Affairs, allowing the government to monitor and exert pressure on local NGOs that received foreign aid funding. Many of the new NGOs created in the wake of Ghana's structural adjustment were created by downsized civil servants or middle class entrepreneurs eager to profit from foreign connections. Others NGOs were closely connected to or even directly created by the military government.[26] PAMSCAD was widely perceived in Ghana as a "huge public relations exercise" for the Rawlings regime, one in which local NGOs and their foreign partners participated in–and profited from.[27]

In the wake of structural adjustment and its attendant political repression, Ghana's NGOs rarely challenged the regime or its accommodation to neoliberalism. In 1992, World Bank representatives, top-level government officials and NGO leaders met to discuss strategies to involve NGOs in achieving the goals of the SAP. With few exceptions, the NGO leaders present did not provide "credible criticism or alternatives to the reform programme." "Many were willing handmaidens of structural adjustment and complained most loudly about not having a larger slice of the PAMSCAD cake." Far from creating a vibrant and independent civil society that could act as a check on arbitrary government power, Ghana's NGO boom led to a greater control over civil society by the military regime and the donors.[28]

Measured by inequality, jobs or access to social services, PAMSCAD was a failure. PAMSCAD was largely ineffective at creating jobs to compensate for the gutting of public employment by the SAP. Economist Frances Stewart estimated that Ghana's PAMSCAD created about 7,000 person-years of employment, "only a fraction of the 61,000 redundancies in the civil service and the education service."[29] The informal sector grew accordingly and many NGO initiatives focused on helping the poor start their own small businesses. As more and more jobless Ghanaians entered the informal sector, especially in urban areas, prospects for making a living from activities like street vending became increasingly gloomy, due to high levels of competition and low levels of demand.[30] The use of child labour also grew along with the rise of the unregulated informal sector. Rural women traders were one of the few "winners" of adjustment among the poor, yet even here the victory was Pyrrhic. The success of traders was a result of the flood of imports that followed trade liberalization. While low priced imports produced short-term profits for traders, these same imports caused the hollowing out of industry, with the result that "under the impact of liberalization, Ghana was progressively 'turned into a nation of shoppers and storekeepers with very little manufacturing or industrial activity.'"[31]

Despite the growth of NGOs, access to public services like health care and education continued to decline. Enrolment rates fell and primary school dropout rates climbed to as high as 40%. In 1990, 80.5% of children reached fifth grade, but by 2000 the figure had fallen to 66.3%. Access to health care was also severely constricted, especially in rural areas. Visits to clinics and hospitals fell by as much as 33%.[32] Performance reviews of PAMSCAD and other NGO-led projects reported massive waste and inefficiency in directing funds to the poor. One study of Ghana's adjustment experience marveled at "how haphazard and ad hoc the siting and focus of development initiatives appeared to be." The multiplicity of donors and NGOs, all working largely in isolation, precluded a rational, well-organized response to the pain of the SAP. "Whether projects are initiated by individual community leaders or a government organization or an NGO, success in attracting funds … appears random to say the least: a Canadian NGO here, the Catholic Church there, PAMSCAD, among others, somewhere else."[33] The World Bank reviewed PAMSCAD in 1990 and echoed the sentiment that the targeting of the social fund was problematic. The political influence of the Rawlings government was evident in PAMSCAD's selection of projects, which rarely benefited the most vulnerable but overwhelmingly went to former public employees. The World Bank review concluded that "PAMSCAD had not shown significant benefits in terms of mitigating the social costs of adjustment."[34]

Thanks in part to PAMSCAD, Ghana remained a star pupil of the IMF and the World Bank. The opening of Ghana's market produced a profit bonanza for Canadian mining corporations, which capitalized on the newly liberalized mining law to buy up huge gold mining concessions and privatized state mines. While the mining-led boom produced impressive economic growth on paper, Ghanaian economist Eboe Hutchful was skeptical of the long-term benefits of the "wild capitalism" ushered in by structural adjustment: "This form of 'recovery' also exacted a significant environmental cost (not to mention rising debt obligations), in terms of the continuing devastation of Ghana's forests and the pollution of land, water, and air by hazardous wastes (mercury and arsenic) from the gold-mining industry."[35] And while GDP grew, it led to a "boom for the few and a bust for the many," NGO worker Ian Gary explained:

> Ghana's traditional sources of income–gold, cocoa, and timber–have benefited from the programme, but this has only exacerbated the colonial legacy of dependence. Nearly all of the $1.5 billion worth of private foreign investment has been in mining, with most of the profits being repatriated overseas. "User fees" for health care services and education have been introduced. Disincentives to food producers, and the damage caused to local rice producers by cheap rice imports, have led to increased malnutrition and lower food security. Rapid and indiscriminate liberalization of the trade regime has hurt local industry, while cutbacks in the public sector have shed 15 per cent of the waged work force.[36]

Structural adjustment had the same impoverishing, socially unbalancing effect in Ghana as in other parts of the globe.

The principle preoccupation of the Ghanaian regime and the international donors was not to tackle seriously poverty and inequality, but to mitigate the *political* costs of adjustment. In this respect, PAMSCAD and other poverty alleviation schemes involving NGOs were actually quite effective. The temporary influx of aid made it easier for the military government to permanently cut back social services, allowing it to divert funds towards debt repayments. Simultaneously, responsibility for social services was shifted from the central government to NGOs and local communities, establishing a new relationship between Ghanaians and the institutions that provided social services. Ghanaians were transformed from citizens demanding social rights into depoliticized "beneficiaries" requesting outside charity: "Help from PAMSCAD is appreciated but not expected: it comes as no surprise to those who apply that PAMSCAD money is not forthcoming, that supplies run out, that resources are withheld. If help comes it is seen as a 'blessing', if it does not then people just shrug their shoulders."[37] The shift from public to NGO service provision initiated by the SAP and PAMSCAD allowed the Ghanaian state to abandon previous social responsibilities towards its citizens. Even as Ghana's government enacted policies that systematically harmed the poor, the regime was nonetheless able to present itself as concerned with their suffering by pointing to the projects financed by the social fund.

The Disappointments and Successes of Social Funds

Social funds proliferated in the late 1980s and 1990s. Reddy and Cornia counted at least 70 social funds, as of 2001, with Latin America and other areas effectively "saturated."[38] As in Ghana, social funds typically failed to address the impacts of neoliberalism. Aid expert Judith Tendler writes, "the findings of evaluations by the donors themselves on Social Funds–let alone of others–have been quite mixed."

> In particular, *impacts on poverty and unemployment have often been found to be insignificant*, sometimes even when compared to more traditional and longer-lived employment-generating schemes. ... To offer them to national leaders as a "safety net" to catch those hurt by economic crisis can also provide these leaders, in certain ways, with a way out of facing the poverty challenge more seriously.[39] [emphasis added]

Providing political cover to "reforming" leaders was, to the functionaries charged with implementing neoliberalism, precisely the point.

Learning the political lessons of Ghana's adjustment experience, the IMF, the World Bank and other the donor agencies began to see NGOs "as important vehicles for ... constituency building for a variety of macroeconomic efforts including structural-adjustment programs."[40] A 1990 World Bank document suggested that poor countries "can often usefully involve their NGOs in efforts to mitigate the social costs of adjustment." By giving NGOs a role in designing and implementing SAPs, governments could "develop political support for the adjustment program generally, and especially for its anti-poverty dimensions."[41] In 1991, the World Bank announced "an institution-wide effort to expand its work with NGOs," largely on the basis of the Bank's experience with social funds.[42] The senior vice-president of the World Bank praised NGOs as "important coworkers in a common cause."[43] Other proponents of structural adjustment praised NGO projects financed by social funds for helping to cultivate "new coalitions for reform."[44]

Social funds allowed political elites pursuing neoliberal reforms to reach down to the grassroots via NGOs dependent on their patronage. Social funds were often administered by the executive branch of government, rather than the usual government ministries. This helped to directly bolster the image of "reforming" leaders, who used social funds to win supporters that would otherwise have been alienated by the harsh impact of structural adjustment. According to Tendler, the political impact of social funds "does not necessarily work directly through their actual impact on the poor [which was minimal], but through their use by elected leaders to selectively court groups of voters, whether among the poorest or not." In Peru and Mexico, social funds' numerous small grants for individual projects were "an excellent vehicle for such patronage," wielded with great skill by ruling politicians to defuse opposition to reforms.[45] In Bolivia and Uganda, social funds spurred the growth of NGOs, which provided jobs for civil servants and other downsized members of the middle class.[46]

Leaders were able to deploy social funds to buy off or isolate critics. In El Salvador, the government used its social fund to marginalize critics of structural adjustment. Funds were given only to NGOs with proven links to business groups, while "NGOs allied with the popular sectors during the 1980s … found themselves largely shut out of government plans." In Chile and the Philippines, governments recruited the leaders of progressive NGOs to manage social funds, effectively decapitating organizations and silencing voices that might otherwise have been critical of neoliberal policies. "Some NGO activists fear that this type of cooptation may lead to the end of the progressive NGO as a distinctive organization."[47] With social funds operating across Latin America in the 1980s and 1990s, the growth of NGOs absorbed the leadership of many Left organizations, according to sociologist James Petras:

Many of the former leaders of guerrilla and social movements, trade
union and popular women's organizations have been co-opted by the
NGOs. Some have undoubtedly been attracted by the hope–or the
illusion–that this might give them access to levers of power which would
allow them to do some good. But in any case, the offer is tempting:
higher pay (occasionally in hard currency), prestige and recognition by
overseas donors, overseas conferences and networks, office staff, and
relative security from repression.[48]

Once accustomed to middle class lifestyles, many ex-leftist leaders grew
distant from social movements and were neutralized as a source of potential
opposition to SAPs. Their NGOs were only in exceptional cases involved
in popular struggles against privatization, social spending cutbacks, attacks
on unions, or reductions of agricultural subsidies for small peasants.
According to Petras, their ascension into the aid system came at the price
of "the freedom to challenge the political and economic system."[49]

Perhaps the main difference between Ghana's pioneering social fund
and subsequent funds was the level of resources donors committed.
PAMSCAD was one of the few funds to which donors provided sufficient
resources to maintain–albeit temporarily–aggregate levels of social
spending, making its failures all the more glaring. For subsequent social
funds, however, donors provided far less money than what governments
were cutting back. With aid levels stagnant or falling for the rest of the
Third World, there was "little chance of major resource transfers, at least
on the scale necessary to offset the adverse social impact of structural
adjustment." CIDA officials admitted as much at the time, recognizing
that "we cannot afford another PAMSCAD."[50]

A Versatile Tool

Structural adjustment and the neoliberal development paradigm it brought
into being are often described as "failed" or "flawed." Neoliberalism was
indeed a terrible failure in development terms, causing greater suffering
and hardship for the world's poor. It was also a failure in terms of objectives
of the economists who designed the SAPs, since the debt burdens of poor
countries increased and–except for a handful of exceptions like Ghana–
economic growth stagnated. Throughout the 1980s and 1990s, much of
the Third World remained stuck on the "treadmill of reform," forced to
go back regularly to the IMF for new loans, each time with new, more
onerous conditions attached.

Neoliberalism was, however, a bonanza for the financial and economic interests that promoted and implemented it. The IMF and the World Bank managed to stave off widespread defaults by debtor nations, while foreign capital and local elites reaped huge profits from the turn to privatization, liberalization and deregulation in the Third World. Multinational corporations gained new markets for their products, and new sources of raw materials and cheap, easily exploited labour. Politically-connected elites in the Global South enriched themselves by buying up state industries and even public infrastructure (e.g., telecommunications, water utilities, electricity generation plants) at fire sale prices from financially distressed governments. Mining corporations and agribusiness giants thrived in unregulated market spaces where mineral resources and agricultural exports were no longer controlled by state monopolies or regulated by state marketing boards.

Canada was not a mere bystander to the sea change in development that occurred in the neoliberal era. In Ghana and elsewhere, the NGO boom was fuelled by the desire of CIDA and other donors to contain the political backlash against structural adjustment and smooth the transition to neoliberalism. In the process, government officials and political and corporate elites discovered in NGOs a versatile tool.

3

Faith-based Solutions
The gospel of self help and grassroots capitalism

"[A]t the very foundation of the theory and practice of the development industry ... is the modernist premise that the causes of Third World poverty reside not in the forces that enrich and empower a few of the world's people and immiserate the rest but lie in the deficiencies and delinquencies of poor people and the communities in which they live."
–Jennie M. Smith [1]

On the morning of November 8, 2008, residents of Port-au-Prince, Haiti, awoke to the sounds of shattering concrete and screaming children. The first floor of *College La Promesse* had collapsed during classes, trapping hundreds of students and teachers beneath the rubble. Several NGOs arrived on the scene to help. As hours dragged on into days, families of the victims and other onlookers became frustrated with the slow pace of the rescue effort. The crowd grew impatient and finally exploded. Community members stormed the rubble pile, removing debris and even concrete slabs with their bare hands, only to be driven back by riot police and UN troops occupying the country since June 2004. Speaking afterward to journalists, one father revealed a deep and long-standing resentment towards those ostensibly there to "help":

> No one cares about the children, living or dead ... Government officials and people from all the NGOs, they all come, take pictures, make speeches and they leave us with nothing. We need action! ... Watch, after 15 days, no one is even going to be talking about this. Only the victims and the families will be talking about it. The government and

some other people will get some money out of the disaster, and the children and their families and the community will see none of it.[2]

The November 2008 school collapse was a microcosm of the epic tragedy that befell Haiti on January 12, 2010 when a 7.0 magnitude earthquake levelled several cities, including much of the capital, Port-au-Prince. While the sturdily-built homes and schools of the wealthy mostly survived the quake, the city's slum neighbourhoods were devastated. Like *College La Promesse*, the tiny, concrete homes of the poor precariously perched on hillsides were instantly destroyed, killing countless thousands in a matter of seconds.

NGOs stampeded into the disaster zone immediately after the 2010 earthquake, but as months passed and reconstruction efforts stalled, many Haitians felt these organizations were exploiting their poverty and suffering for their own benefit. Dr. Paul Farmer, who had worked in Haiti for over 30 years, reported that popular frustration with NGOs was at an all-time high. "The Haitian people are seeing the money coming in, and the resources aren't coming to them. ... There's graffiti all over the walls in Port au Prince right now saying, 'Down with NGOs,'" Farmer said in a speech at Barry University in Florida. "I think people in the NGO sector need to read the writing on the wall."[3] In a demonstration on the 1-year anniversary of the earthquake, Haitians marched behind a banner reading: "*12 Janvye 2010 = Misé pou Ayisien, Milyon pou ONG*" (January 12, 2010 = Misery for Haitians, Millions for NGOs).[4] Government and UN officials decried the undue influence of these "do-gooder" organizations over the country.

Long before the earthquake brought popular resentment to the surface, close observers of Haiti had been aware of the discontent brewing in the "Republic of NGOs." In Haiti, NGOs are a regular subject of political discussion, much of which is quite hostile, from all ends of the political spectrum. Haitian researchers described the astounding growth of these foreign-funded organizations over the last 30 years as an "invasion" of NGOs, resulting in the "NGOization" of Haitian society. A report by Haitian academic Sauveur Pierre Étienne concluded that NGOs "constitute obstacles to development of the country."[5] From the perspective of ordinary Haitians, NGOs and their employees had become just another layer of corrupt *gran manje* ("big eaters") living at the expense of the nation without benefiting it, hardly different from Haiti's political class or its tiny, rapacious economic elite.

Why have Haitians grown poorer, hungrier and more desperate over the last 30 years, despite the huge number of NGOs out to "Save the Children," to take "Action against Hunger," and to bring "Development and Peace" to the country? Why have the good intentions of NGO workers and volunteers produced only resentment and suspicion among the vast majority of Haitians, 80% of whom live on less than $2 per day?

The case of Haiti may be extreme, but it is not exceptional. Anger and disillusionment with NGOs is widespread in the South and part of a more general phenomenon: the failure of NGO-inspired self help and the institutionalized corruption that came with it.

Favoured Children

The NGO boom persisted long after the tumultuous early years of structural adjustment. "Although the 1980s were described as the 'NGO decade'," political scientist Julie Hearn noted in 2007, "growth continues apace: the bubble has not yet burst."[6] Fuelled by ever-growing shares of development aid, NGOs have taken over provision of employment opportunities, social services and basic infrastructure (health care, education, roads, housing, water and sanitation) from structurally-adjusted governments of the Global South. In the process, development NGOs have become a ubiquitous feature of everyday life throughout the poorer parts of world.

With the ascendance of neoliberalism as the dominant development ideology, note NGO scholars Michael Edwards and David Hulme, NGOs became "the *preferred channel* for service provision, in *deliberate substitution* for the state."[7] (emphasis in original) In 2000, local NGOs and churches provided a third or more of the clinical health care in Cameroon, Ghana, Malawi, Uganda and Zambia. Over a quarter of the health facilities in Bolivia's three largest cities were run by NGOs.[8] In Bangladesh, one NGO–the Bangladesh Rural Advancement Committee (BRAC)–has grown "so powerful that it is commonly termed Bangladesh's second government." Critics accuse BRAC of acting like a parallel state, but one that is accountable to no one. "Government dependency on its services has grown to the extent that they almost can't run the country without it," a former employee told the *Guardian* (UK).[9]

As governments gutted public programs meant to deal with unemployment, NGOs were funded to devise "income generating" projects, typically aimed at helping the poor set up or expand micro-enterprises. NGO interventions designed to help poor individuals to seize opportunities in the marketplace came in many forms–teaching a new skill to fishermen, organizing a marketing cooperative of basket weavers, providing seeds to farmers eking out a living on tiny plots of land, etc.–but none was more popular than microcredit. "Virtually every development project I see these days," writes veteran international development worker Tom Dichter, "from maternal and child health, to women's education, to soil conservation, to social forestry, to old fashioned integrated rural development, has a 'microcredit component,' and everyone from camel herders in Mauritania to peasants in rural China can speak the lingo."[10]

The donors' preference for NGOs was justified based on two major assumptions. The first was that NGOs are superior to the public sector when it comes to providing social services to the poor. NGOs were, the architects of aid claimed, more efficient and better able to reach the poor while the public sector was bloated, bureaucratic, inefficient and corrupt. The rollback of the state's social welfare functions was welcomed by donors because it cleared the way for NGO service provision. NGOs actively involved the poor in the design and implementation of projects, so NGO service provision was expected to be lower cost and higher quality. Encouraging community participation was also seen as a way of making NGO projects "sustainable." Donors celebrated these "comparative advantages" of NGOs for providing social services "better, cheaper and faster" than governments.

The second assumption was that NGO support for micro-enterprises was superior to government-led efforts to promote economic development. Neoliberal policies occasioned an explosion of unregulated economic activity in the "informal" sector, especially in fast-growing urban areas, as more people turned to petty trading, services and other kinds of micro-enterprise as a means of survival. In the past, development economists of all ideological stripes had viewed the informal sector as a form of disguised unemployment. They considered an increase in formal sector jobs essential to dealing with poverty. Proponents of micro-entrepreneurialism challenged these ideas, arguing that the poor were in fact repressed entrepreneurs.

Prominent NGO figures spearheaded the change in thinking by embracing the informal sector as an engine for "bottom up" growth. Grameen Bank's Mohammed Yunus became a development industry icon by suggesting that tiny loans could free the poor from the oppression of the moneylender and unleash their entrepreneurial instincts, breaking the cycle of poverty and indebtedness. Peruvian economist Hernando de Soto famously declared he had solved the "mystery of capital": the poor were sitting on mountains of untapped informal wealth, and only needed property rights and a market framework to realize that wealth and escape poverty. De Soto and his NGO, the Institute for Liberty and Democracy, promoted the idea that once the poor had property rights for their informal assets (such as homes built on illegally-squatted land), they would instantly have the legal collateral necessary to borrow money. If the state reduced regulations and provided title for such assets, the poor would be able to start or expand micro-enterprises and a wave of investment would ensue. Yunus and de Soto's influential writings suggested that with a little push from NGOs–in the form of training, loans and start-up capital–the poor could easily create successful micro-enterprises that would uplift the community in a virtuous cycle of reinvestment and job-creation.

Underpinning donors' enthusiasm for such programs was the ideology of "self help" as a remedy to the problems of the poor. NGOs were not supposed to replace the state so much as to help the poor to provide their own jobs, infrastructure and social services. By initiating these kinds of projects, NGOs were supposed to spur the process of self help and then withdraw, leaving self-sufficient, healthy communities in their wake. NGOs became "the 'favored child' of official agencies and [were seen] as something of a panacea for the problems of development."[11] In the poorer, more aid-dependent countries of Africa, Asia and Latin America, NGOs almost entirely supplanted the social welfare functions of the local state.

Built on "Foundations of Sand"

Self help programs were widely considered to be a pragmatic–even "empowering"–way to meet the needs of the poor. But the hype surrounding NGO-assisted self help as a poverty reduction strategy was established well before any serious research on its effectiveness had been done. When greater attention was paid to the issue, the assumptions behind self help proved to be flawed.

Generalizations about the superiority of NGOs-provided services were difficult to sustain in the face of the facts. At the height of the NGO boom in 1996, for instance, Edwards and Hulme observed that "there is no empirical study that demonstrates a general case that NGO service provision is cheaper than public provision."[12] Based on an extensive review of documentation on NGO service provision in the Global South, UN researchers Andrew Clayton, Peter Oakley and Jon Taylor found "a number of common deficiencies" with having NGOs act as a surrogate social safety net for the poor, including "limited coverage; variable quality; amateurish approach; high staff turnover; lack of effective management systems; poor cost effectiveness; lack of co-ordination; and poor sustainability due to dependence on external assistance." The review found little evidence for the presumed superiority of NGOs over governments, whether it was with respect to quality of services, reaching the poorest, or efficiency.[13] Other assessments came to similar conclusions: "NGO service provision was frequently characterized by problems of quality control, limited sustainability, poor coordination and general amateurism."[14] According to NGO researcher David Lewis, "even when the quality of services is high, most NGOs offer limited, piecemeal or patchy provision which can never compete with the state in terms of coverage."[15]

At a time of growing need, the shift to NGOs as service providers created a social safety net that was uneven, inadequate, and vulnerable to the fluctuations in notoriously volatile aid levels from the West. The results in terms of the lives of the poor were underwhelming, even in best-case scenarios:

> In Bangladesh, where the NGO sector contains some of the most large-scale, influential NGOs anywhere in the world, the total combined NGO effort may only reach about 20 per cent of the functionally landless population (which numbers about a half of Bangladesh's 130 million people)–leaving about 40 million people out altogether. And that is with diverse, unsystematic services.[16]

Research also established that NGO income-generating projects typically failed to improve the situation of the poor in measurable ways. The main reason was that NGOs and other self help enthusiasts promoting micro-entrepreneurialism had vastly overrated the business prospects available in the informal sector. The informal economy was home to countless tiny, labour-intensive "businesses"–roadside vegetable stands, home-based artisans, open-air repair shops, street corner hawkers–whose prospects for growth were severely limited. These small-scale economic activities of the poor had low levels of technology and little or no fixed investment. With virtually no scope for productivity-enhancing investments, competition between ever-growing numbers of micro-entrepreneurs produced an endless subdivision of the local market. The poverty-reducing potential of micro-entrepreneurialism was also constrained by the neoliberal context, such as competition from foreign imports and limited domestic demand, which made the chances of success for poverty-stricken businesspeople even slimmer.[17]

The growth of the informal sector was itself a symptom of the lack of opportunities faced by the poor under neoliberalism.[18] In both rural and urban areas, with few options for employment in the formal economy and without any social security systems to fall back on (welfare or unemployment insurance), poor people had little choice but to seek a living in the informal sector. As Thomas Dichter explains, micro-entrepreneurialism was a survival tactic of the poor, not a solution to poverty as the self help enthusiasts misleadingly implied:

> The informal sector in most places is in fact a default mode, a function of failing economies. It is not the incubator of economic growth but a holding action where everyone (including government employees) is forced to go since little else is available to them. *These markets are not the way out of poverty; they are driven by it.*[19] [emphasis in original]

An exhaustive review of microfinance impact studies commissioned by the UK's Department for International Development (DFID) found that the buzz around microcredit as a powerful poverty-fighting tool was built on "foundations of sand." "No clear evidence exists that microfinance programmes have positive impacts," whether with respect to income, social well-being or women's empowerment, the review concluded. The research team led by Maren Duvendack concluded that proponents of microcredit based their claims on "weak methodologies and inadequate data," and suggested that the "ill-founded enthusiasm for microfinance" may have been driven by "other powerful but not necessarily benign, from the point of view of poor people, policy agendas."[20]

Microcredit expert Milford Bateman confirms these assessments, arguing that tiny loans for the poor have only produced "hyper-competition and self-exploitation."

> For perhaps the saddest reflection of generalised microcredit failure, however, we need look no further than the iconic village of Jobra in Bangladesh, the location for Muhammad Yunus' pioneering Grameen Bank, and so the effective starting point for the global microfinance movement. In spite of an unparalleled availability of microcredit since the late 1970s, Jobra and its neighbouring villages remain mired in deep poverty, unemployment and underdevelopment. Moreover, a new social problem haunts the region thanks to the ubiquity of microcredit—growing levels of personal over-indebtedness.[21]

Hernando de Soto's favourite intervention, land titling, fared no better under scrutiny. In Turkey, Mexico, South Africa, Colombia or even de Soto's home country of Peru, titling did not increase the flow of formal credit to the slums or produce the anticipated burst of informal sector investment.[22] According to urban researcher Mike Davis, titling "accelerates social differentiation in the slum and does nothing to aid renters, the actual majority of the poor in many cities." Titling proved to be a double-edged sword even for homeowners, who gained property rights but were also made more visible to tax collectors and municipal utilities. Davis cites a number of studies demonstrating that "titling by itself is hardly an Archimedean lever to raise the fortunes of the great mass of poor urban dwellers."[23]

On their own, NGO programs are at best inadequate, limited and temporary palliatives for the severe and deepening poverty of the world's majority. Reviewing the evaluation literature on NGOs, aid expert Roger Riddell concludes that NGO projects have made "only a small contribution to improving the lives and enhancing the well-being of the beneficiaries."[24] The incremental improvements, moreover, rarely lasted beyond the life of the project, as Riddell observes: "The bulk of the NGO evaluation material … has concluded that most NGO projects are not financially sustainable without the continued injection of external funds. Nor is it surprising that the poorer the beneficiaries, the less likely they are to be able to pay for the services, training or goods provided to them."[25] As long as NGO projects are constrained by the adverse economic conditions created by neoliberalism, Riddell notes, these meagre results are unlikely to change through better project design or other kinds of technical fixes: "Especially when the environment beyond the project does not provide the context in which narrower projects gains can be exploited, it has proven exceptionally difficult for discrete NGO projects on their own to enable poor people … to live free from poverty."[26] NGO expert Tina Wallace relates how at a European NGO conference, participants questioned by a journalist were forced to sheepishly admit, "we have few stories of development success to tell."[27]

The Privatization of Welfare

Dismal results did little to dampen donor support for NGOs and their self help approach to development. "The more micro views of how to approach poverty reduction," aid expert Judith Tendler observes, "have gained such strength that they seem to have become impregnable to contrary findings from evaluation research."[28] Couched in a language of pragmatism, the enthusiastic and enduring support of donors for NGOs went hand in hand with the broader pro-market, anti-state thrust of neoliberal ideology. "NGOs were first identified as ... key players that reshaped public action for development away from state-centred approaches towards private, market-based policies," writes David Lewis.[29] Though it had little basis in reality, the myth of self help was ideologically useful in a number of ways.

Bypassing the public sector by redirecting an ever-larger share of development aid to NGOs fit with the donors' larger neoliberal objectives. By draining the state of resources and people, the growth of NGOs accelerated the rollback of the state, especially in poorer, aid-dependent countries with a scarcity of professional expertise. The NGO boom created a multitude of well-paid positions in NGO service delivery systems operating parallel to the state. This tended to lure away qualified personnel from posts in local government, weakening the capacity of the state to design or implement social programs. "In fact, what NGOs end up doing is weakening government in the long run and perpetuating its inefficiency."[30] Perversely, giving aid money to NGOs was subsequently justified with the claim that the gutted civil service and cash-starved ministries lacked the "absorptive capacity" to receive aid. The large subsidies granted to NGOs but denied to governments for public social services threatened to "make the gap between private and public provision a 'self-perpetuating reality'."[31] In *A Brief History of Neoliberalism,* geographer David Harvey calls this process "privatization by NGO," whereby NGOs functioned as "Trojan horses" for neoliberalism, as their expansion "helped accelerate further state withdrawal from social provision."[32]

Claims that NGO service providers could magically do "more with less" were attractive to donors because they eased the way for further cutbacks while placing greater burdens on poor communities. "It may be the desire to cut costs, rather than an interest in improving effectiveness," David Lewis and social policy analyst Nazneen Kanji conclude, "that lies at the heart of a decision to make greater use of NGOs to deliver a particular service."[33] According to sociologist Shelley Feldman, the preoccupation with "sustainability," "cost recovery" and avoiding subsidies, "whether with regard to banking for the poor, healthcare, or education, signals the appropriation of the rhetoric of privatisation and individualism as cornerstones of NGO operations."[34]

Ideologically, NGO income generating projects fit perfectly with neoliberalism. In part, microcredit and other similar initiatives were attractive because they promised to create employment "on the cheap," without public employment programs, the creation of state-owned enterprises, or any kind of industrial policy. The emphasis on micro-entrepreneurs meant the poor were conceptualized, not as oppressed peasants or exploited workers, but as budding micro-capitalists. To escape poverty, the poor did not need land reform, higher wages or more generous terms of trade—just property rights and the proper market framework. Neoliberalism, by getting the state out of the way, was a victory for the little man. Simultaneously, by exaggerating the opportunities in the informal sector, NGOs shifted the blame for poverty onto the poor themselves and away from social, political or structural factors. If the poor failed to pull themselves up by their bootstraps, it was due to their own deficiencies rather than any inherent unfairness of the social structure.

The shift to NGOs was part of the privatization of welfare, taking issues of public services and employment out of the realm of politics and de-linking them from questions of social justice. Self help naturalized the existing distribution of wealth and reinforced the neoliberal premise that long-term transfers of resources to poor communities were unnecessary or even harmful. "Self-sufficiency, the idea that 'left to their own devices' (and their current resources) poor communities would lift themselves out from poverty just fine, makes for an attractive myth but a regressive policy," warn Erhard Berner and Benedict Phillips. "The shift towards self-help can be seen as a masking defence against calls for redistribution."[35]

The spread of NGOs transformed poor people in the Global South from citizens demanding social rights into charity recipients, as Arundhati Roy argues:

> NGOs give the impression that they are filling a vacuum created by a retreating state. And they are, but in a materially inconsequential way. Their real contribution is that they defuse political anger and dole out as aid or benevolence what people ought to have by right. NGOs alter the public psyche. They turn people into dependent victims and blunt political resistance.[36]

"We Live like Kings": Institutionalized Corruption

The turn to self help may have done little for the poor, but it had a major impact on the living standards of NGO professionals. NGOs often tout their low administrative costs, placed in the 5-15% range, and imply that the rest of the funds go "directly to the poor." According to aid expert Roger Riddell, these figures are misleading, since it is only "agency-wide" costs incurred by the head office (fundraising, advertising, etc.) that are counted as administrative costs in such calculations. The "support" costs incurred for individual projects–administration costs by any other name–are typically excluded. Yet these support costs for projects make up the bulk of NGO expenditures: they include the salaries of both foreign and local NGO employees, travel and living expenses, and the cost of field offices in the South incurred in the course of a project. Riddell conservatively estimates that over 70% of aid money spent by NGOs goes towards these support costs, along with training and "institutional strengthening" activities. In fact, less than 30% of development money flowing through NGOs reaches the ultimate beneficiaries.[37]

With the growth of NGOs, the illicit corruption of state officials was replaced with the institutionalized corruption of the NGO system. Anthropologist David Mosse, who worked as a technical expert on a British rural development project in India, found a degree of dishonesty in the way those working on the project talked about it. In official discourse, the development project was celebrated as a "gift," but this language "concealed a more complex economic reality in which those honored as donors (DFID officials, consultants, ourselves) were proportionately the far greater beneficiaries of aid money in a project system that 'redistributed' at least 25 per cent [and as much as 37 per cent] of funds to UK institutions and consultants."[38]

Living in cloistered expatriate ghettos, the international development set often takes the huge salary disparities and lavish lifestyles that set them apart from the poor for granted. In his study of development workers in Honduras, anthropologist Jeffrey Jackson found that expatriate development personnel, while emphasizing the "sacrifice" they were making by working abroad, enjoyed luxuries that they never could have afforded back home (e.g. maids, gardeners, chauffeurs etc.) and freely admitted that they "lived like kings."[39] Daniel Jordan Smith noted the hypocrisy of expatriate development workers in Nigeria, who relished outlandish tales of local corruption while enjoying privileges that a government bureaucrat could only dream of. "At parties, and over drinks and dinner at the expensive restaurants in Ikoyi and on Victoria Island, the upscale areas of Lagos where the development and diplomatic communities entertained themselves in the early 1990s, expatriates told seemingly endless stories about Nigerian corruption."[40]

Those in the "receiving" countries are not blind to the contradiction between the NGOs' rhetoric of giving and their reality of getting. In Liberia, it is the foreign NGOs themselves that Liberians see as benefiting the most from development activities in the country. According to the *Sunday Independent*, a South African newspaper, "Liberians say the benefits of this massive international investment are far more obvious in the parts of town inhabited by the foreigners themselves. The number of pools is burgeoning. Casinos are opening. Beach-side bars are springing up or being spruced up." With the arrival of aid, new stores sprung up selling imported products at prices that often exceed the monthly salaries of Liberians fortunate enough to have a job, and some upscale bars and nightclubs even have specially-designated "NGO nights."[41]

On a smaller scale, local NGO employees in the South participate in the institutionalized corruption of the aid system as well. Local NGO workers receive salaries that are often far higher than civil servants in the public sector. Researcher Peter Uvin estimates that an average of one third of all development project costs go to "a handful of technical assistants, experts, and consultants." "It has often been said–and I largely concur–that the prime impact of development projects is to create jobs for the lucky few who manage to obtain them." Local NGO employees benefit from the significant sums spent on "four-wheel-drive vehicles, villas, foreign travel, and hundreds of small, daily status symbols." In Rwanda, NGOs tended to exacerbate local inequalities, as the privileges that accrued to development workers, both foreign and local, created "a permanent reminder of the life that could be but that never would be for the majority of the population."[42]

Haiti: Discontent in the "Republic of NGOs"

Everywhere you look, you see projects piling up … in every little corner of the country, projects. But they're not really benefiting the country … it's not development you see here, but envelopment!
  –Leader of a peasant women's organization speaking to anthropologist Jennie M. Smith about foreign aid in Haiti [43]

Haiti has been dubbed "The Republic of NGOs" and it is an appropriate moniker. Over the past 30 years, development NGOs have become a ubiquitous presence in the country. White 4x4 SUV bearing the logos of various organizations clog the streets of Port-au-Prince, while billboards declare, "Avis is the preferred rental car company of NGOs!" In Haiti's largest and oldest daily newspaper, *Le Nouvelliste*, 74.5% of "help wanted" classified ads were for jobs with NGOs or international organizations (such as the UN) in 2005. Of the remainder, 29% were for private-sector jobs and only 8% were for positions within Haiti's government. According to anthropologist Mark Schuller, NGOs have carved up the country, claiming parts of it as their "turf":

> I have seen signs with an NGO logo welcoming me to a particular provincial town. More often, this marking of territory was accomplished through a sign mentioning a particular project: "food for work," "road rehabilitation," or others.[44]

Haiti is estimated to have the world's highest concentration of NGOs per capita, with over 900 foreign development NGOs and an estimated 10,000 NGOs overall operating in the small Caribbean nation of 8 million inhabitants. Their presence has even been felt in the capital's real estate market: Rising housing prices in the wealthy neighbourhood of Petionville have been attributed NGOs seeking setting up shop in this posh neighborhood of the capital. The country is literally blanketed by organizations there to "Save the Children," to "Feed the Poor," to wage a "War on Want" and so on.

"Privatization by NGO" has advanced further in Haiti than any other nation. Over 90% of foreign aid money is channeled through NGOs and nearly 80% of Haiti's basic services (healthcare, education, sanitation etc.) are provided by NGOs. NGOs operate in nearly every field of activity–healthcare, education, sanitation, reforestation, microcredit, agricultural assistance, etc.–and often enjoy budgets larger than those of the corresponding Haitian government ministries. Agriculture provides an indication of just how far the loss of sovereignty has gone. In 2006-2007, the Ministry of Agriculture controlled only $6 million of the $91 million budgeted for public investment in agriculture. The remaining $85 million–some 93% of total public investment in agriculture–was managed by over 800 NGOs working in parallel to the Ministry and pursuing priorities over which elected officials have little influence.[45] "Fuelled by North-Western coffers, political agendas, and expertise, NGOs [and other foreign organizations] … have amassed a great deal of power in Haiti during recent years," observes anthropologist Jennie M. Smith. Especially in rural areas and the urban *bidonvilles* (shantytowns), NGOs have all but supplanted government agencies. "In many ways, in fact, they seem to constitute a sort of shadow government."[46]

Given what came before the NGO boom, Haiti should have been a showcase for the "comparative advantages" of NGOs over the public sector. Under the rule of the US-backed Duvalier dictatorships (1957-1986), corruption in the public administration was rampant and the government provided virtually no services to the population. The peasantry was relentlessly taxed while state coffers were looted for the benefit of the ruling clique and its hangers-on. Haiti was a notorious sinkhole for international development aid and the *modus operandi* of the Haitian state in this period earned it the label "predatory state." Haitians expected the situation to change with the advent of democracy in 1990. Haiti's elected leaders were voted into office on a platform of "investing in human beings," primarily through increased education and health care spending. Public investment in Haiti's long neglected countryside was another priority of ordinary Haitians, who hoped to reverse the decades-long decline in agricultural production.

Before this mandate could be put into practice, the government was overthrown in a coup d'état from 1991-1994. When elected officials returned to power, the IMF and the World Bank announced they had other plans for Haiti's development. "NGOs will continue to play a major role in service design and delivery, especially in remote rural areas and among the urban poor," noted a 1997 World Bank report, "where the [Government of Haiti] has scarcely any autonomous delivery capacity." Privatization of Haiti's state enterprises–a key source of revenue for the government–would force the further abandonment of the social responsibilities of the state to NGOs, the report explained. "The agreed privatization of key para-statal organizations is likely further to limit Government's engagement in most sectors, and to provide additional scope for NGOs and the for-profit private sector."[47]

The growth of the non-governmental sector precipitated the decline of the state's capacity to implement programs, as NGOs "raided" the public sector of whatever talented or trained individuals remained. Haitian staff working for development NGOs receive salaries at least 10 times higher than local civil servants with similar levels of training and responsibility.[48] A 20-year veteran of the Ministry of Agriculture estimated that with the same amount of money, the government could do nine times the amount of work that an NGO could. Ironically, this long-time civil servant left his post to work for an NGO because of a higher salary.[49] The internal "brain drain" created by the growth of NGOs became a self-fulfilling prophecy: the weaker and more hollowed out the state became, the more justification the donors had for routing aid around the government. A December 2004 evaluation noted that CIDA's "emphasis on non-governmental actors as development partners also undermined efforts to strengthen good governance ... [and] contributed to the establishment of parallel systems of service delivery, eroding legitimacy, capacity and will of the state to deliver key services."[50]

Pressed to sell off state assets and pay down debts accumulated by the Duvaliers, and at the same time deprived of skilled personnel and resources by the NGO sector, the democratic government's hands were all but tied. In the late 1990s and early 2000s, CIDA and other donors consistently starved Haiti's elected governments of funds–precisely because of its reluctance to privatize state enterprises.

Macro Problems, Micro Solutions

There is perhaps no place on earth where the devastation caused by neoliberalism has been greater than in Haiti. According to political scientist Alex Dupuy, neoliberal reforms "led to the steady deterioration of the Haitian economy" and transformed it into "an essentially labour-exporting economy increasingly dependent on remittances from Haitian migrants, foreign aid, and drug trafficking."[51] Trade liberalization and privatization wiped out industries producing for the domestic market, but industries producing for export never materialized and economic indicators plummeted: "[R]eal per capita GDP fell an average of 2.4 percent per year in the 1980s and continued to decline in the 1990s at an average annual rate of 2.6 percent."[52]

Although Haiti's turn to neoliberalism produced deepening misery for the poor majority, it simultaneously created additional riches for the already-wealthy minority:

> Missing from most media accounts is that while Haiti is the "poorest country in the hemisphere" by economic measures–80% live on less than US$2 per day, and around half have an income of $1 or less–it is also the most unequal. It is second only to Namibia in income inequality, and has the most millionaires per capita in the region.[53]

Since independence in 1804, Haiti has been divided between a poor, black, largely rural majority and a wealthy, light-skinned urban elite. After decades of neoliberal reforms, "the polarization between the dominant class and the rest of the population was even larger."[54] Privatization had the effect of concentrating wealth even further in the hands of Haiti's tiny light-skinned elite. Using their monopolistic control over the domestic market, the Haitian elite enriched themselves via import-export trading enterprises and in partnership with foreign investors bought up public companies at a fraction of their value. Haiti's skewed income distribution reflected this reality: In 2002, the top 1% of the population received over 50% of the country's income, while the bottom 70% received only 20% of Haiti's declining national revenues.[55]

Haiti's embrace of neoliberalism was harshest for the country's peasants, who were dealt a series of blows in the 1980s and 1990s. The first came in 1983, when an African Swine Flu scare hit Haiti. The U.S. government pressured the Duvalier dictatorship to eradicate all the indigenous "Creole" pigs on the island. The hardy Creole pigs subsisted on food waste and foraging, and functioned as a savings bank for peasants to pay for expenses like funerals, doctor's visits or school fees: when the time came, they could slaughter or sell the pig. The eradication program effectively wiped out the savings of virtually the entire peasantry. School enrollment fell by nearly 50% following the kill-off of the pigs.[56] A repopulation program funded by USAID and CIDA was a failure; the American-imported pigs were unadapted to the harsh conditions of Haiti.

The next blow came from the liberalization of agriculture, which was devastating to Haiti's peasants. Though the Duvalier dictatorships had never invested in agriculture, peasant smallholders had been protected by tariffs from foreign competition. When tariffs were cut in 1986 and again in 1995 as part of IMF-negotiated trade liberalization, cheap imported food flooded the market. Facing competition from mechanized and heavily-subsidized U.S. farms, Haitian agriculture collapsed. Rice farmers from the fertile Artibonite Valley were hit particularly hard. Though Haiti had been self-sufficient in rice production up until the 1980s, imports of "Miami rice" from the U.S. grew from 5,000 tons in 1984 to 200,000 tons in 1995. American food conglomerates' forays into Haiti's liberalized markets also decimated the small-scale poultry industry, which was wiped out by dumping of surplus frozen chicken parts on the Haitian market.[57] Local dairy production was eliminated by imported powdered milk. Once domestic agricultural capacity was cut down, Haitians were exposed to the wild swings of the world commodities markets and price gouging by local elite-owned importers. In April 2008, food riots broke out over the rising price of imported rice and other basic staples.

The destruction of Haiti's agriculture was foreseen as a consequence of going through with neoliberal reforms. A 1995 USAID report stated: "An export-driven trade and investment policy has the potential to relentlessly squeeze the domestic rice farmer. This farmer will be forced to adapt, or he [sic] will disappear."[58] Rural Haitians adapted by either retreating into archaic forms of subsistence farming or moving to the cities in search of work. Trade liberalization also accelerated the problems of deforestation and soil erosion, because one of the few profitable "crops" left for rural Haitians was charcoal made from felled trees and sold as cooking fuel in the cities.

Rural migrants descended on Port-au-Prince in droves. The city's population grew from 732,000 in the early 1980s, and to approximately 3 million in 2008, or nearly one-third of Haiti's population of 9.8 million. Yet just as peasants were arriving, formal sector jobs were disappearing. Public sector employment contracted under the impact of privatization. When state-owned companies like the flour mill, the cement factory, and the sugar refinery were privatized, they were shut down, their workforces laid off and their machinery sold. Their production was replaced by imports. Even in the apparel assembly factories, which were supposed to provide jobs for displaced peasants and act as a motor for export-led growth, employment shrank as foreign investors shifted sweatshop production to other, more "politically stable" low-wage locations. By 1999, Haiti's urban formal sector employed only 114,000 workers.[59]

The rural-urban migration created a huge oversupply of labour in the cities, which translated into falling wages and working conditions and a growing informal sector. In the apparel assembly sector, wages fell continuously over the 1980 and 1990s. Wages dropped by 56% from 1983 to 1989, and by 2000 were at less than 20% of their 1980 level.[60] The fortunes of those in Haiti's informal sector, where a staggering 93% of the non-agricultural working population was trying to make a living, were not any better.

Even the most innovative and well-conceived NGO projects could do little against the adverse economic forces bearing down on the Haitian poor. Despite the support offered to Haiti's urban micro-entrepreneurs by NGOs, the overcrowded informal sector was characterized by "low wages and precarious employment conditions" and continued to function "primarily [as] a means of survival rather than an alternative engine of growth for the Haitian economy," writes Alex Dupuy.[61] Projects to reforest mountainsides or to help cultivators to eke out a living on their tiny *mouchwa* ("handkerchief" sized) plots could not save Haiti's peasants. According to Jennie M. Smith, NGO development efforts "left little more than the shells of unfinished projects" in rural Haiti.[62]

Some NGO programs actually contributed to the flooding of Haiti's domestic market. Food aid from Canada, the U.S. and the EU tripled in the 1980s. World Vision, CARE and other major NGOs were contracted to distribute "Miami rice" and other foreign food commodities through food-for-work and food distribution programs. Implemented at peak seasons, these programs undermined small producers by further undercutting their prices and drawing away farm labour at harvest time. At their height in the early 1990s, these programs were feeding some 600,000 to one million Haitians with food commodities purchased abroad.[63]

Corruption or Overhead?

Watching acronyms, projects and development panaceas parade through the country, many Haitians concluded that their poverty was being exploited for the benefit of foreigners and a tiny, educated middle class in the NGOs. While the notorious corruption of Haiti's government often served to justify favoring NGOs to deliver aid, from the perspective of Haiti's poor, there was little difference between the petty corruption of government officials and the institutionalized corruption of NGO elites. "A sour Haitian joke says that when a Haitian minister skims 15 per cent of aid money it is called 'corruption' and when an NGO or aid agency takes 50 per cent it is called 'overhead.'"[64] As one activist passionately explained to Mark Schuller, "NGOs live in luxury, with new cars and big air-conditioned offices that just get bigger and bigger, and what do we get? We're supposed to be grateful for everything."[65]

Working in rural Haiti, Jennie M. Smith heard similar biting criticisms over and over again from Haitians who accused NGOs of exploiting their poverty for personal and institutional gain. When talking about development NGOs, rural Haitians would often repeat the proverb: "They put the pot on the fire in the name of the children, but it comes off in the name of the adults."[66] A woman hired to wash and cook for a group of Canadian expatriates told Smith:

> We are like a calf they put up to its mother's teat to suckle, but push aside when the milk begins to flow. We are allowed only to taste the milk; they collect the rest in the bucket to drink themselves.[67]

A spiritual healer in one of the villages Smith studied explained that the real beneficiaries of development were not the rural poor, but the educated urbanites running the NGOs themselves:

> The people who benefit from development are those who sit with their big vests, big neckties in the city. ... You hear them talking about doing

deeds for the poor, but when you take a good look, you see the poor
never get anything there.[68]

To the outsider, ordinary Haitians might seem ungrateful to those there
to help, but their perspective cannot be dismissed lightly. NGOs failed
to arrest the long and excruciating downward slide in living standards
among the poor majority. Discussing the impact of self help development
schemes, Jennie M. Smith observed:

> [O]ther than the handful of nationals working for international
> organizations (most of whom already were better off than most
> citizens), few Haitians have benefited more from this most recent series
> of program plans than they had from those of the past. In fact, the
> situation of the 'targeted populations' (for the most part, the peasantry
> and the urban poor) seems to be declining as rapidly as ever.[69]

CIDA came to similarly pessimistic conclusions about the effectiveness
of NGOs in a December 2004 evaluation of 450 projects it had funded in
Haiti. The initiatives of Canadian NGOs and their partners were described
as "small," "fragmented" and "widely dispersed," and as a result, "no critical
mass of results was achieved."[70] "As a structure–yes, there are notable
exceptions–NGOs have failed Haiti," Mark Schuller argues, "particularly
the *pèp la*, Haiti's poor majority." Though the lion's share of foreign aid
went to NGOs, the only bright spots in development terms were the result
of concerted public programs enacted by Haiti's democratic governments,
Schuller notes:

> All development indicators have seen a steady decline from 1980 to
> 2007, as of the last data I methodically examined, except for two. These
> two indicators–the incidence of HIV/AIDS and literacy–are exceptions
> precisely because they were mutual priorities of the elected governments
> of Haiti and donor groups. ... Haiti's success in combating the disease is
> a ray of hope: in just over a decade since 1993, the seroprevalence went
> from 6.2 percent to about 3.2 percent.[71]

The failures of the "Republic of NGOs" came into full view with the
January 12 earthquake. The government was incapacitated after years
of reforms, and the catastrophe revealed the dysfunction of the NGO
system and its alienation from the population. On March 5, 2010 Haiti's
Prime Minister Jean Max Bellerive openly aired his frustration with the

government's near-total loss of sovereignty to NGOs, due to the way the aid money is being delivered. "The NGOs don't tell us ... where the money's coming from or how they're spending it," Bellerive told journalists. "Too many people are raising money without any controls, and don't explain what they're doing with it."[72] UN representative Edmond Mulet chimed in, complaining that Haiti's chaotic patchwork of NGOs had undermined the government. NGOs were not coordinated, took on too many roles and swarmed well-known neighbourhoods while leaving others untouched–doing what Mulet called "little things with little impact." "We complain because the government is not able to [help the people], but we are partly responsible for that," admitted Mulet.[73]

In a grimly ironic turn, the same forced liberalization that brought the NGOs also made a significant contribution to the scale of the disaster. Haiti's rapid urbanization had led to chaotically-built slums sprouting everywhere: on garbage dumps, next to the airport, on floodplains–and on hillsides. Organizer and advocate Beverly Bell explains:

> Unable to compete with imported goods and thus unable to survive, Haitian farmers have flocked into the overcrowded capital in search of a living. They have joined the ranks of the underemployed or been welcomed by sweatshops. And they have taken up residence in shoddily constructed housing built on insecure lands, like ravines and the sides of steep mountains. The devastating toll from the earthquake, with anywhere from 250,000 to 300,000 killed in and around Port-au-Prince, is in part due to farmers' inability to remain in their rural homes.[74]

Conclusion: Downsizing and Narrowing

In response to the onslaught of neoliberalism, poor people throughout the Global South found innovative ways of surviving. The resources provided by NGOs have helped some of the poor in Haiti and elsewhere to cope with the damage done by neoliberal reforms. The populist rhetoric of NGOs, however, depicted these desperate adaptations to worsening poverty to be the last word in "bottom up" development. Western governments embraced the idea of self help and lauded NGOs as "a 'magic bullet' that can be fired off in any direction and will still find its target, though often *without leaving much evidence.*"[75] (emphasis added)

Behind rhetoric about NGO-aided self help was a downsizing of entitlements and a narrowing of politics. While local elites and multinationals enriched themselves, NGOs and their perpetually upbeat

"success stories" provided a "human face"–a Potemkin village-style façade–
to cover up the brutal conditions of poverty created by neoliberalism. NGOs'
unjustified optimism regarding empowerment through participation and
"self reliance" in the place of wealth redistribution made them complicit
in this process. Governments of the Global South were relieved of their
responsibilities by NGOs, and donors got an alibi for the harm their
policies caused.

Widespread enthusiasm for NGOs and their self help approach to
development was a result of ideology and money rather than pragmatism
in the service of development. NGOs fit snugly with neoliberal ideology
and practice, and were funded accordingly. Self help programs helped
the poor to cope with and integrate into the harsher and more unequal
market-oriented societies created by neoliberalism, instead of struggling
against exploitation and marginalization. The growth of NGOs aided in
relieving the state of its responsibility for social welfare and accelerated the
erosion of the state's capacity in these areas. NGOs' emphasis on individual,
entrepreneurial efforts in the informal sector as the route out of poverty
resonated with the market ideology of neoliberalism. "The rise of NGOs
within the world of international development has ... helped create a space
in which the more intrusive impulses of neoliberal development policy
have gained further ground."[76]

Ultimately, the enthusiasm for the informal sector and NGO-provided
services did not amount to much more than the re-labeling of a problem
as a solution. "The self-help campaign risks being transformed from a
survival strategy in the face of government unconcern into a defence of
such unconcern," write development researchers Benedict Phillips and
Erhard Berner.

> The idea that poor communities can "develop themselves"–if it means
> that they require no redistribution of resources ... [and] that the macro
> structures of wealth and power distribution can be ignored–is flawed to
> the point of being harmful. It harms calls for realistic levels of funding
> for tackling poverty ... and it risks legitimising inequity, reinforcing the
> complacent view that the poor are poor because they have not helped
> themselves. To knock all resource transfers as "welfare" or "charity" is
> to accept unquestioningly the current distribution of wealth as both
> optimal and fair.[77]

Some NGO insiders may still hope that the scatter of piecemeal
interventions by NGOs will add up to a comprehensive response to

the needs of the poor. Most are not so naïve, recognizing that the wider conditions structuring the poor's lives, and reproducing their poverty, must be radically transformed if long-lasting improvements are to be made. John Clark, a former director of Oxfam UK, writes that NGO projects, while still important, can "do no more than create islands of relative prosperity within an increasingly hostile sea," that is in a growing "wealth gap between nations and within nations" created by neoliberalism.[78] Former CUSO director Ian Smillie puts it bluntly: "development writ large will not occur on the basis of aid, projects or the work of NGOs." While NGO projects may help, Smillie argues, the lot of the poor will not improve if the overarching structures that reproduce poverty do not change.[79]

Though they issue from people who have worked in the heart of the NGO world, these conclusions run counter to the promotional messages of virtually all development NGOs. Today, NGOs continue to imply that their projects do indeed constitute durable solutions to the problems of the world's poor. "Romantic visions in which individual communities can somehow resolve problems of livelihood and sustainability on their own are politically misguided and a political disservice."[80] By suggesting that their rural women beneficiaries are just one goat, or one $10 loan away from escaping poverty, the marketing messages of NGOs constantly do violence to the true sources of world poverty.

4

Who Pays the Piper?

Structure, funding and autonomy

The foundational myth of development NGOs is that they are autonomous institutions that express and embody the altruistic impulses of Canadian society. NGOs are understood to be operating on a higher plane, governed by values and morality and unsullied by the economic and political interests that motivate business and government. Autonomy means NGOs are institutionally free from the imperatives of both the state and the market. "The optimism of the proponents of NGOs derives from a general sense of NGOs as 'doing good,' unencumbered and untainted by the politics of government or the greed of the market."[1] NGOs' approach to development is seen as essentially guided by the goodwill of their donors and staff on the one hand, and the needs and interests of poor people in the Global South on the other.

NGOs believe this myth and describe themselves as "values-driven" organizations. In their 1988 study of Canadian NGOs, *Bridges of Hope?*, Tim Brodhead and Brent Herbert-Copley identified "autonomy" as one of five deeply held self-perceptions—or "articles of faith"—of the voluntary sector. The study gives a clear explanation of what are commonly understood to be the sources of NGO autonomy:

> In democratic societies, this independence flows from their juridical status, their financial autonomy, and their capacity to articulate their own goals and to pursue appropriate ways to achieve them.... Drawing on their own motivation and resources, NGOs have been to a considerable extent insulated from official priorities and shifting development dogmas.[2]

This position is itself a dogma; it is false in nearly every meaningful sense, yet it remains unquestioningly believed. Far from securing their independence, the juridical status of NGOs as charitable organizations curtails it. Far from enjoying financial autonomy, NGOs suffer from a deep financial dependency on government funds. The ability of NGOs to articulate and pursue their own goals has been constrained and in some cases suffocated, leaving them increasingly subject to official priorities and development dogmas imposed from above. The relationship between NGOs and the state is so close-knit that one can legitimately ask: In what ways are these institutions in fact non-governmental?

The idea of NGO autonomy can be considered a *legitimizing myth*, in that it is essential to the perpetuation of these organizations. If NGOs were perceived to be self-seeking institutions or simply extensions of the government, ordinary people in Canada would naturally be less inclined to support them. The Canadian public would also treat NGOs' claims to speak on behalf of the "poorest of the poor" more skeptically. In the Global South, communities and governments would regard NGOs with a much greater degree of suspicion (and possibly place greater restrictions on their activities) were they not considered to be independent organizations.

Charity Law and Anti-Politics

Most development NGOs in Canada are incorporated as registered charities. Obtaining charitable status with Revenue Canada benefits NGOs by making private donations tax-exempt, as well as exempting the organization itself from income taxes. Charity law thus makes giving less costly to individuals and represents a significant hidden subsidy–in the form of foregone tax revenues–by the state to NGOs.

In exchange for charitable status, there are important restrictions placed on what kinds of activities NGOs can engage in. In Canada, registered charities can use their resources only for "charitable" goals, defined as relieving poverty, advancing education or religion, or other activities "that benefit the community as a whole." Charitable organizations are restricted from engaging in "political" activities. Prohibited activities include involvement in partisan politics, but also things as vague as the promotion of "political or socio-economic ideologies" and carrying on charitable works in a "political" way.[3]

Until 1986, NGOs were prohibited from engaging in any activities aimed at influencing the political process (e.g. organizing letter-writing campaigns, suggesting legislative changes, etc.). They were limited to presenting written briefs or representations to a government minister or their staff. The law has since been changed to allow NGOs to engage in advocacy, provided such activities remain "ancillary and incidental" to the organization's charitable endeavors. Activities recognized as charitable must continue to employ "substantially all" of the organization's resources, defined as at least 90% over a five-year period.[4]

The line between charitable works and political activities is often unclear and can change according to the prevailing political climate. The Canadian branch of the International Defence and Aid Fund for Southern Africa (IDAFSA) was for many years denied charitable status on the grounds that its activities in South Africa were too political. Yet in 1988, following the Mulroney government's endorsement of the fight against apartheid, the legal aid provided by the IDAFSA to black political prisoners became "non-political" in the eyes of Revenue Canada and the organization was granted charitable status.[5]

Speaking out against government policy–even if it pertains to the NGO's area of activity–can draw the attention of those overseeing the charitable status of organizations. On several occasions, the Charity Commissioners for England and Wales targeted Oxfam UK for censure because of its critique of British government aid policies.[6]

That said, the application of the law is subject to much discretion[7] and revocations of charitable status typically occur only after a formal complaint. Yet this is precisely why many NGOs are reluctant to take public stands or engage in activities overseas that might disturb powerful interests in Canadian society (be it the government, the media or corporations) with the legal and political wherewithal to mount such a challenge, lest they find their charitable status brought into question. In the lead-up to the 2006 federal election, Revenue Canada received a "flood of complaints" lodged against organizations with charitable status, journalist Murray Dobbin reports:

> Many environmental organizations were audited–that is, investigated by Revenue Canada for how they spent their money and staff time. It is by all accounts a very intimidating and time-consuming process. Preceding the 2006 election, all charities received a warning letter from the Charities Division of Revenue Canada, saying that they should not comment on or participate in elections. It had an immediate chilling effect on advocacy from groups with charitable status. Virtually all charitable groups responded cautiously–they interpreted the warning to mean a charity could not even publish a survey on party policies.[8]

Individual Donors: Empathy and Apathy

NGOs are generally perceived as manifestations of Canadian civil society, expressing the desire of their supporters to contribute to the fight against world poverty. The influence of private, small-scale donors over the shape of NGOs' activities in the Global South, however, is miniscule.

Individual donors get little information on the activities of NGOs beyond what the NGOs themselves choose to give and have virtually no sources of independent verification. Competition for funds leads NGOs to carefully manage the flow of information in order to project an image of effective, efficient operations to the donating public. When it comes to describing their activities abroad, "only successes–often highly situational– are disseminated, usually in a public-relations format," reports former Canadian University Service Overseas (CUSO) Executive Director Ian Smillie. The successes themselves, and the role of the NGO in bringing them about, are often exaggerated, while "failures are downplayed or concealed." The information that NGOs give to their donors is far from an honest, objective picture of the organization, and "the relatively few serious NGO evaluations that do exist remain confidential."[9] Controlling the flow of information may be an effective way to win a bigger share of the public's generosity, but it makes meaningful, democratic control of these organizations by their supporters all but impossible.

NGO marketing strategies tend to reinforce apathy and disengagement among individual donors. Child sponsorship and other tried and tested charity marketing tactics are effective at mobilizing the pity of the public, but fail to educate supporters about the root causes of poverty. Instead, they offer easy solutions requiring little engagement ("For just $1 per day …") and encourage a paternalistic attitude towards the poor. Over time, emotionally manipulative NGO appeals are self-defeating. They reinforce the cynicism and callousness of the public, producing "a growing antipathy towards any kind of aid but for the most heart-wrenching plights."[10]

Politically, NGOs often find themselves trapped by their own marketing messages. According to NGO scholar Alison Van Rooy, charity fundraising and the broad but shallow public support it cultivates has produced a "notable timidity" on the part of many development NGOs. Fearful that controversial positions on public policy or less "sexy" or telegenic work might "dry up public support," most NGOs "have limited their scope of work to 'safer' projects." Van Rooy cites John Foster, a former head of Oxfam Canada, who has said that "a number of organizations have engaged in self-censorship for fear that advocacy work may scare away conventional [private] donors who want every charitable dollar to be spent on relieving poverty on the ground."[11]

Information that addresses the structural or political roots of poverty, or that may disturb the "feel-good" aspects of an NGO's image, is therefore filtered out. As Ian Smillie points out, "even the most activist NGOs are cautious in their fund-raising and their advocacy ... in part because political and economic messages seem to drive all but the most committed donors into the arms of feel-better NGOs." On the whole, development NGOs are "not selling ideas, change, or reform to their [individual] donors ... They are selling salve for the troubled conscience, small feel-good opportunities for busy people living in a crass, materialistic world."[12]

Overwhelmingly, NGOs are not seeking to transform their donor base into an active and informed membership, able to weigh in on the direction of the organization. "For many organizations, the most consistent contact they have with their public is for fundraising," according to a 2006 report by the Canadian Council for International Cooperation (CCIC), an umbrella organization representing over 100 Canadian development NGOs. NGOs have few other interactions with their supporters, the report noted. Some NGO members felt they had "missed opportunities to engage Canadians more fully."[13]

Despite the stated commitment of many NGOs to the ideals of transparency and participation, they remain opaque, distant institutions for the ordinary Canadians who support them: "[I]t is in practice virtually impossible for [individual donors] to hold an agency accountable in other than the most general sense."[14]

Putting the Government in Non-Governmental Organizations

Contradictory though it may seem, the bulk of the funds for non-governmental development initiatives come from government agencies. These funds come from a variety of sources, from provincial governments to international bodies like the World Bank and various UN agencies. The largest single funding source for development NGOs is the Canadian International Development Agency (CIDA), the federal government body that administers Canada's aid program. CIDA funding to NGOs is primarily channeled through two branches of the Agency, the various Geographic (or country-to-country) branches, and the Canadian Partnership branch.

Since the mid-1960s, when the federal government began offering funding to voluntary organizations working in the Global South,

Canadian NGOs have steadily increased their financial dependence on the government. In 1975, only 39% of NGOs relied on CIDA for more than half of their revenue. By 1984, this figure had risen to over 59% of NGOs.[15] A 1994 survey of 18 large NGOs in Canada found that one third relied on CIDA funding for at least 67% of their income, and two thirds received 25% or more of their income from the government.[16] Today, most NGOs get more than 50% of their funding from CIDA, and in some cases as much as 80%, as demonstrated in Table 1.* As NGO experts Michael Edwards and David Hulme note, this is part of a worldwide trend: "NGOs that are not dependent on official aid for the majority of their budgets are now the exception rather than the rule."[17]

Even for NGOs with a substantial base of individual donors, such as the Canadian branches of Plan International, World Vision and CARE, the influence wielded by CIDA over these organizations is greater than their relatively low reliance on government funds might indicate. Individual donors are a large, disorganized group and possess few means of exercising oversight over or applying sanctions to NGOs. CIDA, on the other hand, possesses elaborated objectives and priorities and exercises ongoing, organized surveillance over the NGO sector. CIDA also has the means to demand accountability; it can–and does–apply sanctions when NGOs fail to conform.

Who Is Responding to Whom?

Funding from the Canadian Partnership branch of CIDA is often referred to as "responsive" funding because it allows NGOs–in theory–to design their development intervention themselves, deciding where to work and what to do, before requesting funding. If approved, CIDA agrees to match the funds raised by the NGO on a 1-to-1 to 3-to-1 basis, meaning CIDA covers 50% to 75% of the costs for a given activity. In 2005-06, CIDA's Canadian Partnership Branch disbursed over $194 million to NGOs and other Canadian organizations, comprising 38.4% of the CIDA funds received the voluntary sector.[18]

The assumption underlying responsive funding is that since NGOs work at the "grassroots," close to those whom the development effort is supposed to help, they are better placed than CIDA bureaucrats or distant

---

* The figures in Table 1 likely understate the level of dependence, as in many cases budgets for humanitarian aid and development work could not be disaggregated. Humanitarian aid tends to draw proportionately larger amounts of funding from individual donors.

Table 1 CIDA funding as a percentage of annual budget

Organization	% of budget (year)
Canada World Youth	81.1% (2011)
Canadian Bureau For International Education	81.0% (2010)
CHF Partners in Rural Development	76.6% (2010)
SOCODEVI	75.7% (2010)
Canadian Crossroads International (CCI)	75.6% (2011)
CUSO-VSO	75.0% (2008-09)
Oxfam Quebec	70.7% (2008)
World University Service of Canada (WUSC)	70.0% (2010)
Inter Pares	67.5% (2010)
Save the Children Canada	63.0% (2009)
Canadian Organization for Development through Education (CODE)	61.6% (2011)
USC Canada	53.8% (2011)
Centre d'étude et de coopération internationale (CECI)	50.5% (2010)
Alternatives	48.6% (2007)
Centre de coopération internationale en santé et développement (CCISD)	47.7% (2010)
Développement international Desjardins	47.4% (2010)
Oxfam Canada	44.5% (2010)
Canadian Lutheran World Relief	42.0% (2009)
KAIROS	41.4% (2009)
Development & Peace	38.5% (2008-09)
CARE Canada	21.6% (2010)
Mennonite Central Committee of Canada (MCC)	13.2% (2009-10)
Plan Canada International	9.4% (2010)
World Vision Canada	4.9% (2009)

Source: authors' calculations, based on various NGOs' annual reports.

government officials (at the "treetop" level) to ascertain the needs of the people. The close and collaborative relationship that development NGOs claim to build with poor people is one of their major selling points to

CIDA and the public. By conducting community meetings, involving those affected by poverty in needs assessments and using other "participatory" techniques, NGOs are able to craft proposals for development activities that more accurately reflect what poor people really want. CIDA is thus "responding" to requests from the NGOs, which are themselves "responding" to the desires of poor people in the Global South.

CIDA, however, still has the final word over what gets funding. A proposal for responsive funding is accepted or rejected based upon, among other things, "how well it fits with CIDA ... programming priorities."[19] Given the degree to which they are financially dependent on government funds, NGOs cannot afford to thumb their noses at CIDA for too long. NGOs must submit projects that match CIDA's priorities if they are to survive intact. The agenda-setting power of the government is evident in the great lengths to which voluntary organizations go in tailoring their proposals to fit CIDA's priorities. Shifts in CIDA thinking and priorities are watched closely by NGOs, who must stay current with the latest "development dogmas" or risk being left out in the cold. "Smaller organizations (and many large ones as well)," notes Ian Smillie, "spend inordinate amounts of time and efforts simply reacting to changes in CIDA thinking, programmes and regulations."[20] In July 2008, for example, *Embassy* magazine reported that uncertainty about how to please CIDA–and thus secure funding–had left a number of NGOs feeling "jittery." Robert Fox, Executive Director of Oxfam Canada, was quoted as saying he had been "told by CIDA officials that when making proposals [for international projects] to be mindful of CIDA's 'priority countries.'" The "frustration" expressed by Fox and other NGO representatives was not caused by the imposition of CIDA's priorities on their putatively independent organizations, but rather by the "lack of clarity" at CIDA as to what exactly its officials wanted.[21] The power to set development agendas is one of the most significant yet subtle forms of control that CIDA exercises over NGOs.

When KAIROS, Alternatives and the CCIC had their funding cut in 2009, the incident revealed how accommodating seemingly oppositional, left-leaning NGOs can be in order to secure CIDA funding. All three organizations publicly declared their close adherence to CIDA's demands in the past and their willingness to adjust their programs further in order to restore funding. Such arguments may have highlighted that the government's claim that their programs did not fit CIDA priorities was merely a pretext concealing other motives. But it was a curious stance to take for organizations nominally defending their independence in the face of Conservative government cuts.

KAIROS contested the cuts by pointing to its positive evaluations by CIDA officials in the past and underlining that, for the refused 2009 funding application, the organization had "made all adjustments to the program requested by our program officer."[22] The organization also tried to distance itself from more activist stances on foreign policy. Mary Corkery, Executive Director of KAIROS, defended her organization by insisting that it had never been involved in the Boycott, Divestment and Sanctions campaign targeting Israeli Apartheid.

In November 2010, KAIROS submitted a new $6 million funding proposal intentionally geared to the government's priorities. "We are addressing the issue that the minister raised," Jennifer Henry, KAIROS's dignity and rights manager told *Embassy*. "We have demonstrated in our new proposal that we can meet those priorities and can put forward an effective program related to those priorities." In order to hew more closely to CIDA's priorities, KAIROS made substantive changes to overseas programs to directly link the activities of its local NGO partners to these goals.[23] Despite these changes, KAIROS was turned down a second time.

After his organization lost its CIDA grant, CCIC head Gerry Barr admitted that he had considered curbing CCIC's advocacy efforts, which mostly revolved around aid policy questions, but complained that the Harper government had not given the organization a chance to change its tune. "We had no sign, no signal, nothing," Barr told journalists. "Not a single word suggesting that we should somehow shift or change the program or name this country more or this country less."[24]

When Alternatives got the axe, Executive Director Michel Lambert described the cuts as "incomprehensible" given how closely Alternatives had tailored its programs to fit CIDA's wishes and the government's foreign policy priorities. Alternatives had, for instance, withdrawn a funding application for an education project in Palestine at the request of CIDA.[25] It was not enough to save Alternatives, however, which had almost all of its federal funding cut. The injustice caused much anguish to Lambert:

> How could CIDA, after having positively evaluated and audited us and above all after having worked in collaboration with us to define our future projects that we were going to finally integrate into our three-year program, now tell us that these projects didn't fit with their priorities any more? Why are countries like Afghanistan or Haiti, which are at the heart of Canadian interventions, now no longer essential for the Canadian government?[26]

Afghanistan and Haiti, Lambert neglected to explain, were at the heart of Canadian *military* interventions where Canadian troops had overthrown existing governments to establish more pliant, pro-Western regimes, in concert with U.S. forces. The Harper government, perhaps seeing the logic in Lambert's pleas, re-established a small amount of CIDA funding for Alternatives' programs in Afghanistan and Haiti, though funding for development education at home or projects in Palestine remained shut off.

Whither Participation?

While NGOs must be particularly mindful of CIDA's inclinations when designing programs, the amount of decision-making power given to poor people through consultations or other participatory techniques is slight. According to NGO scholars Tina Wallace and Lisa Bornstein, decisions taken at community meetings organized by NGO are typically non-binding, and development plans are finalized without community oversight. Proposals for development activities are typically written by a handful of NGO staff or consultants, "working with a vague mandate from local people and a clear set of strategic objectives from potential donors." Opinions expressed at community meetings that do not fit with current development thinking at CIDA are likely to be left out. "Participative and responsive approaches ... rarely challenge too deeply or overturn the strategies, programmes or projects funded–and often designed–by external donors and NGOs."[27]

Other studies echo these observations about the thinness of participatory input. A literature review of research on community development commissioned by the World Bank found little basis for the claim that participation "enables primary stakeholders to 'drive' development interventions." "The evidence suggests that while rhetorically the emphasis is on devolving control to communities, these usually enjoy no control over project design, and very limited decision-making power over project implementation and resources. ... Mechanisms for downward accountability to citizens and communities were also found to be weak, if at all in place."[28] Surveying the last 25 years, Michael Edwards concurs, noting that "little concrete attention is paid to downward accountability [i.e. to the grassroots]" by Northern NGOs.[29]

Poor people participating in consultations are not oblivious to the fact that the broad development agenda has already been set without them. Participation is often perceived less as a chance for genuine expression than as a cynical charade, in which locals must say what NGO personnel want to hear in order to unlock development funds. In his study of a rural development project in India, anthropologist David Mosse discovered that "participatory consultation exercises were both a strategic game whereby villagers tried to second-guess the resources to be won, and simultaneously important events in legitimizing the programme for audiences of powerful outsiders."[30] Mark Waddington describes in similar terms the effect that this power imbalance has on the outcomes of participatory rural appraisals:

> Consequently, village communities identify needs and problems and tailor their prioritisation of them to the services which they perceive the local NGO is offering. Subsequent to this, the local NGO amends the prioritisation and, more often than not, the nature of the project itself to what they believe its northern partner will fund.[31]

CIDA's agenda-setting power produces a certain uniformity of approaches to development, despite the bewildering diversity that exists on the surface. There is no clearer indication of the distorting, homogenizing pull of funding power than the fads that periodically afflict the world of development NGOs. Tina Wallace reports that fads affect even the grassroots, where "the language of aid management has become universal," in a process akin to cultural imperialism:

> Right down to the village level you will hear development discussions interspersed with the English words for goals, aims, objectives, mission and vision, outcomes and so on: "Instead of a diverse, heterogeneous mix of projects, ideas and practices, which are locally derived and designed, we see powerful waves of global development fashions sweeping everything before them." Indeed it could be argued that northern NGOs, together with their partners–those they fund and support in the south–have become highly effective distributors of a set of approaches and procedures for development that could be said to rival Coca Cola in reaching down to the grassroots.[32]

Participation rarely does more than provide a little "local colour" to the otherwise formulaic programs of development NGOs; it most certainly has not overturned the massive power imbalances between the various actors (CIDA, Canadian NGOs, Southern organizations, poor people) along the "aid chain." Participation is not to be confused with democratic control over aid money. "While there is constant talk of downward accountability in the aid chain," Wallace concludes, "the reality for most NGOs is that accountability is upward. Meeting the needs of the next level up in the chain overrides the needs of all other stakeholders."[33]

Off the CIDA Leash?

Initially, CIDA's responsive funding was only available for discrete projects, which meant CIDA officials weighed in on the "blueprint" design of each project directly. "The NGOs were thus on a fairly short 'leash,' with a fair measure of CIDA supervision and control."[34] Yet as the number of NGO projects funded by CIDA expanded rapidly in the early 1980s, the administrative burden of dealing with micro-level details for so many different projects became overwhelming. To ease the stress on CIDA's bureaucracy, responsive funding for NGOs was expanded to include entire programs of activities and support for the organization itself.

Program funding meant NGOs could now submit proposals, usually for a three-year period, specifying the countries they would work in, the sectors they would concentrate on and the people and groups that would be their partners overseas. Institutional or core funding likewise meant CIDA would fund the NGO itself, leaving the detailed planning work with the NGO. On the face of it, these new forms of funding devolved greater responsibility (and hence autonomy) to the NGOs for their development work. Reduced involvement in the routine administrative and programming work of NGOs, however, did not diminish CIDA's control of aid funds. Quite the opposite, according to Ian Smillie, who explains how program funding is ultimately more invasive:

> [Rather than individual projects,] the entire NGO will now be open to full CIDA scrutiny: its structure, management, programs, policies and attitudes. ... CIDA managers will continue to make field trips "to review activities of organizations and their southern partners on the ground"; there will be regular discussions and contact with the NGO, and CIDA program managers will attend the NGO's board meetings "at least once a year to discuss issues of mutual concern."

Hence, Smillie concludes, "[i]nstitutional funding represents a step forward in the ability of government to manage and control Canadian NGOs and a step backward from the concept of NGOs as independent expressions of civil society."[35]

Funding from CIDA's Geographic branches is awarded to NGOs whose activities are in line with the government aid agency's predefined priorities for a given country or region. Whether through contracts or projects or programs, CIDA has the power to define the nature of NGO activities funded through the Geographic branch. The name often given to this type of funding, "directive funding," reflects this reality. As one internal government document described it, "CIDA will devise frameworks for development activities (the 'WHAT' to do) while letting agents (business, NGOs, institutions) determine the 'HOW' to do it."[36] NGOs accepting these arrangements take on a role closer to that of a public service contractor than of an autonomous organization setting its own objectives. Directive funding was first introduced by CIDA in the 1980s and has expanded rapidly since then. Today, directive funds make up a sizable chunk of NGO revenues: in 2005-06, CIDA's Geographic branches disbursed over $227 million, comprising 44.9% of the total CIDA funds received by NGOs and voluntary sector organizations.[37]

"Ideas Contrary to the Political Direction of the Day"

NGOs must also be mindful of the attitudes of politicians, whose good will can sometimes be the deciding factor in obtaining funding. Both the responsive and directive funding channels for NGOs have long been open to politicization. CIDA routinely clears NGO proposals with the Canadian embassies of the countries concerned. After passing through CIDA, proposals still require approval by Minister of Foreign Affairs and the Treasury Board–a committee of cabinet ministers–before going forward. In his history of CIDA, David R. Morrison notes that in the 1980s, the procurement process for contracts "offered scope for political intervention at both the short-listing and final-selection stages. Ministers have had even greater discretion in the responsive programs for business, NGOs and NGIs [non-governmental institutions]."[38]

Three decades later, the vulnerability of NGOs to the whims of their political overseers is greater than ever. The June 2008 *Embassy* magazine report on CIDA-NGO relations cited above identified

> an overwhelming sense among federal civil servants that ideas contrary to the political direction of the day could cause unwanted headaches. Others say the process of project approval has also become more politicized than in the past, noting that intervention by a politician has increasingly become the solution.[39]

Fierce Competition

Despite frequently describing their work as "development cooperation," NGOs are in fact an intensely competitive bunch–at least in relation to one another. "The competition between NGOs is legendary, and pushing for increased profile, funding and market share drives many boards and directors."[40] In many ways, this is a matter of arithmetic. Growth has been exponential: In 1960, there were only 25 development NGOs in Canada, while in 1980 there were 107; by 1990 this number had risen to 240, and today the number is somewhere in the neighborhood of 500. Though charitable donations and government funding have also grown, they have not kept pace with the rapid proliferation of NGOs. The result has been an increasingly intense scramble for scarce resources. Compounding the impact of competition is the notorious volatility of the aid budget, and the unpredictability of donations from the public. Not surprisingly, many organizations report being financially unstable.

According to Brian K. Murphy, former policy analyst with Inter Pares, the exigencies of organizational survival and growth can become an overwhelming preoccupation for Canadian NGOs, especially "when the original mandates of the organizations involved have lost relevance and the organizations themselves have lost some of their original impetus and moral force."[41] Michael Edwards and David Hulme point to "the seeming obsession of many NGO managers with size and growth as indicators of success."[42] This growth obsession of the top NGO managers has meant that the political compromises implied by taking large amounts of government money have been accepted uncritically, Tina Wallace argues: "The drive for growth ... appears to override any serious discussions about whether official funding can subvert an NGO's values, mission, or even its advocacy work."[43]

The competitive environment increases the vulnerability of financially-dependent NGOs to pressure from CIDA, giving it even greater leverage over its so-called development partners. Each NGO is disciplined by the possibility that CIDA will simply choose to fund one of the over 500 other organizations working in international development. The predominance of one major "buyer" (CIDA) and many different competing "sellers" (NGOs) makes the market for development projects very much a buyer's market, with the government playing "an increasingly pro-active role in determining program directions."[44] Getting on CIDA's bad side or failing to keep up with its shifting funding priorities may lead to a loss of revenues, with all the unpleasantness (program cutbacks, staff reductions, closure of offices etc.) a smaller-than-expected budget entails. The result is a tendency towards opportunism on the part of NGOs. Lacking "a strategic or sufficiently-analytical view" of how to achieve development, Michael Edwards notes that NGOs "tend to drift into and out of different roles and relationships according to development fashions, the availability of resources, or donor demands—adult literacy one year and micro-finance the next."[45]

Organizations that don't closely follow CIDA priorities quickly discover the limits of government-sponsored "pluralism." A phone call or a stern lecture from CIDA officials will usually suffice, the threat of revoking funding and charitable status lurking in the background. Dissident organizations, i.e. groups that are vocally critical of the government or don't accept to work within CIDA parameters, are marginalized and ignored where possible, and vilified, attacked and shut down when necessary. Funding cuts are a last resort, and CIDA is usually discrete when bringing agencies into line. The experience of the Canadian University Service Overseas (CUSO), an organization which had a conflictual relationship with CIDA in the 1970s, typifies this approach: "The occasional CIDA budget cuts were usually effected without explicit reasons or admonishments; so *CUSO was left to draw its own inferences and to act accordingly.*"[46] (emphasis added)

These cuts serve not only to discipline the targeted NGO, but also to send a message to the entire NGO community, who also draw their own inferences and act accordingly. "Altering funding levels is one means available to a government to express its confidence or displeasure in an NGO," according to Smillie.[47] From the perspective of CIDA, cuts have the added benefit of deterring further dissidence by spreading fear throughout the voluntary sector.

In the unending search for funding, the pressure to conform eventually leads NGOs to internalize the norms and constraints placed on them. Instead of CIDA policing the behaviour of NGOs, the NGOs police themselves. Censorship becomes self-censorship; discipline, self-discipline.

Corporate Ideals

While the image of development NGOs as fly-by-night operations run by a bunch of idealistic, scraggly amateurs was always something of an exaggeration, it certainly does not hold today. NGOs are bureaucratic, hierarchical and professionally-staffed organizations. A creeping conservatism has accompanied the growth of the NGO bureaucracy.

Over time, CIDA demands for reporting and accountability and increasing competition for funds have spurred major organizational changes. In an effort to establish their credibility in the eyes of donors as reliable and efficient conduits of aid funds, NGOs have adopted hierarchical management structures and hired professional staff. Many NGO directors have begun to rearrange their organizations in the image of the private sector:

> This ethos has been embraced by and is now aggressively–sometimes ruthlessly–promoted by senior managers in many of our leading NGOs, convinced that restructuring our organisations along corporate lines is the ticket to successful integration in the new trilateral global order that sees the public, private, and voluntary sectors somehow as partners in development. ... Increasingly the model for the 'successful' NGO is the corporation–ideally a transnational corporation–and NGOs are ever more marketed and judged against corporate ideals.[48]

Development NGOs are increasingly focused on producing measurable outputs and results to demonstrate their short-term achievements to CIDA. In the process, warns Brian K. Murphy, NGOs are taking on "precisely the values and methods and techniques that have made the world what it is today."[49] While bureaucratization has been welcomed as improving NGOs' effectiveness, the narrow, technocratic focus has limited the attention paid to wider political and social structures that reproduce poverty or longer-term efforts to transform these structures. Brodhead and Herbert-Copley enumerate the downsides that have come with the transformation:

> Larger budgets and more specialized knowledge may have significantly reduced the role of volunteers, concentrating decision-making power in the hands of staff. Increasing reluctance to take risks and greater reliance on established procedures may have made NGOs more predictable, and therefore more acceptable partners of government; they may also have become vulnerable to criticism that they have grown too ponderous, protective and rigid.[50]

The bureaucratization of NGOs has transformed the profile of NGO personnel. As NGO researcher David Lewis observes, "development has become a professional field rather than simply a value-driven calling or a voluntaristic pursuit," which has "strengthened concerns with career and salary issues among NGO staff." Gone are the early days when volunteers played a prominent role in running NGOs. In their place are development professionals, whose demands for remuneration "rarely reflect tangibly improved performance in the work that they do," Lewis remarks.[51] In a similar vein, political scientist Mark Duffield notes that with the rapid expansion of the NGO sector since the 1990s, "new staff have tended to be university graduates lacking direct experience [working in the Global South] but having degrees in development studies. One reflection of this change has been a growing technocratic culture within the NGO movement."[52] With the influx of career-oriented NGO personnel, maintaining the organization (and its paid positions) has become an end in and of itself, independent of how faithfully the NGO fulfills its mandate. And maintaining the organization is synonymous with maintaining friendly relations with CIDA.

Beyond the question of job security, being on good terms with the government offers many other perks for NGO staff, from subsidized participation in UN summits and other international conferences, to CIDA consultancy contracts, to improved "access" to Canadian policy makers (though influence is another story, as we discuss in Chapter 9). At the apex of the NGO world, the inducements of pay, power and prestige are even more alluring. A top NGO management position can serve as a stepping stone to brighter vistas: World Bank Presidential fellowships, high-level positions in the development agencies of the United Nations, even a career at CIDA, where many senior and middle management positions are filled by former NGO workers.[53] The revolving door between CIDA and NGOs is yet another factor tying the interests of NGO personnel, who naturally want to avoid souring relations with a potential future employer, to government priorities.

Incestuous relationships between NGOs and the government have created a culture of silence among development professionals. Those whose conception of development conflicts with the priorities of the Canadian government are likely to encounter friction within their organizations. Their more prudent colleagues will appreciate the need to stay on good terms with CIDA and will not be inclined to endanger the security of the organization (and their jobs) for the sake of a "political crusade." Capacity for controversial or politically "risky" work by NGOs has suffered as a result. "Many staff have been forced to leave NGOs they felt committed to," Tina Wallace reports, "as the values they held dear appear eroded by the new incorporation of NGOs into global agendas."[54]

Even consultants hired to evaluate projects have been "rendered incapable of taking deficient aid programmes seriously to task," due to their dependence on those they are evaluating, reports author and former consultant Tom Lines:

> How many complaints did I hear from other consultants and consultancy firms about the absurdities of the aid system! Yet almost no one would voice open criticism, however mild, for fear of losing the next contract: a pernicious consequence of the commercialisation of aid projects. ... What a waste of the North's public money; what a deception played on the people of developing and transition countries alike.[55]

Unequal Partners and Willing Captives

"Partnership" is the term often used by both CIDA and NGOs when discussing NGO-government relations. Yet the power imbalance that exists between the two development "partners" betrays any notion of genuine partnership. NGOs depend on government funds for a large and growing share of their budgets, with CIDA exercising surveillance and an increasingly direct influence over NGO activities. The politicization of the funding approval process, the intense competition for funds amongst financially precarious organizations, and the development of a career-oriented NGO bureaucracy with close ties to CIDA, have served to reinforce this relationship of dependence on–and deference to–the government. Meanwhile, the need to preserve charitable status leads NGOs to avoid activities that may be considered too "political."

CIDA is well aware of the power it wields over the NGO sector. Although in public CIDA officials extol the values of NGO independence, Canadian foreign policy scholars Cranford Pratt and Tim Brodhead note that internally, "CIDA discourse routinely (and revealingly) talks of 'using' partners to accomplish one or another of CIDA's objectives."[56] In 1995, NGOs were informed that they would be "expected to conform to CIDA's programming priorities," and that any "renewed relationship between CIDA and Canadian voluntary organizations [would be] based on the principle of complementarity of action."[57] For CIDA, "complementarity" is a one-way street.

NGOs' growing dependence on government funding–and "the consequent overriding need to maintain harmonious relations" with

CIDA[58]–produces two major results. First, NGOs tend to avoid criticism of the Canadian government, or confine criticism to polite lobbying and other routine political channels. Second, NGOs pursue development work in the Global South which is broadly consistent–or which at the very least does not openly conflict–with Canadian foreign policy positions in a given country or region.

Over time, NGOs and their personnel internalize these structural constraints. This process creates invisible mental barriers when thinking about development, in much the same way as the ideological "filters" internalized by journalists identified by Noam Chomsky and Edward Herman in their analysis of the political economy of the corporate mass media. Swapping references to journalism for those of development work in Chomsky and Herman's analysis sheds some light on this process:

> [The] marginalization of dissidents that results from the operation of these filters occurs so naturally that [development workers], frequently operating with complete integrity and goodwill, are able to convince themselves that they choose and interpret [development activities] "objectively," on the basis of professional [development] values. Within the limits of the filter constraints, they often are objective; the constraints are so powerful, and are built into the system in such a fundamental way, that alternative bases of [development] choices are hardly imaginable.[59]

There remain a handful of development NGOs that are mildly critical of the government, but they too are marked by dependence on government funding. They may criticize Canada's international stance occasionally, but they always presume Canadian policy makers to be guided by benevolent motives, and never point to the close links between corporate wealth and political power in Canada. Neoliberalism is criticized as a set of misguided policy ideas that are bad at achieving the shared objective of poverty reduction, rather than a rational set of policies designed to further Canadian economic interests in the Global South. "Such organizations," remarks Murphy, "can exist unmolested only as long as neither their purpose nor their methods are perceived as radical, that is, as having the capacity to promote, let alone achieve, significant political or economic change."[60] Their ability to oppose the neoliberal orthodoxy, and Canada's role in promoting it, is strictly bounded.

The structural power of the state over NGOs cannot be equated with absolute control. CIDA's authority is not monolithic, and its bureaucracy simply doesn't have the resources to directly oversee the huge multiplicity of NGO projects and programs throughout the Global South. CIDA priorities often shift with the changing political context in a given country, leadership changes in Ottawa or a new international consensus on development among the wealthy donor countries. NGOs do not always adjust automatically and CIDA must reassert itself from time to time to enforce these shifts. We can also expect that the intensity of CIDA's oversight will correspond to the importance of a given country or region to Canadian foreign policy.

CIDA is not totally intolerant of dissent from the NGOs it sponsors. Chomsky and Herman's analysis is again germane: they argue that there is plenty of debate in the mass media, but only within a narrow spectrum of acceptable opinion. Likewise, CIDA accepts criticism from NGOs that provides "a certain diversity of tactical judgments on how to attain generally shared aims." However, when NGOs start to articulate "views that challenge fundamental premises or suggest that observed modes of exercise of state power are based on systemic factors," CIDA becomes far less indulgent.[61] Criticism, in other words, must remain focused on the how, but not the what–and certainly not the why–of Canadian foreign policy.

Most NGOs are what we might call "willing captives" of CIDA, content to work within the broad outlines of Canadian foreign policy and enjoy the many perks offered for their compliance. NGOs' views on development have–with few exceptions, discussed in Chapter 7–been solidly within the dominant ideology; which is to say, in line with the current thinking at CIDA. Liberal internationalism has been "by far the most prevalent" political orientation of Canadian NGOs, as Cranford Pratt and Tim Brodhead note: "These values enjoin caring towards the poor, but within a context set by the powerful presence of liberal economic values."[62] Most NGOs are unlikely candidates for challenging the neoliberal worldview, never mind the injustices of the Global South's debt bondage or of capitalism in general. NGOs tend to take a minimalist approach to empowerment, seeing the solution to poverty in individualized, market-based approaches. NGOs may see the status quo as requiring some rebalancing in favour of the poor with the help of "civil society," but they share the dominant faith in the inherent fairness of the market.

Paradox or Self-Serving Myth?

Surveying trends in government and NGO relationships in 1994, Pratt and Brodhead predicted that "CIDA will increasingly assert closer policy control over the NGOs that it assists."[63] Tina Wallace argues that whatever their initial intentions, "as northern NGOs increasingly rely on official donor funding and goodwill, and as the conditionalities attached to that aid increase, they are inevitably drawn into supporting and even spreading many aspects of the dominant global agenda."[64] The NGO community claims the wide diversity of organizations and approaches to development that it represents as one of its greatest strengths. But Murphy argues that much of the talk of pluralism belongs to the "realm of self-serving myth":

> There is a plurality but general homogeneity among the mainstream agencies in the voluntary sector, to the extent that many have become relatively secure extensions of government programs.[65]

Even proponents of the myth of NGO autonomy such as Brodhead and Herbert-Copley are forced to admit to what they call a "paradox":

> Indeed, it is a paradox that within Canada the single dominant presence on the non-governmental scene since the late 1960s has been the federal government. Government funding, policies and procedures for NGOs, more than any other single factor, have determined the pattern of Canadian NGO activity.[66]

This constitutes a "paradox" only if we insist on taking the "non-governmental" label and the myth of autonomy at face value. Behind their carefully-maintained veneer of independence, development NGOs are ensnared in a web of governmental relationships that place severe limits on what they can say and do. They are creations of government, not by-products of an altruistic Canadian society. NGOs cannot be said to be "insulated from official priorities and shifting development dogmas." The very name "non-governmental organization" itself constitutes a form of mystification about the actual nature of these institutions.

5

Empowerment or NGOization?

Partnership, capacity building and social movements

When I gave food to the poor, they called me a saint. When I asked why the poor were hungry, they called me a Communist.
–*Dom Hélder Câmara*

The question is whether one can talk about poverty without talking about wealth–and, more specifically, whether one can struggle against poverty without also struggling against wealth.
–*Gilbert Rist* [1]

Plan International's ubiquitously-advertised "Because I am a girl" campaign claims to have found the key to "break[ing] the cycle of poverty in the developing world." In one TV advertisement, the campaign depicts Plan's efforts to provide education for girls as sparking positive social change–represented by blooming flowers–literally around the globe. Another advertisement explains how giving one girl the opportunity to get an education will rapidly produce multiplier effects that culminate in development and prosperity for all. "Soon," the text on the screen states, accompanied by an uplifting piano score, "more girls have a chance, and the village is thriving." Once the effect reaches "600 million girls in the developing world," the screen says, "you've just changed the course of history."

With evidence of the failures of self help quietly accumulating, the NGO world has shifted its emphasis away from the direct benefits of projects and towards their less obvious social by-products. Assessments that dwell on measurable impacts miss the bigger picture, aid expert and NGO insider Roger Riddell insists, since they "tend to ignore or give insufficient prominence to the empowerment dimensions of NGO development projects, which, for many, constitute a core purpose of NGO development interventions." The language of "empowerment" and its corollaries, "civil society" and "capacity building," pervade the current discourse of development NGOs. "What matters most to many NGOs is whether poor people have greater control over their lives–greater power and more voice–to influence future patterns of development," writes Riddell.[2]

How do development NGOs promote the empowerment of the poor? There are as many answers to this question as there are NGOs. The language of empowerment is used liberally by NGOs, with nearly every NGO project proclaimed to be "empowering" in some way. The "Because I am a girl" campaign is perhaps the most prominent example of the rhetoric of empowerment, but it is far from unique. An Internet search for "NGOs" and "empowerment" yields over 10 million results, with a mind-boggling number of NGO websites advertising their plans to "empower" everyone from rural women in Zimbabwe to children in Bangladesh to health workers in Indonesia.

The greatest claims of empowerment are made on behalf of development NGOs' collaboration with local organizations in the Global South. Many NGOs have shifted their focus away from directly implementing projects towards jointly carrying out development initiatives and conducting "capacity building" activities with Southern organizations. NGOs' Southern partners in turn engage in lobbying, advocacy and campaign work and encourage the poor to organize collectively. NGO enthusiasts claim the end point of this work is a vibrant, independent "civil society" which defends the interests of the poor and promotes the "democratization" of the Global South. At their most exuberant, proponents describe NGOs as working in collaboration with social movements and refer to their capacity building activities as international solidarity work.

Empowerment: A Fundamental Contradiction

Fighting poverty by supporting organizations and movements in the South that struggle for the interests of the poor is an eminently sensible approach to empowerment. Individually, the poor are victims of their circumstances, but collectively they have tremendous strength. Historically, poor people have realized their power in numbers through social movements that fight for a more just distribution of wealth and power. Social movements employ a variety of tactics, ranging from signing petitions to organizing strikes and demonstrations, from campaigning in elections to waging armed struggle. The struggles of social movements play out over decades, or even generations, punctuated by uprisings, revolts and rebellions. Whether they choose guerrilla warfare or civil disobedience, social movements depend on winning strong popular support to succeed.

Independent organizations of the poor are essential to the struggle for social justice. Organizations playing a leading role in social movements have taken a multitude of forms: trade unions, cooperatives, political parties, peasant federations, neighbourhood committees, grassroots religious communities, and guerrilla armies. Where such organizations are weak, dependent or nonexistent–crushed by state repression, co-opted or hollowed out by elites or fragmented by racial or ethno-religious divisions–progress for the poor is slight. "If and where poverty will be reduced is a question of the poor's own demand-making power," as sociologists Erhard Berner and Benedict Phillips explain. "If and where powerholders have no price to pay for neglecting the needs of the poor, they will very likely do precisely that."[3] Behind every concession won from elites, one invariably finds years of patient, painstaking organizing among the poor.

Whether reformist or revolutionary, whether seeking to tip the balance of social power in favour of the oppressed or to overturn the existing social order completely, social movements face serious obstacles to realizing their goals. Empowering poor people means challenging the disempowering status quo, which brings social movements and their organizations into conflict with the powers that be. Those who profit from the current forms of development have no interest in a shift towards a "pro-poor" approach. Elites who stand to suffer from diminished influence and wealth naturally seek to preserve existing social arrangements, and resist social movements with all the means at their disposal–including violence in many cases. Social movements that seriously challenge the status quo are often labelled by elites as "dangerous," "extremist," and even threatening to "national security."

Any attempt to help poor people realize their collective power is therefore bound to be "political," not necessarily in the sense of party political (though it often takes such forms), but in the sense of disturbing the social order. Sociologist Jeremy Gould stresses that poverty must be thought of as a political problem, which raises questions like:

> [A]re "the poor" ever treated equitably before they organize themselves into an irrepressible political force? Do genuinely "pro-poor" policies

ever get carried out without effective political demands for social justice on the part of the assigned beneficiaries? The best documented experiences of poverty reduction … all suggest that the answer is no: the haves share their wealth and influence only when the have-nots can force them to do so.[4]

As the "Because I am a girl" ad campaign implies, empowering the poor involves "changing the course of history" and can have revolutionary consequences. Development NGOs, however, claim to be able to empower the poor without provoking political or social upheaval. Anthropologist James Ferguson calls this "a fundamental contradiction in the role 'development agencies' are intended to play."

> On the one hand, they are supposed to bring about "social change," sometimes of a dramatic and far-reaching sort. At the same time, they are not supposed to "get involved in politics"—and in fact have a strong de-politicizing function. But any real effort at "social change" cannot help but have powerful political implications, which a "development project" is constitutionally unfit to deal with.[5]

Plan International's recipe for global revolution through education, sponsored by CIDA and other donors and featuring visuals produced by the Nike Foundation, epitomizes the contradiction.[6]

In reality, development NGOs do not build the power and self-determination of poor people in the Global South. The expansion of NGOs programs proclaiming to "build capacity" and support "civil society" have in fact rendered Southern organizations more accountable to donors and less responsive to their constituencies. Once-radical organizations increasingly become "apolitical" creatures of the aid system, in the sense that they do not question the political priorities of the donors. The "empowered" poor, meanwhile, are marginalized and rendered powerless over organizations that supposedly represent them. Canadian NGOs play a key role in what might be called the "NGOization" of the Global South, the cumulative social and political effect of which is to stabilize the neoliberal status quo.

Partnership: Transmission Belt for Managerialism

With the epochal shift of development aid towards non-governmental channels, Canadian NGOs and other development NGOs from Northern countries (Northern NGOs) expanded into new countries and new regions, establishing partnerships with local organizations in the South. For Southern organizations, the experience of partnership is rarely an empowering one. According to geographer Giles Mohan, Northern NGOs' need to satisfy the donors tends to "breed conservatism and a wariness to hand over the reins to local partners." Indeed, Northern NGOs "are so wary of upsetting their funders that they tightly circumscribe the activities on the ground," trapping their Southern partners in the "irreconcilable position" of claiming to represent local people while in reality answering to outsiders.[7] Canadian foreign policy experts Cranford Pratt and Tim Brodhead report that demands by many Southern organizations for greater control over aid resources and a greater sharing of decision-making with their Canadian NGO counterparts have "produced only token gestures."[8]

In fact, these partnerships have served to spread the influence of the donors down to the grassroots. "Since the mid-1970s, and with special force after 1989," aid experts John Degnbol-Martinussen and Poul Engberg-Pedersen observe, "NGOs in the North have exerted pressure on their partners to make them live up to increasingly comprehensive demands, both regarding development goals and their internal organization."[9] As NGO expert David Lewis argues, "increasingly dense transnational networks of NGOs are serving as a kind of transmission belt for managerialism, acting as nodes that link international donor agencies down to [Southern organizations] and their projects."[10] In her study *The Aid Chain*, Tina Wallace found that "many so-called partners in Africa feel more like supplicants or dependents."

> For many this language of partnership denies the relationships of power, but in reality these are strong and defined by some as the new colonialism. References to [anti-colonial theorist Frantz] Fanon were heard in discussions, especially in Uganda, where many said aid relationships echoed their colonial past: those at the receiving end dissemble, fall in line and play their part convincingly. Some commit to their recipient roles with enthusiasm because there are many financial and status gains to be made by participating in the international aid process, and ideas from outside Africa are believed by some to be superior and more professional.[11]

Competition between Southern organizations seeking to enter into such partnerships, no matter how one-sided, is intense. For Southern organizations, funding from CIDA or a CIDA-funded NGO can increase the size and scope of activities that they engage in dramatically.

With more field workers and greater financial resources, programs reach more poor people, operations expand into new areas of activity, and the organization's stature and visibility increases. For poor communities, attracting NGO projects can help to cope with chronic problems such as unemployment and a lack of basic services. Not surprisingly, Southern organizations and the communities they represent are often willing to sacrifice their independence for the sake of outside resources. As Degnbol-Martinussen and Engberg-Pedersen note: "Cooperation is seldom based on organizations in equal need of each other."[12] Masked by rhetoric of "partnership," ties between Northern NGOs and Southern organizations are suffused with unequal power relations, mimicking at a lower level on the aid chain the relationship between CIDA and Canadian NGOs.

Capacity Building: Mechanisms of Self-regulation

Northern NGOs often refer to their work with Southern organizations as "capacity building," but a more accurate term might be "NGOization." Southern organizations that want access to aid money must supply donors with applications, planning documents, financial reports, evaluations and quantified results, all tailored to donor agencies' specifications. As sociologist Jeremy Gould notes, "the internalisation of a rigorously formalised aesthetic for the production of such documents is considered a prime indicator of improved capacity."[13] More generally, according to a senior CIDA policy analyst, donors expect Southern organizations to have "eloquent, personable, English-speaking, charismatic leaders" and to be "professionally equipped, full of the latest financial and rhetorical skills."[14] In order to live up to these expectations and produce the mountains of paperwork required by the aid system, Southern organizations are obliged to take on the same hierarchical, bureaucratic, professionalized structures as their Canadian partners.

Professionalization and bureaucratization creates a growing divide between those who run the organization and its putative base, the poor. Even with formally democratic structures in place, Southern organizations gradually lose touch with the grassroots as they restructure to meet the bureaucratic imperatives of the aid system, according to Tina Wallace:

> Groups may have to organise in new ways and develop plans, accounts and monitoring that fit the donor organisation's needs, even when they have little or no literacy and have to bring in outsiders to help them with this. Thus they lose control and even understanding of the processes of development work.[15]

Within the organization, power gravitates to a leadership and staff fluent in the language of the development scene. Language in the most literal sense, in many cases. In Honduras, for instance, learning English or another foreign language is "an essential skill for Honduran development workers because their work with international development organizations often requires them to read or write non-Spanish documents and communicate with expats whose Spanish language skills are poor."[16] Effective control of Southern partner organizations tends to shift to highly-educated professionals from an upper- or middle-class background as a result. Both organizationally and sociologically, Southern organizations selected for partnerships by Northern NGOs cease to be representative of the poor.

Much of the training and consulting done by Northern NGOs in the name of "capacity building" focuses on helping their partners to acquire the skills and organizational set-up necessary to meet the punishing bureaucratic demands of the donors.[17] "While other training courses are also provided–for example in participatory techniques, in gender analysis, in advocacy work–far more time is spent on aid management training than any other kind of training."[18] In practice, writes Jeremy Gould, capacity building often boils down to helping Southern partners to be "able to perform reliably the (self-)management routines required by the exigencies of the aid industry."[19]

Once properly structured and outfitted for the aid routine, Southern organizations find themselves addicted to foreign aid money and controlled by a new NGO class, with interests distinct from those of the grassroots. With the entire structure premised on a continuous flow of donor dollars, organizational dependence on outside funds increases. How could the impoverished membership possibly afford to pay the salaries of the professional managers and their project staff, let alone foot the bill for the organization's other costs: rent for office space, salaries for ancillary staff (secretaries, security guards, drivers etc.), gasoline, phone bills, internet access, and other utiliy bills? And who else but Northern donors would provide the SUVs, the new laptops equipped with accounting software and the international travel opportunities?[20]

Unable to function without new sources of financing, Southern organizations find themselves on the treadmill of seeking grants and projects. This process creates "mechanisms of self-regulation" within Southern organizations, which "become (self-)disciplined clients of donor agencies." Through their capacity building activities, Northern NGOs "are becoming an instrumental link in establishing these disciplinary mechanisms," according to Jeremy Gould.[21] Southern organizations, which may have once been independent organizations with close ties to poor communities, are transformed into organizations that are bureaucratic, professionally-staffed and financially dependent on a continued flow of outside funds. In short, Southern organizations are transformed into Southern NGOs. Indeed, in much of the Global South, "the very definition of a non-governmental organization is that it receives foreign funding."[22]

As economist Eboe Hutchful argues, the end point is the creation of a donor-funded "civil society" that is largely unrepresentative of and unaccountable to the grassroots it claims to serve:

> Organizations that insist on autonomy and primary accountability to the membership are likely to be excluded. What we may then witness ... is a growing hierarchy and differentiation of civil organizations through selective "NGO-ization." The NGOs anointed by the international organizations and donors, and reflecting the priorities of donor agencies rather than those of local communities, have been privileged at the expense of the thousands of grass roots organizations with much better claims to local development and empowerment.[23]

Priorities: "You Risk Closing"

One consequence of NGOization is that Southern organizations become oriented to the fads and fashions of the international development set. According to Degnbol-Martinussen and Engberg-Pedersen, Southern NGOs have suffered from "the imposition of norms and values by outside partners, as well as fluctuations in priorities influenced by what is 'in'." Most don't resist because they are "forced to accept [these impositions] for economic reasons." Many leaders of Southern NGOs have felt a "considerable erosion of their independence" as their organizations adapt to meeting the demands of the donors.[24] Southern NGOs must adjust their development activities to fit with the priorities of their Northern "partners," regardless of whether they align with the needs and interests of the poor or not.

Even when a "glut" of donor funds in a given country allows Southern NGOs to "shop around" between funding sources, the result is still a far cry from freedom to determine priorities independently. In Senegal, NGO scholar Sarah Michael found that although Senegalese NGOs could pick and choose between donors and occasionally turn down funding, organizations were nonetheless forced to follow the latest development fads in order to please foreign donors. "The focus of local NGOs ... are decided, or at least heavily influenced, by donors." As one NGO president put it in an interview with Michael, his organization had been "splintered" from its objectives:

> [Donors], sometimes you don't find them [focused] on your needs. They also have their own objectives. At times, they say it's women that they're working on, you must help women. At times they say there are problems with the environment, someone must take care of the environment. At times they say there are diseases, sexually transmitted diseases, AIDS, someone must [work on these]. So if you want your structure to endure, because there are costs–your office, secretaries, there are these things which arise, you have to at least manage these programmes. You have to have programmes to run. If you say, [you only work on] employment, but employment is not financed, you risk not working on employment and you risk closing.[25]

Clientelism: Footloose NGOs

Northern NGOs partner with Southern organizations because of their perceived closeness to poor communities and their understanding of local development needs. But sociologist Shelley Feldman argues that donor funds erode accountability to the grassroots. Southern NGOs "become more focused on generic coverage rates than on long-term commitments to individual members … and unwilling to risk the loss of funding, even if it means losing legitimacy among their members."[26] If poor communities are uncooperative or if their needs or demands don't fit with current development fashions, Southern NGO can simply move on to another community:

> Like their private-sector counterparts the footloose firms, NGOs can withdraw resources from a community when they find limited support within the constituency, or when they fail to meet the targets they have negotiated with donors. This means that … few means exist whereby NGO participants can ensure long-term programme involvement or hold NGOs accountable for the kinds of programmes they offer and for the relations they structure among members and between members and programme workers.[27]

Similarly, Degnbol-Martinussen and Engberg-Pedersen observe that as Southern organizations become NGOs, "connections to grassroots organizations and the poor ... become weaker." These groups cease to be "primary partners" and are transformed into "clients and consumers of NGO services," while accountability shifts upward to the donors.[28]

Relations between Southern NGO and the grassroots are highly unequal. The scale of poor communities' unmet needs always outstrips the availability of development dollars. But because Southern NGOs have no responsibility for equal coverage of services or programs, poor communities must vie with one another to attract the attention of Southern NGOs and their projects. Those controlling Southern NGOs can use their discretionary control of aid money to cement their own social standing or advance their political interests by building up networks of loyal followers. NGO aid is thus a uniquely flexible form of patronage. As Giles Mohan points outs, in many instances Southern NGOs behave in "patronising, dictatorial and bureaucratic ways towards the villages they represent." Indeed, some NGOs "become fiefdoms for local elites to further their material and political status."[29] Urban theorist Mike Davis is even more scathing, denouncing the NGO boom as a form of "soft imperialism":

> For all the glowing rhetoric about democratization, self-help, social capital, and the strengthening of civil society, the actual power relations in this new NGO universe resemble nothing so much as traditional clientelism ... with the major NGOs captive to the agenda of the international donors, and grassroots groups similarly dependent upon the international NGOs.[30]

The divisive competition at the grassroots has disorganized and weakened the poor. Eboe Hutchful notes that the growth of NGOs in the South has "discouraged the building of horizontal relationships and broad alliances between civil associations."[31] According to sociologists James Petras and Henry Veltmeyer, the jousting over NGO projects has prevented the poor from even perceiving their common interests:

> The NGOs' 'aid' affects small sectors of the population, setting up competition between communities for scarce resources, generating insidious distinctions and inter- and intra-community rivalries, and undermining class solidarity. ... The net effect is a proliferation of [Southern] NGOs that fragment poor communities into sectoral and subsectoral groupings unable to see the larger social picture that afflicts them and even less able to unite in struggle against the system.[32]

Instead of building a committed, informed and politicized membership base, with real influence over how their development activities are conceived and pursued, Southern NGOs create an anonymous, disconnected and apolitical client base, which may benefit from NGO largesse, but is in no position to control the organization. Instead of building up horizontal relationships that allow the poor to realize their collective power, Southern NGOs create vertical relationships that divide and frustrate the unity of those on the receiving end. "When it comes to aid," Latin America scholar Laura Macdonald argues, "small is not necessarily beautiful. In fact, assistance from Northern NGOs to small development projects can be even more dangerous than aid from state agencies because it penetrates into the very fibres of a community, creating new forms of clientelism and cooptation."[33]

The Politics of Being Apolitical

The most significant effect of NGOization in the South is political. The political impact of NGOs, however, is often masked by the claim that these organizations and their programs are "apolitical." Out of respect for the political sovereignty of countries in the South, Northern NGOs and donors are not supposed to support "political" groups and activities. Southern NGOs are therefore expected to remain formally "apolitical," which means that organizations receiving funding should not support or ally with political parties or get directly involved in political issues more generally. In this narrow, non-partisan sense, most Southern NGOs are apolitical. In a broader sense, partnerships with "civil society" are anything but politically neutral. Even when Southern partners scrupulously avoid involvement in party politics, Northern support inevitably goes to certain groups and not others, altering the balance of power between groups in society. Funding can extend the reach and influence of some organizations beyond what their local support would allow, while marginalizing others.

In practice, being "apolitical" means that Southern NGOs steer clear of stances that might be controversial with their foreign patrons. "To ensure their funding is not jeopardised and that the governments of the countries they work in will allow them to function," observes Indian author and activist Arundhati Roy, "NGOs have to present themselves in a shallow framework, more or less shorn of a political or historical context (an inconvenient historical or political context anyway)."[34] CIDA recognizes that many of the organizations it supports in the South are in fact involved in politics. A senior policy analyst at CIDA explains that Southern NGOs "must not be *seen to be beholden* to outside funders and political patrons, even when that may be the only way to get any work done."[35] CIDA's main concern is for recipient organizations to maintain the illusion of purity and independence.

The need to remain "apolitical" limits the empowerment strategies of Southern NGOs to the most inoffensive–and therefore ineffectual– means. Many Southern NGOs simply label their self help projects as the last word in empowerment and deny that development has any political implications at all. Other Southern NGOs claim to advocate on behalf of the poor, but reject the politics of confrontation in favour of lobbying. They support marginal, piecemeal micro-reforms rather than broad political programmes that address the structural causes of poverty. They seek to convince elites to help the poor through moral pleas and rational dialogue. They speak on behalf of the poor, rather than seeking to organize and mobilize the poor to speak for themselves. According to Eboe Hutchful, NGOs' notions of empowerment are "almost completely devoid of any activist political connotation." Efforts to "empower the poor" are invariably limited to NGOs speaking on their behalf in sector-specific government policymaking consultations (e.g. concerning agriculture, health care, education) and "specialized, micro-level action by affected groups, rather than broad political processes and alliances."[36]

Even when NGOs recognize that advancing the interests of the poor "requires empowering them in relation to better-off and politically stronger groups and especially in relation to a locally or nationally dominant economic and political elite," few are willing engage in disruptive tactics or take up controversial issues:

> Many NGOs are reluctant to involve themselves directly in conflicts and power struggles. Instead, they base their strategies on the assumption that they can strengthen their partners without confrontations with other groups. *In this respect, they follow the thinking that prevails among official aid organizations.*[37] [emphasis added]

From the perspective of the donors, organizations or movements in the South are deemed to be "apolitical" (or "democratic" or representative of "civil society") to the degree that they work within the political framework of neoliberalism. Tina Wallace argues that donors oblige Southern NGOs to water down criticisms of neoliberalism. "Donor agencies often require [Southern] NGOs to take on reformist approaches to advocacy even though their commitment is to rejecting global [neoliberal] policies."[38]

Southern NGOs are sometimes permitted to take a nominally anti-neoliberal stance, but only as long as their "radicalism" is ineffectual and lacks political mobilization to give it force. Southern NGOs are only exceptionally involved in opposition movements against privatization, user fees for public services, or other neoliberal policies, and rarely support militant trade unions or peasant organizations struggling for labour rights and land reform.[39]

With few exceptions, Southern NGOs have not been allies in poor people's struggles for justice and dignity.[40] Shelley Feldman observes that Southern NGOs are "more concerned with compromise than with challenging structural and institutional problems that contribute to poverty and gender inequality."[41] NGO expert Sangeeta Kamat argues that NGOization has produced organizations that regard development work "as apolitical and disconnected from larger social and economic processes, such as structural adjustment or international debt policies, even when they directly impact the poor." Professionalization has inclined Southern NGOs to adopt the "functionalist problem-solving approach to social issues of inequality and poverty" of their Northern partners, which has more often than not "translate[d] into paternalism towards the poor."[42] Even if Southern NGOs were committed to mobilizing the poor, their tenuous links to the grassroots and their upper- and middle-class character would make such an approach difficult. As civil society expert Mary Kaldor notes, the principal weakness of NGOs is that "they are largely composed of an educated minority and they lack the capacity for popular mobilization."[43]

"Beware of NGO Money"

Development NGOs have often been harmful to poor peoples' struggles, serving to dampen challenges from below and stabilize the neoliberal status quo. Southern organizations confronting elites or opposing neoliberal policies are typically excluded from funding. In addition, these radical but cash-strapped organizations are faced with artificially-strengthened NGO competitors urging the poor to seek more modest, more "realistic" reforms. The proliferation of NGOs, Mike Davis argues, has politically neutralized the poor and their movements. "Third World NGOs have proven brilliant at co-opting local leadership as well as hegemonizing the social space traditionally occupied by the Left."[44] Eboe Hutchful echoes this assessment, suggesting that the spread of Southern NGOs and their "apolitical, particularistic 'community-based' approach" to empowerment has dispersed the political influence of the poor, resulting in "the strengthening of the state at the margins."[45]

The influence of foreign funding can also tilt segments of Southern civil society away from "unacceptable" ideas and stances towards political commitments more in line with those of the donors. As Southern organizations are sucked up into the aid system and NGOized, Arundhati Roy remarks, funding "begins to dictate the agenda."

> It turns confrontation into negotiation. It depoliticises resistance. It interferes with local peoples' movements that have traditionally been self-reliant.[46]

Under the influence of NGOization, once-radical organizations drift away from "their original mandate to organize the poor against state and elite interests," observes Sangeeta Kamat. "This is a clear case in which market demand determines supply," as Southern NGOs "emerge and flourish to meet the demand of international aid agencies, thereby restructuring political engagement at the local level in completely new ways." Southern organizations that started out struggling for "development with social justice" rapidly "moved away from empowerment programs that involved political organization of the poor and education about unfair state policies or unequal distribution of resources." Kamat cites an account of Mexican NGOs that transitioned from being "organizations geared towards 'deep social change through raising consciousness, making demands, and opposing the government,' to organizations aiming at the 'incremental improvement of the poor's living conditions through community self-reliance.'" In her research in Western India, Kamat noted a similar funding-driven shift "from consciousness-raising and political-organizing work to an emphasis on skills-training for economic livelihood projects." Donor funding has had "an enduring impact on the political capabilities of NGOs," Kamat concludes.[47]

In some cases, NGOs have been part of a conscious strategy of Western donors to blunt popular opposition to neoliberalism. James Petras points to a "direct relation between the growth of social movements challenging the neoliberal model and the effort to subvert them by creating alternative forms of social action through the NGOs." The latter are "funded to provide 'self-help' projects, 'popular education,' and job training, to temporarily absorb small groups of poor, to co-opt local leaders, and to undermine anti-system struggles." According to Petras, NGOs have become "the 'community face' of neoliberalism," whose main effect is to "strengthen neoliberal regimes by severing the link between local struggles and organizations and national/ international political movements."[48] But more often than not, the harm done by NGOs has been the result of the unconscious pressures exerted on Southern organizations as they integrate into the aid regime. According to Davis, "the broad impact of the NGO/'civil society revolution,' as even some World Bank researchers acknowledge, has been to bureaucratize and deradicalize urban social movements."[49]

Whatever the intentions of the donors, the outcome of their support for "civil society" in the South has been the exact opposite of the stated goal. With Northern NGOs "passing on the tight conditionalities of their funding" and "increasing their hold on local organisations and NGOs in the south," Tina Wallace argues that the ultimate effect of these partnerships has been to create of a set of tamed organizations that stabilize the unjust status quo:

> *These processes and demands are forcing southern NGOs to learn and comply with northern agendas, creating a set of dependent organisations, not a vibrant and independent sector.* This fits well with government agendas in the south, where NGOs are appreciated for their role in providing much-needed services to the poor, but not for creating independent organisations able to engage robustly with their governments and donors.[50] [emphasis added]

Grassroots activists in the Global South are increasingly wary of NGO funding and the political constraints that come with it. In a statement issued shortly after the 2008 sub-prime housing market crash, the Western Cape Anti-Eviction Campaign, a South African housing rights organization, gave a word of warning to their sisters and brothers in the U.S. engaged in similar struggles: "Beware of money, especially NGO money, which seeks to pacify and prevent direct action." Democratic control by poor people over the organizations leading their struggles was essential, the activists stressed. "Make sure poor communities control their own movements because, as we say, no one can lead without us. ... This means that NGOs and development 'experts' should stop workshopping us on 'world-renowned' solutions ... we refuse to be a 'stakeholder' and have our voices managed and diminished by those who count."[51]

Oslo and the NGOization of the Palestinian Left

Palestine after the Oslo Accords provides a clear example of the negative depoliticizing impact of NGOization, and the way NGOs can serve to contain popular movements. The Palestinian Left, which played a key role in the First Intifada, was severely weakened and disoriented by Palestine's post-1993 NGO boom. The NGO sector absorbed large swaths of the Left, including much of its urban intellectual leadership, opening the way for Islamic resistance movements like Hamas to take over leadership of the national liberation struggle.

The First Intifada began in 1987, an unprecedented and overwhelmingly non-violent popular uprising against Israel's decades-long military occupation of the West Bank and the Gaza Strip. Organized by a vast network of popular committees and supported by left-wing organizations, Palestinians held general strikes and demonstrations, refused *en masse* to pay taxes, and organized boycotts of Israeli goods to protest the ongoing theft of their land and Israeli military control of their lives and territory. Throughout the West Bank and Gaza, Palestinians fought to keep the Israeli army out of their villages and towns by setting up barricades and blocking roads with large boulders while youths threw stones at soldiers.

The Palestinian Left (composed of the Democratic Front for the Liberation of Palestine, the Popular Front for the Liberation of Palestine, and the Communist Party) played an important leadership role at the local level in the popular committees. Left activists founded numerous grassroots groups to support local organizing efforts and sustain the Intifada. Activities to promote local self-sufficiency were seen as intimately connected to the national struggle, serving to break the population's dependence on wage labour in Israel and thus remove a key lever of influence. Left activists spoke of developing "socialist autonomy" in the Occupied Territories.[52]

In response to the uprising, Israel aggressively cracked down, arresting huge numbers of Palestinians, torturing prisoners, deporting activists, and shooting children throwing rocks. The Israeli leadership realized, however, that the occupation could not continue as it had in the past in the face of an insurgent population. In addition to using violent repression, Israel sought to make a deal with elements of the Palestianian leadership to contain the Intifada. Yasser Arafat and the Palestinian Liberation Organization (PLO) had played little role in sparking the uprising, which made the exiled official leadership of Palestine's national liberation struggle was uneasy about the growing influence of popular organizations that they did not control. Activists in the Occupied Territories had called into question the pre-eminent role of an increasingly corrupt and bureaucratic PLO. Anxious to re-assert his leadership, Arafat and a coterie of his closest advisors entered into secret negotiations with Israel arranged by the Norwegian government, which culminated in the signing of the Oslo Accords in September 1993.

The deal initially inspired great hopes that a just settlement of the longstanding Israel-Palestine conflict was at hand. As details leaked out, however, it became evident that the Oslo Accords represented a one-sided peace that overwhelmingly favoured Israel. Under the agreement signed at Oslo, the PLO transitioned into the Palestinian National Administration (PNA), but it was a far cry from statehood. Israel did not commit to return any Palestinian lands beyond the internationally recognized (1967) borders and the accord did not block any future illegal Israeli settlements. Conflicts over water resources or the right of return for Palestinian refugees were left unresolved. Crucially, Israel's military occupation effectively remained in place. In the West Bank, the PNA was given direct control over only 3% of the territory, and its decisions could be overruled by Israel. The rest of the territory remained more or less in Israel's hands. In Gaza, the PLO would control 30%. Arafat also effectively ceded control of all of Jerusalem to Israel, including East Jerusalem, where Palestinians are the majority. Oslo gave the Israeli leadership nearly everything it wanted while granting them effective control over the Occupied Territories. Arafat and the PLO leadership claimed victory, but it was a major capitulation. The Oslo Accords formalized Israeli domination, with the PNA operating more like a colonial administration, policing the local population on behalf of a conquering power.

Palestine's Post-Oslo NGO Boom

As staunch allies of Israel, Canada and other Western donors enthusiastically endorsed the Oslo Accords and redirected their aid programs to ensure that the population accepted Arafat's deal. The central element of the donors' agenda was a determination to stifle or mollify popular opposition to the Oslo Accords. To this end, the donors sought to build up the PNA into a state-like apparatus controlled by Arafat, to improve living conditions and to bolster those elements of wider Palestinian society that were supportive of Oslo. NGOs were key vehicles for this agenda, and CIDA funds flowed accordingly. According to sociologist Benoit Challand, CIDA's support for Palestinian civil society was "rather monolithic," placing "a strong emphasis on the success of peace agreements" through programs concentrated in the urban zones of the Occupied Territories.[53]

Western funding for Palestinian "civil society" grew exponentially after 1993, and the number of Palestinian NGOs skyrocketed from 444 in 1992 to over 1,400 in 2005. Palestinian NGOs benefiting from the deluge of Western funding became some of "the largest, and therefore the most significant" organizations in the Occupied Territories.[54] By 2005, the NGO sector employed more than 20,000 people, and NGO service provision covered over 60 percent of all health-care services, 80 percent of all rehabilitation services, and almost 100 percent of all pre-school education. Some of the largest Palestinian NGOs exerted "virtual monopolies" in certain fields, like agriculture, health and training, while becoming "heavily dependent on outside financial support … a fact that has affected their development and evolution in more than one way," according to Allam Jarrar.[55]

The post-Oslo flood of money for Palestinian civil society had a huge impact on the politics, activities and structure of the organizations on the receiving end. Prior to Oslo, many of Palestine's leading NGOs were deeply political "mass organizations" whose focus was "mostly mobilizational, that is, activities were initiated, decided on and carried out with grassroots involvement."[56] In the early 1990s, however, with the collapse of financial support from the Soviet Union and Arab nations, the Palestinian Left and its allied popular organizations faced a major funding crisis.[57] Many urban leftist intellectuals founded their own NGOs, while some popular organizations formalized their structures and became legally-recognized NGOs in order to tap into Western funding. Although Palestinian NGOs created in the post-Oslo period "generally ha[d] leftist roots" and in particular were often connected to the Palestinian Communist Party, (later renamed the Palestinian People's Party after 1991), donor funding provoked the "absorption of donor ideas and norms."[58]

From Activists to Technocrats

Under the influence of donor funding, Palestinian NGOs transformed into professionally-led bureaucratic organizations, more oriented to the donors than to the local population suffering from the continuing effects of Israeli apartheid. According to sociologist Asef Bayat, "after the Palestinian National Authority was set up the conditionalities of foreign funding turned NGOs into professional, elite organizations, with particular discourses of efficiency and expertise. This new arrangement tends to create distance between NGOs and the grassroots of society."[59] Foreign funding rapidly led to the "predominance of English speaking university graduates with financial skills" while reducing the importance of Arabic-speaking field managers and specialists within Palestinian NGOs. Political activists were also increasingly marginalized as Palestinian NGOs professionalized and drifted away from the social movement focus they had during the First Intifada. Their staff "is no longer associated with pure activism or activists, but is composed of the technically trained, university-educated activists and technocrats, who did not previously have any connection with militant Palestinian activism."[60] The location of NGO headquarters, often chosen for the convenience of international visitors rather than local constituencies, was symbolic of their growing distance from the grassroots. In Jerusalem, for instance, Palestinian NGOs clustered their offices near the World Bank complex, far from the Arab quarter.[61] Researcher Cheryl Rubenberg interviewed women in rural areas and refugees camps of the West Bank and found that the policy agendas advocated by internationally-funded women's NGOs in the urban centres "bore little or no resemblance to what village and camp women articulated as their problems or how to resolve them." Indeed, few of the 175 women interview by Rubenberg had even heard of any of the prominent women's NGOs and "fewer still had made use of their services."[62]

NGO programs were realigned away from struggle against the occupation to an "apolitical" agenda of service provision and state building. Service provision was no longer connected to the struggle against Israeli domination or for a wider socialist transformation of Palestinian society. Palestinian NGOs shifted from mass mobilization and political action to less politicized, less confrontational "advocacy," civic education, and awareness-raising activities. "The shift from mobilization to advocacy, I had been informed by various Palestinian development practitioners," reports Palestinian planner Mufid Qassoum, "has been triggered by northern NGOs."[63] Though most NGOs worked side by side with the PNA, some Palestinian human rights NGOs clashed with Arafat's regime. At the behest of donors, they shifted their focus from Israeli abuses to those of the PNA. "[A] Palestinian human rights NGO, LAW, recently changed its mandate from reporting on Israeli violations of human rights to reporting, almost exclusively, on the PNA's violations, since this was the express interest of several major funders."[64] Other NGOs focused on building up the PNA's administrative apparatus. NGOs worked on projects designed to strengthen the legal system and otherwise support the "institutional capacity for the fair administering of justice," to promote human rights and fundamental freedoms, as well as "the enhancement of the rule of law" in the West Bank and the Gaza Strip.[65] NGOs implemented "peace-building" and development projects encouraging Palestinians to accept the terms of Oslo, while ignoring "the Israeli practices that have obstructed Palestinian development options and political independence."[66]

While NGOs and the PNA concentrated on quixotic efforts at development and state building, Israel's mechanisms of control over the West Bank and Gaza expanded:

> During the ten years following the conclusion of the Oslo Accords, Israel's exercise of control over Palestinians not only deepened, but metamorphosed into an apartheid regime of checkpoints, a permit system, settler by-pass roads, and settlements encircling and besieging Palestinian cantons of "territoriality." By late 2003 there were 83 separate "bantustans" in the West Bank and Gaza from which travel to and from was only possible for those Palestinians with permits. This was all carried out as money flowed into the occupied Palestinian territories, ostensibly for laying the groundwork of statehood.[67]

The PNA was given the role of local police force, while NGOs generally collaborated with the PNA to try to make life tolerable for the population. This proved difficult because promoting development and maintaining Israeli control of the Occupied Territories were contradictory objectives. Encroachments continued and even accelerated after the signing of the Accords, with Jewish settlements on Palestinian land increasing in size by 65% from 1993 to 2003. Military controls routinely disrupted access to the Israeli market for Palestinian trade and labour, while Israeli goods entered local markets of the Occupied Territories unimpeded. Internal trade (between the West Bank and Gaza) and foreign trade were also obstructed, further weakening the Palestinian economy. The World Bank itself noted that the influx of aid only barely compensated for the economic losses due to Israeli border closures and other restrictive controls. According to Middle East scholar Sara Roy, the combined result was stagnant investment, rising unemployment and the balkanization of the economy: "The years since the Oslo agreement have seen a marked deterioration in Palestinian economic life and an accelerated de-development process."[68]

Palestine, like other aid-dependent regions, developed its own NGO class, with interests that diverged from that of the anti-occupation struggle. Even though certain factions of the Palestinian Left (the Popular Front for the Liberation of Palestine and the Democratic Front for the Liberation of

Palestine) rejected the Oslo Accords as a betrayal of the national struggle by Arafat, few NGOs with roots in the Left joined them in this stance. In line with the views of Canada and other Western donors, Palestine's NGO elite steadfastly supported the peace process and opposed active resistance. As Israeli journalist and activist Roni Ben Efrat observed in 1999, "many of the agreement's potential opponents found work in the NGOs, where–dependent on outside funders–they were politically neutralized."

> Because most funders today have no interest in rocking the [PNA]'s boat, the NGOs must toe Yasser Arafat's line … Apart from plugging up gaps and solving individual problems, there is little left for their members to do but grimly endure the relatively stable lifestyle–and perks–of the elite group to which they belong.[69]

Western funding was conditional on supporting the Oslo process and existing NGOs that refused to compromise their politics "suffer[ed] from diminished funding while new NGOs continue[d] to mushroom."[70] Despite frequent Israeli provocations and ongoing land grabs, much of the NGO sector considered the national liberation struggle effectively finished after the signing of the Oslo Accords and the creation of the Palestinian National Authority.[71] NGO employees tended to either "accept projects without rigorously questioning the politics of donor policies or critically assessing the ideological implications of the project," or "perceive and interiorize the donor agenda as … a natural and self-evident agenda."[72] Palestinian NGOs became disconnected from the national struggle as "an educated class of Palestinians with university degrees and wishes of upward social mobility came to dominate the NGOs."[73] Ordinary Palestinians were not oblivious to the change; Benoit Challand reports on "widespread critiques in the Palestinian streets against NGOs which are often labelled *dakakeen*, or 'boutiques', to mock their business-like approaches."[74]

Second Intifada: Radical Islam Fills the Political Void

When the Second Intifada erupted in September 2000, it was "propelled by people who did not gain from the peace process," and led by groups left out of the Western donor funding networks. The uprising took place "in the refugee camps and remote towns in the north and south of the West Bank and in the south of Gaza, rather than in urban centres like Ramallah," where Palestinian NGO personnel and their programs were concentrated.[75] In return for their collaboration with the Oslo peace process, NGO staff had been insulated to a degree from the economic consequences and political repression of the military occupation. While unemployment and living conditions remained difficult for the majority of Palestinians due to Israeli encroachments and controls, the NGO class enjoyed generous salaries paid in hard currency, protecting them from inflation.

The Second Intifada exposed Palestinian NGOs "as isolated and lacking an organic base in society." In contrast to the First Intifada, "when activists, intellectuals and community leaders were embedded within the popular struggle and bound up in a mass-based national movement," during the Second Intifada the NGO-ized segments of the Palestinian middle class were reduced to "spectators," criticizing the conduct of the uprising from the sidelines but unable to articulate–let alone mobilize around–alternative strategies of resistance. Leadership of the second Intifada came from Islamic charities and resistance groups such as Hamas and Islamic Jihad, which had opposed to Arafat's deal with Israel and were thus systematically excluded from Western funding.

While some Palestinian NGOs worked to provide medical aid to those injured by Israeli military incursions and documented and communicated abuses by the occupiers, they failed to give vocal support to the local and regional boycotts of Israeli goods, and did not attempt to strengthen community initiatives or aid popular committees to sustain the population socio-economically, as they had during the First Intifada.[76] Palestinian NGOs did little "to mobilise people, encourage voluntarism or direct the public by providing a leadership role."[77] Many NGOs feared that if they openly supported the Second Intifada, even in non-violent ways, they risked being accused of supporting "terrorism" and thus losing funding from Western donors. Others defended their passivity or lack of support for the uprising by claiming their "apolitical" organizations could not take a stand on the issue, though such considerations had not prevented them from supporting, both materially and ideologically, the Oslo Accords.

Funding for civil society served as one of the major fulcrums used by Western donors to pre-empt resistance to the Oslo Accords. Though they had played a crucial role in the First Intifada prior to receiving development aid, Palestinian NGOs became an integral part of Israel and the West's pacification strategy in the post-Oslo period, undermining their legitimacy and roots within Palestinian society. "Palestinians now look upon aid somewhat more warily, realizing the way donor assistance can undercut and prefigure local development strategies, options and vision, often according to donors' practical and political agendas."[78] By the time of the Second Intifada, Palestinian NGOs had been effectively incorporated into the occupation. Palestinian NGOs were "wedded to a 'peace process' that in real terms had become a ruse for unfettered Israeli power–a cover under which Israel has achieved its most massive land grabs and infinitely increased its destructive control over all aspects of Palestinian life."[79]

Palestinian groups were required to halt their resistance to the occupation in return for funding, but Western support for Israel (diplomatic, military, and economic) came with no political conditions attached. Israel was given a free hand to violate the Oslo Accords, expand settlements beyond the internationally agreed 1967 borders and assassinate the leadership of the Palestinian resistance. According to Palestinian scholar Rema Hammami, the Western donors' double standard in aid-giving was blatant, since "the victims are punished for not acting as they should while the occupier is given free reign."

> Instead of using their leverage to deal with the core cause of the conflict, namely Israel's colonization of the occupied territories, [Western donors] routinely use their leverage on the occupied population to ensure malleability and little resistance.[80]

Western support for civil society succeeded in absorbing and neutralizing a large part of the Left into the Palestinian NGO sector (and the PNA). The post-Oslo NGO boom created a political space that was ultimately filled by Hamas and other Islamist resistance groups. These groups never accepted the Oslo peace process as legitimate and increased their popular standing as a result, while the growth of NGOs hastened the disintegration of the Palestinian Left.

Honduras and Interforos: The Class Contradictions of NGOization

Honduras offers an interesting example of the tensions and conflicts that can arise between the grassroots and Southern NGOs advocating on their behalf. After Hurricane Mitch devastated the country in October 1998, Honduras experienced an NGO boom. Foreign aid poured into the country and the Honduran government and the World Bank organized a series of consultations to get input on the reconstruction plan, institutionalizing participation by "civil society" in many areas of public policymaking. Foreign donors and Northern NGOs provided financing for Honduran

NGOs to participate in these venues and were "essential in opening and consolidating political space for NGO sectors in policy formulation."[81] Though offered as a more "inclusive" mode of policymaking, consultations excluded the poor, their organizations and their demands as before. Instead, consultations "helped to consolidate a small non-state policy elite with its technocratic habitus and international connections, creating at the same time a fracture along class, religious and geographical lines within nascent 'civil society'."[82]

One of the most prominent Honduran NGOs engaged in advocacy was *Foro social de la deuda externa de Honduras* (FOSDEH–Social Forum for Foreign Debt). In 1995, a group of predominantly urban, left-leaning economists founded FOSDEH to study questions of poverty and Honduras's foreign debt. FOSDEH and other foreign-funded advocacy NGOs lobbied the government and the donors on development policies, using statistical definitions of poverty in an attempt to gain access for Honduras to the limited debt relief being offered by the World Bank and the IMF. Though irritated with FOSDEH's aggressive lobbying, the Honduran government was obliged to tolerate the organization due to its strong links with the donors. Following Hurricane Mitch, FOSDEH's influence increased even further: "The leading figures of FOSDEH became part of every public debate and committee where the presence of 'civil society' was required."[83]

Hurricane Mitch had provoked a surge in grassroots self-organization among the poor, especially in rural areas badly hit by the catastrophe. In reaction to the "profound deficiencies" of the government's response to Hurricane Mitch, grassroots associations in Honduras's rural regions multiplied and began working together to provide emergency aid and start reconstruction. Though many of these groups were linked to the Catholic Church, the wave of grassroots organizing occurred largely independently of the NGO boom and rarely benefited from foreign funding.[84] Like the urban NGOs, the grassroots associations hoped to influence the shape that reconstruction would take.

In this context, FOSDEH and other urban advocacy NGOs formed an alliance with predominantly rural grassroots associations to establish the Interforos coalition. Interforos was a "rational marriage" for both parties, who sought to seize the political opportunity presented by post-Mitch reconstruction. Politicians hostile to FOSDEH's advocacy had often accused the group of representing no one but themselves. By allying with rural activists, FOSDEH and other middle class NGOs were able to point to Interforos as proof that they spoke for the people and could not be dismissed as unrepresentative. For the grassroots associations, they hoped their voices would be amplified by linking with the technically-competent policy NGOs and their transnational networks in the aid system, giving them access to public debates and policy making.[85]

In the early phases of the consultations for the post-Mitch reconstruction plan, both NGOs and popular organizations like peasant associations and trade unions were optimistic that the consultations might give them real decision-making power over the issues that mattered to them. But the popular organizations quickly became disillusioned, as they discovered the government and the donors were not willing to even hear their demands. The government refused to allow land reform, income redistribution, electoral reform or any other "politically complex" issues to be raised at the consultations, citing donor-imposed time constraints. In response, many peasant organizations withdrew from the process. When a prominent Honduran businessman was appointed to lead the consultation process, *Bloque popular*, a trade union federation waging a fierce battle against privatization and neoliberal globalization, also refused to participate, stating that the union "did not want anything to do with an enemy of the people." The neoliberal macro-economic framework was excluded from discussion in the consultations and was not even made public before the Honduran government submitted its final plan to the donors. "The trade unions and peasant organizations, and their demands, were totally absent."[86]

The exclusionary and limited nature of the consultations did not bother the leaders of the urban NGOs, who continued to consult with the government on behalf of the Interforos coalition. "Thanks to the existence of Interforos, key persons within FOSDEH were able to establish themselves as part of the Honduran policy elite."[87] FOSDEH and other NGO members of Interforos were part of a "very small and uniform" group of elites, who shared more in common with Honduran government officials and donor staff than with the rural grassroots they were nominally representing in the consultations. FOSDEH's economists had "gone to the same one or two schools, studied at the same faculty" as their counterparts in the Honduran government and the local staff of the IMF and the World Bank. Despite some ideological differences with the donors and government, the NGO leaders never contested "the technocratization of policy formulation." Interforos's NGO members shared the arrogant attitude of the IMF and World Bank experts, who considered economic policies to be "technical issues, subject to expert knowledge, not subordinated to democratic scrutiny."[88] Rather than advancing the demands of Honduran social movements, FOSDEH's leadership and other NGO policy experts focused their high-level lobbying on obtaining the IMF's limited debt relief programs, even if these programs left the neoliberal model in place. Representatives of the grassroots associations within Interforos shared the frustration of the trade unions and peasant organizations, and felt that the coalition "should have activities beyond merely one or two persons sitting at negotiating tables with the government."[89]

The Struggle for Interforos

In April 2001, Interforos withdrew from the consultations, despite the misgivings of its NGO members. Tired of technocratic policy discussions with the government that did little to support the grassroots' wider social and political demands, rural representatives pushed Interforos to organize its own series of grassroots consultations to formulate an alternative, popular reconstruction plan. Encouraged by the success of this process, the rural activists grew more assertive. At Interforos's 2001 convention, rural activists voted to shift the organization's emphasis from advocacy, "requiring rapid reaction and full time monitoring of policy developments," to movement-building, "the slow and invisible strengthening of capacities and civic consciousness at the grassroots." They also pushed to decentralize the organization. Interforos's technical unit, which housed FOSDEH and other policy-oriented NGOs, was assigned to assist regional leaders in the task of movement-building. Due to Interforos's limited human resources, it had to make a choice between elite-level policy advocacy and building the organization at the grassroots. As a result of the reorganization, the issues that originally filled Interforos' agenda, such as lobbying for limited debt relief, took a back seat to regionally-identified issues. "The leaders of Tegucigalpa-based NGOs, controlling the technical unit and the leadership of the organization, were opposed to the decision … [and] insisted on the national scope and role of their advocacy."[90] The NGOs, however, were in the minority, and the grassroots representatives at the convention stood their ground.

It was a rude awakening for the NGOs, whose representatives had far outnumbered the rural activists at previous gatherings. In the first years of Interforos, FOSDEH and the advocacy NGOs had effectively set the agenda of the organization and "often responded more to the immediate political context of the nation's capital than to the situation on the ground in poor communities." NGO professionals had also lobbied in the name of Interforos with little accountability to the base.[91] Following the reorganization, the NGO professionals found themselves working in rural regions far from the capital city of Tegucigalpa and out of the media limelight.

Unhappy with being subordinated to peasants and other rural leaders with a "low cultural level," the educated urbanites of the NGO policy elite revolted. At the August 2002 annual convention, FOSDEH leaders and other NGO representatives staged a dramatic walkout and withdrew their organizations from Interforos. FOSDEH's representative with Interforos lamented the "loss of visibility" and complained that the uneducated rural activists who felt that lobbying was a waste of time were unable to "distinguish the wood from the trees."[92] Delegates from the rural grassroots associations declared they were "fed up" with the NGO representatives, who "publicly despise us and claim that technical policy matters cannot be discussed with 'the people' because the people do not understand economic policies." They accused FOSDEH of "usurp[ing] the name of Interforos" and denounced the NGO representatives for not bothering to inform the other members of Interforos about their activities.[93]

NGOs and the Grassroots: An Inevitable Divorce?

Behind the disagreements on the direction of Interforos's activism lurked the insidious pull of donor dollars. For some rural activists, the split was clearly driven more by questions of status and money than by differences over strategy. The desire of the NGOs to focus on policy advocacy in spite of the limited and exclusionary nature of the consultations was tied to the availability of donor funding. "NGOs are like swallows," remarked Lorenzo Cruz, representative of an umbrella group of community-based associations in Interforos. "When there are dollars to be made, they are here. When there are no dollars, then the NGOs are nowhere to be found."[94] For the NGO professionals, obtaining funding for their advocacy work depended on media exposure, so the shift to movement-building "ultimately threatened their recent elevation to membership in the Honduran policy elite." By walking out, FOSDEH and other NGOs had "opted to try and maintain their position as members of the policy elite instead of pursuing the longer-term work for grassroots civil society building in collaboration with the provinces."[95]

The conflicts in Interforos reflected class divisions in wider Honduran society, divisions which had been accentuated by increased funding for "civil society." The influx of development funds benefited mainly professional or middle class-led organizations while largely excluding organizations rooted in poor communities, such as trade unions and peasant organizations, especially those opposed to the neoliberal agenda in Honduras. Anthropologist Jeffrey Jackson found Honduran development workers possessed "an important characteristic" in common: "their middle- or upper-class position."

> Almost all of the Honduran development professionals I interviewed reported coming from a relatively affluent background. Many of them had studied abroad or attended private schools. Most were college educated (placing them among the top 1 percent most educated in Honduras). In addition, many of them came from families with significant political or business connections. If not members of the Honduran upper class (made up of a small number of families who own and control the majority of the country's wealth), they were certainly in the next highest tier.[96]

For university graduates and other members of the middle class who could no longer find employment in the public sector, founding an NGO or seeking employment as a development professional became a common career path. As aid resources shifted to civil society, Honduras's NGO sector was increasingly used for "clientelist purposes." "A politician could tell a follower that there were no jobs available in the public sector, but that there were funds to be channelled to NGOs."[97]

Class differences between NGO personnel and poor Hondurans were overlaid with religious and cultural differences. Elite Honduran NGO professionals were typically Protestants living in the capital city of Tegulcigalpa, while the poor on whose behalf they frequently spoke were from rural areas and were overwhelmingly Catholic. Despite the social gulf between their staff and the poor, Honduran NGOs were increasingly called upon by government and the donors to speak on behalf of "civil society" in the policy-making circles of the 1990s. Indeed, the NGO elite began to "consider themselves to be 'civil society,' excluding trade unions and peasant organizations which would have much to do with poverty reduction strategies."[98]

While FOSDEH's university-educated economists were not willing to be subordinated to lower class individuals, rural activists objected to being spoken for by unaccountable professionals:

> The split within Interforos was a rebellion by 'the people' against the technocratic NGO policy elite. Their refusal to be dismissed as

uneducated ... can be seen as an emancipatory awakening, an indicator of a slow but deep change in political subjectivity at the Honduran grassroots.[99]

The growing political assertiveness of the Honduran grassroots was confirmed by a CIDA-funded review of Honduras's reconstruction process. According to the review, government consultations after Hurricane Mitch with "proactive civil society organisations" had temporarily reduced "the risk of grassroots actors resorting to radical and obstructive activism." But the effect did not last, the review explained: "The recent resurgence of popular activism disconnected with the [consultation] process suggests that large numbers of grassroots members of civil society have become disillusioned," as evidenced by mass protests against mining projects, privatization, unrestricted logging, and in favour of agrarian reform in 2003 and 2004. Popular frustration was largely driven by issues such as "inequity as a root cause of poverty," and "environmental management," which had been "inadequately included" in the consultations.[100]

The report called on donors "to exercise constructive influence" over civil society to "help to open (or re-open), doors to participation in the [consultation] process, if, that is, the credibility of the process has not already been irrevocably affected by developments to date." CIDA's efforts "to promote broader participation of civil society" were cited as an example for donors of ways of "bringing polarised actors back to the negotiating table and ... ensuring that dialogue does not again become derailed as a result of mistrust and political factors."[101] Popular mistrust was more than justified: the World Bank-sponsored consultations were never intended to make room for demands that challenged the dominant neoliberal approach, but were instead a way of containing or pre-empting such demands.

The frictions between NGO representatives and grassroots associations within Interforos were far from unique. In an interview with geographer Maaria Seppänen, leaders of a peasant union "spontaneously expressed a good deal of reserve towards NGOs who are 'self-appointed' representatives of civil society in the name of which they negotiate even when 'nobody has given them the right to represent us'."[102] According to anthropologist Adrienne Pine, Honduran NGOs working with women in the *maquila* sector are "often beholden to international funding interests." Consequently, local NGOs tended to focus on individual agency rather than structural questions when addressing poverty, often against the wishes of their members. Elena, a member of a women's organization "with a profoundly political, anti-imperialist agenda," explained to Pine how funding eroded the group's original commitments. "Members increasingly found that only their 'soft' projects (e.g., empowerment seminars and crisis and career counselling) received funding, to the exclusion of their antimilitary and anticorruption activities." Tensions within the group led to an "upheaval," provoking Elena and other members to leave. "They've lowered their profile," Elena told Pine years after leaving the group. "They've entered into alliances with the government. They are no longer so confrontational." A member of another women's organization, frustrated by her group's lack of an overt political agenda, told Pine, "I get tired of so much self-esteem."[103]

Bangladesh and the Perils of Institutionalization

The political trajectory of Bangladesh's NGO community reveals much about the limits set by governments and donors on the politics of NGOs. When NGOs have stepped beyond the bounds of their assigned "apolitical" role of helping the poor to cope with their condition and sought to help the poor to organize themselves politically in order to change it, governments and donors have used the many levers at their disposal to bring errant organizations into line. The meteoric rise of microcredit in Bangladesh exemplifies the power of donors to shift the priorities of Southern NGOs.

NGOs sprang up in the wake of Bangladesh's 1971 war of independence, funded by foreign donors to deal with the humanitarian crisis that followed. NGOs gradually moved from relief and rehabilitation work towards integrated community development, only to discover that the poorest rarely benefited from these activities. "Through their own field experience, NGOs realised that 'poverty [was] not simply a problem of income differentials but also of the power relations which constitute rural society.'"[104] Rural elites in Bangladesh drew power from their control of land, local relationships (such as kinship and patronage) and from their political influence over key development resources coming in from outside the village such as employment programs and relief distribution. The poor in rural Bangladesh possessed little or no land and relied on livelihoods based on wage labour, self-employment and forms of agricultural tenancy. Survival thus depended on subservience to the existing power structures. There were "few alternatives to forming dependent bonds with the wealthy in order to secure access to employment or land," even if such relations worsened their condition in the long run.[105] NGO staff witnessed first-hand the ability of rural elites to frustrate or pervert community development efforts directed at the poor.

By the 1980s, many NGOs had been radicalized by these experiences and turned to a Freirean model of "consciousness-raising" to help the poor to break out of the grip of rural elites. Concentrating on adult literacy and education, NGOs organized groups of landless peasants and day labourers, teaching their group members how to read and educating them about their legal rights. The ultimate goal was to encourage their poor membership to assert themselves politically and organize to overcome structural inequalities. Nijera Kori and other NGOs denounced the impact of structural adjustment and other donor policies on their poor members while calling for land reform and the development of rural industries to help the growing landless population. Indeed, before they made the shift to microcredit, virtually all of the major Bangladeshi NGOs (Association for Social Advancement (ASA), Bangladesh Rural Advancement Committee (BRAC), Proshika) followed this radical, mobilizational approach to development.

The "development as struggle" vision of Bangladesh's NGOs led to tensions with rural elites and government officials. NGO empowerment activities which encouraged the poor to "analyse poverty in terms of structural causes and define their objectives in terms of structural transformation" were inevitably seen as threatening by elites and government officials committed to preserving the status quo. While charitable works or development programs like microcredit are non-threatening to the social order, "when the poor are organised to articulate their demands, fight for their rights and struggle to change the structural basis of their subordination, a challenge to the status quo is definitely implied." Government officials "developed an increasing suspicion of NGOs," and by 1992, NGO-government relations had "degenerated into all-out confrontation."[106]

"When the Poor Get Uppity"

The tipping point came with clashes between *Gono Shahajjo Sangstha* (GSS), "one of the most important NGOs in Bangladesh," and rural elites in North Bengal. GSS was critical of microcredit and other individualized attempts to promote economic welfare because of the divisive competition between the poor they engendered, breaking down class solidarity and thus sustaining the status quo. Instead, GSS sought to help the poor "to set up their own class-based organisation, with the eventual aim of contending for political power."[107] In early 1992, a slate of candidates from the poorest sections of the peasantry backed by GSS won the local elections in one village and were poised to win in a number of others.

The modest success of the GSS slate sent a shiver of fear throughout the Bangladeshi power structure, which responded quickly and violently. With the complicity of the police, local elites unleashed a "reign of terror" against the organization, burning down GSS's schools, going house-to-house confiscating GSS publications and beating up their supporters, including women. Many of the group's staff and supporters were forced into hiding while others were rounded up and jailed. The government banned GSS's literacy materials and the police accused GSS of "organising the poor," which in their eyes was "tantamount to fomenting a revolution." As the police chief for the area said, "all of us want to help the poor and provide charity for them. But when the poor get uppity and want to sit on the head of the rich, when they want to dominate, that cannot be allowed."[108]

The reaction against GSS was not limited to the local level; it quickly became a national campaign targeting NGOs following a similar strategy. Later that year, leaders of radical NGOs were summoned to the Prime Minister's office and chastised for their political involvement. Bangladesh's NGO Affairs Bureau, the national regulatory body responsible for oversight of local NGOs, accused many of the country's leading NGOs of being "anti-state and dangerous" and threatened to rescind the licence to operate of a number of NGOs. The government also used NGOs' reliance on foreign funding to score political points against them. Appealing to nationalist sentiment, officials claimed (rather disingenuously) that the NGOs had been acting at the behest of foreign powers to undermine the government.[109]

GSS and other intransigently radical NGOs also faced pressure from the donors to change their tune. According to economist Syed Hashemi, GSS "was forced to move away from its strategy of confrontation."

> The new strategy involves working with civil society rather than helping poor people organize on their own. A model of class harmony has replaced the previous model of class struggle. GSS's economic activities now substitute for its previous political activities. ... The shift in the focus of GSS from raising the consciousness of the poor to working to strengthen civil society seems also to be the result (in part) of donor-driven rethinking.[110]

Donors did not want NGOs which challenged the power of rural elites, criticized structural adjustment or tried to organize the poor into a political force. Bangladesh's government was dutifully applying IMF reforms, deregulating economic activity, privatizing state-owned industries, and establishing union-free Export Processing Zones. As Hashemi notes, NGO funding was increasingly skewed towards organizations which pursued "democratic" agendas and espoused a sanitized, conflict-free ideal of civil society, which in the eyes of the donors "has come to mean systemic class harmony in which the situation of less privileged groups can be improved through gradual readjustments in the system." "What is explicitly (and deliberately) missing from this definition of civil society are the political parties, trade unions and peasant organisations that have consistently fought against exploitation in Bangladesh."[111] Adult literacy, rights education and other mobilizational strategies pursued by GSS and other radical NGOs were either marginalized or dropped altogether "due to the lack of donor interest in such programmes."[112] As a CIDA official in Dhaka explained, aid was channelled through NGOs because they "are very good in identifying, responding and prioritizing the [country's development] needs *in line with donor expectations.*"[113]

Instead of organizing the poor, donors encouraged Bangladesh's NGOs to take up microcredit programs. Microcredit in Bangladesh was pioneered by Mohamed Yunus, a U.S.-educated economist who founded the Grameen Bank in 1983. For Yunus, it was not the unequal distribution of wealth but inadequate access to the credit market that held back the rural poor of Bangladesh. Against the dominant NGO approach of "development as struggle" of the time, Yunus conceived of the poor as oppressed micro-capitalists strangled by lack of affordable credit, rather than oppressed peasants strangled by exploitative landowners. Yunus argued that by giving small loans to poor women, his Grameen Bank could make capitalism work for the poor, and the poor work for capitalism (or in Yunus's terminology, make the poor "bankable" i.e. investment material). Unlike the radical NGOs, the Grameen Bank was deeply enmeshed in the status quo, and maintained its freedom of operation by "closely following politics." Yunus did this by "managing a set of elite relationships and a public image so that the Bank is prominent but non-controversial and creating an image of being non-political."[114] Yunus's message of salvation through microcredit fit perfectly with the neoliberal "self help for the poor" ideology and quickly caught on with the donors. Indeed, Yunus himself was a strong proponent of privatization and market liberalization.

With CIDA and other donors re-directing hundreds of millions of development dollars towards microcredit programs, Bangladeshi NGOs competing for donor funds were compelled to replicate Grameen's model.[115] The result was a sea change in development priorities for Bangladeshi NGOs. In 1985, only 13 NGOs in Bangladesh were involved in microcredit, but by 1990 the number had jumped to 59 organizations. By 1995, Bangladesh was home to 301 NGOs devoted exclusively or principally to microcredit. Today, virtually all of Bangladesh's 2,000 NGOs are "involved in microfinance in one way or another," estimates microcredit insider S. M. Rahman.[116] "Micro-credit, once an initiative to empower the poor, has come to be seen as a means of empowering the organization."[117] Even the peasant wing of the Communist Party of Bangladesh became an NGO offering micro-credit! In addition to microcredit, other development programs taken up by NGOs such as non-formal education, immunisation and diarrhoeal disease control were "all due to donor pressure," according to Syed Hashemi.[118] NGOs were expected to work with the poor to help them cope with their poverty, not organize them to overthrow their oppressors.

From Social Change to Self-perpetuation

The combined impact of state repression and donor pressures led Bangladesh's once-radical NGOs away from "mobilization and 'anti-hegemonic' programs," which "became less and less common."[119] As Bangladeshi NGOs increased their dependence on foreign funding, they "slowly moved away from their role as critics [of structural adjustment] and began to work more closely in association with international donor agencies."[120] Bangladeshi scholars remarked on "the 'de-radicalization' of the NGO sector away from its Freirean roots of 'conscientization' towards the almost universal pursuit of micro-finance delivery by almost every major NGO in the country."[121] As Kendall Stiles notes, despite the "strong mass movement tradition among NGO founders in Bangladesh ... few of these organizations have been able to maintain it."

> One by one, each has been pressured by donors to set aside their radical messages. Nijera Kori experienced this pressure in the early 1990s. GSS was recently pushed to the point of bankruptcy by donors concerned about the extent of the organization's reach. ... NGOs are careful not to challenge the state directly, or especially the strong role of foreign capital in the country. Although some NGO leaders still claim to be Marxist

(as do virtually all Bangladeshi social scientists), they have taken great pains not to criticize globalization or its effects on the poor.[122]

The process of NGOization was also a factor in the shifting politics of the NGOs. In the 1990s, with the advent of large-scale funding for "civil society," Bangladesh's NGOs grew larger and more bureaucratic and their priorities shifted from social change to self-perpetuation. "As payrolls grew into the tens of thousands and the number of clients swelled into the millions, the major NGOs became primarily concerned with keeping the funds flowing."[123] Organizations followed the easy money by adopting programs popular with donor agencies. In particular, managing microcredit programs required professional staff and rigid bureaucratic procedures, which forced NGOs to transform organizationally. As NGOs professionalized, their approach to the poor changed.

NGO staff were typically drawn from the urban middle classes or the local village elite and were increasingly university educated, putting them on different social plane from the poor Bangladeshis they worked with.[124] For Bangladesh's middle class, the NGO sector became "one of the principal job markets in the country, particularly for professional women."[125] "Posted to a rural area, government officers and NGO salaried staff often find that their social backgrounds and career orientation give them more in common with each other than with the local population."[126] Poor people became clients demanding financial services rather than members struggling for justice. NGO-organized *samity* groups, previously focused on literacy and consciousness raising activities, were converted into borrowing circles. As clients, poor people had little influence over budgets or program design of the professionally-run NGOs, their input "limited to relatively inconsequential areas of decision making."[127]

NGO staff gradually took over the role of patron to the poor, acting as power brokers "speaking on behalf of their members rather than mobilising people to speak on their own behalf."[128] At the same time, NGO fieldworkers tended to avoid confrontation with local power structures, be it the village elite or state officials, preferring to "modify their aims and programmes so as to accommodate the existing power structures, rather than attempt to challenge them."[129] In some villages, NGOs *are* part of the power structure. David Lewis, an expert on Bangladeshi NGOs, noted "the phenomenon of 'NGO-ing' in which members of elite families set up new organisations that help them to pursue and maintain their position and influence."[130] According to sociologist Shelley Feldman, NGOs "serve as buffers between citizens and states, militating against rather than encouraging people to struggle on their own together with others who share their interests."[131]

Once they set aside their radical views and embraced microcredit, Bangladesh's NGOs were able to patch up their relations with the government and donors. Despite the radicalism of their youth, the leadership of Bangladesh's NGOs came from the educated elite, sharing more in common with the country's rulers than its poor, rural majority: "NGO directors and high officials belong to the same social milieu as top government bureaucrats, military generals, and ministers."[132] Shafique Chouwdry, the head of ASA, justified his organization's turn away from radical politics to a commercialized microcredit model as the only way to grow the organization. Chouwdry, and politically astute NGO founders like him, knew donors would never give more than a tiny fraction of their funds to NGOs engaged in mobilizing activities. Organizations that stuck with such an approach would remain small and marginal players of the NGO scene.[133] ASA and other like-minded organizations prospered because their leaders were "able to build strategic relationships both with the state and with global forces. … While working outside the domain of the state, these leaders and their organizations do not necessarily challenge or diminish state power."[134]

The New Zamindars

While the Bangladeshi NGOs that made the turn to apolitical microcredit undeniably benefited, the gains for Bangladesh's rural poor are harder to discern. Evaluations have not produced any serious evidence of income gains, nor has the widespread adoption of Grameen-style microcredit "translated into a substantial gain for the borrowers in terms of their socio-political empowerment."

> Many complain that the weekly meetings of borrowers have devolved into mere discussions about how payments will be made. The rather heavyhanded approach to payment collection has aroused concerns among many intellectuals in Bangladesh that NGOs have come to resemble feudal zamindars more than modern development agencies. After 15 years, few borrowers have been able to move out of poverty, although a growing number of women have become active in local politics. It is also clear that managing these programs has absorbed a tremendous proportion of most NGOs' energy, to the exclusion of more traditional development and mobilization activities.[135]

Despite the improvements in agricultural productivity due to the spread of shallow tube-well irrigation and other investments, inequality and landlessness in the countryside have grown. Whereas 80% of rural households owned land in the 1960s, by the turn of the century, almost 65 million Bangladeshis were functionally landless, accounting for nearly half of the country's population. Observers close to the ground note that "life for the average rural Bangladeshi remains harsh and insecure." Wealthy landowners are still able to "combine and convert their power into different forms–such as economic power, physical power and prestige–in order to bribe the police, steal land or extract money [from the poor]."[136] While the chastened NGO sector flourishes, rural Bangladeshis continue to leave the countryside to work in the sweatshops of the cities or as migrant construction workers in the Gulf states, despite extremely dangerous working conditions and derisory pay.

Recalling Bangladesh's long history of peasant-led struggles against colonialism and for independence, Hashemi stresses the "great capacity" of poor people "to rise up and shake the foundations of the kingdom of oppression."

NGOs have to make a choice: between the four-wheel drive vehicle that comes with government licensing and donor funding, and the much harder conditions involved in living alongside poor people. The choices made by NGOs will determine which side of this struggle they are on.[137]

The near-universal conversion of Bangladesh's NGOs to the gospel of microcredit demonstrates that they have chosen to ride in the passenger's side of the donors' white SUV, while the faces of the landless poor whiz by in a blur. Bangladeshi NGOs are in no position to challenge the status quo; indeed, they have become a part of it.

6

Damming Democracy
Haitian NGOs confront "the flood"

In Haiti the proponents of democracy have always been illiterate, while its opponents have been among the best-educated people in the country.
–Jean-Claude Bajeux [1]

Even progressive Southern NGOs can become neoliberal globalization's unwitting partners ... [and] can provide institutional layers against grassroots social change movements and even grassroots development.
–Mark Schuller [2]

From 1994 to 2004, Haiti was the scene of one of the most massive government-funded "democracy promotion" campaigns ever, with legions of NGOs descending on the country to teach Haitians about "civil society" and "human rights." On the face of it, the timing of the U.S.- and Canada-funded effort was a deeply surreal phenomenon. Hundreds of thousands of grassroots Haitian activists had just defeated a three-decade long, U.S.-backed dictatorship and forced the country's first free elections. Suddenly, democracy's long-time enemies in Haiti proclaimed themselves the champions of civil society. In reality, funding for "civil society" channelled through Canadian NGOs worked to politically marginalize or co-opt Haiti's popular movement. When that failed, NGOs were used to destabilize a popularly-elected government, and then to justify the brutal repression of the pro-democracy movement.

In the shadow of brutal dictatorships and military governments and with little outside help, ordinary Haitians had created a massive and vibrant popular movement called Lavalas (meaning "the flood" in *Kreyol*). Lavalas grew out of grassroots religious communities called the *ti legliz* (the little church) formed in the 1970s and linked to the Catholic Church. The *ti legliz* movement was inspired by the teachings of Liberation Theology, a radical interpretation of the Bible, and saw the role of the church as helping the poor to organize and struggle against social and political injustice. These groups combined community development work with literacy training and political education. Despite pervasive political repression, the *ti legliz* movement and its countless offshoots of peasant organizations, trade unions, neighbourhoods associations, women's organizations and student groups drew in millions of poor and middle class Haitians in the countryside and the cities. The struggle for democracy intensified as the 1980s progressed, and on February 7, 1986 in the midst of near-daily street protests and strikes, President-for-Life Jean-Claude "Baby Doc" Duvalier was forced to flee the country. "Not long after the demise of Baby Doc Duvalier, one could drop a pencil anywhere on a map of Haiti and, where the point made its mark, identify at least one organized group in its vicinity." By 1991, an estimated 2 million Haitians (out of a population of 7 million) belonged to, or were affiliated with, these grassroots groups.[3]

With the exception of a handful of church-linked organizations, development NGOs did not contribute to the rise of Lavalas. Although Haiti's modern NGO sector arose alongside the democratic movement, funding for civil society from Canada and other Western donors prior to 1991 went disproportionately to "elite-driven NGOs," bypassing Lavalas-affiliated popular organizations almost entirely.[4] As Haiti expert Robert Maguire observed in 1992, the "civil society" built by the donors shared little in common with the popular organizations of the Lavalas movement:

> Both Haitian and international NGOs are distinct from grassroots membership groups in that they usually are urban- rather than community-based, are managed by professionals, and are organized to service grassroots constituencies.[5]

Unlike popular organizations, Haitian NGOs "tend to shut out the common people," according to political scientist Terry F. Buss. NGOs are controlled by members of the educated middle and upper classes, those who "have the wherewithal to participate" and therefore "set the agenda" in conjunction with the donors. Far from insulating aid from the corrupt practices typical of Haiti's traditional political class, NGOs served to reproduce these practices within civil society. "[N]umerous studies of NGOs in Haiti in the 1980s showed that corruption was just as rampant in NGO service delivery as it would have been for government."[6]

Election Aftermath: Elite Panic and Repression

Although a military-led transitional government took power after Duvalier left, it could not contain Lavalas for long. When the country's first democratic elections were held in 1990, Jean-Bertrand Aristide, a Catholic priest associated with the *ti legliz* movement, was swept to the presidency, powered by the massive electoral participation of the poor. Aristide had risen to national prominence as a key figure in the protest movement that overthrew Duvalier. A gifted orator who served a parish in the seaside slum of La Saline, Aristide campaigned on the slogan of "transparency, participation, justice" and enjoyed the backing of the popular movement. The victory of Aristide, a fearless critic of the Duvalier regime and U.S. imperialism, set off a panic among the island's tiny elite and their local and international associates.

For nearly 200 years, Haiti's tiny, French-speaking, light-skinned urban elite had dominated the country's political and economic system; a handful of influential families had accumulated tremendous wealth under the Duvaliers. Prior to Aristide's election, the *Kreyol*-speaking, predominantly rural poor majority, some 80% of the population, were excluded from the political life and the wealth of the nation. Members of Haiti's elite felt their grip on power slipping and worried that a government led by a proponent of Liberation Theology talking of redistribution and justice for the poor might expropriate their riches. The military and other Duvalier loyalists feared they would be brought to justice for crimes they had committed in service of the dictatorship.

Western donors, especially the U.S., were not pleased with the election results. The dictatorship and the subsequent military governments of the 1980s had dutifully applied the neoliberal recipe to Haiti's economy, receiving approval and financial support from the U.S., Canada and other Western donors, who thought of them as bold "reformers." Under their protection, a "stable business climate" was established. In the Haitian context, this meant the growth of a low-wage, union-free, unregulated and hyper-exploitative subcontracted sweatshop industry, producing textiles, sporting goods and the like for foreign multinationals. In the 1990 elections, the U.S. had hoped to contain the popular movement's demands to strictly political reforms, while keeping the neoliberal economic model intact, by backing another candidate: former World Bank economist Marc Bazin. For Haiti's impoverished masses, however, neoliberalism came to be known as "the American plan" and sometimes, due to its devastating effect on the poor and especially the peasantry, "the death plan." The popular movement was opposed to the privatization, liberalization, and deregulation agenda. When Aristide registered his candidacy at the last minute and defeated the U.S.-backed Bazin at the polls by a crushing margin of 67% to 14%, donors began to fear that with a radical priest issued from the Lavalas movement in the Presidential Palace, the "progress" made on economic reforms might be halted or even reversed.

These fears were heightened when Aristide's government stepped up tax collection on the rich, opened investigations into prominent human rights violations, raised the minimum wage, initiated land redistribution and began dismantling parts of the repressive apparatus of the Duvalier era. In particular, raising the minimum wage and increasing subsidies for basic commodities consumed by the poor were looked upon as an intolerable violation of the neoliberal model of development. The stability of the status quo seemed to be crumbling. Freed from the yoke of repression, popular organizations were rapidly gathering strength and advancing more radical demands. Sweatshop owners and USAID officials were disturbed by the inroads union organizers were making in the factories; landowners were outraged by the boldness of peasant land occupations under the democratic government. After only seven months in power, President Aristide was overthrown on September 30, 1991 in a military coup d'état financed by leading members of the Haitian business elite.

Led by General Raoul Cedras, the military regime conducted a merciless campaign of terror against the popular movement, killing some 5,000 people during the 1991-1994 coup. Although the U.S. officially opposed the coup, its support for UN sanctions against the Cedras regime was weak and filled with loopholes. Investigative journalists later revealed that Cedras and other high-ranking military officials had been on CIA payroll for years. In 1993, the CIA actively supported the creation of *Front pour l'avancement et le progrès haitien* (FRAPH–Front for the Advancement and Progress of Haiti), a far-right death squad which murdered Lavalas supporters with impunity.[7] Many grassroots leaders went into hiding or fled the country by boat towards Florida, causing a refugee crisis in the U.S. The violence forced the popular movement underground, but did not destroy it. "Despite the coup leaders' best efforts–including terror tactics and severe violence–they were unable after three years to consolidate their power within the country."[8] With international and domestic pressure building to resolve the situation, the U.S. government negotiated Aristide's return to the presidency. The Cedras regime went into exile and U.S. troops occupied the country to oversee the transition. The return of Jean-Bertrand Aristide and his government-in-exile came with a heavy political price. When negotiating the return of the democratically-elected government during the 1991-1994 coup, the U.S. extracted serious compromises from Aristide, a key element of which was agreeing to carry through the privatization of nine state-owned enterprises, as mandated by the IMF. In effect, the U.S. restored the democratic government to power on the understanding that it would pursue the same neoliberal economic policies as its authoritarian predecessors. Aristide was to serve as a figurehead president, leaving in place the power structure he had vowed to transform during his 1990 campaign.

Once he was returned to office in October 1994, however, Aristide demonstrated a stubborn independence that infuriated Western donors and the Haitian elite. Although his government adopted some of the IMF-recommended economic reforms, Aristide blocked the privatization of nine state-owned enterprises by dismissing Smarck Michel, the U.S.-selected Prime Minister. Before the end of his mandate in February 1996, Aristide also raised the minimum wage, re-established diplomatic ties to Cuba and disbanded the murderous Haitian army to prevent future coups d'état, an overwhelmingly popular move.[9] Aristide's refusal to obey U.S. strictures, with the backing of Lavalas and the Haitian population, was the political backdrop of Haiti's NGO boom.

The NGO Invasion

Unable to achieve their objectives through repression, the U.S.–with Canada rapidly increasing its participation–refocused efforts to contain and undermine Aristide and the Lavalas movement. On the heels of U.S. troops came a flood of money for NGO projects, which journalist Jane Regan described as "institutionalizing a more permanent, less reversible invasion."

> The troops of this intervention–called 'democracy enhancement' by USAID [and CIDA] and 'low intensity democracy' by others–are technicians and experts. Their weapons are development projects and lots of money. ... As in other countries, this democracy promotion industry will support those projects and people willing to go along with its agenda and will mould them into a center. In the crude old

days, grassroots organizers unwilling to be co-opted would have been tortured or killed. Now, they will simply be marginalized by poverty and lack of political clout.[10]

The NGO invasion that followed the October 1994 restoration of the democratic government sparked a frenzied round of NGOization of Haiti's civil society. The number of Haitian NGOs registered with the government had begun to grow in the 1980s, but after 1994 there was an explosion of NGOs following an exponential trend, with the number of registered organizations doubling over the next decade.

Funding for civil society was a form of "politics by stealth." According to Terry Buss, donor-funded "civil society organizations" in Haiti "tend to be dominated by elites, or people who soon become elites" who use their organizations "to further their own political careers."

[NGOs] composed of only a handful of people can exert power and influence considerably out of proportion to the size of their membership. Often they are used by political actors as surrogates, while the actors themselves appear to remain at arm's length from the political arena. ... [NGOs] can cause great havoc in the political system.[11]

By channelling money to NGOs, the donors were "trying to build a grassroots movement complete with hand-picked leaders" willing to go along with the neoliberal agenda to ensure that political power remained in elite hands.[12] Though the major beneficiaries of the post-1994 NGO boom continued to be NGOs linked to Haiti's business elite and figures associated with the *ancien regime*, significant funds also were directed at co-opting elements of popular movements to build a "left" opposition to Aristide and the anti-neoliberal political movement he represented. Instead of crushing the popular movement, the lure of NGO money served to corrupt and co-opt opportunistic sections within Lavalas.

Funding the Bourgeoisie and the Right

After the restoration of democracy in 1994, much of the funding channelled through major development NGOs to "enhance" Haiti's democracy found its way into the hands of conservative groups tied to the business elite or close to the old regime and thus hostile to social change. A landmark report published in 1998 by Grassroots International described the "consistently negative role" played by CARE and other large

Figure 1 Growth of NGOs in Haiti

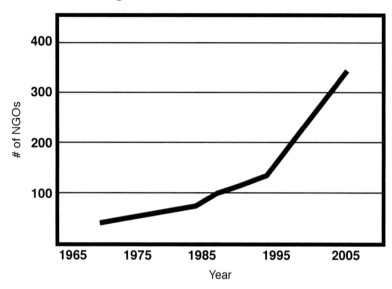

Source: Mark Schuller, "Invasion or Infusion? Understanding the Role of NGOs in Contemporary Haiti," Journal of Haitian Studies *Vol. 13, No. 2 (2007).*

NGOs in rural Haiti. After the coup, CARE and several other NGOs were contracted by USAID to manage a short-term employment creation program for 50,626 jobs. The NGO-managed jobs program was plagued by "rampant" waste and corruption and failed "to coordinate with local and regional Haitian government bodies, thereby creating projects at odds with stated Haitian priorities." The report found that major development NGOs in Haiti continued to work with discredited right-wing forces that had supported the coup d'état, rather than the popular movement. Foreign NGOs disproportionately selected local Haitian partners "who not only lack community support but are closely associated with the former military government," according to the Grassroots International report.[13] CARE, for instance, was "often working in conjunction with local partners cited as linked with the coup regime," while the Pan-American Development Foundation (PADF) and other foreign NGOs selected conservative Protestant missionary operations as their local partners. Their connection to aid resources gave these discredited or conservative local actors greater influence in the community while discouraging grassroots organizing, the report explained:

The fact that NGOs worked with tainted local partners to hand out jobs and associated benefits gave massive economic–and therefore political and social–power to these anti-democratic forces. ... The PADF/CARE work strengthened Haiti's anti-democratic sector and demonstrated to farmers that collective organizing was not advisable. Many residents ... have learned that, when resources become available, authentic community groups are not likely to be recipients.[14]

In some cases, these local partners also used their control over resources to build up a base of dependent political followers, and to mobilize people to vote against Lavalas in the 1995 Parliamentary elections. Deputy Ronald Deshommes, representing Grand Saline in the rural Artibonite region, claimed CARE and their local rightwing allies "seek to ... pull the bases away from popular leaders with the prospect of a job. They create divisions, and make it impossible to organize people." The corrosive impact of NGO projects threatened to "destroy" local peasant organizations, according to Deshommes. CARE and other major NGOs, the report concluded, were "feeding dependency and starving democracy."[15]

Perhaps the most notorious example of conservative forces empowered by civil society funding is the medical NGO *Centre de développement et de santé* (CDS). Headed by Dr. Reginald Boulos, a member of Haiti's light-skinned elite, CDS operated a network of community clinics that functioned as little more than instruments of social control. During the 1991-1994 coup, Boulos worked with the right-wing death squad FRAPH and used his CDS clinics to keep tabs on the pro-Lavalas populations of slums like Cité Soleil. With members of FRAPH on the payroll of CDS, medical services and other benefits were denied to individuals if they were known to support Lavalas:

After a December, 1993 FRAPH rampage in Cite Soleil–in which dozens of homes were torched and at least 37 people died–U.S. Embassy officials took a photo-op tour of the site to announce that CDS would have complete control over $100,000 to rebuild houses and care for victims. That aid was dispensed by CDS community health workers who were members of the local FRAPH chapter. Supporters of Aristide–by far the majority of victims–could not safely claim any aid.[16]

Despite its sordid role during the coup and its management's blatantly anti-democratic political inclinations, CDS received $4-5 million per year in international funding in the post-coup years, including seven

USAID-funded make-work projects, where its agents were responsible for awarding jobs to over 17,000 Cité Soleil residents and another 5,000 to Ouanaminthe residents in the North. The stated purpose of the program was to reduce "social disturbances" while the government implemented the American plan. Another of the program's objectives was to "bolster faith in the democratic process," though giving power over desperately-needed employment opportunities to a notorious institution associated with the military regime and its death squads may not have helped.[17]

According to anthropologist Jennie M. Smith, many Haitians, "particularly those involved in the popular movement," came to see the foreign-sponsored building of civil society "as being aimed primarily at breeding dependency and undermining grassroots efforts directed at real change." As such, NGO-led efforts to "democratize" Haiti were perceived as just one of the many "inherently exploitative strategies" designed to impose neoliberalism on Haiti.[18]

Funding a "Left" NGO Opposition

Some civil society funding went to the left wing of the Haiti's NGO sector. In the post-1994 period, human rights activists, women's movement leaders, agronomists, university professors and other middle class* sympathizers of Lavalas founded NGOs engaged in development work with unions, peasant organizations, women's groups and other grassroots organizations. Much of Haiti's educated, French-speaking middle class had opposed the dictatorship in the 1980s and was aligned with the poor in the struggle for democracy. SOFA, PAPDA, MPP, NCHR-Haiti and other organizations

---

* Between the handful of ultra-wealthy light-skinned families who control virtually the entire economy and the poor, black, *Kreyol*-speaking majority are the educated middle classes. "Middle class" is something of a misnomer, since it includes only the top 10% of Haitians, who speak French and possess a higher level of formal education than most Haitians. Historically, these relatively privileged Haitians became part of what is locally known as the "political class," referring to those people "who are always working for the state or competing with one another for power." See Schuller, "Gluing Globalization," 98. With most of the country's wealth monopolized by the light-skinned elite, a career as a politician or civil servant was often the only way to gain entry to the middle class. As Haitian scholar Robert Fatton Jr. explains: "In a country where destitution is the norm and private avenues to wealth are rare, politics becomes an entrepreneurial vocation, virtually the sole means of material and social advancement for those not born into wealth and prestige." Fatton, *Haiti's Predatory Republic*, xi. With the growth of civil society funding, development likewise became an "entrepreneurial vocation" for Haiti's educated elites, though as we saw in Chapter 2 it did little to improve the lot of the poor. Many career politicians and other members of the political class formed their own NGOs and became members of the "NGO class."

coalesced into the "social democratic" wing of Haiti's NGO sector, thanks largely to financial support received through partnerships with Northern NGOs. By mid-1996, it was apparent to seasoned observers of Haiti's popular movement that almost all of the assorted "liberal-professional 'revolutionaries and professors' who had once played a role in the struggle against Duvalier … had been absorbed in various NGOs." According to veteran Haitian activist Patrick Elie, these middle class sectors "are comfortable, well-paid, and have the impression that they are continuing to pursue the revolution."[19]

With greater access to outside funds, the development activities of Haitian NGOs–even those championing "participation" and the popular movement–were increasingly biased towards what the donors were willing to fund and away from the priorities of the poor. During fieldwork studying women's NGOs in Haiti, anthropologist Mark Schuller observed, "the NGO class is entirely dependent on outsiders, foreign donors, and their short-term contracts."[20] In an interview with Schuller, one NGO director was blunt about his organization's orientation to the donors: "essentially, we follow the money."[21] At another large NGO Schuller studied, the technical director lamented that due to funding constraints passed on from donors, the organization was forced to ignore the concerns of the poor to keep development dollars flowing: "Often, when people make demands, you feel powerless to respond."[22]

However, even Haitian NGOs that worked more closely with poor communities and "enjoyed a measure of autonomy and defended their *politik* (the same word for either politics or policies)," vis-a-vis the donors were nonetheless "unable to promote community interests if different from donors' interests." For instance, access to foreign funds quickly led one Haitian women's NGO to become more top-down and donor-driven. Despite the organization being "more open, autonomous, and participative" than most, "spaces for member discussion and decision were gradually diminishing, in part because of the changing landscape of aid financing, with greater emphasis on numerical 'results'." The "results" donors wanted were for HIV/AIDS prevention work, which became the NGO's central focus in spite of differing priorities expressed by its members. "As a result, several ideas for projects arising from member participation remain unimplemented [and] … aid recipients' requests for other programs–such as support for public transport, unions, or neighborhood associations–remain unaddressed."[23] "When you're put in the position of begging," Frisline, a member of a women's group linked to the NGO, explained to Schuller, "you are obliged to accept whatever they give you, whether it's what you need or not."[24]

The growing influence of donors was evident in political drift of the social democratic NGO class away from the popular movement. Prior to founding NGOs, middle class activists had been staunch opponents of the 1991-1994 coup d'état and the neoliberal agenda of the donors. Indeed, these middle class Lavalas activists were often among the most vocal critics of U.S. imperialism and many had advocated armed struggle rather than negotiations with the U.S. during the coup. Many were Marxists and maintained political ties with Cuba. In the post-1994 period, however, many educated elites turned their backs on the popular movement and adopted "apolitical" stances, in order to enjoy the comfortable lifestyle that administering an NGO offered. According to Stan Goff, a U.S. Special Forces officer who witnessed this transformation first-hand while serving in Haiti:

> These Haitians [employed by NGOs] are generally young and educated and very bright, and this work gives them the impression that they are doing a lot of good—which at one level they are, but they are contained, as it were. We all have the tendency to rationalize our actions, and the tendency that emerges among this group is to mistrust or oppose direct political agitation and class struggle, that systemic resistance, because it threatens their "thing," then to adopt ideologies of so-called civil society, self-help and other non-revolutionary, and anti-revolutionary, modes of thought, to rationalize their collaboration with the status quo.[25]

The end result was the "de facto containment of revolutionary initiative" by creating "a "brain drain" from community-based and class-based modes of resistance to the status quo, into these NGOs," according to Goff. The political disconnect between the social democratic NGO class and the grassroots fully emerged during the struggle against privatization in the late 1990s.

Privatization and the Lavalas-NGO Split

Privatization became a polarizing issue in the years following the return of the democratic government, provoking a bitter political split within the Lavalas movement. Most of the popular movement vehemently opposed privatization, fearing that the workers would be laid off and the assets would simply end up in the hands of the small clique of families that own

Haiti, concentrating wealth further. (The privatization of the flour mill in 1997 and the cement factory in 1999 amply confirmed these worries.) While in office, President Aristide blocked the IMF-backed privatization plan, but key figures in his party at the time, *Organization politique Lavalas* (OPL–Lavalas Political Organization) accepted the donors' demands as the price to be paid for getting international aid.[26] After Aristide stepped down in February 1996, leading OPL parliamentarians disregarded popular opinion and resumed the push to privatize Haiti's state enterprises. In reaction, public sector unions and popular organizations repeatedly paralyzed the capital with strikes, demonstrations and roadblocks protesting the announced plans. Aristide and a number of his close associates split from OPL and in November 1996 founded a rival political party, Fanmi Lavalas. Rooted in the *ti legliz* groups, Fanmi Lavalas immediately joined the anti-privatization struggle.[27]

With Haiti's parliament divided over the issue, the country sunk into political paralysis. As the privatization plan stalled, Western donors withheld promised aid and bemoaned what they saw as Aristide's "duplicity."[28] In a bipartisan U.S. Congressional report from June 1997, American lawmakers were greatly troubled by Aristide's continuing political influence:

> The lack of a strong leader–particularly given Aristide's renewed prominent role in economic and political questions–poses a serious threat to U.S. interests in privatization and economic reform in Haiti. Aristide's criticisms … are based on anti-U.S. and anti-international community slogans which suggest a re-emerging nationalism.[29]

Given donor hostility to Aristide, the choice for NGOs allied to the Lavalas movement was clear: side with Fanmi Lavalas and risk sacrificing a career as an NGO administrator, or side with the OPL and continue to receive funding. Social democratic NGOs were unanimous in their hostility to Fanmi Lavalas and joined OPL leaders in criticizing Aristide as a "demagogic populist" who was misleading the people. This was even the case for social democratic NGOs that held onto their radical rhetoric and continued to claim to speak on behalf of the *mouvement populaire*. "By the end of the 1990s, most of the anti-neoliberal NGOs had much closer links with Suzy Castor's OPL than they did with FL, despite the fact that in reality the OPL was more aggressively neo-liberal than FL."[30] Many NGO leaders were in fact prominent members of OPL.

Emblematic of the split was the *Mouvman peyizan Papaye* (MPP–Papaye Peasants' Movement), a peasant movement with a significant regional following in Haiti's Central Plateau. Chavannes Jean-Baptiste, who founded the MPP in 1973, was a close ally and advisor to Aristide and became a master at attracting development funding. In the post-1994 period, the MPP transitioned from a militant peasant movement demanding land reform and fighting against IMF economic conditions into an NGO managing countless projects throughout the Central Plateau. Thereafter, as author Peter Hallward notes in his magisterial study *Damming the Flood*, the MPP's base of support around Hinche was "sustained in large part by the regular and growing flow of NGO patronage that passes through Chavannes' hands."[31]

The MPP's organizational transformation was accompanied by a political shift. Though Jean-Baptiste retained his anti-imperialist, class struggle rhetoric, he became a bitter enemy of Aristide. The MPP abandoned the Lavalas movement in the late 1990s and "allied closely" with the OPL.[32] The rest of the population of the Central Plateau evidently did not share Jean-Baptiste's enmity towards Aristide and Fanmi Lavalas. Dr. Paul Farmer, who worked in Cange since 1985 treating tuberculosis and other poverty-related diseases, saw countless peasants from the Central Plateau come to his clinic for treatment and remarked that "almost all of the ones around these parts are members of Fanmi Lavalas (Aristide's party)."[33] When the MPP ran candidates in the May 2000 elections, its candidates fared poorly, polling well behind Fanmi Lavalas and lagging even the defeated OPL.[34]

Solidarité Famn Ayisyen (SOFA–Haitian Women's Solidarity) a women's rights NGO, underwent a similar transformation. SOFA had participated in the struggle for democracy in the 1980s and 1990s and had documented human rights violations against women during the 1991-1994 coup d'état against Aristide. As SOFA gained greater access to foreign funding, their leadership turned against the popular movement and Aristide's government. SOFA was funded by Montreal-based NGO Development & Peace and received "technical support" from the *Centre canadien d'étude et de coopération internationale* (CECI). "SOFA failed to negotiate the tension that exists between organizational management and popular representation," argues Anne Sosin, an American women's rights activist living in Haiti who worked with the organization. According to Sosin, the disconnect between the views of the organization and the views of the poor was typical of Haiti's social democratic NGOs, which had "failed to evolve into a truly democratic and representative citizen sector." "Like many civil society organizations in Haiti, SOFA is led by educated, French-speaking women from the Haitian middle class, and has become politically aligned with the elite political movement." SOFA's leadership "used its position to reach the international community. ... Their position [on Aristide] was not derived from a vote of a dwindling membership, but rather reflects the sentiments of a small handful of paid leaders."[35] Alienated by the leadership's anti-Aristide stance, most of the group's original members eventually left to join more grassroots popular organizations.

At the grassroots level the strategy had some success, as "a number of the formerly militant popular organizations ... have been slowly co-opted by the steady trickle of project dollars flowing through the almost interminable list of non-governmental organizations (NGOs) infesting every corner of Haiti."[36] Though a handful of local leaders joined the social democratic NGOs who turned against Aristide, the main consequence of civil society funding was "a growing split between the two kinds of organizations, with the grassroots remaining supportive of Lavalas and Aristide, and the NGOs mostly opposed."[37] NGO funding fragmented the popular movement along class lines, co-opting many of the middle class activists and intellectuals while marginalizing most of Haiti's poor and their popular organizations.

Regime Change by NGO

In the decisive legislative and local elections of May 2000, the OPL paid a high political price for its stance on privatization. Fanmi Lavalas won strong majorities at all levels of government, taking 89 of 115 mayoral positions, 72 of 83 seats in the Chamber of Deputies and 18 of the 19 Senate seats contested. The OPL, by contrast, won only one seat in the legislature. In response to its crushing defeat, the OPL accused the electoral commission of organizing a "massive fraud." Organization of American States (OAS) observers, however, did not support the OPL's claims, calling the May 2000 elections "a great success for the Haitian population, which turned out in large and orderly numbers to choose both their local and national governments." According to the OAS, an estimated 60% of registered voters went to the polls and there were "very few" incidents of either violence or fraud. Jean-Bertrand Aristide easily won the subsequent November 2000 Presidential elections. Though the OPL and other losing parties boycotted the presidential elections, no political analysts seriously doubted Aristide's popularity. "For the anti-Aristide opposition, the elections proved that there was no chance of defeating [Fanmi Lavalas] at the polls for the foreseeable future."[38]

With Haiti's government firmly in the hands of a political movement opposed to neoliberalism, the U.S., Canada and other Western donors unleashed a massive destabilization campaign against Aristide and his government. Professor of Caribbean Studies Tom Reeves explained:

> The game is low-intensity warfare, a policy mix long familiar to observers of U.S. policy towards "undesirable" regimes in Latin America and elsewhere. The mix includes disinformation campaigns in the media; pressure on international institutions and other governments to weaken their support of the 'target' government; and overt and covert support for rightist opposition groups, including those prepared to attempt a violent overthrow.[39]

The dilemma for the Western "democracy promoters," according to a U.S. official interviewed by journalist Anthony Fenton, was "a very weak opposition, a very fragmented opposition with no platform, unwilling to come together and form some sort of coalition by ideology or program or anything ... you know, Aristide really had 70% of the popular support and then the 120 other parties had the thirty per cent split in one hundred and twenty different ways, which is basically impossible to compete [with]."[40] Donors mobilized Haiti's NGOs, on both the left and the right, as part of a concerted campaign to bring down the government.

First, the donors looked for ways to erode the incoming Fanmi Lavalas government's popular support–economic strangulation played a key role. Even before taking office, the government faced an aid embargo from the World Bank and the Inter-American Development Bank, which blocked $500 million in already-approved loans for Haiti at the behest of the U.S. and Canada.[41] These loans were equivalent to over half of the Haitian government's annual budget, and the embargo sent the Haitian economy into a tailspin. According to economist Jeffrey Sachs, the cut-off had the effect of "squeezing Haiti's economy dry and causing untold suffering for its citizens."[42]

In its desperation to get aid flowing again, Aristide's administration made a number of concessions to the IMF and the World Bank. "The Lavalas government never yielded, however, to U.S. pressure to privatize Haiti's public utilities," writes Peter Hallward, continuing to implement its modest program of "investing in human beings":

At the same time, and with drastically limited resources, it oversaw the creation of more schools than in all the previous 190 years. It printed millions of literacy booklets and established hundreds of literacy centres, offering classes to more than 300,000 people; between 1990 and 2002 illiteracy fell from 61 to 48 per cent. With Cuban assistance, a new medical school was built and the rate of HIV infection–a legacy from the sex tourism industry of the 1970s and 80s–was frozen, with clinics and training programmes opened as part of a growing public campaign against AIDS. Significant steps were taken to limit the widespread exploitation of children. Aristide's government increased tax contributions from the elite, and in 2003 it announced the doubling of a desperately inadequate minimum wage.[43]

Next, the Western powers sought to create a united opposition front. Under the guidance of the International Republican Institute, a U.S. government agency affiliated with the Republican Party, the OPL merged with other parties hostile to Lavalas–an eclectic mix of neo-Duvalierist, rightwing fundamentalist Christian and business-linked parties–to create the *Convergence démocratique* (CD). The CD demanded that the May 2000 elections be annulled, that Aristide resign and that the Haitian military be revived. The U.S. and Canada insisted on a political settlement between CD and the elected government over the elections before restoring aid, while instructing CD leaders behind the scenes to maintain their intransigent stance.[44]

Due to the unpopularity of the defeated political opposition, the U.S., Canada and the EU funded the creation of a parallel, "independent" civic opposition movement. The importance of ordinary people mobilizing against the status quo to assert their rights was suddenly central to Western aid funding. A large portion of spending was for "human rights, democracy, and good governance" projects that fuelled vociferous NGO criticisms of alleged human rights abuses by the Lavalas government and its supporters. Haitian NGOs were funded to produce radio shows claiming the elections had been "fraudulent," unite the opponents of the "dictatorship" and organize anti-government demonstrations.

According to a CIDA report, its spending in Haiti during the 2000-2002 period "was characterized by a shift in support to civil society," while aid to the elected government was reduced to a trickle.[45] CIDA spent $67.3 million in Haiti, almost exclusively channelled to NGOs. Though this funding was ostensibly "apolitical," virtually without exception, Haitian organizations receiving CIDA funding–either directly or indirectly via

Canadian NGOs–were political opponents of Aristide and the Lavalas movement.[46]

Under Aristide's second government, Development & Peace, for instance, aimed to assist its Haitian civil society partners "to become players to be reckoned with and to help put an end to the political chaos caused by the current regime." Through its Haitian NGO partners, Development & Peace spent $1.4 million in Haiti from 2000-2003 working with over 70 local organizations "to improve the … external circulation of information," and "to develop action and training plans, and to mobilize." Development & Peace also organized a national symposium on strategies for fighting the "dictatorship," attended by representatives of 40 Haitian groups. The symposium led to the creation of several regional networks of groups opposed to the government, which "started coordinating their activities closely to develop synergy in action."[47]

USAID was also reoriented its development funds towards unifying and galvanizing "civil society" opposition to Aristide's government, spending an average of $68 million per year through thousands of NGOs from 2000 to 2003.[48] In Jacmel, for instance, students, women and union organizers openly boasted to a U.S. human rights delegation of the guidance given by USAID and other "democracy promoters." Bankrolled by the U.S. government, they had formed anti-Aristide groups to specifically demand the ouster of the government. "They trained us and taught us how to organize, and we organized the groups you see here to demand the corrupt government of Aristide be brought down."[49]

In December 2002, the crown jewel of the "civic" wing of the opposition was unveiled: the Group of 184, a coalition of NGOs and grassroots groups. The Group of 184 presented itself as a broad-based citizens' movement encompassing 184 organizations representing Haitians from all walks of life: not only the business elite, but intellectuals, human rights groups, women, peasants, labour, students, etc. Claims of pluralism notwithstanding, the Group of 184 was dominated by a wealthy, slender segment of Haitian society. The Group of 184 had grown out of the *Initiative Société Civile*, "a collection of business and religious elite organisations" funded by USAID and CIDA that according to the Haiti Support Group in the UK was "wholly unrepresentative of the Haitian majority."[50] Light-skinned members of Haiti's elite, such as Andy Apaid Jr. and Charles Henri Baker, dominated the Group of 184's leadership. These men were also some of the country's leading sweatshop industrialists, and were strongly opposed to Aristide's raising of the minimum wage.

Lawyer and human rights researcher Thomas Griffin describes how the Group of 184 grew directly out of USAID-funded groups like the International Foundation for Electoral Systems (IFES), which invested millions in building up the "civic opposition":

> IFES ... formulated groups that never existed, united pre-existing groups, gave them sensitization seminars, paid for people to attend, paid for entertainment and catering, and basically built group after group. ... They reached out to student groups, business ... [and] human rights groups–which they actually paid off to report human rights atrocities to make Aristide look bad. ... They bought journalists, and the IFES associations grew into the Group of 184 that became a solidified opposition against Aristide.[51]

A significant amount of Canadian support went directly to the Group of 184 and its member organizations. CIDA spent $13 million on "civil society, democracy and human rights"-themed projects implemented by NGOs affiliated with the Group of 184, and Canadian aid money helped to pay for the elaboration of the Group of 184's "social contract."[52] Some social democratic NGOs joined the Group of 184. After Aristide re-election in 2000, the MPP's Jean-Baptiste immediately sided with the CD. He joined their campaign for Aristide's overthrow, and called for a return of the army. The MPP subsequently joined the Group of 184 and Jean-Baptiste became one of its spokespersons.[53] Member organizations that were not created out of whole cloth tended to be foreign-funded Haitian NGOs, or local groups dependent on their patronage.

The CD and the Group of 184 staged numerous demonstrations denouncing the government and calling for Aristide to resign. Students at the State University (where many NGO leaders worked as professors) turned against the government. Clashes between pro- and anti-government demonstrators were increasingly frequent, as pro-Lavalas popular organizations mobilized in support of the government to counter the (typically much less numerous) Group of 184 demonstrators. Violent confrontations escalated from throwing bottles and stones to attacks with weapons, and on rare occasions firearms, on both sides.[54] Tensions led to isolated cases of political killings, such as the murder of journalist Brignol Lindor by members of a pro-Lavalas group, in response to the killing of one of their members by opposition supporters in Petit-Goave.

As political scientist Robert Fatton Jr. argues, some pro-Lavalas popular organizations began "threatening the opposition because they believe that it is purposefully exacerbating the crisis to generate a chaos that would nurture the return of the military."[55] The popular organizations' concerns were not only theoretical: In July and December 2001, former soldiers had attempted to overthrow the government, and from 2001-2003 conducted a low-level war against the government and its supporters through cross-border raids from the Dominican Republic. The wealthy elite and leading members of the CD were in fact secretly bankrolling the "insurgency" which combined former soldiers of the disbanded military and notorious FRAPH leaders of the 1991-1994 coup.

Civil society groups supported by CIDA seized on these incidents as proof that Aristide was an unpopular "dictator" who ruled by force. When pro-Lavalas popular organizations clashed with anti-government protesters, the civic and political opposition accused the government of using violent gangs to crack down on dissent. The opposition also cited gang violence and drug trafficking as further evidence of the nefarious designs of the Lavalas government and its supporters. These problems, however, afflicted the country–and especially its fast-growing slums–both before and after Aristide's second mandate. Nonetheless, since the opposition and its foreign donors assumed that "Aristide controlled everything," the President could be held accountable for any of the problems suffered by the country. His supporters from the slums were relentlessly demonized as "*chimères*" (thugs) and "Lavalassian hordes" no different from Duvalier's notorious *Tonton Macoutes*, or neo-Nazi followers of Hitler. Some members of the civic and political opposition called Aristide a "fascist" and accused his government of committing "genocide."[56]

Less partisan observers found that the systematic human rights violations and political repression that had characterized the Duvalier dictatorship and the military juntas were completely absent during the decade of the democratically-elected adminstrations led by Préval and Aristide (1994-2004). In the context of rising political tensions, regular paramilitary attacks from the Dominican Republic and foreign economic strangulation of the country, Amnesty International's reports showed that at most 30 political murders could be attributed to the police or pro-Lavalas groups (only tenuously linked to the government). There was no basis for comparison with previous (or subsequent) governments, according to Peter Hallward. "Remember the basic numbers: perhaps 50,000 dead under the Duvaliers (1957-1986), perhaps 700 to 1,000 dead under Namphy/Avril (1986-1990), 4,000 dead under Cedras (1991-1994) and then at least another 3,000 killed under Latortue [2004-2006]."[57] Human rights lawyer Brian Concannon Jr. argues that the opposition's claims of political persecution simply did not align with the reality on the ground:

> The press was so free in [Aristide's second] term that in the lead up to the coup d'état of 2004 you had the press openly calling for the overthrow of the government. In the US, that would not be tolerated. That would be beyond free speech. My expectation is that it would be illegal in Canada as well. There was immense freedom of assembly. There were assemblies that would definitely have been controlled in the U.S. or Canada because they were violent and illegal. But because they were done by the opposition, the Aristide government didn't touch them. So it's curious that someone like that is called a dictator.[58]

The dramatic change was due to the democratic transition Haiti had undergone, according to Concannon, as the human rights violations of democracy (non-systematic police brutality, judicial corruption, failures to protect citizens from other citizens) replaced the human rights violations of a dictatorship (large-scale killings, censorship of dissent, torture of political opponents).[59]

What gave the opposition's accusations an apparent credibility was that they came from so many different "independent" sources at both ends of the anti-Aristide political spectrum. With much of the private media owned by prominent Group of 184 leaders, opposition messages dominated Haiti's radio and television stations during the 2000-2004 period. These accusations were widely repeated in the international media as well, since two of Haiti's largest human rights groups, the National Coalition for Human Rights (NCHR-Haiti) and the *Centre oecuménique des droits de l'homme* (CEDH–Ecumenical Centre for Human Rights), were members of the Group of 184. Suzy Castor, a leader of the OPL, accused Aristide of trying to install a "Pol Pot-ian" system and claimed that Haitians had been under the thumb of a Lavalas "dictatorship" since 1990. Castor's NGO, CRESFED, was a member organization of the Group of 184 and received a $54,000 grant from CIDA for its "social action centre on human rights." The MPP's Chavannes Jean-Baptiste described Aristide as "a criminal, an assassin, a thief, a liar, a traitor, a gang leader," and, of course, "a dictator."[60]

Even social democratic NGOs that did not join the Group of 184 echoed its criticisms about Aristide's "totalitarianism," and at times put a "radical" spin on the anti-government campaign. SOFA's leaders accused Aristide of being "worse than Cedras or Duvalier," though as Professor

Tom Reeves noted following an April 2004 delegation to Haiti, their exaggerated claims of political repression did not match the situation: "I met these women in hiding during the previous [1991-1994] coup period and found them terrorized. I saw them last year [2003], under Aristide, openly functioning from their office in downtown Port au Prince."[61] Loud, public and deeply exaggerated criticism of the Lavalas government seemed to be a requirement for receiving foreign funding.

In a December 2002 press release, ICKL, ITECA, PAJ, and SAKS, four partner organizations of Development & Peace in Haiti, claimed, "since 1990, Lavalas has done nothing but betray the masses and disorganize the popular movement." In addition to having "reestablished censorship, fear and repression among the population," the four training NGOs charged that Aristide's government was acting "in the service of imperialism." The communiqué ended by celebrating the resistance of the IFES-trained student protestors as the vanguard of the "popular masses" and appealed to the popular movement to join in demanding that Aristide step down.[62] In a January 27, 2004 press release, PAPDA also saluted the university students, declaring that the struggle of the "social movement" to force Aristide's resignation was part of the Haitian people's historic struggle "against dictatorship, foreign domination, IMF dictats, the dictatorship of financial markets, capitalist globalization and every policy of destruction of our country."[63] Despite the aid embargo and the other manifestations of the destabilization campaign, in October 2003 the CIDA-funded coalition of women's NGOs CONAP called on the international community to "assume, without ambiguity, their responsibilities and withdraw their support for the government."[64]

Despite previously maintaining close ties with the Lavalas movement, social democratic NGO leaders had no qualms about calling for the overthrow–by any means necessary–of Haiti's elected government. Brian Concannon Jr. explains:

> The ease with which Haiti's leftist elite and its foreign supporters joined sweatshop owners, Duvalierists and the Bush administration in a crusade to overthrow Aristide says more about the fluidity of their own political commitments than about Haiti's government. The real cleavage in Haiti has always been not left-right but up-down. When push came to shove, class allegiance trumped any professed commitment to social equality or democracy.[65]

The Second Coup: Three Reasons

In a December 2004 assessment of Canada's "difficult partnership" with Haiti, CIDA remarked that by "identifying a change driver," "engaging a coalition of key players" and "providing sufficient resources," (i.e. by generously funding the Group of 184 and other opponents of the government), Canada's support for "civil society initiatives and Canadian NGO partners produced relatively good qualitative results." The shift to civil society had "contributed to building the capacity of non-governmental actors to generate grassroots [sic] demand for reform."[66]

Even with massive funding, however, the anti-government opposition could not expand its support beyond a small urban, middle class base. "Everybody knows that Aristide was bad," as Paul Farmer explains. "Everybody, that is, except the Haitian poor–85 per cent of the population." Aristide's popularity remained solid in spite of a deteriorating economic situation and NGOs' and the political opposition's relentless vilification. Polls commissioned by USAID from 2002 and 2003 and obtained by *New York Times* journalist Tracy Kidder showed consistent popular support for President Aristide.[67] Group of 184 demonstrations were regularly dwarfed by pro-Lavalas counter-rallies. According to Tom Reeves, social democratic NGOs such as PAPDA "do not represent the poor people of Haiti, based on their record and the evidence of their growing lack of connection to the base."[68] By the end of 2003, the artificially inflated opposition movement had managed to turn only a small segment of the population against the government. "To the distress of the Group of Friends [Canada, U.S., France]" observed David Malone of Foreign Affairs Canada, "Aristide remains the most potent political force in Haiti."[69] The NGO class, the Group of 184 and the discredited CD could not mount a serious political challenge to the government.

Ultimately, the fate of the Fanmi Lavalas government was decided by military force, with NGO subversion relegated to a supporting role. As NGOs in Haiti agitated unsuccessfully against Aristide and Fanmi Lavalas, the Canadian government organized a "high-level roundtable meeting on Haiti" held on January 31-February 1, 2003 at Meech Lake to discuss "the current political situation in Haiti." The "Ottawa Initiative" brought together Canadian, French and American representatives, who decided that Aristide had to go and that they "weren't ready to wait for the 2005 elections for the regime to change." The return of Haiti's disbanded military and the option of imposing a Kosovo-like UN "trusteeship" on Haiti were also discussed.[70]

In the fall of 2003, former soldiers intensified their cross-border attacks against government targets, and were joined by a coalition of gangs in Gonaives led by a former death squad leader. On February 5, 2004 the "rebels" launched a full-blown assault on the country. The heavily-armed force rampaged across Haiti, slaughtering police, emptying jails and burning down public buildings. Aristide's request for "a couple dozen peacekeepers" from the international community to prevent the former military from once again taking over the country received no reply. By late February, the rebels were nearing the capital city, Port-au-Prince. Government supporters built barricades around the city and braced themselves for the rebels' offensive. Jeffrey Sachs recounts the events of the night of February 29, 2004:

> According to Mr. Aristide, U.S. officials in Port-au- Prince told him that rebels were on the way to the presidential residence and that he and his family were unlikely to survive unless they immediately boarded an American-chartered plane standing by to take them to exile. The U.S. made it clear, he said, that it would provide no protection for him at the official residence, despite the ease with which this could have been arranged.

> Indeed, says Aristide's lawyer, the U.S. blocked reinforcement of Aristide's own security detail and refused him entry to the airplane until he signed a letter of resignation.

> Then Aristide was denied access to a phone for nearly 24 hours and knew nothing of his destination until he was summarily deposited in the Central African Republic.[71]

Canada played a lead role in the kidnapping and coup d'état: Joint Task Force 2, an elite Canadian commando force, was on the ground in Haiti on February 29, 2004, securing the airstrip which U.S. Marines would use to abduct President Jean-Bertrand Aristide. Canada, along with France and Chile, also provided troops for the subsequent U.S.-led and U.N.-approved occupation, the Multinational Interim Force (MIF). In an interview with journalist Naomi Klein after he was overthrown for the second time, Aristide gave three reasons for the internationally-sponsored coup against him: "privatization, privatization, privatization."[72]

Part II

From idealism to imperialism

Sgt. Jerry Kean

A Canadian soldier hands out radios in Kandahar in 2005.

7

The Idealism of Youth
Rise and fall of the NGO radicals

*Pluralism often means a smug tolerance among the powerful—a kind of
non-aggression pact which presumes that "I won't question or criticize
what you are doing, if you don't question me," while otherwise it's every
man (usually quite literally) for himself. ... The limits of pluralism are
defined by the most powerful, and the commitment to pluralism rarely
survives divergence among, or a challenge to, the self-interests of those
who espouse it.*
 –Brian K. Murphy [1]

If there is anything in the whole history of Canada's development NGOs
that explains the perception of NGOs as fierce critics of government
policy, as passionate activists fighting in solidarity with the Third World,
as institutions seeking to "do development" differently, it is the rise of the
NGO radicals. Canadian development NGOs were caught up in the wave
of student radicalism that swept the world in the 1960s and 1970s, and
politicized youth became a major force within a number of prominent
NGOs.

Driven by the prevailing spirit of confronting authority and a thirst for
more participatory, less bureaucratic ways of functioning, the Canadian
University Service Overseas (CUSO), Oxfam Canada and a handful of
church organizations shifted their focus to building solidarity with Third
World struggles, and activists developed solidarity-oriented approaches
within many other NGOs. At home, NGO radicals drew the ire of policy
makers with their sharp criticisms of Canada's foreign policy.

The radicalization of development NGOs took Canada's political
leaders by surprise. Prior to the late 1960s, NGOs had been firmly within

the political and development mainstream, and government support was decisive for the creation of the development NGO sector. Politicians saw these organizations not as critics but rather as domestic allies of the government's foreign policy, and of the development aid program in particular. When the NGO radicals turned to solidarity activism, conflicts with the government erupted. CIDA repeatedly used its funding power to discipline the errant development NGOs. Over the course of the 1980s and 1990s, the NGO radicals were ultimately defeated and the solidarity currents stamped out. The history of Canada's NGO radicals at once demonstrates the potential of solidarity activism and the political limits of government-funded pluralism that constrain development NGOs.

Wanted: Cheerleaders for Canada's Aid Program

Canada embarked upon an international aid program in 1950 with the Colombo Plan, a development effort targeting Sri Lanka, India and Pakistan, and soon extended aid to other former British colonies. Until the mid-1960s, however, public support for Canada's development aid program was "modest."[2] Canadian politicians like Mitchell Sharp, Secretary of State for External Affairs from 1968 to 1974, understood that if Canada was to fulfil its international responsibilities in the U.S.-dominated post-1945 international order, building strong domestic political support for the development aid program was key:

> [A]t a time when the total flow of official development assistance from major donor countries is declining, it is essential that public support in Canada be maintained, stimulated and increased. This is particularly true of governmental programmes where there is a great distance and many administrative steps between the taxpayer and the ultimate beneficiary. The value of a new road through a tropical jungle, or of a more modern and effective system of teaching science in an African country, is hard for many of us here to fully grasp as the live reality it actually is ... Increased popular awareness in Canada of this world-wide problem is a condition for the necessary public support of and involvement in the large development assistance programme to which the Canadian Government is committed.[3]

Canada's aid program was born in the midst of the Cold War, and it served two fundamental purposes. First, Canada and other Western nations sought to keep the rapidly decolonizing South in their geopolitical camp. At the time, socialist and nationalist movements in the emerging Third World were aggressively fighting for greater economic sovereignty by imposing stringent controls on multinational investors and in some cases nationalizing entire sectors of their foreign-dominated economies. Development aid served as an inducement for fence-sitting regimes to ally with the West and to not slam the door on foreign business interests, or worse, on capitalism itself. The West supported–and in some cases imposed–corrupt and repressive right-wing dictatorships to fight back the tide of Third World revolt. Canada's aid also helped to prop up Western-backed autocrats.

Second, the West wanted to promote capitalist-friendly industrialization efforts and maintain access to raw materials on favourable terms. Development was accordingly conceived as a process of adopting Western norms and technology, led by strong "modernizing" elites over the objections of the tradition-bound lower orders. With most of Canada's aid "tied" to the purchase of Canadian products and services, the aid program also acted as an outlet for surplus commodities and a source of contracts for Canadian exporters and multinational corporations. From its inception, Canada's aid program was driven by economic and geopolitical interests.[4]

Initially, ordinary Canadians shared little of policy makers' enthusiasm for this expansionist, business-oriented Cold War agenda. Canadian political elites looked for credible grassroots allies in the voluntary sector to impress upon Canadians "the imperatives of active growing programmes of development assistance" that the struggle to control the Third World entailed.[5] They found such allies in war charities, missionary societies and university-based organizations, which were searching for a continuing relevance in the post-war period. Though "commercial and diplomatic advantages were anticipated from expanding links between Canadians and Third World peoples resulting from greater NGO activities," the principle motive for Canadian policy makers in spurring the creation and growth of Canada's development NGOs was to consolidate domestic public opinion behind the aid program and Canada's broader international role.[6] With government support, these organizations became the core of Canada's early development NGO community, rallying to the slogan of the UN's Development Decade launched in 1960: "Give a man a fish and feed him for a day; teach him to fish and you feed him for a lifetime."[7] For Sharp and other politicians, their most important work was at home converting Canadians to the secular gospel of development and aid.

War Charities, Missionaries, Universities

Some of the most prominent development NGOs started out as private humanitarian organizations reacting to the suffering and deprivation caused by wars and revolutions in Europe during the first half of the twentieth century. These "war charities" raised money to send relief supplies such as food, clothing and medical items to people in distress throughout continental Europe. With the end of the Second World War and the economic recovery of Europe in the 1950s, many of these efforts ended, as their supporters felt their work was done. A handful of war charities, however, shifted from relief work in Europe to development work in the Third World. Some of the war charities that made the transition to development were Save the Children Fund Canada, Plan International, Oxfam Canada, CARE Canada and the Unitarian Service Committee, now known as USC Canada.*

The first church-based development organizations grew out of the missionary societies that preceded them. Missionaries had helped to extend and consolidate European rule in the colonies, with the goal of "civilizing" and Christianizing local populations. Decolonization implied an end not only to political and economic oppression but to cultural and religious domination by Europeans as well; the legitimacy of the entire missionary enterprise was put into question. In response, missionary societies "changed their ideological outlook, replacing the overt racism of the past with a new discourse about 'development' that was just beginning to take shape in the international arena."[8] Canadian NGOs with religious or missionary roots include the Catholic Canadian Organization for

---

* Save the Children Fund Canada's first activity in 1921 was sending relief to starving Russian children in the wake of the Russian Civil War (1919-21). Foster Parents Plan (now known as Plan International) started during the Spanish Civil War (1936-39) as a child sponsorship program for orphans in Spain. The Oxford Committee for Famine Relief, today know as Oxfam, began sending supplies to famine-stricken Greece in 1943 as the Second World War was coming to a close. The Cooperative for Assistance and Relief Everywhere (CARE) was founded in 1946 to send humanitarian relief to post-war Europe. The acronym "CARE" originally stood for "Cooperative for American Remittances to Europe," and the parcels of surplus U.S. Army rations sent to Europeans were known as "CARE packages." (I finally understood that the "care packages" of cookies and other gifts my mother would send my sister and me while on camping trips with the Scouts were in fact "CARE packages."–NBS) Though some were founded in Canada, like the Unitarian Service Committee established in 1945, most originated in the U.S. or Britain and only established Canadian fundraising branches later in the 1950s or 1960s. Oxfam Canada, for instance, was created in 1963. The Canadian branches would, however, come to be independent NGOs in their own right over time in most cases.

Development & Peace, Canadian Lutheran World Relief, the Mennonite Central Committee (MCC), World Vision Canada and the *Centre d'études en cooperation international* (CECI).* Today, the affiliated NGOs of major religious denominations still occupy a prominent place on the international development scene.[9]

University-based organizations, such as the World University Service of Canada (WUSC), Canadian University Service Overseas (CUSO) and the Canadian Bureau for International Education (CBIE), were the third type of early development NGOs. Often founded upon the initiative of university administrations, the university-linked NGOs were eager to share the knowledge of the academy with the Third World. They initially concentrated their activities on volunteer programs, student exchanges and sending educators, technicians and experts abroad. Like the war charities, many of these organizations had participated in relief efforts during the War.

"Made in Ottawa" NGOs

Political connections were key to the growth of Canada's development NGOs, and in some instances, NGOs were virtually direct creations of the state. In 1961, Mitchell Sharp, a Liberal politician and future External Affairs minister, organized the Freedom From Hunger Campaign (FFHC), whose members included most of the major Canadian NGOs at the time. According to historian Matthew Bunch, the Canadian government "initiated and supported the development of a Canadian [FFHC] committee." Ministers of government departments, usually from the Department of Agriculture and Department External Affairs, "cooperated directly" with the FFHC Committee on development projects and the government "loaned FFHC some personnel and the use of the offices of the Department of Agriculture, and provided direct capital assistance until 1963." Lester B. Pearson and other prominent political figures–as well as leading Canadian industrialists and bankers–were also "directly associated" with the Campaign. "One of the central goals of the Freedom From Hunger Campaign was to develop an increased profile for NGOs in the work of international development."[10] Canadian Friends Service Committee, Canadian Lutheran World Relief, Canadian Save the Children Fund, CARE Canada, Caritas Canada, the Mennonite

---

* CECI, though now a secular organization, was founded in 1958 as the Centre d'études missionaires.

Central Committee, Unitarian Service Committee Canada, and other NGOs linked to the FFHC undertook a wide range of public awareness and fundraising activities to boost support for development aid, including "Walks for Development, gift coupon and voucher campaigns, educational materials, poster campaigns, photo contests, art exhibits, cultural activities of all kinds, and personal appeals by prominent individuals."[11] In 1964, the Canadian Hunger Foundation (CHF) was created to carry on the work of the Campaign, and today is one of the largest Canadian NGOs.

Prominent Canadian politicians actively supported the fundraising of many Canadian NGOs in the 1960s. In 1967, for instance, Prime Minister Lester B. Pearson led the first "Miles for Millions" walkathon, an annual fundraising event that became a significant source of income for Oxfam Canada and other development NGOs. The External Aid Office, a precursor to CIDA, "provided logistical and financial support for [the 'Miles for Millions' walks] and for associated speaking tours and community gatherings."[12] Thus, even before formal funding channels for NGOs were established within the aid program, the Freedom From Hunger Campaign and other such government-initiated efforts had "served to unify a broad but disparate voluntary movement in Canada, and contributed directly to a proliferation of Canadian NGOs and a corresponding increase in the number of 'voluntary' overseas projects."[13]

Official support to the NGO sector increased dramatically in 1968, when the External Aid Office was reorganized as the Canadian International Development Agency (CIDA). A NGO Division within CIDA was established and received a $3 million budget, which was distributed in the form of matching grants to more than 50 organizations for various small-scale development projects. Some of the first CIDA-funded NGO projects included educational radio programming in Tanzania, community development activities in Jamaica and India, and a clean water project in Peru. Influencing domestic attitudes was, however, the principle concern. Financing NGO activities was seen as a way of eliciting support for an expanding aid program and an interventionist foreign policy. "Unless Canadians could have a sense of participation, this whole thing would seem very remote from them," Lewis Perinbam, the founding Director General of CIDA's NGO Division, explained.[14] By giving NGOs a piece of the aid pie, the government effectively tied their interests to CIDA's. Through their public activities and the involvement of their staff and volunteers, NGOs in turn created a domestic constituency in support of development aid.

These voluntary organizations possessed a number of advantages over politicians or CIDA officials in making the case for aid. They were, for instance, familiar to the Canadian public. In the late 1960s and early 70s, opinion polls showed that while Canadians were familiar with large NGOs such as CUSO, UNICEF, CARE and Oxfam, only 6% even knew that CIDA existed.[15] Voluntary organizations also enjoyed a favourable public image due to their previous humanitarian activities and could pose more credibly as disinterested advocates for the poor when calling for an increased aid budget.

NGOs helped to put a human face on the aid program by associating it with images of young Canadians digging wells, teaching in rural schools and feeding children in the Third World. NGOs played a key part in the successful effort to shape public attitudes towards Canada's foreign aid program, as "throughout the 1960s and 1970s Canadians became increasingly supportive of government aid, and tens of thousands of individual Canadians were involved in a wide variety of development activities at home and abroad."[16]

The public relations value of development NGOs has been a major reason for CIDA's continuing support. A leaked 1982 strategy paper suggested that CIDA counter criticism about waste and corruption in the aid program by recruiting "opinion leaders" within NGOs and other institutions to "convince Canadians that [CIDA] is an efficient, effective and responsible institution." CIDA officials recognized that Canadians "will have to be told this by sources … outside government if it is to be believed."[17]

In the campaign to win over the Canadian public to development aid, the NGOs were also a perfect fit ideologically. Most NGOs accepted the orthodox view of development as "modernization" and Westernization: "In the period before 1970 NGOs, by and large, shared the dominant faith of the post-war era that progress could be equated with economic growth: development was a relatively linear process of adoption of Western values and technology."[18] CIDA hoped Canadian NGOs would strengthen voluntary organizations in the Third World that promoted "individual responsibility" and "private initiative," which CIDA President Maurice Strong described as values "basic to the Canadian way of life."[19] NGOs shared the government's view that the Third World's poverty was not due to the history of colonial exploitation, but instead attributable to the poor's irresponsibility and lack of initiative:

On this basis, the so-called 'developing world' and its inhabitants were (and still are) described only in terms of what they are not. They are chaotic not ordered, traditional not modern, corrupt not honest, underdeveloped not developed, irrational not rational, lacking in all of those things the West presumes itself to be. White Westerners were still represented as the bearers of 'civilization' and were to act as the exclusive agents of development, while black, post-colonial 'others' were still seen as uncivilized and unenlightened, destined to be development's exclusive objects.

The early NGOs, like their missionary predecessors, tended to believe the problem "was not injustice, but being 'uncivilized' and suffering from the 'native' condition."[20]

Canadian development NGOs were often hostile to movements that challenged the injustices of colonialism or promoted inward-oriented or non-capitalist strategies of development. Like Canadian foreign policy makers, NGOs were apprehensive of the tremendous social and political upheaval that accompanied decolonization, and saw the radicalism of Third World national liberation movements as evidence of the "Communist menace" preying on the sufferings of the world's poor. Some organizations, like CARE and World Vision, were "active anti-communist crusaders in the Cold War years," and many saw development as part of the ideological struggle between "freedom" and "totalitarianism" in the Third World.[21] Throughout the early years of the aid program, "[t]he alliance of CIDA and the NGOs … [was] rooted in shared objectives and common interests."[22] Ironically, government support to NGOs increased substantially just as important segments of the NGO community were about to turn away from the Cold War development orthodoxy.

Youth Radicalism and the "Ideology of Solidarity"

Increasing youth participation in development via NGOs was a priority of the government, and students and other young people entered the NGOs in droves. But radicalized youth were sceptical of the Cold War jingoism of Canada's political elite and their arrogant, technocratic approach to development. Many students were engaged in anti-war activism on campus and were disgusted by the relentless U.S. bombing of Vietnam, Cambodia and Laos, its terrible human consequences, and Canada's "quiet complicity." Student radicalism was strongest in Quebec, emerging as part of the *souverainiste* movement fighting for independence from

Canada. Left nationalist ideas critical of Canada's close alignment with the U.S. also gained much currency in young radical circles in English Canada. The May 1968 student-led insurrection in Paris was a touchstone, demonstrating the huge political impact that radicalized youth could have in the West.

Inspiration also came from movements in the Third World. Some radicalized youth active in NGOs were influenced by Third World religious currents concerned with social justice. Catholic priests in Latin America and other parts of the Third World, for instance, involved themselves in political and social struggles and developed a radical interpretation of Christian scripture called "Liberation Theology," which preached a "preferential option for the poor." Other radicals were drawn to the heroic struggles of leftist guerrillas like Che Guevara in Latin America and national liberation struggles in South-East Asia and Southern Africa.

The rejection of the reigning development orthodoxy coalesced into a new and radically different approach, dubbed the "ideology of solidarity." Development was no longer conceived of simply as a process of economic transformation happening "out there," but a political and social struggle implicating both First and Third World actors. For proponents of the "ideology of solidarity," it was impossible to do development in an apolitical or neutral way. Commitment to social change at home was as important as working on the ground in poor countries. As one young volunteer put it: "In the global struggle for development, isolated, individual actions are no longer enough; they must express a sustained commitment to overturn structures which permit the rich to profit from the poor, a commitment as relevant to our own societies as to others, as much reflected in our daily attitudes and lives as in exotic activities in far away places."[23]

This new conception proposed that development required an uprooting of unjust political and economic structures and systems, both within nations of the Third World and the industrialized world, including Canada. Development was about choices, and one could either choose the side of the oppressed or the side of the system. The development radicals therefore felt projects in the Third World should strengthen those fighting for the rights and interests of the poor, and be designed with the direct participation of poor people if they were to do any good.* Canadian

---

* The roots of participatory development can be traced to the works of the Brazilian priest Paolo Freire, a Marxist educator and well-known proponent of Liberation Theology, who was hugely influential with NGO radicals, though the revolutionary content of his ideas have been stripped out as they are applied by the development industry today.

NGOs had a responsibility to stand with those resisting injustice, whether they were priests in Brazil denouncing the military dictatorship, peasant organizations in Bangladesh fighting for land reform, or guerrillas in Angola struggling against Portuguese colonialism.

In Canada, radical NGOs would work to raise awareness and develop links between ordinary Canadians with these resisters, and to draw out the connections between local issues and international questions. For Judith Marshall and other young radicals, the rich countries were part of the problem, rather than part of the solution:

> "Imperialism" as a world system was the problem. People's struggles in the third world–Vietnam, Mozambique, Angola, Nicaragua–were "lopping off its tentacles." The corporate elite was tapping into "open veins" of the third world, sucking out mineral and agricultural resources for fabulous profits on the basis of cheap labour. The "development of underdevelopment" and "dependency theory" were new concepts. Nationalist movements fought to control their own resources as the basis for self-sustained development. Solidarity work in the 1970s seemed straightforward. Our interventions were threefold–information, campaigns on corporate and government targets and material support for liberation movements. Information was key.[24]

The "ideology of solidarity" was a gamble, betting that ordinary Canadians could be convinced to see in their own problems and issues an affinity with those of the Third World, and identify with those fighting for social change. "Solidarity with struggles for social justice and change, whether in Southern Africa or Central America or the Caribbean brings a recognition of the dimensions and linkages of these same issues within our own society and the realization of Canada's actual economic and political relationship with the Third World."[25]

By engaging youth in NGO development work abroad, policy makers had hoped to exploit their energy and idealism to advance Cold War political ends. The leaders of the FFHC, for instance, "actively sought to 'piggy back' on the growing youth movements of the 1960s." They expected involvement in development NGOs to help steer the young baby boomer generation away from troublemaking at home. By "involving youth in positive action in international development," the Campaign's leaders hoped to lessen their "potential for disruptive behaviour." "Idealism is the essence of youth, but unless there is opportunity for the idealism to be expressed in concrete action," warned one proponent of the FFHC, "it often turns to anger and revolt."[26] Support for NGOs had the intended effect of cultivating young Canadians' interest and participation in development, but the government's attempt to contain their rebellious energies backfired. Under the influence of politicized youth, a number of development NGOs adopted the more radical, anti-Establishment agenda of the "ideology of solidarity."

"We've Created a Monster": CIDA Wakes up to the Problem in Rome

The 1974 United Nations World Food Conference in Rome awakened CIDA to the trouble radicalized youth within the NGOs could cause. Its fallout left relations with the Canadian Council on International Cooperation (CCIC), an NGO umbrella group, seriously frayed. The Rome conference was called to address the world food crisis of 1972-73, provoked by rising food prices and failed harvests that were swelling the ranks of the hungry in much of Africa and Asia. Between 1971 and 1974, however, Canadian officials substantially cut back the volume of food aid shipped to the Third World, in line with other grain exporting countries. "As a result there was a dramatic fall in global food aid levels just at the moment when greater volumes of food aid were needed by recipient governments."[27] In the midst of the crisis, Canadian officials were busy reducing food aid to the Third World in order to give precedence to Canadian grain exporters eager to take advantage of higher world prices.

UN organizers and Canadian officials did not anticipate public criticism from the usually complacent NGOs. The organizers of the UN Conference welcomed NGOs in Rome, expecting them to play a "constructive" role. As the Secretary-General of the Conference explained, the organizers "wanted [the NGOs] here from the first ... they are the ones who form public opinion at home, and we need them."[28] Although the Canadian government took the Conference "very seriously" and had sought to ensure that Canada's participation in the Conference would go smoothly, it was "the complexities of Canadian federalism" that the government expected to cause the greatest difficulties, not criticism from NGOs.[29] CIDA provided $23,000 in funding for the Canadian NGO delegation led by the CCIC.[30]

The CCIC's youthful delegates–with the help of opposition MPs and the media–exposed the government's shameful position, unleashing a scandal back in Canada. NGO conference participants demanded greater food aid in a time of crisis, but also pushed for Canada to support a host of reforms championed by many Third World countries at the Conference. The large CCIC delegation pressed for land reform and income redistribution combined with international commodity agreements to stabilize the prices paid to Third World producers and other reforms to the international trading system to address the structural roots of the food crisis.

Although the official Canadian delegation dismissed the NGOs' wider demands as lacking "credibility," the CCIC obtained a number of concessions on food aid from bewildered government negotiators. Embarrassed officials pledged one million tons of food aid annually for three years and committed to make greater use of multilateral channels to distribute it, which reduced their ability to use food aid to influence recipient countries.[31] The vocal activism of the CCIC in Rome "had a direct and measurable influence on Canada's position on development issues as expressed at the 1974 Conference,"[32] and as a result of the negative attention, the entire food aid program was overhauled over the next few years.

The Canadian government reacted with shock and hostility to the activism of the boisterous CCIC delegates. Canadian negotiators were "irritated by the young, 'unreasonable' demonstrators in the corridors," and felt harassed by the intense political pressure mobilized by the NGOs. Over the course of the Conference, "a mood of hostility" set in between the government and the CCIC delegates.[33] Politicians and civil servants in the official delegation "were infuriated by NGO activities that were largely financed by CIDA," and in the aftermath demanded an explanation from the Agency. CIDA had financed the creation of the Canadian Council for International Cooperation (CCIC) in 1968, expecting the NGO umbrella group to coordinate relations with the growing NGO network and build domestic political support for the aid program.[34] "The experience of having ... preferred constituents create serious problems," CIDA officials later wrote, led them to conclude that they had "created a monster" that "was threatening to worsen the political security of the Agency within government." In 1975, CIDA cut funding to the CCIC to appease External Affairs and to teach the young radicals a lesson.[35]

A decade later, due to "the Council's (and NGOs') growing dependence on government," the CCIC had toned down its politics considerably, according to John S. Clark. "CCIC's advocacy has avoided broader development issues and focused instead almost exclusively on NGO/CIDA relations," Clark observed in 1985.[36] The subsequent "chill effect" was evident in failed attempts by the CCIC to establish common positions on public policy amongst its members. These efforts were "paralyzed by fear" due to the concerns of many member agencies that the advocacy of the NGO umbrella group "might harm their funding base, public or private."[37]

CUSO: "A Great Idea to Help Canada Save the World"

The most spectacular and telling conflict with radicalized development NGOs was the government's power struggles with the Canadian University Service Overseas (CUSO) in the late 1970s. CUSO began life as the favoured child of the NGO scene, thanks to its founders' deep political connections to the Liberal party. To create the organization, Keith Spicer, one of CUSO's founders, claimed to have "convinced everybody who needed to be convinced, from the Prime Minister on down."[38] With the help of university administrators, Spicer had unified a variety of campus-based volunteer-sending efforts into a single structure and turned to the government for help getting the nascent organization off the ground. Spicer described CUSO to Prime Minister Lester Pearson as "a great idea to help Canada save the world." By sending Canadian university students abroad as volunteers, Spicer argued, CUSO would contribute to the anti-Communist crusade. Spicer's inspiration was derived in part from the ideas of Dr. Donald Faris, a Canadian missionary in Asia, who thought such a program could supplement the wider aim of the aid program—to keep the Third World in the Western orbit:

> Our youth possess a tremendous potential of energy, idealism and enthusiasm, just waiting to be tapped. … To this end, visualize placing not just a few thousand balding experts in the field *to cope with the advancing enemy*, but a hundred thousand young people to supplement the other more seasoned men and women … [39] [emphasis added]

The payoff from Spicer's high-level political lobbying came in 1965 when CUSO was given a $500,000 grant, becoming the first voluntary organization to receive direct government funding for its development work. In addition to financial support, the government arranged for early CUSO volunteers to be flown to their destinations in Canadian military aircraft.[40]

   True to its name, CUSO recruited student volunteers from university campuses across Canada for placements in the Third World, typically for work as teachers or health care workers. Initially, CUSO's approach to development was characterized by the patronizing view of non-Western peoples common to most Canadian NGOs, which was not lost on those being "helped." Following a visit to volunteer placements in Asia in the early 1960s, Lewis Perinbam found that Asians were insulted by CUSO's activities, which were interpreted as a calculated display "of the superiority of the west over the non-westernized world."

> There was a strong feeling that young Canadian graduates were, in a sense, coming to 'civilize', and that this was why many of them wanted to work in villages rather than in towns where life might be more sophisticated. This emphasis on poverty and technical backwardness is very much resented among Asians, but there is little doubt that it is uppermost in the mind of many westerners.[41]

Throughout the 60s and into the 70s, the volunteer-sending organization obtained the lion's share of funds earmarked for NGOs in CIDA's rapidly expanding budget. CIDA's NGO Division, of its initial budget of $3 million, gave $2.3 million to CUSO in the form of a block grant, while the rest was shared among numerous other organizations in the form of matching grants for various small-scale projects. The number of CUSO volunteers abroad tripled from 341 working in 29 different countries in 1966 to 1,110 working in 42 countries in 1970. Throughout its history, 80-90% of CUSO's budget has come from government funds.[42]

CUSO's spectacular growth had a major impact on Canada's development NGO sector. "Latter-day Canadian NGOs, gingerly following in CUSO's footsteps, found a well-blazed trail ... [and] many of their staff were former CUSO volunteers and field staff."[43] "Many of the leaders of today's NGOs," writes Alison Van Rooy, "are returned volunteers from CUSO's first forays into West Africa in the 1960s ... [who] have spent the whole of their career in NGOs, often hopping among NGOs and in and out of CIDA."[44] CUSO also indirectly spurred the creation of the NGO Division in CIDA, which was established in response to growing demand from other NGOs jealous of the organization's substantial government funding. By 1967, CUSO was receiving $1.8 million from the government, and "other voluntary organizations were lining up at the trough."[45]

The CUSO Kids Shake Things Up

Despite the intentions of its founders, CUSO's politics changed dramatically over the course of the 1960s and 1970s. Inspired by political struggles in the Third World, many of CUSO's young volunteers and staff members became proponents of the "ideology of solidarity." CUSO's relatively autonomous Quebec branch, the *Service universitaire canadien outre-mer* (SUCO), became even more radicalized throughout the 1970s. The "CUSO kids" were out to shake up the development world:

> Many were annoyed by CUSO's growing bureaucracy, its increasing dependence upon the Canadian government, its apolitical stance in the face of growing Third World problems and by what they saw as the complicit apathy of the industrialized world. Many wanted to slap the rose-coloured glasses off the technocratic face of development and say loudly what they had seen: that the gaps, rather than narrowing, were widening to reveal a terrible chasm of poverty and despair that demanded urgent attention.[46]

CUSO Executive Director Murray Thomson noted in 1974 that a "large segment" of CUSO's members wanted "a shift of direction and of emphasis … towards more public identification with the unrepresented of the world; the poor, oppressed, the powerless."[47] With SUCO's members in the lead, the radicals progressively won over more and more adherents to their point of view. Their influence within CUSO grew, reflected in both the organization's activities and its structure.

Early on, youthful radicalism found expression at the organization's Annual General Meetings. CUSO's membership passed resolutions expressing solidarity with anti-colonial struggles and liberation movements throughout the world while denouncing Western-supported dictatorships and criticizing Canada's foreign policy. Though non-binding, the resolutions soon "became an annual source of friction between CUSO and CIDA."[48] CUSO also investigated Canadian corporate ties with the apartheid regime in South Africa and established links with the liberation movements in southern Africa (Angola, Mozambique, Zimbabwe and South Africa). At a time when support for Israel spanned the political spectrum, SUCO criticized Israel's treatment of Palestinians. SUCO also made connections between the struggle for liberation in Angola and the sovereignty struggle in Quebec.

One of CUSO's most effective actions was in the wake of the bloody 1973 coup d'état in Chile. Democratically elected in 1970 on an explicitly socialist platform, President Salvador Allende had infuriated the Chilean oligarchy by nationalizing the country's hugely profitable copper mines and other major industries. Allende's *Unidad Popular* government had also drawn the enmity of the U.S. government, whose multinationals held substantial investments in the country. On September 11, 1973, Chile's experiment with democratic socialism was cut short when Allende's government was overthrown in a brutal CIA-backed military coup. Allende was killed as the army stormed the Presidential Palace and a military junta led by General Augusto Pinochet took power. The Pinochet dictatorship reversed the socialist policies of the deposed government, banned political parties, unions and popular organizations of the Left, and savagely persecuted those who had supported Allende.

Following the coup in Chile, CUSO organized a cross-Canada speaking tour for Hortensia Allende, wife of the slain Chilean president. To packed auditorium halls, the Chilean First Lady spoke of the terrible suffering of her husband's supporters, who were being rounded up, tortured and killed by the thousands. The public sympathy generated by Mrs. Allende's tour and other actions in solidarity with Chile forced a reluctant Trudeau government to open its doors to thousands of Chilean political refugees. The government had initially welcomed the coup d'état, and Canadian mining companies were some of the first multinationals to take advantage of the red carpet rolled out to foreign capital by the dictatorship. But public pressure obliged the government to curtail its more overt support for the military junta. CIDA, for instance, did not offer aid to Chile following the 1973 coup d'état. A confidential 1974 cabinet document lamented that "the attention ... focused on the Chilean Government's use of repression against its opponents has led to an unfavourable reaction among the Canadian public—a reaction which will not permit any significant increase in Canadian aid to this country."[49]

Lights Out for CUSO

As solidarity-minded voices grew within CUSO, Ottawa's enthusiasm for the organization declined. Both in public and in private, CIDA officials and parliamentarians expressed displeasure with CUSO's radical take on development and its criticism of Canada's foreign policy. Media hostility to CUSO's solidarity orientation added to the pressure on the organization. CIDA exerted pressure on CUSO, placing tighter controls on some activities and limiting funding for others, such as development education programs that were often critical of the government. The organization's grant submissions to CIDA also came under greater scrutiny, delaying the release of money and forcing CUSO to borrow from private banks at high interest rates in order to cover ongoing expenditures. CUSO's Executive Directors bore the brunt of the government's fury. CIDA president Michel Dupuy (1977-1980), for instance, once summoned the heads of CUSO and SUCO to his office to issue a warning: "I know the difference between development and politics, and I hope that you do too."

In 1978, a firestorm of ill-informed (and often ill-intentioned) media criticism engulfed CUSO's work in Zimbabwe, then called Rhodesia. CUSO was working with the liberation movements to provide humanitarian aid as the final stages of the armed struggle against the white settler-dominated regime played out. Canada had voted in favour of providing humanitarian relief to the liberation movements of Southern Africa at a 1973 Commonwealth gathering, and CUSO's activities were strictly non-military; one project was a CUSO-supported farm growing food for refugees displaced by the Rhodesian military's assaults. Nonetheless, media commentators claimed that CUSO was supporting "terrorists" with Canadian tax dollars and demanded that the program be shut down immediately. Fear of a political scandal cascaded down the bureaucracy onto CUSO: "In Ottawa there was unmitigated panic at CIDA, as junior officials, blasted from above, telephoned CUSO to find out what had gone wrong. Negotiations on the CIDA grant ... came to an abrupt standstill."[50] Evidently, the government hadn't expected anyone to act on its empty words of solidarity with liberation movements.

CUSO's Executive Directors were under intense pressure to rein in the youthful radicals, but by the late 1970s, top management no longer had the control necessary to deliver the demanded changes. To accommodate rapid organizational growth and the youthful membership's "passion for social action and participatory democracy," CUSO had decentralized its operations in the late 1960s. Overseas local committees, composed of CUSO staff and volunteers, and regional groupings were given greater control over programs in the Third World. Greater authority was also vested in democratic decision-making bodies such as the Inter Regional Meeting, which twice a year brought together staff representatives from the overseas committees, as well as delegates from the Ottawa head office and the various Canadian sections of CUSO.

With staff and volunteers assuming a bigger role in determining CUSO's day-to-day operations and overall direction, the traditional hierarchy of the organization was turned upside down. On paper, the Board of Directors was responsible for governing CUSO, determining budgets and producing policies that the Executive Director and the staff would carry out. Authority was supposed to flow down and responsibility up. Instead, decentralization placed authority and decision-making power in the hands of overseas committees coordinated through the Inter Regional Meeting, which "had largely subsumed the role of both the Board and the Executive Director by the late 1970s."[51] While even critics of the CUSO kids acknowledged that the activities of the overseas committees were "more often than not beyond reproach," CIDA was unhappy about the influence of radicalized students and staff, and pressured CUSO's top managers to reassert control.

In 1978, Robin Wilson assumed the post of Executive Director at CUSO, determined to re-establish his position's authority. Wilson sought to diminish the influence of staff with "militant leftist views" within the organization, which he knew was "a guarantee ... of sure disaster in the CIDA cheque-writing department."[52] To patch up relations with the government, Wilson tried to push through a series of management reforms recentralizing power in the hands of the Executive Director and divesting the democratic structures of any real influence. Staff members were immediately hostile and denounced the undemocratic and authoritarian nature of the reforms, setting off a period of strained and uneasy relations between Wilson and distrustful staff. After a tense debate about the internal conflict, the Board of Directors decided to replace Wilson in January 1979.

Wilson's firing proved to be the crisis the government was waiting for. CIDA cut CUSO's entire funding of over $10 million. 95% of its budget disappeared overnight. The head of the NGO Division at CIDA publicly complained that "rads" (radicals) and "trots" (Trotskyists) had overrun the organization, and announced that no more funding would be forthcoming until major changes were made.[53] Over the next year, CIDA dictated a total overhaul of the organization. The membership-elected Board of Directors was sacked and a new Board composed of civil servants, municipal politicians and university presidents parachuted in. CIDA also reserved the right to approve the two chairmen of the Board.[54] Following a CIDA-imposed management audit, the overseas committees, the Inter Regional Meeting and other participatory management structures were stripped of power, which was given to a CIDA-approved Executive Director. Chris Bryant, a CUSO staffer, testified to the rapid growth of bureaucracy following the government-imposed reorganization: "[Before] CIDA gave us the money and we spent our time programming. ... Now ... all my time is spent filling out forms and calculating the telephone bills."[55] Radical currents in CUSO remained, but under assault from inside and outside of the organization, their influence was drastically reduced.

The fate of the more radical SUCO was harsher still. SUCO was jettisoned from CUSO in 1981, and when the same tactics of financial intimidation failed to convince SUCO's members to adopt a less strident political stance, CIDA shut off all funding indefinitely. Without government backing, SUCO's annual budget dropped from $6 million to only $400,000 and staff levels fell from 45 employees to 4. By 1984, the Quebec-based organization had effectively collapsed.*

When CUSO forced policy makers to "look over their left shoulder" on international questions, the tolerance of the Canadian state disappeared. CIDA did not want to fund a democratically-run NGO that worked to address the world's inequalities. Pious expressions about "pluralism" and "autonomy" notwithstanding, they wanted a bureaucratic organization accountable and responsive to CIDA.

CIDA's Tightening Noose: Central America and South Africa

The humbling of CUSO–Canada's largest NGO at the time–was part of a wider assault launched by CIDA against NGO radicals in the 1980s. Increasingly, CIDA demanded greater "accountability" and "transparency" from NGOs. This generally translated into exhaustive activity reports, detailed project plans and an ever-growing paper trail for money spent. CIDA also pressed for greater "professionalism" on the part of NGO personnel. In response to these pressures, NGOs centralized decision-making in the hands of top managers in close contact with officials in CIDA and other government agencies. Development NGOs became more bureaucratic and hierarchical, ultimately resulting in a decline in volunteer involvement.[56]

CIDA added stringent political controls on aid money, freezing out NGOs working with leftist movements and regimes. In 1979, CIDA cut all funding to NGO projects in Cuba, Vietnam, and those supporting liberation movements in Southern Africa like Nelson Mandela's African National Congress. Shrinking political space and suppression of radicalism was evident in the roles NGOs played in the Central American solidarity movement and the anti-apartheid struggle in Canada, the two major solidarity movements of the 1980s.

In the 1980s, a massive Central America solidarity movement emerged in Canada to support the region's popular movements, with Canadian churches playing a leading role. For decades, radical priests, peasant

---

* After 4 years in the wilderness, SUCO was able to re-establish CIDA funding in 1988. Known today as Solidarité union coopération, SUCO received 72% of its funding from CIDA in 2011. See SUCO's website for more details:
http://suco.org/suco/solidarite-union-cooperation/historique/

groups and other popular organizations in the region had demanded a more equal distribution of land and an end to corrupt and authoritarian regimes. When the elite-dominated governments turned to death squads and military repression to eliminate these Liberation Theology-inspired oppositional groups, peasant-based insurgencies exploded in the 1960s and 1970s. In Nicaragua, the Sandinista guerrillas overthrew the Somoza dictatorship and established a socialist government in 1979, while in Guatemala and El Salvador U.S.-backed regimes used extreme violence to stamp out opposition, peaceful or otherwise. Instead of denouncing human rights abuses against popular organizations or supporting their demands for social justice, however, the Canadian government aligned its aid with the counter-insurgency strategies of the violent U.S.-backed regimes.

NGOs working in Central America in the 1980s were often forced to choose between their politics and their CIDA funding.[57] According to Brian K. Murphy, church-based NGOs and other progressive Canadian NGOs working with popular organizations in Guatemala had to decline funds from the Canadian government "for security reasons–that is, to protect the lives and work of project partners–because it was known that the government sometimes shared Canadian project information with the Guatemalan government and the U.S. embassy." The U.S. military was closely involved in training and advising their Guatemalan counterparts in counterinsurgency warfare. Nonetheless, at least 20 other Canadian NGOs had no qualms about their projects potentially serving to extend the gaze of a military carrying out a genocidal campaign against indigenous people in the countryside, Murphy reports.[58]

In El Salvador, the situation was largely the same, except that NGOs were much more united in their opposition to the government. In 1984-85, the radical NGOs carried out a concerted campaign against CIDA re-opening bilateral aid to the government of El Salvador. The CCIC even passed a resolution forbidding its members to accept funds for development work with the Salvadorean regime. Nonetheless, when CIDA offered a contract for managing a development fund in collaboration with the government of El Salvador, the Canadian Hunger Foundation broke ranks and signed the contract. The agreement establishing the fund, to which communities could submit project proposals, stipulated that all projects were subject to the approval of the government of El Salvador and all project information was to be available to the government.[59] As in Guatemala, there was "profound concern" among popular organizations in El Salvador about the way Canadian aid was serving to increase surveillance of poor communities by a repressive state.[60]

In testimony before Parliament on the issue, radical NGOs were harshly critical of the move, and of Canada's foreign policy in the region more generally. The government reacted strongly to the NGOs' criticism. In a subsequent report based on the hearings, Members of Parliament claimed that a few established organizations "have been known to support inappropriate political activities in the Third World." The MPs denounced these "violations of the public trust" and called on CIDA to "take effective remedial action."[61] CIDA became "very sensitive to ... the use of government funds to directly or indirectly criticize government policy."[62]

As the civil wars ended, a group of NGOs spent two years crafting a proposal to create a Central American Peace and Development Fund. The fate of the proposed Fund was indicative of the new funding atmosphere:

> Unfortunately, CIDA was less than wholehearted in its support of the proposal. Some within the Canadian government saw certain NGOs as ideological and programmatic supporters of left-wing movements in Central America. These NGOs were unable to build a constructive working relationship with CIDA.[63]

According to Tim Brodhead and Cranford Pratt, CIDA and the NGOs failed to reach an agreement in part because of Canada's geopolitical ties to the U.S. "The region, unlike Angola and Mozambique but very much like Zimbabwe and South Africa, was politically too important for CIDA to accept any real delegation of power to NGOs, especially when they included many that were strongly critical of U.S. policy in the area. A Central American monitoring agency set up by the NGOs took on an exclusively policy focus but received no CIDA funding."[64]

The creeping conservatism of NGOs was on display in the last stages of the decades-long struggle against South African apartheid. Apartheid was a system of institutionalized racism installed to control and exploit the native black population. South Africa's white regime had expropriated land belonging to blacks for the benefit of white commercial farmers. The former residents were herded into isolated, overcrowded villages called "Bantustans." Pass laws restricted the freedom of movement of black South Africans, and access to social services was segregated by race. Cheap black labour was used on plantations, in mines and factories, and political or labour organizing among blacks was illegal.

To bring down apartheid, opponents both inside and outside the country were demanding comprehensive economic and political sanctions against South Africa. Though the Canadian government often expressed its opposition to apartheid, this rhetoric did not disturb its "flourishing economic relations, loopholes on military exports and full diplomatic relations with the white regime."[65] Canada's policy appeared to change when Prime Minister Brian Mulroney announced his government's support for comprehensive sanctions in October 1985, but it was a hollow pledge. Mulroney's government maintained diplomatic relations with South Africa throughout the 1980s, and Canada's "economic sanctions were neither comprehensive nor mandatory."Trade sanctions affected only a quarter of Canadian trade with South Africa and imports continued to increase after Mulroney's announcement. Canadian banks continued to make loans to South African firms, as financial sanctions "remained voluntary and, at times, ignored."[66]

With the "enormous increase" in aid funding to South Africa and the region following Mulroney's announcement of support the anti-apartheid cause, "an artificially inflated network of NGOs emerged to coordinate work on southern Africa."[67] CUSO, Oxfam and WUSC, organizations which had been one set of players among many in Canada's anti-apartheid movement in the 1970s, took on increasingly dominant roles in the late 1980s thanks to the clout they enjoyed due to growing budgets and field staff. In South Africa, CIDA "by-passed some NGO players and induced others into existence ... while keeping a firm hand on the reins."[68] CIDA established the South African Education Trust Fund, for instance, at the behest of External Affairs because officials "did not think the strong NGOs already active vis-à-vis South Africa sufficiently sensitive to Canadian foreign policy concerns."[69]

Though the government started backsliding almost immediately on sanctions, a "kind of self-censorship" set in amongst NGOs in the anti-apartheid movement.[70] Mulroney's support for sanctions was haphazard and measures that might hurt corporate interests were rarely binding or enforced, but Canadian NGOs in the anti-apartheid movement avoided criticizing the hypocrisy of their patron. One example was the International Defence and Aid Fund for Southern Africa (IDAFSA), which had previously been denied charitable status because Revenue Canada deemed its work defending political prisoners "too political." Following the Mulroney government's rhetorical embrace of the anti-apartheid cause, IDAFSA was granted charitable status and it established a "cordial relationship" with Ottawa; thanks to an $8 million injection of funding from CIDA, IDAFSA massively expanded its work. Access to aid money, however, came at the cost of its political independence. "Not surprisingly," notes historian Linda Freeman, "this transformation was accompanied by a dramatic change of attitude towards the state and to critics of state policies."[71]

NGOs not only abstained from criticism, but also pressured other voices in the movement to follow suit. NGOs used their growing financial clout to tone down the politics of the anti-apartheid movement in Canada, according to activist Judith Marshall. Independent, radical groups critical of the Mulroney government experienced "strong tensions" working in coalition with development NGOs, who "at times pitt[ed] the value of dollar inputs over against inputs of lobbying, education and analysis." As NGOs acquired prominence on the anti-apartheid issue, "what was increasingly lost was the sharper resonance of a left solidarity politics that went beyond liberal repugnance at racism to a deeper critique of the workings of international capital."[72]

According to Freeman, NGOs' newfound political prudence "came into full view" at the final national anti-apartheid conference in May 1990:

> The taming of what had been an independent pressure on the state was evident in matters trivial–the change of the title of the conference from "Taking Stock" to "Taking Strides"–to the attempt to bar critics of government policy from attending the conference. In discussions of Canadian policy, the conference organizers gave an exclusive platform to the External Affairs official in charge of the task force on southern Africa, but none at all to independent opinion. Key organizers explained privately that they felt the confrontational style of previous anti-apartheid conferences was 'old-fashioned' and that a 'conciliatory' approach to the Canadian government was in order.

"To some extent," concludes Freeman, "the process of depoliticization and co-optation scattered the energy and focus of the movement as a whole, making it less effective as a centre for pressure on the government."[73]

ICFID and "Murder by Ignorance"

Neoliberalism became the reigning development paradigm at CIDA in the 1980s, a change which had profound effects for Canadian NGOs. From 1986 on, CIDA made more and more of its aid conditional on a country's acceptance of IMF/World Bank reforms, and reoriented the aid program towards facilitating the reform process. CIDA President Margaret Catley-Carlson explained that supplementary CIDA aid would be available to countries that "put their house in order," meaning those that "put together

a program of economic stabilization and better [sic] policy measures."
Boasting of the transformations that aid programming to the Third World
had undergone in recent years at CIDA, Catley-Carlson stated, "Our
programs are very much keyed to ... discussions with the IMF and the
World Bank."[74]

Though some NGOs criticized the World Bank and the IMF, they
rarely challenged the Canadian government on its support for structural
adjustment. And NGO criticisms of structural adjustment rarely pointed
out the manifest injustice of squeezing the poor in order to bail out
insolvent Western banks. Even when NGOs were pushed by their Third
World partners to become more "forthright critics" of CIDA's neoliberal
stance, most held their tongues.[75]

One of the few Canadian NGOs to criticize CIDA for pushing
policies that deepened poverty and inequality was the Inter-Church Fund
for International Development (ICFID). In an October 1991 evaluation
of Canada's aid program the ICFID condemned "the closer and closer
integration of CIDA's thinking and policies with those of the IMF."[76]
They singled out CIDA president Marcel Massé for criticism as the official
most responsible for the Agency's neoliberal drift. Massé was livid and
responded by publicly branding the ICFID report "murder by ignorance."
According to Massé, NGOs that criticized CIDA's embrace of free market
ideology were undermining public support for the aid program, which led
to budget cuts. This, Massé told an audience of NGOs, took food out of
the mouths of the hungry:

> In money terms, the intervention by a group of NGOs [opposed to
> neoliberal policies] ... has cost me a billion dollars in my budget over
> the next five years. That's not a billion dollars to me. It is a billion dollars
> to starving people who need it.[77]

CIDA went on the offensive against anyone with the temerity to
question its support for structural adjustment. In 1992, under Massé's
leadership CIDA began to use NGOs' evaluations and additional controls
"to ensure greater ideological cohesion among the activities that it was
supporting."[78] In the next budget ICFID's funding was severely reduced.
Although CIDA denied the cuts were related to their criticism of Massé,
but NGOs received the message: Don't challenge the neoliberal direction
of Canada's aid policy.[79]

At the same time, the NGOs were pushed into the Agency's arms
by their growing dependence on CIDA funds. In the early 1990s, with

looming budget cuts threatening CIDA, the NGO community "had an interest in mobilizing public opinion behind the aid program" and therefore "tempered its criticisms of CIDA."[80] Development NGOs like CUSO organized public campaigns in support of CIDA's budget. Publicly, most NGO statements were restricted to pleading with CIDA, the IMF and the World Bank to take greater account of the suffering of the poor, while never questioning the neoliberal thrust of adjustment policies. In practical terms, this amounted to little more than calls for greater aid for poverty alleviation schemes—a position tinged with self-interest given that NGOs were the preferred channel for that type of aid.

The Nail in the Coffin: CIDA Kills Off "Dev Ed"

The final blow to NGO radicalism came in 1995, when CIDA abolished funding for development education. Established in 1971, the Public Participation Program (PPP, originally called the Development Education Animateur Program) provided grants for NGOs and other organizations to carry out community-based educational projects with ordinary Canadians. On the basis of these grants, the first development education centres (or learner centres) were created by CUSO. Development education centres were modeled on CUSO's Mobile Learner Centre, which featured a wide array of educational materials pertaining to development and the Third World. They encouraged self-directed learning and provided users with hard-to-find information and materials, ranging from books, magazines, and collections of newspaper articles, film clips and other resources. By 1984, there were more than 30 CIDA-funded development education centres in operation.[81]

As CIDA conceived it, "development education" would provide the public with an understanding of the social and economic problems faced by the Third World while simultaneously explaining how development aid helped to overcome these problems. CIDA "wanted 'development education' to emphasize Canada's contribution to technical assistance in developing countries and to defend the case for 'foreign aid.'"[82] According to David Morrison, CIDA expected development education activities to "generate support for CIDA's work."[83] It was not an unreasonable expectation since NGOs' public activities prior to 1970 had focused on "building support for the aid program in general and NGOs in particular."[84]

To CIDA's chagrin, development education was often critical of Canadian corporations and aid, focusing on how they "supported the very structures which perpetuate underdevelopment and poverty."[85]

Development education departments at CUSO, the CCIC and other NGOs became the strongest advocates of the "ideology of solidarity." Development education centres were also typically radical in outlook and encouraged political engagement. They stressed that development was not just happening "out there" in the Third World, "concentrating instead on a more political approach and attempting to focus on local concerns and issues which could be linked to international problems." One development education centre in Saskatchewan discussed the impact of the international grain trade on both Prairie farmers and peasant producers in the Third World. Other development education initiatives investigated the labour practices of Canadian corporations operating abroad, encouraged support for the Nicaraguan Revolution, and opposed U.S. Cruise Missile testing.[86]

Intended as a propaganda tool to "educate" the public about the wonders of Canada's aid program, CIDA-funded development education instead became a source of sustained criticism of Canada's conduct on the world stage. As a result, CIDA worked to undermine the program it had created. Funding for development education was constricted, and the Agency placed increasingly detailed controls on what NGOs and development education centres could do with PPP funds: "CIDA specified, for example, that CUSO could not use CIDA funds to criticize Canadian foreign policy or to draw parallels between struggles against oppression in developing countries and struggles by powerless groups in Canada."[87] In 1980, CIDA tried to bypass existing organizations working in development education by setting up an alternative organization called Futures Secretariat. While the organization ultimately failed to get off the ground, it was seen by the CCIC and other NGOs as "an effort to undercut their own 'dev ed' [development education] work," which was felt to be too radical.[88]

Politicians and CIDA officials were unhappy with the politics of development education efforts. A 1988 Parliamentary report on the aid program was extremely hostile to development education's emphasis on international solidarity, claiming it was "based more on ideology than practical experience," and urging CIDA to lay down funding rules to "differentiate clearly between education and legitimate debate on the one hand and propaganda on the other." The Parliamentary report derided development education centres as "politically marginal" or "fringe" and claimed they were only "preaching to the converted."[89] Nevertheless, a 1989 government-commissioned report concluded that development education centres did a good job in their outreach to the public, despite being "underfunded and understaffed." The real problem, the report noted, was lack of funding: "In fact, a great many development education groups are victims of their own success. They have sensitized their target groups so successfully that demand for their services has grown beyond the resources available."[90]

By the 1990s, development education centres were among the last bastions of support for the "ideology of solidarity" within an increasingly depoliticized NGO community. Unable to flush out the solidarity-minded activists from development education centres, CIDA pulled the plug on the Public Participation Program altogether in March 1995. In another round of government cuts, CIDA slashed the PPP's entire $11 million budget, eliminating funding to over 100 development education organizations. The PPP absorbed 24.7% of the reductions in CIDA's voluntary sector funding, although development education comprised only 4.5% of the budget for NGOs. "Upwards of ninety community-based organizations–always funded 'on the cheap' compared to other CIDA activities–lost their major, and in many cases sole, source of financial support." Dozens of development education centres folded shortly after the funding cut, with many more "facing the prospect of extinction." Learner centres outside of major urban centres were particularly hard hit.[91] Among development NGOs, the cuts to the PPP severely compromised their development education activities as well. A 2006 CCIC report based on interviews with Canadian NGO personnel reported that the infrastructure for engaging the public had been "fatally weakened" by PPP's termination.[92]

Supporters of the Centres protested vigorously, sending over 2,000 critical letters to Foreign Affairs, "more than the minister, his staffers or CIDA officers had anticipated." The government, however, stood by its decision. The PPP cut was driven by the "growing impatience and irritation felt within CIDA towards politicized NGOs." Development education centres were among the few NGO voices that criticized CIDA's free market policies in the 1990s, and Canada's political elite was aggressively choking off funding to any "activist groups (women's, aboriginal, environmental, etc.)" and other "oppositional elements" that "mobilize and articulate popular opinion." In explaining why the PPP had been closed, Janet Zukowsky, vice-president of CIDA's Canadian Partnerships Branch, derided development education's emphasis on solidarity and struggle as hopelessly *passé* in a globalizing world. "[The] entire development education community ... was essentially stuck in a rut on a dead-end street trying to get across a mix of messages that were fresh and relevant in the 1960s but are increasingly out of sync with realities of the 1990s."[93]

Reluctant Converts to Capitalism

In many ways, the fate of CUSO and the NGO radicals was a death foretold. As early as 1968, Normand Tellier, a CUSO volunteer to Rwanda, perceived the corrupting influence of bureaucratization at work. If CUSO was not driven by committed people actively putting their ideals into action, Tellier warned, in time the organization would become a "perfectly running but purposeless machine." "If we are not attentive, this bureaucracy will make civil servants of our leaders, mere files of our volunteers, and of CUSO a skeleton."[94] It was precisely the imperatives of organizational self-preservation and self-interest that drove the political surrender over the coming years.

Hemmed in by CIDA's political policing of NGO funding and suffocated by bureaucratization, the radical currents in the development NGOs were eventually defeated. "From the 1980s onwards the language changed: globalisation in place of imperialism, governance in place of politics, social capital and trust in place of struggle, community in place of class, and civil society in place of 'revolutionary imaginings', and NGOs in place of popular mobilization."[95] The NGO radicals either succumbed to the pressures and adopted more "reasonable" stances or left the NGOs altogether to join smaller, independent organizations like the Latin America Working Group or the Toronto Committee for the Liberation of Southern Africa (and Canada).

Voices within the NGO community called for abandoning the "ideology of solidarity" in favour of a more moderate stance. In the influential 1991 book *Democratizing Development*, Oxfam UK's John Clark issued a clarion call for moderation, suggesting that the worsening situation required not a radicalization and politicization of NGOs' approaches to poverty and inequality, but rather "a new pragmatism." Instead of mobilizing the public in the North in solidarity with Third World struggles, NGOs should concentrate on lobbying government officials and political elites, Clark argued. The change in strategy would require a change in ideology as well. "A world view that is restricted to flagging ideas of neo-imperialism and conspiracy theory is no longer adequate if it is to catalyze change in the thinking of governments." In their reasonable advocacy for "human values" and "environmental sustainability," Clark urged his NGO colleagues to become, like him, "reluctant converts to capitalism." NGOs, Clark warned, "will make little headway unless their ideas are well grounded in economic reality and unless they search for positive as well as negative lessons within the programs of the World Bank and other practitioners of development orthodoxy."[96]

Although Clark disavowed any belief in "free markets with a human face" and denied "that the Thatcherite free market offers any sort of solution to the problems I care about," his "more pluralist approach" was scarcely any different from the neoliberal orthodoxy. Clark advocated "harnessing the creativity of private enterprise" while balancing out the free market with a more "caring and guiding role" for the state. Indeed, Clark expressed enthusiasm for UNICEF's "adjustment with a human face." For Clark, representing Oxfam's leadership in the once-radical wing of the NGO world, there was no choice but to capitulate to the neoliberal status quo. "The world has changed," Clark concluded. "Our ideas must keep up with the times."[97]

In many ways, Clark's even-handed voice was that of the NGO bureaucracy and their opportunism. Official aid agencies everywhere "were looking to NGOs to deliver people-oriented programming."[98] Development NGOs comfortably reconciled themselves with the rising neoliberal orthodoxy, and were rewarded with a bigger slice of the aid pie and a cozy relationship with donors. By the late 1980s, NGOs had acquired "too many institutional interests that reduce their ability and willingness to 'speak truth to power'."[99] In 1992, Clark moved from Oxfam headquarters in the UK to Washington, D.C. to lead the World Bank's NGO Unit.

Canadian NGOs followed a similar ideological trajectory. Relations between CIDA and Canadian NGOs in the era of structural adjustment were "warmer ... than at any time since the late 1960s," when CIDA first began funding NGOs, according to historian David Morrison. CIDA's leadership held frequent consultations, and "praised the work of NGOs at every opportunity." By the end of the 1980s, CIDA funding had come to account for 40% of NGO revenues.[100] There was no denying that development NGOs had profited institutionally from CIDA's turn to neoliberalism. Not surprisingly, NGOs were reluctant to disturb their close relationship with CIDA. In 1988, Brodhead and Hebert-Copley observed the effect of growing assimilation into the state apparatus on the discourse of development NGOs:

> Increasingly, the vocabularies of government and NGOs have become indistinguishable. As the gap narrows it has become difficult to determine from the pronouncements of Canadian voluntary development agencies how 'different' they now view themselves to be from government.[101]

Political disillusionment and the deceleration of Third World popular struggles was another factor in the turn away from the "ideology of solidarity." Disheartened by the collapse of "actually existing socialism" in the USSR and awed by the apparent global triumph of capitalism, a sense of hopelessness and general malaise afflicted much of the Left during the 1990s. Hopes for pursuing more egalitarian and environmentally sound development paths were at a low point and there seemed to be no alternative to the existing system. "Another, more human factor contributing to the switch," writes Marcia Burdette, was that by the mid-1980s many NGO development professionals "had lost faith in the previous models and approaches ... [and] were in despair about turning around conditions for the poorest countries."[102]

Though many aging NGO radicals continued to work within the aid system, they gradually accepted and internalized its constraints. In such a political climate, perhaps it is not surprising that many NGO radicals chose to reject the "childish" radicalism of the "ideology of solidarity," and reluctantly embrace neoliberalism. They took on a consensual stance, opting for dialogue and consultation with the powerful over conflict and confrontation, despite the manifestly small returns such methods produced. Unable to pose a credible threat to elite interests within the constraints they accepted, they rationalized surrender by arguing that the best that could be hoped for was to alleviate the worst of the suffering caused by neoliberal capitalism. The reaction was similar to previous generations of "failed rebels from below" in times of political retreat, as described by political scientist Corey Robin:

> With much of the world renouncing everything they once fought for, ex-leftists, repentant leftists, and liberals subject themselves and former comrades to an anxious scrutiny ... these critics imagine a Left less histrionic, more moderate and inclusive, able to do what had never been done before: change the world without provoking a howling backlash.[103]

The rise and fall of the NGO radicals revealed the political elite's ostensible commitment to pluralism for what it was: a smug tolerance of the powerful, a tolerance that reached its limits when radicalized NGOs began challenging Canada's foreign policy. Unable to imagine carrying on outside of NGO structures, these "failed rebels from below" gave up on real struggles for social change and the "howling backlash" that inevitably follows.

8

"Does the Doormat Influence the Boot?"

Civil society and the anti-globalization movement

> *[F]ear and bewilderment have seized governments of industrialised countries as they struggle to draft rules for the treatment of foreign investment. To their consternation, their efforts have been ambushed by a horde of vigilantes whose motives and methods are only dimly understood in most national capitals.*
>
> *This week the horde claimed its first success and some think it could fundamentally alter the way international economic agreements are negotiated.*
>
> *The target of their attacks was the Multilateral Agreement on Investment (MAI) being negotiated at the Organisation for Economic Co-operation and Development, the attackers a loose coalition of non-government organisations (NGOs) from across the political spectrum.*
>
> –Financial Times, *April 30, 1998*

Negotiated in secret between the 29 members of the Organisation for Economic Co-operation and Development (OECD), the Multilateral Agreement on Investment (MAI) was an attempt to enshrine investors' rights in a binding international treaty. The "ambush" against the agreement began in January 1998, when a secret draft copy of the proposed economic agreement was leaked. An internet campaign publicizing the draft agreement's contents succeeded in arousing strong public hostility to the deal. Opponents bitterly denounced the MAI as an attack on democracy, sovereignty, and countries' ability to enforce environmental and human rights standards. It began to dawn on "veteran trade diplomats" that the days when they could "do deals behind closed doors and submit them for rubber-stamping by parliaments," were long gone, the *Financial Times* explained. "Instead, they face pressure to gain wider popular legitimacy for their actions by explaining and defending them in public," which might be difficult since the impact of trade agreements "on ordinary people's lives ... risks stirring up popular resentment."[1] In May 1998, protesters in Montreal demanded that Canada withdraw from the secretive negotiations and conducted a blockade of the hotel where MAI negotiators were scheduled to meet. The protest disrupted the negotiations for over 5 hours, ending only when police made over 100 arrests. By the end of 1998, public hostility in Canada combined with strong opposition in France forced the proponents of the MAI to shelve their plans.

The defeat of the MAI marked the first victory for the nascent "anti-globalization" movement.[2] Participants in this wave of activism–also dubbed the global justice movement–accused governments of placing the rights of investors above those of working people and the environment. Greater freedom for capital, they argued in teach-ins, publications, street theatre performances, chants and graffiti, would translate into a race to the bottom for wages, working conditions and environmental controls. They blamed the "globalization" agenda for the growing poverty and widening inequality of the previous decades. Denouncing agreements like the MAI and institutions like the World Bank as undemocratic and illegitimate, anti-globalization protesters increasingly turned to civil disobedience and other forms of "direct action" protest to shut down or disrupt the meetings of the globalizers. The movement's targets were the international institutions and trade agreements responsible for spreading the neoliberal agenda: the International Monetary Fund (IMF), the World Bank, the World Trade Organization (WTO), the Group of 8 (G8), Asia-Pacific Economic Cooperation (APEC), the MAI, and the Free Trade Agreement of the Americas (FTAA). Rallying behind slogans like "People Not Profit" and "The World Is Not For Sale," hundreds of thousands of people on multiple continents, overwhelmingly youth, were drawn into the movement in a few short years.

Who were these mysterious "network guerrillas" terrorizing the global elite, and where had they come from? According to the *Financial Times*, the MAI's defeat was the result of opposition mounted by "NGOs." Academic Theodore Cohn likewise describes the revolt against the MAI as having been "launched by a wide-ranging coalition of civil society NGOs." A report by the French government described opposition to the MAI as heralding "the emergence of a 'global civil society' represented by NGOs which are often based in several states and communicate beyond their frontiers."[3]

These views reflect a consensus of countless observers–both sympathetic and hostile–that the movement was a consequence of the growth of NGOs. *The Economist* complained that institutions like the WTO had been paralyzed by a "swarm of NGOs" and attributed the rise of the anti-globalization movement to the government-financed NGO boom. Journalist Sebastian Mallaby referred to the anti-globalization movement as an "NGO movement" and explained the watershed November 1999 Seattle protests against the WTO as a result of the fourfold growth of international NGOs over the preceding decade. Researcher Alison Van Rooy linked the "dramatic prominence" of NGOs on the UN conference circuit with the growth of anti-globalization activism, tracing its origins to the 1992 Rio Summit. "The snowball," Van Rooy explains, "was gathering lots of NGOs, and *new* NGOs, in its roll down the mountain." Even journalist and movement chronicler Naomi Klein described it as "a by-product of the explosion of NGOs, which, since the Rio Summit in 1992, have been gaining power and prominence."[4]

Although the unique alliance of trade unions, think tanks, environmental advocates, churches, anarchist collectives, social justice groups, and Indigenous nations which formed at the close of the 1990s in opposition to global trade agreements and international financial institutions could be termed a coalition of "non-governmental" organizations, development NGO were in fact marginal to the rise of the movement. According to former CUSO director and development consultant Ian Smillie, development NGOs played virtually no role in building the anti-MAI movement. A joint declaration against the MAI was endorsed by 560 organizations from 67 countries, including many labour organizations and environmental groups in Canada. Development NGOs made up only "one-third of one per cent" of the signatories overall and only one Canadian development NGO–Development & Peace–signed on.[5]

Development NGOs arrived on the scene much later, presenting themselves as the "respectable face of dissent" while working as reliable government collaborators within a threatening movement.[6] In a critique of NGOs' role in the movement entitled "This is What Bureaucracy Looks Like," Jim Davis writes: "To the media it seems that NGOs and protestors are virtually interchangeable and synonymous. In reality elite decision-makers evaluate the NGO world with a quick and pragmatic eye and see potential allies in the delicate work of diffusing this new opposition." Having acquiesced to the neoliberal status quo and the political constraints imposed by funding relationships with the government, development NGOs in the 1990s were precisely such allies. Once swelling protests became large and militant enough to scare Western elites pushing trade agreements, development NGOs donned the mantle of "global civil society." They tried to steer the movement in the direction of polite lobbying and reforms, away from the militant direct actions and radical visions that had shaken the status quo in the first place. NGOs lent their credibility to elites as part of an effort to "rebrand" neoliberalism while denouncing direct action protesters in the same terms they used to describe police violence. Their involvement in the movement became "a device for the containment of political dissent."[7]

The "Globalization" Agenda

The scuttling of the MAI was the first in a series of setbacks that would take the neoliberal "globalization" agenda by surprise in the late 1990s and early 2000s. The corporate and political elites backing the MAI assumed that opposition to these kinds of policies had died, and with good reason. The Soviet Bloc had collapsed in 1990, the social democratic parties of the West reconciled themselves to the market, and nationalist and socialist approaches to development in the South had been all but stamped out by the force of structural adjustment. Controls on the flow of capital had been loosened and sectors of the globe hitherto off-limits were now open for business. Basking in the glow of the market-friendly post-Cold War era, the political and economic elites triumphantly proclaimed that "There is No Alternative" to neoliberal capitalism.

In spite of their confident declarations, the globalizers were taking no chances when it came to consolidating their gains. Multinational corporations had massively expanded their foreign investments in the 1980s and 1990s, and were now seeking safeguards for their interests abroad. Their plan was to enshrine the freedoms and privileges gained by investors in binding economic treaties like the MAI. To keep Southern nations on the neoliberal path, the globalizers sought to perpetuate the treadmill of debt, and thus maintain the supervision and authority of the IMF and the World Bank over poor countries.

The MAI was the first of many agreements attempting to safeguard the newfound freedom of action of multinational business, in what some have called the "constitutionalization of neoliberalism." Written in opaque, legalistic language, the agreements sought to not only reduce tariffs, quotas and other barriers to trade, but also to take away governments' powers to regulate business more generally. Misleadingly billed as "trade agreements," treaties such as the WTO and NAFTA extended to matters like investment, services and intellectual property rights.[8] The agreements were designed to roll back regulations on any supposedly "trade-related" areas of the economy. Many contained provisions for supra-national tribunals that would enable corporations to directly sue governments for any laws or regulations that harmed the future profitability of their operations. In these "Free Trade Agreements," the rights of investors consistently took precedence over the decisions of democratic governments. The crafting of the agreements was itself undemocratic: negotiations occurred behind closed doors and draft texts of the deals were carefully guarded secrets. Political scientist David McNally writes, "the globalizers are trying to design an 'economic' model that is immune to democratic politics. ... At the heart of these 'trade' agreements, in other words, are laws designed to prevent the people of any nation from democratically making inroads against the immense and unaccountable powers of capital."[9]

Rhetoric about "free trade" and "globalization" mainly served to conceal a double standard. Rich countries had no intention of doing away with the subsidies they provided to their leading industries, such as agriculture, defence, aerospace, pharmaceuticals and automobiles, and made explicit exemptions for their subsidies. Most trade was not free but administered— by globe-spanning multinational corporations controlling markets through endless mergers and acquisitions. Some agreements increased restrictions on the free flow of ideas and innovations by requiring signatory nations to apply stringent intellectual property rights protections for the benefit of pharmaceutical firms, media conglomerates and other high-tech corporations. "These deals aren't about trade," explained Eugene Whelan, Canada's former Agriculture Minister. "They're about the right of these guys to do business the way they want, wherever they want."[10]

In the Global South, these investors' rights agreements threatened to severely limit options for development policy. By creating legal obstacles to future governments that might attempt to reverse the forced market liberalization of the South, the agreements also served to lock in these changes and effectively block a return to nationalist and socialist development policies, or any other development approach that would constrain the freedom of foreign investors. "Free trade" deals promised to further entrench and deepen the neoliberal agenda of liberalization, deregulation and privatization.

"Globalization" was presented as an inexorable, technology-driven phenomenon. Behind the buzzwords, however, corporate and political elites were pursuing a carefully-crafted agenda.

Canada's Anti-Globalization Hordes

In Canada, a kaleidoscopic mix of groups and issues coalesced under the anti-globalization umbrella. Opponents of earlier free trade deals were an important source of popular opposition to neoliberal globalization. Labour unions and membership-based organizations like the Council of Canadians built upon their previous experience mobilizing against the Canada-U.S. Free Trade Agreement (1988) and NAFTA (1994). A key change was the transition from nationalist rhetoric towards the politics of international solidarity. The Council of Canadians in particular played a key role in the fight against the MAI by mobilizing opposition within Canada and creating international alliances.

Groups opposed to the economic policies imposed on the Third World by the IMF and the World Bank presented another key element. These included progressive church groups which in 1998 launched the Jubilee 2000 campaign, calling for cancellation of Third World debt by the year 2000. Solidarity groups formed to support leftist movements against Western-backed authoritarian regimes in Latin America, the Philippines and Southern Africa in the 1980s were another important component, as they shifted their focus to opposing structural adjustment and free trade in the 1990s.

Another strand of the movement grew out campaigns against specific corporate abuses or harmful "development" projects in the Global South. Anti-sweatshop campaigns targeting Nike and other major brands for their exploitation of Third World workers were emblematic of these single-issue struggles. The focus of many anti-corporate campaigners gradually shifted from the misdeeds of the multinationals to the globalization agenda that enabled them to commit these harmful acts. Anarchist groups were influential among youth, especially in Quebec, and were active in student struggles and anti-poverty activism. Anarchist ideas and practices were a major influence on the decentralized organizational structure of many anti-globalization demonstrations.

Though often derided as "protectionist," anti-globalization activists were overwhelmingly internationalist in outlook, and drew inspiration from struggles in the South against the "free trade" agenda, such as the Zapatista rebellion in Chiapas, Mexico. All of these groups were wrestling with various facets of the rapidly globalizing capitalism unleashed through neoliberal policies.

The movement increasingly adopted "direct action" protest tactics, partly out of a sense of urgency and partly out of frustration. Many protestors felt that if these agreements weren't stopped there would be no going back. Organizers attempted to disrupt meetings through tactics like blockades, sit-down protests and confrontations with police because many believed that nothing less would compel politicians to listen. Groups had tried lobbying and routine protests that allowed business to go on as usual, and these tactics had failed to exert any real influence. The secret nature of the proceedings indicated contempt for the public on the part of elites.

Over time, the movement's analysis and demands became more radical. Many activists began to ask hard questions not only about globalization but capitalism itself and a significant anti-capitalist current grew within the movement. Ironically, the radicalism of the movement was provoked by the increasingly limited options offered by the system. Labour economist Sam Gindin explains:

> If small changes were—as business, politicians, and editorial writers kept reminding us—impossible, then maybe it was time again to start thinking big. … Where "globalization" had become a weapon brandished by business, politicians, and the media to explain what we *couldn't* do, placing capitalism itself up for discussion and criticism was part of insisting that the limits we faced were socially constructed, and could therefore be challenged, stretched, and one day overcome. The protesters raised the stakes because enough of them didn't want *in*, but demanded something *different*. The term "anti-capitalism" arrived on the public agenda.[11]

David McNally suggests that there was an inherently radical dynamic to the movement's demands: "When protesters refuse to accept that issues like health care, jobs, provision of water, access to education and housing should be left to private actors in the market (and their global representatives, like the IMF and the World Bank), they are implicitly challenging the privatization of economic power that lies at the heart of capitalism."[12] At the same time, development NGOs were following the opposite political trajectory.

Development NGOs: Inclusion Without Influence

By the 1990s, the activist spirit and "ideology of solidarity" that had animated Canada's once-radical development NGOs had all but disappeared. Under the successive blows of funding cuts and government restrictions, the militancy of the NGO radicals had withered, and NGOs were now settled into a less confrontational stance towards the government and the world system. In contrast to the disruptive protest tactics favoured by the anti-globalization movement, NGOs sought to change the world by presenting policy briefs and hobnobbing with diplomats at UN conferences, World Bank consultations and other international gatherings of the global policy elite. By the mid-1990s, NGOs were enjoying "a significant increase in access to decision making in development and foreign policy departments … NGO and government staff are now spending significant amounts of personal time together."[13]

Increased access for NGOs, however, came with a price: it implied that "controversial and embarrassing tactics have been dropped in favour of a more 'reasoned' approach to an issue." As Alison Van Rooy explains, access to meetings was only provided to "reasonable" organizations, which the Canadian government defined as those sharing its neoliberal assumptions and worldview. Radical alterations to the governance of the IMF and the World Bank, fundamental critiques of structural adjustment or the reform of international trading practices–the issues that animated the anti-globalization movement–were not the kind of demands raised by NGOs seeking the ear of policymakers.[14] Criticisms voiced by NGOs, even those with a more activist bent, Tina Wallace notes, "are limited to attacking specific aspects of the neoliberal agenda; there is almost no deep questioning of the roots of that paradigm."[15] Brian K. Murphy argues that the development NGO community had become "an intrinsic part of the system that it was once committed to transform." NGOs had become "indoctrinated in the assumptions" of the globalizers and had "internalised the language and myths" of neoliberalism:

> Many NGOs, … convinced that 'globalisation' is inevitable and irreversible–that indeed, we are at the end of history–have joined with its acolytes, ironically without much critical analysis of what 'it' really is or means. What the corporate PR manager understands implicitly as economic propaganda, NGO people often repeat as articles of faith.[16]

The gains made by NGOs through "reasonable" advocacy were quite small. Van Rooy describes NGOs' influence through advocacy as limited to "low policy" issues, i.e. those which are "fairly cheap," "unknown" or "broadly noncontroversial."[17] Other scholars refer to the participation of NGOs in trade policy making as "inclusion without influence." The inclusion of NGOs was nonetheless politically useful for governments and institutions, which could always claim that civil society groups had been consulted, and their input taken into consideration. Even if the outcome was boilerplate neoliberal policy, it could be presented as a compromise between multiple stakeholders. NGO scholar Michael Edwards caustically summed up the impact of NGO "advocacy" strategies by asking: "Does the doormat influence the boot?"[18]

Many within Canada's anti-globalization movement were aware of the shortcomings of NGO advocacy. Development NGOs and other civil society groups had participated in a number of government-sponsored consultations on development and foreign policy in Canada with disappointing results. According to Council of Canadians' leader Maude Barlow: "Over and over again ... groups would offer the benefit of their expertise in these consultations, only to find that their advice had been entirely omitted when their governments issued final policy positions."[19] Elizabeth Riddell-Dixon's study of Canadian NGO involvement in UN negotiations concludes with the observation that "government-sponsored mechanisms to facilitate NGO participation do little to influence policy outcomes but are significant in serving the interests of the governing elite."[20] "Unquestionably, stakeholder politics is an excellent tool of political management for state officials," argues professor Richard Kim Nossal. By sitting down at the table with government officials, NGOs and other "civil society" groups that participate in consultations are lending their legitimacy to the policy-making process. Stakeholder politics serves to protect state officials "against future claims by stakeholders" and "binds the stakeholders more tightly to the policies eventually adopted."[21] Canadian foreign policy scholar Cranford Pratt is even more blunt, describing government strategies for consulting with NGOs as "exercises in public relations, in the erosion of dissent, and in the co-option of dissenters" rather than as opportunities for NGOs to exert real influence.[22]

Development NGOs had no reason to expect that such an approach could win any serious concessions. What the approach did win them was funding and continued access to high-level meetings. Once development NGOs jumped on the anti-globalization bandwagon in the late 1990s, they consistently sought to divert the movement away from radical demands and confrontational protests, and towards their preferred strategy of polite lobbying for minor reforms. This strategic debate became the dividing line in the movement, according to Maude Barlow:

> The greatest divergence exists between those who believe non-governmental organizations (NGOs) should be in dialogue with governments and institutions like the WTO and those who contend that such interactions will co-opt the movement, taking the wind out of its sails and transforming it into a mere "reformist" agenda.[23]

Despite having played virtually no role in building popular protest against neoliberal globalization, development NGOs positioned themselves as the movement's respectable interlocutors with governments, corporations and international organizations. They criticized protesters who engaged in direct action as endangering "civil society's" chance for a seat at the table. They were joined by some social democratically-oriented groups such as union leaders and mainstream environmental and feminist groups, who mobilized their supporters not to defeat the neoliberal agenda outright, but to win limited reforms and a seat for themselves at the globalizers' table. Development NGOs did not create this radical vs. reformist divide, but they pushed the movement towards the latter position.

"SprayPEC" in Vancouver: Axworthy Opens the Steam Valve

The first significant anti-globalization protest in Canada was at the November 1997 Asia-Pacific Economic Cooperation (APEC) meeting in Vancouver. Protesters targeted APEC as a venue through which government leaders sought to advance the neoliberal agenda. Christopher Butler, Chair of the APEC Committee on Trade and Investment, described negotiations as concerned with "not only well-established border questions ... [but also] a number of new issues arising from the globalisation of economic activity such as services, intellectual property, investment, competition policy and deregulation."[24] The summit featured leaders from 18 countries, including Indonesian dictator Suharto. Protesters also attempted to draw attention to the tens of thousands of deaths resulting from the Indonesian occupation of East Timor under Suharto's rule. The plethora of issues that were represented would become a signature of anti-globalization demonstrations in the years to come.

In anticipation of the protests, the Canadian government financed a "People's Summit" alongside the leaders' APEC summit. Ottawa provided

$100,000 to the parallel conference, organized by a coalition of trade union federations, mainstream environmental groups and development NGOs.[25] Though relatively few development NGOs had even nominally joined the anti-globalization movement at this point, Rights & Democracy, the Canadian Council for International Cooperation (CCIC), and Development & Peace were among the organizers. Why would the government fund a gathering of organizations aiming to "challenge APEC's business-driven agenda"?[26]

The "challenge" issued to APEC by the NGOs and their allies was in fact quite limited, playing directly into the stakeholder strategy that had already been established by the Canadian government. The People's Summit organizers did not oppose the neoliberal APEC agenda as such but rather criticized APEC's "one dimensional" focus on economic issues, to the exclusion of human rights and development. Instead of mobilizing opposition to the negotiations, the purpose of the People's Summit for the NGO organizers was "to ensure that diverse views on APEC are heard in accordance with the Canadian pluralist tradition."[27] The NGOs' preferred way to influence policy-makers was to present working papers couched in the same technical language and economic assumptions as the APEC leaders, appealing to their common concern for "sustainable development" and "human rights." As a result, the NGOs' and their allies' central demand was for a seat at the table for "civil society," i.e. for themselves. "Many of the organizations most invested in the People's Summits had no links with, or intentions to build or support mass-based counter-power to neoliberal policies," explains Aziz Choudry, a scholar and activist involved in anti-APEC organizing in both New Zealand and Canada.[28]

By financing an NGO-controlled conference, the government hoped to marginalize more radical groups opposed to APEC and redirect the energies of the movement towards lobbying strategies. As internal documents revealed, the government maintained "ongoing discussions" with "constructive elements" among protesters, which "we hoped would be helpful to vent steam," according to then-Deputy Trade Minister Len Edwards.[29] Rights & Democracy in particular was in regular contact with government officials and played in a major role in the organization of the People's Summit. Foreign Affairs Minister Lloyd Axworthy described "dialogue" as "one way of offsetting radical NGOs."[30] Working with NGOs and other moderate groups allowed the government to present a façade of openness.

Other protesters, according to the Department of Foreign Affairs and International Trade (DFAIT), were "involved in a less constructive process that could undermined [sic] both the efforts of Canada to engage civil society and efforts of the latter to have its voice heard by APEC."[31] Their ranks included Indigenous groups demanding respect of their land rights, a coalition rooted in the Philippine-Canadian activist community and a coalition of students and Vancouver activists working on local social justice struggles. These protesters rejected closed-door trade negotiations with murderous dictators as fundamentally illegitimate, and some planned to engage in civil disobedience. Unlike the NGOs, they regarded the Canadian government's claim that such negotiations would help spread "Canadian values" in Indonesia and other East Asian countries with scepticism. The Canadian Security Intelligence Service identified them as "a potential security risk." Police spied on these groups and pre-emptively arrested several leading activists in the days before the Leaders' Summit.[32]

Though the organizing committee for the People's Summit claimed to "not to take a stand" on political and strategic debates within the movement, "but to offer a venue to which all sides would feel welcome," radical critics found that the organizers' actions fell short of their rhetoric.[33] Aziz Choudry attended the counter-summit in Vancouver and witnessed first-hand how NGOs and their allies used their substantial resources to influence the Summit's political direction. By shaping of the agenda and framing, and chairing plenary sessions and other events, Rights & Democracy and other NGOs "attempted to orient People's Summit discussions towards reforming APEC."[34]

One of the criticisms raised by the NGO-led organizing committee was that "the decisions made at the APEC table ... would be made without the voices of those most affected being heard."[35] According to Choudry, however, those directly affected by neoliberalism–such as landless peasant farmers or Indigenous women or rank-and-file labour unionists from Asia– were seldom selected to address the People's Summit. In the rare instances where they were allowed to speak, they were "pigeonholed into talking about their 'sector' or their 'plight.'" Trade unionists and other Southern activists who held "more militant rejectionist positions" were shut out despite their years-long involvement in contesting APEC. By contrast, the conference organizers gave ample space to NGO professionals, Northern academics and Southern speakers who shared their reformist outlook. These speakers were "given free rein to address what ever issue that they like and treated as an authority on the subject."[36]

At the People's Summit, NGOs took on the role of movement gatekeepers. Many activists described to Choudry how the NGOs, along with the mainstream leadership of the trade unions, had shaped the agenda to squeeze out or marginalize more radical critiques of APEC and the Canadian government. NGOs watered down political demands, seeking repeatedly "to direct the People's Summit forums away from blanket condemnation of APEC." The organization of the event itself left little space for more radical critiques to be voiced. The People's Summit was divided into a number of different workshops and themes, which corresponded to "NGO compartmentalization of issues," rather than "broader social movement visions, preventing much important and deeper discussion." Summit moderators "rigorously policed" the narrow, sectoral focus of workshops or invoked time constraints as reasons for avoiding broader political questions. "For all of the claims that NGO conferences on APEC were democratically organized 'people's' spaces," argues Choudry, "they were tightly controlled, and quite hierarchical."[37]

NGOs were able to contain the radicals at the People's Summit, but they could not corral the protests that followed. Many of the 1,500 to 4,500 protesters participating in the "Walk for Global Justice" decided to block roads on the University of British Columbia campus leading to where APEC leaders were meeting. These acts of civil disobedience were met with what was at the time an unprecedented level of violence. Dozens of protesters—and some members of the media—were indiscriminately pepper-sprayed and 49 individuals were arrested by police in an attempt to clear the way for Suharto's motorcade. The protests were dubbed "SprayPEC" in the media and a government inquiry was established to deal with the 52 formal complaints filed against the police, citing humiliating strip searches and other rights violations. A 453-page report released four years later described the police response as excessive and unconstitutional and pointed to political pressure from the Prime Minister's office to crack down on the protesters.[38]

For most protesters, the police actions indicated that the government intended to pursue trade deals with dictators like Suharto regardless of public opinion. For the NGOs behind the counter-summit, Canadian politicians had proven that they were willing to listen to the voice of civil society. "For the Canadian government," a post-protest People's Summit statement read, "it became clear that their constituency want human rights on the table." Despite the repression, NGO organizers declared a partial victory: "In the end, even Lloyd Axworthy, Canadian Minister of Foreign Affairs and International Trade, spoke of the dangers of two-dimensional (business and government) trade discussions." With one verbal acknowledgement of the importance of human rights, the steam had been vented.[39] Choudry suspects that People's Summit declarations were less expressions of serious opposition to neoliberal capitalism than "an exercise in lobby-oriented NGOs establishing credibility with governments and the private sector."[40]

The 1997 APEC summit marked the unveiling of what Choudry calls the government's "co-opt and clampdown" strategy for dividing the anti-globalization movement into "good protesters" and "bad protesters," funding and consulting with the former while demonizing the latter as "violent" and subjecting them to heightened police repression. Ottawa, Choudry concludes, "had no genuine commitment to truly open democratic debate on APEC, and ... its support for the People's summit was a cynical exercise in staging a non-threatening NGO Summit while preparing draconian security measures for those who dared to speak or mobilize outside very limited parameters."[41] NGO participation was essential for defining and maintaining this division, which remained the centrepiece of government strategies to counter the anti-globalization movement in the years to come.

In 1997, the pattern had been set for the role the NGOs would play in the anti-globalization movement as it rose to global prominence for a few brief years.

The WTO in Seattle: "A Festive of Resistance"

If the defeat of the MAI was the first real victory of the anti-globalization struggle, the "Battle of Seattle" was the moment it achieved global prominence. Images of this moment circulated around the globe: young people with their arms locked together, chanting and blocking access to the World Trade Organization Ministerial that was to take place; riot cops dousing sit-down protesters with pepper spray at close range; burly trade unionists marching beside skinny vegan anarchists, the street-level manifestation of the "Teamsters and turtles" alliance; crowds of young people chanting "the whole world is watching" and "this is what democracy looks like," as they dodged tear gas canisters; and WTO conference rooms featuring rows of empty chairs and a handful of confused delegates.

Over 60,000 protesters swarmed into the city, marking Seattle as the largest anti-globalization gathering in North America at the time. On November 30, as the WTO talks were about to begin, protests turned downtown Seattle into "a festival of resistance," according to activist David Solnit. "Tens of thousands of people joined the nonviolent direct action blockade that encircled the WTO conference site, keeping the

most powerful institution on earth shut down from dawn until dusk ...
Long shore workers shut down every West Coast port from Alaska to
Los Angeles."[42] The blockades prevented trade officials from entering the
convention centre. The police, under pressure from the Mayor and an irate
President Clinton, responded with a massive but panicked show of force.
They pepper-sprayed those who refused to leave blockades, filled the city
with tear gas, imposed a curfew outside of business hours, and arrested
hundreds of peaceful demonstrators. (A brief lull occurred when police
ran out of tear gas, and more canisters had to be flown in from a military
base in Montana.) The repression was not enough to save the far-reaching
liberalization agenda at the WTO, as talks collapsed due to the combined
force of militant street protests and opposition from Southern delegates.
The globalization juggernaut had been stopped in its tracks.

The corporate media went to great lengths to demonize protesters.
News outlets described police actions as a legitimate response to "anarchist"
vandals. TV networks showed hours of repetitive footage of smashed
store windows, neglecting to mention that these incidents occurred several
hours *after* the police violence against peaceful-but-inconveniently-placed
civil disobedience actions.[43] The *New York Times* falsely reported that
protesters had thrown excrement, rocks and Molotov cocktails at police
and WTO delegates.[44] Denunciations of protesters as naive, ignorant and
violent flowed freely in news reports.

Despite hostile media attention, the WTO protests forced the anti-
globalization debate into the mainstream, and it soon became clear that
the protesters were winning the battle of public opinion. Jeff Crosby, who
brought a delegation of workers from the International Union of Electrical
Workers to the Seattle protests, reported that there was growing support
for the anti-globalization movement amongst ordinary people:

> This is a period when on certain issues, massive, non-violent direct
> action is in order, as the demonstration in Seattle shows. Every member
> who went on our trip reports that support for the demonstrations, even
> with the disruptions, is overwhelming. And not just from other workers
> in the shop, but family and other friends, regardless of what they do
> for a living. 'Since we came home, we're being treated like conquering
> heroes,' marveled one of our group.[45]

Opinion polls after Seattle confirmed that public support for the movement
was widespread. An opinion poll conducted by *Business Week* a month after
the November 30 demonstrations found that 52 percent of Americans

"sympathized with the protestors at the WTO in Seattle."[46] Surveys also found that ordinary people in both Canada and the U.S. were increasingly hostile to trade agreements and the politicians that pursued them and shared the same concerns about corporate power as the movement.[47]

The "battle of Seattle" and the movement that had fought it put the champions of the status quo on the defensive. The business press expressed horror at the radicalism of the movement. *Forbes* magazine observed that with unemployment low and "capitalists ... still savoring their triumph over communism," the movement seemed to have come out of nowhere. But while "the past two decades have witnessed a surge in prosperity for corporations," the hollow boom of the neoliberal years had "also set the stage for the inevitable backlash." The "enemies of profits" had gained a hearing beyond the fringe, *Forbes'* editors worried, as "resentment against U.S. corporations ... has boiled over into the American mainstream." Capitalists were advised to take heed: with the movement gaining strength, "anti-capitalist demonstrations" could no longer be safely confined to college campuses.[48]

As news of the victory in Seattle spread, the movement took on an increasingly radical flavour. Teach-ins and books by authors like Vandana Shiva and Noam Chomsky gained popularity among young people. Suddenly, the system had a name—capitalism. Pundits on CNN and editors at the *New York Times* and the *Globe and Mail* were sufficiently worried that they began to invoke the "c-word," if only to defend it. "After more than a decade of unchecked triumphalism," Naomi Klein remarked a few months after the Seattle demonstrations, "capitalism (as opposed to euphemisms such as 'globalization,' 'corporate rule' or 'the growing gap between rich and poor') has re-emerged as a legitimate subject of public debate."[49]

The movement gained huge momentum following the collapse of trade talks at the WTO. "Post-Seattle, the world of international politics was put on notice: wherever you go, wherever you meet, the antiglobalization movement will be there."[50] Over the next two years, hundreds of thousands marched at IMF and World Bank meetings in Washington (April 2000), the Republican Convention in Philadelphia and the Democratic Convention in Los Angeles (July-August 2000), the World Economic Forum in Melbourne and the IMF/World Bank meetings in Prague (September 2000), G20 meetings in Montreal (October 2000), the Summit of the Americas in Quebec City (April 2001), a European Union summit in Gothenburg, Sweden (June 2001) and G8 meetings in Genoa, Italy (July 2001).[51]

As the redefining effect of the anti-WTO protests became clear, NGOs jostled to take credit for the incredible shift in Northern public opinion. Jim Davis notes that "the Seattle victory was revised by many NGO and union leaders as the outcome of a great collaboration between them."[52] Yet the massive protests owed little of their success to the reformist, lobby-oriented forces. As Alexander Cockburn and Jeffrey St. Clair report, "even in the run-up to WTO week in Seattle, the genteel element–foundation careerists, NGO bureaucrats, policy wonks–was raising cautionary fingers, saying that the one thing to be avoided in Seattle this week was civil disobedience." With a promise from Bill Clinton of a "seat at the table" at future WTO negotiations, the leadership of the trade unions took a similarly cautious approach. The large labour rally was held far from the downtown core, and the march route steered union members away from the blockades where direct action protesters were battling lines of riot police.[53] After the protests, some NGO representatives criticized the police as much for failing to "identify and arrest these few anti-social individuals" who had smashed the windows of Niketown as for their egregious abuses against peaceful protesters.[54]

Without the direct action approach shunned by NGO and union leaders, the protests in Seattle would have amounted to very little. As Maude Barlow argues:

> It was not the many thousands of the official march who shut down the opening ceremonies of the WTO in Seattle or captured the media attention of the whole world, but the several thousand young people, many of them high school students, who claimed the streets in the name of democracy.[55]

Cockburn echoes this assessment: "If the direct action protesters had not put their bodies on the line throughout that entire week, if the only protest had been that under official AFL-CIO banners, then there would have been a 15-second image of a parade on the national news headlines that Tuesday evening and that would have been it."[56] Jim Davis emphasizes that in Seattle it was "the 'street warriors' who did the heavy lifting."[57] Though the NGOs had acted as a drag on the movement up to this point, they were poised to benefit from the movement's growing strength.

The Globalizers Strike Back

Rattled by the surprising ferocity of the demonstrations in Seattle and the resonance of the movement with the public, elites were determined to learn from their mistakes. Larger quantities of repressive force, they decided, would be needed to contain future protests. "Security agencies at Seattle," the Canadian Security Intelligence Service (CSIS) noted in a 2000 briefing sizing up the movement, "were caught off-guard by the large number of demonstrators and scope of representation, combined with the use of sophisticated methods and technology that effectively shut down the Conference."[58] To prevent protesters from disrupting future meetings as they had in Seattle, entire sections of host cities were closed down and huge fences were erected to block protesters from getting anywhere near the summit gatherings. Summits were increasingly militarized, with massive "security cordons" patrolled by phalanxes of police dressed in body armour and gas masks. The intensifying brutality with which police responded to protests served to eliminate the space for civil disobedience of the type that had been used in Montreal against the MAI or in Seattle against the WTO. "By the time of the April [2000] protest in Washington," Cockburn and St. Clair observe, "any talk of constitutional rights to assembly and protest was a joke."[59]

Politicians and the media tried to criminalize the movement in the public mind, and police authorities began treating activists accordingly. Police systematically labelled anyone using disruptive or confrontational protest tactics to shut down the globalizers' meetings as "violent," even if these consisted only of non-violent direct action or civil disobedience. In an August 2000 report titled "Anti-Globalization–A Spreading Phenomenon," CSIS warned of the security risk posed by "violent extremists" engaged in direct action and linked civil disobedience and minor acts of vandalism with terrorism. Increasingly, anti-globalization activists "found their meetings infiltrated [by undercover cops], their public gatherings disrupted, their phones tapped, and police posted outside their homes and offices."[60] "Lots of people have been getting these calls and we think it's a scare tactic to keep us away from the protests," said Jodi Hazen, a Windsor activist who had been questioned by an RCMP officer in the days before a May 2000 protest against the FTAA.[61]

Simultaneously, corporate and political elites scrambled to deal with the legitimacy crisis afflicting the WTO, the IMF and the World Bank and other institutions dedicated to the neoliberal agenda. The editors of the *Economist* lamented "the poor public image that these technocratic, faceless bureaucracies have developed," and warned of the risk that they "will become paralysed in the face of concerted opposition."[62] Improving the image of these institutions and agreements and the multinational corporations that profited from them was thus imperative. As *Business Week*'s editors put it, "until marchers are convinced that the issues they feel so passionate about get a fair hearing, they'll go right on making life difficult for governments and companies alike."[63]

Facing a public increasingly aware of and hostile to the neoliberal agenda, the globalizers began cultivating an image of a kinder, gentler capitalism. Corporations announced their commitment to Corporate Social Responsibility with new (but non-binding) "codes of conduct" laying out labour and environmental standards for operations in the Global South. There was a huge jump in mentions of "Corporate Social Responsibility" or "CSR" in major news sources, from 28 articles over the 1988-1998 period to 561 from 1998-2003.[64] Government leaders, while meeting behind three-metre fences to negotiate economic agreements, proclaimed their deep commitment to openness, transparency, and democracy. They expressed concern for the plight of the poor excluded (as opposed to exploited) by globalization. The head of the World Bank declared his commitment to "social justice," while the director of the IMF conceded that his organization must be "willing to change." Paul Martin, Finance Minister at the time, called the protesters "sincere" and "allies of Canada."[65] Cockburn and St. Clair describe the sea change in rhetoric that had occurred among the globalizers:

> A decade, even five years ago, officials of the World Bank and International Monetary Fund were florid with righteous self satisfaction at the good works their institutions were performing round the world. By the spring of 2000 these same officials were apologizing for the sins of their past and nervously contending that they are re-engineering themselves as forces for good.[66]

Corporate and political elites would need some help in the marketing department if these sudden epiphanies from the very institutions and politicians leading the neoliberal charge were to convince a sceptical public. Post-Seattle, "dialogues" and consultations with "civil society" proliferated. Politicians and trade bureaucrats invited NGOs to sit down at the table, dangling promises of debt relief for poor countries and offers of side-agreements on labour rights and the environment. Corporate executives unveiled CSR partnerships with NGOs to demonstrate their newfound commitment to "sustainable development." Development NGOs became key allies in the campaign to put a human face on neoliberalism.

The business press openly discussed how to use NGOs to re-establish the legitimacy of the system and divide the anti-globalization movement. "Assaulted by unruly protesters, firms and governments are suddenly eager to do business with the respectable face of dissent," the *Economist* observed in a September 2000 editorial entitled "Angry and Effective." The business magazine noted that "the movement has changed things–and not just the cocktail schedule for the upcoming meetings." Protests, which had scuttled the MAI and frustrated the launch of global trade talks in Seattle "amid street scenes reminiscent of the 1960s," had also "dramatically increased the influence of mainstream NGOs, such as the World Wide Fund for Nature and Oxfam."[67]

In a similar vein, after the July 2001 protests in Genoa where Italian police killed one demonstrator and relentlessly attacked protesters, *Business Week* argued that "smart CEOs should proceed in opening a dialogue with the reformers."

> The violence that has been intensifying since the first Seattle demonstrations finally split the anti-globalization movement, with reformers of the international capitalist economy distancing themselves from the anarchists who simply want to destroy it. This could open an opportunity for corporations to sit down and negotiate compromises with groups willing to reason.

In addition to saving the capitalist economy from destruction at the hands of anarchists, using the good name of NGOs to rebrand their business operations as ethical endeavours could also be profitable. "It may be hard," the editorial noted, reflecting on recent CSR deals struck by Nike, Home Depot, Starbucks and other multinationals with various NGOs, "but by working with reasonable reformers of the global system, corporations can not only help others, they just might help themselves."[68]

Through their official aid agencies, Western governments made it clear to development NGOs that their coveted seat at the table and their funding might be taken away if the "respectable" protesters failed to rein in or were in any way connected to the "extremists" of the movement. Speaking to an audience of donor agency representatives, one of CIDA's senior policy analysts remarked that the growing intensity of global protest had provoked a "backlash" from donors, as "funding for NGOs came under scrutiny after a good couple of decades of enthusiastic spending." "It rapidly became evident–particularly in the aftermath of the 1999 Seattle demonstrations–that some voices were more welcome, more legitimate than others."

As the CIDA policy analyst explained, donors had a set of "hidden rules that are also applied to our relationships with civil society organizations," above and beyond the "official rules" used for determining "eligibility criteria for funding or for inclusion in an intergovernmental process." These hidden rules required that, in addition to being eloquent, businesslike and able work professionally on a shoestring budget, CIDA's civil society partners "must also not be involved in 'direct action' protests of any kind–anything that may be identified as 'violent,' by anyone–lest they delegitimize the effort of the whole movement." Challenging "the legitimacy of civil society organizations engaged in the anti-globalization movements," donors worked to "weed out bad apples" suspected of "questionable political affiliations" among the NGO crowd.[69]

With their funding and access dependent on their docility, development NGOs gave in to the suspension of democratic freedoms at global trade talks and kept away from anything involving confrontational tactics. NGOs also accepted the authorities' definition of "violence" and denounced any groups using protest tactics that went beyond polite lobbying. To maintain their status as reasonable reformers, NGOs had to be sure to distance themselves as much as possible from the radical elements within the movement. As Jim Davis explains:

> The conditions of negotiation between capital and the NGOs are the unilateral disarmament of the movement's tactics. This is the only thing the NGOs have to offer neoliberalism; a special sort of police power and movement sabotage. In other words, the promise (articulated, indicated or simply understood) that the politics of the street will be replaced by the politics of 'heated' negotiation.[70]

Ironically, NGOs justified their preference for the politics of negotiation over the politics of the street by pointing to the sudden eagerness of elites to sit down with NGOs and other moderate critics. NGOs argued that their patient lobbying approach was finally bearing fruit, and that disruptive protests threatened to distract attention from the NGOs' reasonable demands. As the movement progressed, divergences between radical grassroots groups and development NGOs widened into a chasm.

Friends Like These: Oxfam Versus the "Globaphobes"

No organization better epitomizes the divisive role played by development NGOs than Oxfam.[71] "The example of Oxfam is revealing of the changes in trajectory that many NGOs underwent" as the anti-globalization movement grew, notes academic Pascale Dufour. Oxfam tried to straddle both sides of the globalization fence, claiming to speak for the movement while distancing itself from its demands and tactics. "Without siding with the anti-globalization activists of the late 1990s, they clearly situated themselves next to them in the global space of protest," by advocating a slightly renovated form of neoliberalism.[72]

During the September 2000 protests against the IMF and the World Bank in Prague, Czech Republic, Oxfam's representatives were careful to distance themselves from the rejectionist demands and militant tactics of the movement. "Oxfam's point of view isn't that globalization is bad per se," an Oxfam campaigner explained to *Forbes* magazine. "We don't want to get rid of the World Bank or the IMF, because if you didn't have them the situation would be a heck of a lot worse." While Oxfam's chiefs hunkered down with Bank bureaucrats and 300 other NGO representatives to chew the fat about debt relief and poverty, Oxfam campaigners on the street deplored the "brute force" used by radical demonstrators in Prague. Oxfam was meanwhile silent on the brutish mentality of the Czech leaders who unleashed 11,000 riot police and the ensuing beatings, tear gas and abuses against arrestees. Despite the Czech government's huge mobilization of security forces, direct action protesters managed to get inside the convention centre and force an early end to the meetings.[73]

Forbes lauded Oxfam and other NGOs that preferred to "duke it out in the conference room than on the streets." Oxfam, the business magazine noted, "has had a lot of practice sitting down with 'the enemy' and finding common ground." Its conciliatory approach certainly helped in the fundraising department. Oxfam's U.S. branch, for instance, secured $24 million in 2000 from outfits like the Ford and W.K. Kellogg foundations, as well as from J.P. Morgan, the Calvert Group "and, yes, even AES Shady Point—a unit of Applied Energy Services that has drawn the ire of environmental groups."[74]

Oxfam's position spread discomfort among its staff and supporters within Canada. According to former staffer Rex Fyles, Oxfam Canada "struggled with contradictions" and the "dissonance" generated by its advocacy of "globalization lite," which clashed with the views of its traditional allies and members. Many of these supporters had been drawn to the organization during its more radical heyday of the 1970s and 1980s and were sympathetic to the anti-globalization movement. Staff members were also not happy with the position of the organization's leadership. Though Oxfam had sent staff to Quebec City in 2001 to participate in the People's Summit, the organization did not mobilize its members for the protests. In the aftermath of the Quebec City protests, some staff members frustrated by Oxfam's lack of support for the growing movement wrote a document entitled "Has Oxfam lost its edge?" which was circulated and discussed at Oxfam's Regional Assemblies across the country and at the June 2001 National Assembly in Vancouver.[75]

Oxfam gave the campaign to rebrand neoliberalism as a struggle on behalf of the poor a major credibility boost. In March 2002, Oxfam published a report on global trade entitled "Rigged Rules and Double Standards," which denounced anti-globalization protesters as "globaphobes" whose "anti-trade" views had become "counter-productive." Speaking to the press after the publication of the report, Oxfam's representatives continued to equate popular opposition to neoliberal trade agreements with hostility to trade *per se.* "The extreme element of the anti-globalization movement is wrong," said Kevin Watkins, lead author of the "Rigged" report. "Trade can deliver much more [for poor countries] than aid or debt relief."[76]

What the movement should be fighting for, Oxfam announced, was "inclusive globalization," the central element of which was market access. The movement needed to call for lower tariffs and trade barriers for Third World exporters to First World markets. Furthermore, the report argued, the WTO should be reformed "to give poor countries a stronger voice," not rejected.[77] The expansion of exports of textiles and export-oriented agriculture was central to Oxfam's strategy, bringing it in line with IMF/World Bank development priorities.

Many within the movement expressed shock and anger at Oxfam's position. Arundadha Mittal of the progressive think tank Food First charged that Oxfam's call for market access was "undermining the demands of social movements and think tanks in the South," who were promoting food production for the domestic market, not export-oriented agriculture. South African activist Patrick Bond argued that Oxfam's trade reform strategies were disconnected from the demands of those directly affected, such as trade unions and peasant organizations in the South, making them "dubious" from an international solidarity perspective. In a lengthy written rebuttal, Filipino academic and activist Walden Bello claimed Oxfam's market-access campaign "simply distracts the movement from its real priority at this point, which should be derailing the free trade drive ... [and risks] waylaying the movement into side streets where the results can even be counterproductive." Many activists, Bello wrote, saw the campaign as "an opportunistic ploy that is designed to project Oxfam as taking the rational, sensible middle road between two irrational blocs." The "globaphobe" epithet used by Oxfam demonstrated a lack of gratitude for the protesters in the streets, as it was "the so-called 'globaphobes' that have created the dynamic movement that has shaken the international financial and trade institutions and forced them to listen to the views of organizations like Oxfam." Bello called the organization on its hypocrisy, writing "you can't have it both ways: You can't say you're part of us then score with the Establishment by caricaturing us in the crudest *Economist* fashion."[78]

Oxfam's criticism of the movement and celebration of market access as a panacea for the poor had internal consequences as well. Severina Rivera, one of Oxfam's senior policy advisors in the U.S., quit in protest over the organization's campaigning focus on market access. In her resignation letter, Rivera wrote: "I cannot support Oxfam's trade campaign priority that calls, over the life of its three-year campaign, for more market access and trade for poor countries as the solution to poverty. Nor can I support the year-one campaign objective: market access for textiles from least developed countries as the solution to, or even a solution to poverty in these countries."[79]

The report was panned by activists, but it was immediately recognized as a PR victory for corporate globalization. "Breaking with some of its anti-globalization allies," the *Washington Post* noted with apparent glee, "the aid agency Oxfam International issued a report yesterday that praised international trade as a potentially enormous boon to the world's poor."[80] The right-wing *National Post* praised Oxfam for distinguishing itself from the anti-globalization rabble by rejecting their "protectionist, anti-corporatist view" and "properly conced[ing] that trade is the best way to help poor nations."[81]

Oxfam's stance also won it friends in high places. Mike Moore, director general of the WTO, immediately endorsed Oxfam's call for greater market access for poor countries. One month after its "delusional acceptance of neoliberal pro-trade premises," Patrick Bond notes, Oxfam was attending a closed-door strategy session organized by the World Bank. The focus of this "intensive dialogue" with civil society leaders was how to make the next round of WTO negotiations "work for the poor."[82]

Doomed to Repeat: Oxfam's Track Record

Though Oxfam's denunciation of the movement came as a surprise to many, it was only the latest in a string of betrayals. Oxfam in fact had a long history of playing both sides of the fence–to the benefit of the globalizers. This history is most graphically illustrated by the anti-debt campaigns of the 1990s targeting the World Bank.

As early as 1994, Northern activists were calling for cancellation of Third World debt. The IMF and the World Bank had drawn the ire of environmentalists and development NGOs, including Oxfam. Following protests against the IMF and the World Bank at their 50th anniversary meetings in Madrid, the leadership of the Bank recognized that their economic prescriptions had become "politically toxic." When James Wolfensohn took the helm of the organization in June 1995, he began wooing NGOs intensely. As President, Wolfensohn organized countless personal meetings with development NGOs to convince them that the World Bank shared their values and that he was an ally in their cause, according to Wolfensohn's biographer Sebastian Mallaby: "He would flatter NGOs with his intense listening. He would eagerly talk of partnership. He would use his intellect to enlarge their ideas rather than merely to belittle them."[83]

Wolfensohn's inducements went beyond sweet talk. The dangling carrot of "partnership" meant jobs and contracts for NGOs willing to soften their criticisms. The Bank gave NGO leaders involved in the anti-debt coalition "50 Years is Enough" posts in their Civil Society Unit, and hired over 70 NGO specialists to work in the field offices in the Global South. Bank funding for NGOs expanded rapidly, with over half of the Bank's loans including NGO side-projects.[84] Wolfensohn multiplied the number of consultative bodies, giving NGOs the impression they had influence over strategizing at the Bank.[85] One year into his term in office, the Bank's public image was "improving fast," according to Mallaby. "Wolfensohn had reached out to nongovernmental groups, turning the enemies of the Madrid summit into dinner companions."[86]

Oxfam was one of the first NGOs to fall prey to Wolfensohn's "techniques of seduction." In October 1995, Oxfam broke ranks with its colleagues in the anti-debt campaign "50 Years is Enough." Although Oxfam had been among the protesters in Madrid denouncing the Bank's neoliberal policies, its leaders swallowed their criticisms of structural adjustment and staged a joint press conference with Wolfensohn at the Bank's annual meetings. "In Madrid one year before, Oxfam had denounced the Bank for 'jeopordizing prospects for sustainable recovery and poverty reduction.' Now Oxfam was sharing a platform with the World Bank president." Later in the year, it endorsed the World Bank's "new direction."[87]

This Is What an NGO Campaign Looks Like

Oxfam would repeat this performance in slow motion with Jubilee 2000, an even larger anti-debt campaign. The Jubilee 2000 campaign was officially launched in 1996, first in the UK and then around the world as a coalition effort of churches and NGOs both North and South. The Jubilee movement called on the creditor governments to release the South from its debt bondage and cancel their outstanding debts, in the spirit of the Biblical notion of the Jubilee. The campaign originated with progressive churches in the North taking up the criticisms of Structural Adjustment Policies (SAPs) advanced by their sister churches in the South, joining them in calling for debt cancellation in the mid-1990s. Though churches played a key role in the campaign at the national level, development NGOs enjoyed influence over the direction of the campaign at the international level. Oxfam and other major development NGOs based in the North took on the role of intermediaries, negotiating with the World Bank and the wealthy nations' finance ministers on Jubilee's behalf. The campaign had no formal structure through which grassroots church activists could hold their NGO allies to account.[88] Judged by Jubilee's stated goals of debt cancellation and freedom from IMF / World Bank diktat, their leadership was disastrous.

The NGOs eschewed direct action or any other confrontational forms of public protest. They typically opted for "careful and constructive co-operation" with the authorities in preparing their symbolic and non-threatening protests. In May 1998, Jubilee 2000 campaigners mobilized some 60,000 people to protest the G8 meetings in Birmingham, England, by forming a human chain–representing the chains of debt that ensnared the Third World–around the meeting site. When confronted by British government officials concerned that their protest might embarrass the world leaders assembled in Birmingham, Jubilee's leadership assured them that they "had every intention of running a peaceful, constructive and co-operative event." Jubilee's NGO leaders sought approval from the authorities for the protest, but their abject stance did not pay off. "[A]fter months of endless, exhausting negotiations with the Foreign Office, Birmingham City Council, Birmingham police and the CIA," the organizers were nonetheless forced to divert their human chain behind empty warehouses, into deserted squares and far-away streets, reducing the symbolic protest's media impact. At the last minute, the government moved the leaders' meeting to a secret location away from the protests in what campaigners called "a calculated move to de-mobilise our supporters."[89]

In the hands of Oxfam and other NGOs, the Jubilee movement's demand for justice became a plea for charity. NGOs watered down the original demands of the church activists for debt cancellation on political and moral grounds, which were replaced with calls for debt relief for the "poorest" countries. The more radical anti-debt campaigners pointed to the injustices visited upon the poor through SAPs and emphasized the illegitimacy of the IMF and the World Bank setting economic policy for developing countries and the odious nature of the debt. Their focus was on total debt cancellation with no strings attached. NGOs on the other hand accepted the right of the IMF and the World Bank to dictate conditions to the South and even "accepted the key elements of the IMF's macro-economic austerity programmes." Indeed, NGOs in the Jubilee coalition called for debt relief with more–but better–conditions. Under the NGOs' leadership, the new buzzwords of the global Jubilee movement "became 'civil society participation' and 'democratisation of international financial relations.'"[90] In practical terms, the campaign came to be centred on calls for "civil society" to be given additional seats at the policy-making table. The Jubilee critique of debt as a symptom of the massive power imbalance between rich and poor countries, painstakingly built up by thousands of grassroots activists, was now a request to tweak the existing system.

The divide was most evident in the conflicting stances on the Bank's Heavily Indebted Poor Country (HIPC) program within the Jubilee movement. The HIPC program was unveiled in 1996, which won Wolfensohn "the valuable affection of nongovernmental groups such as Oxfam."[91] Two years later, the HIPC program had provided only 2 of the 40 countries eligible with a trickle of debt relief, access to which was still contingent on the successful application of the Bank's economic reforms. Many Jubilee activists rejected HIPC for providing inadequate debt reductions and carrying the same neoliberal conditionalities that harmed the South in the past. NGOs, on the other hand, called on activists to work with Wolfensohn to make HIPC better. "While Oxfam viewed HIPC as an imperfect process, it continued to advocate within the framework, instead of rejecting it like some other activists."[92]

PRSPs: Poverty Reduction or Public Relations?

The Jubilee 2000 movement quickly became too big to ignore. Churches had conducted extensive popular education and succeeded in mobilizing their adherents, typically an older segment of the population than the more youthful anti-globalization protests. "Churchgoers were the bedrock of the activist base, many inspired by the biblical principle of Jubilee."[93] By 1998, Jubilee activists had gathered over 17 million signatures worldwide calling for debt forgiveness. The campaign was instrumental in raising the issue of illegitimate Third World debt in rich countries, making it one of the issues driving the anti-globalization movement forward. In an article entitled "How to Blunt the Anti-Globalization Backlash," *Business Week* suggested that more debt relief and increased development aid could "help ease protests."[94]

When the rich country finance ministries, led by the U.S. and Britain, deliberated with officials of the IMF and the World Bank on the issue, "the Jubilee campaigners were invited to say what they wanted–given their popular following, any new debt deal would require their endorsement." If the people mobilized by the campaign perceived the rich countries as unwilling to reform the IMF and the World Bank, there was a danger they could tilt towards the radical wing of the anti-globalization movement. Led by Oxfam's representative, NGOs championed a minimalist approach to debt relief in negotiations with the Bank. They demanded even more conditions be added to IMF and World Bank lending, this time undoing some of the damage done by their anti-popular policies. Neoliberalism with a human face was the order of the day.[95]

Following the negotiations with moderate Jubilee campaigners, the World Bank and the IMF unveiled a new public image in June 1999. The World Bank changed the name of the much-reviled Structural Adjustment Policies to Poverty Reduction Strategy Papers (PRSPs) and the Heavily Indebted Poor Countries (HIPC) program was "Enhanced" to give greater access and more substantial debt relief to poor countries. NGO-inspired development buzzwords like participation, social capital, empowerment and civil society filled the Bank's reports and communiqués. The new Poverty Reduction Strategy Papers (PRSPs) required borrowing governments to carry out "participatory" consultations with civil society and to allocate a fixed percentage of their budgets to health care and education, to ensure the money freed up by debt relief would serve the poor.

Oxfam and other NGOs celebrated the debt relief announcement as a victory for insider lobbying. Northern NGO campaigners called the World Bank's announcement an "important first step," though some quietly demurred that the amount of debt relief was inadequate.[96] Oxfam's leadership was overjoyed with the outcome and claimed that James Wolfensohn "deserve[d] a lot of credit" for pushing debt relief, and gushed over his "political conviction, leadership, courage, and–at times–sheer bloody mindedness ... he really opened the door."[97]

Yet the makeover of the Bank's policies fell far short of what the Jubilee campaign had been demanding. Economist Eric Toussaint described Enhanced HIPC as offering "a drop of reduction in an ocean of debts" since the new debt reduction amounted at most to 2.6% of developing country debt.[98] "There remained more than $2 trillion of Third World debt that should be cancelled," wrote Patrick Bond, "including not just HIPC countries but also Nigeria, Argentina, Brazil, Mexico, South Africa and other major debtors not considered highly-indebted or poor in the mainstream discourse."[99]

Even for the countries that did enjoy some of the debt relief offered by HIPC, it was far from the total wiping away of debts called for by Jubilee. The World Bank had seized on the vagueness of the call for cancelling "unpayable" debts, and interpreted this to mean bringing down debts to "sustainable" or "manageable" levels. A decade later, the IMF found that HIPC countries were slipping back into debt, because of their weak economic base and the low prices paid for their commodities.[100] Though social spending increased, it remained well below pre-debt crisis levels in most cases.

From the outset, it was clear that PRSPs continued to impose the same neoliberal prescriptions as SAPs, regardless of their participatory add-ons.[101] Participatory structures were not in any way empowered to address contentious questions like land reform, privatization or user fees for public services, nor were the anti-inflationary macroeconomic policies that severely limited government spending up for discussion. Development economist Ha-Joon Chang found the changes brought about by the World Bank's PRSP consultations with NGOs to be "at best marginal."[102] In a meeting with NGOs to discuss the new "participatory" orientation, the IMF's Executive Director was clear that the changes were more about image than substance. "It's not about abandoning conditionality ... The IMF still leads on macro, the World Bank on social. In reality it's not that big a departure; it's in our *interests* to make it *seem* like a big deal."[103]

In an assessment of the impact that the Jubilee campaign had on the World Bank, Jubilee 2000 Communications Manager Nick Buxton commented on the superficial nature of the reforms achieved under Wolfensohn:

> The change in language on debt and development is still far from being reflected in practical action. ... In reality, there has been very little evidence of creditors and international financial institutions enacting the rhetoric they espouse. Fundamentally there has been no shift in terms of democratization of institutions such as the IMF and World Bank. Power in terms of decision-making is still firmly in the hands of rich creditor nations.[104]

Economist David Ellerman has argued that the World Bank and the IMF are "almost entirely motivated by big power politics and their own internal organisational imperatives." While working alongside Joseph Stiglitz at the World Bank, Ellerman saw countless attempts at internal reform fail, leading him to a pessimistic conclusion: "Intellectual and political energies spent trying to 'reform' these agencies are largely a waste of time and a misdirection of energies."[105]

These cosmetic reforms were enough to satify the Bank's NGO critics. At the April 2000 protests in Washington, D.C. against the IMF and the World Bank, where–in contrast to Jubilee events–direct action protests were planned from the outset, few NGOs were out on the streets. According to Sebastian Mallaby, the absence of NGOs spoke to the success of Wolfensohn's co-optive strategy: "Some groups like Oxfam recognized the [rhetorical] change, and turned from adversaries to allies; other NGOs such as CARE were more interested in delivering aid than in anti-Bank campaigning."[106]

Self-interest was a factor. "Participatory" and "social" conditionalities were attractive to development NGOs like Oxfam, according to Mallaby, since "it was effectively giving NGOs a say in the Bank's choice of projects."[107] Many NGOs were subsequently contracted by the Bank to organize participatory meetings for the development of the PRSPs.[108] In addition to imposing economic policies on poor countries, the World Bank and NGOs now dictated important aspects of their social policy as well. While elected government bodies were further marginalized from policy making, NGOs were given a social policy sandbox to play in, funded by the meagre HIPC debt relief funds.

Jubilee Split: The South Rejects Lesser Evilism

The duplicity of the NGOs and their betrayal of the campaign's original demands for debt cancellation and freedom from IMF / World Bank tutelage was the last straw for many Southern anti-debt campaigners. Resentments had built up after Northern NGOs used their control of resources to marginalize Southern campaigners who were making more radical demands and were more open to militant protests.[109] A coalition of Southern activists and organizations calling itself Jubilee South split from the Jubilee 2000 coalition and denounced its "politically expedient" tactics for undermining their radical and longer-term demands:

> Do not ask us, as we are often asked by debt coalitions and Jubilee Campaigns in the North, to accept the lesser of many evils, to settle for a piece of the loaf and not the whole, to be realistic about the HIPCs as the "only game in town." If that is the only game in town, then the problem is not the game but the town.[110]

The church groups leading Canada's Jubilee 2000 coalition were not taken in by the World Bank's rebranding effort. "We can anticipate a public relations campaign from the Fund and the Bank to sell their agenda," John Dillon of the Canadian Ecumenical Jubilee Initiative wrote in February 2000, "with attempts to co-opt our language and perhaps some NGOs in the process." While Canada's Jubilee coalition officially opposed any debt relief measures that allowed the IMF and the World Bank to continue dictating economic policy to their borrowers, its position was "not universally held by all NGOs in Canada." "There are dissenting voices who still believe that creditors should impose so-called 'positive conditions,'" of the sort contained in the PRSPs, Dillon noted. Jubilee South was joined by representatives of Canadian churches at major protests in Genoa in July 2001. While Oxfam and other development NGOs withdrew from the demonstrations after the killing of a 21-year old protester by Italian police, decrying the "violence" of the protests (but not of the police), Jubilee South continued to protest against the G8.

The World Bank's skilful manipulation of NGOs to deflect criticism and divide its opponents became a template for subsequent efforts to counter the anti-globalization movement. One month after the Seattle protests, the *Economist* suggested Western leaders "could still try to weaken the broad coalition that attacked it in Seattle by reaching out to mainstream and technical NGOs," citing the success of the World Bank in splitting off

Oxfam and other development NGOs from the ranks of its critics.

Take the case of the World Bank. The Fifty Years is Enough campaign of 1994 was a prototype of Seattle (complete with activists invading the meeting halls). Now the NGOs are surprisingly quiet about the World Bank. The reason is that the Bank has made a huge effort to co-opt them.

Through intensified dialogues with the respectable face of dissent, Wolfensohn had successfully "diluted the strength of 'mobilisation networks' and increased the relative power of technical NGOs (for it is mostly these that the Bank has co-opted)."[111]

Fortress Quebec City: Topple the Fence or March to Nowhere?

The protests in Quebec City in April 2001 against the Free Trade Agreement of the Americas (FTAA) were the largest anti-globalization street protests in Canada. Leaders of 34 nations (Cuba was excluded) were meeting at the Summit of the Americas to negotiate a hemispheric trade agreement, which critics dubbed "NAFTA on steroids." Some 60,000 people gathered to oppose the deal and express their outrage at the heavily fortified, closed-door meetings.

The more radical elements were led by the *Convergence des Luttes Anti-Capitalistes* (CLAC–Convergence of Anti-Capitalist Struggles) and the *Comité d'Accueil du Sommet des Amériques* (CASA–Summit of the Americas Welcoming Committee), which brought together anarchists, students, anti-poverty activists, radical feminists and environmentalists. The moderate wing was represented by the *Réseau québecois sur l'integration continentale* (RQIC), a platform of Quebec labour unions and NGOs, and Common Frontiers, its counterpart from English Canada. In contrast to Vancouver, development NGOs had a large presence in Quebec City and were well represented in the moderate coalitions: the RQIC included Alternatives, *Association québécoise des organismes de coopération internationale* (AQOCI), CUSO-Québec and Development & Peace while Common Frontiers included Americas Policy Group of the CCIC, Inter Pares, Oxfam Canada, the Canadian Consortium for International Social Development and Rights & Democracy.

In many respects, the Summit of the Americas was a replay of the APEC summit in Vancouver on a much larger scale. Continuing the "co-opt and crackdown" strategy unveiled in Vancouver, the federal and provincial governments provided over $300,000 in funding to the RQIC to host a parallel People's Summit. Alternatives in particular played a key role in the organization of the Summit. Alternatives negotiated with the government for funding of the Summit, provided the coordination team for the "People's Summit" and had staff working as spokespeople for the RQIC. Alternatives "met frequently" with the prime minister's summit representative as well as with other government representatives in the months leading up to the protests.[112] A government spokesperson explained that the government wanted to "ensure there is a dialogue with the public," and claimed that the parallel summit would "give citizens the opportunity to present their concerns to government."[113]

These groups were courted by the government because they "support the balanced agenda of the Summit of the Americas process but want to see more emphasis on the implementation of commitments made in pursuit of equitable trade and social inclusion," as Marc Lortie, the Prime Minister's personal representative at the FTAA meeting, put it. Oxfam Quebec and Oxfam Canada, for instance, blandly urged the Canadian government to "harness trade for development" and ensure that the Agreement supported "development goals."[114] The RQIC's demands prior to the Summit centred on the inclusion of labour and environmental clauses and its public statements focused on the exclusion of its members from the negotiations.[115] The tactics favoured by the RQIC–"large-scale parallel events and massive, peaceful demonstrations," in the words of Lortie–also aligned with the objectives of the authorities, who desperately wanted to avoid or at least minimize Seattle-style confrontations. Generous government funding allowed the NGOs and their demands for inclusion to occupy the media spotlight in the run up to the protests, marginalizing the views of anti-capitalist organizations calling for a rejection of the FTAA. Thanks to government funding, Lortie noted with some satisfaction, the People's Summit and its organizers, "enjoyed wide coverage, in part because the main media set up on the site of the People's Summit throughout the week, where they covered activities and conducted live interviews."[116]

There was a "Plan B" for those groups that did not support the "balanced agenda" of the FTAA. In anticipation of the protests, the Canadian government mobilized a squad of 6,700 riot police to guard the Summit of the Americas, "wielding an arsenal of tear gas, water cannons, batons, concussion-grenades, pepper spray, and rubber bullets."[117] A fortress-like 3.9-kilometre fence, which came to be known as the "Wall of Shame," swallowed up a major portion of Quebec City's picturesque downtown core. Local jails were emptied and officials ramped up their intimidating rhetoric. "If you want peace, you must prepare for war," Serge Menard, Quebec's Minister for Public Security, explained to the press. With a price tag of over $100 million, policing for the Summit was the most costly peacetime security operation in Canadian history up to that point.[118]

Months before the Summit, tensions between the two tendencies flared up, frustrating attempts to organize a common demonstration or to collaborate on public outreach. Representatives of the RQIC and other reformist groups insisted on tightly-controlled forms of protest. The moderates demanded that all organizations adhere to a strict code of "nonviolent discipline," which was defined as excluding not only physical violence but property damage, wearing masks or hoods and even "verbal violence, including insults."[119] CLAC and other groups refused to accept these conditions and insisted on the right of protesters to stand their ground rather than capitulate when attacked by police. CLAC, CASA and other radical groups argued for "an escalation and a diversification of tactics beyond both the routines of lobbying and of legal, stage-managed demonstrations," and promoted "a return to more militant and confrontational tactics, including direct action and civil disobedience." The NGO members of the RQIC, on the other hand, worked alongside the *Fédération des travailleurs et travailleuses du Québec* (FTQ) and other "traditional allies of the governing *Parti Québecois*" who "wanted to keep the demonstrations under their control and minimize embarrassment to the Quebec government."[120]

Consequently, the radical groups were excluded (and excluded themselves) from the People's Summit. The radicals organized a separate "Carnival against Capitalism." They held their own teach-ins and organizing meetings, and planned their own marches. They made links with the local population and sponsored a popular education caravan against the FTAA that traveled throughout Quebec, Ontario and the Northeast of the U.S. Protester and radio journalist Shawn Ewald claimed that "the most important work (organizing the effort to either stop or disrupt the summit, and build community support) was done by CLAC and CASA." Alternatives and the RQIC, on the other hand, "while having one hundred times the resources of CLAC and CASA, did not do one tenth of the organizing that CLAC and CASA did." Instead, they appeared to have "spent more energy trying to marginalize CLAC and CASA ... [than] doing any real organizing work on the ground."[121]

If the government's purpose in funding the People's Summit was to co-opt the moderate elements of the movement, the People's Summit itself was co-opted by an increasingly radical rank-and-file. The 2,000-3,000 delegates in attendance roundly rejected the draft statement proposed by the organizers calling for the inclusion of social clauses in the FTAA in favour of a position much closer to that of the radical anti-globalization groups. Delegates voted for an unequivocal "No to the FTAA" stance and refused to endorse the RQIC's preferred strategy of *concertation* with government or business.[122] To the embarrassment of the RQIC, the counter-summit's final declaration was "admittedly quite radical and ... rejected not only the proposed FTAA but also the very principle of free trade because of the supremacy of the capitalist system."[123]

A Tale of Two Marches

On Friday, April 20 the radical-led march explicitly set out to shut down the FTAA negotiations, as protesters had done less than two years earlier in Seattle. The People's Summit organizers did not support the demonstration and instead chose to hold a day-long teach-in on the FTAA. The organizers promised the teach-in would "highlight civil society's capacity for resistance" and "deliver a public political challenge" to the FTAA leaders.[124] Some key participants in the People's Summit, however, refused to accept the criminalization of dissent and judged that taking to the streets was a better way of delivering a message to the globalizers than sitting in a day-long conference. Led by the more militant Canadian labour unions and the Council of Canadians, hundreds of People's Summit delegates deserted the teach-in and joined the 10,000-strong march in a show of solidarity with the radicals' opposition to the "Wall of Shame."

The Friday march produced the most iconic image of the Summit, as protesters directed their rage at the chain link fence erected to protect the Summit from the anti-globalization hordes. The crowd quickly toppled large sections of the fence, but was subsequently beaten back by lines of riot cops and volleys of tear gas. The police response was indiscriminate and brutal, targeting not just those engaging in direct action against the wall in the "red zones," but those in the non-confrontational "green" and "yellow" protest zones as well. Police fired over 5,000 tear gas canisters (so many they had to order more from their U.S. supplier during the Summit) and nearly 1,000 plastic bullets at the crowds. Several protesters were seriously injured by police-fired projectiles. Maude Barlow was shocked by the "random, government-endorsed brutality being waged against innocent protesters" she saw after the Council of Canadians' delegation joined the protests at the fence:

For the next two days, into the small hours of the morning, the police directed a merciless tear gas assault against the several thousand protesters anywhere in the vicinity of the wall. Four hundred and sixty-three were arrested, some having been picked up by police in unmarked vans, and were held in filthy conditions inside the jail. Women were stripped and doused with disinfectant by male guards and people were squeezed into tiny cells without toilet facilities or food. ... The terms "green" or "yellow" immediately became irrelevant. Anyone standing peacefully within the vicinity was a target of tear gas, water cannon and even plastic bullets.[125]

After the wall came down and protesters clashed with police, Prime Minister Jean Chretien claimed the action was "carried out by a small group of extremists" and was "contrary to all democratic principles that are so dear to us."[126] The RQIC leadership reacted with much the same horror, publicly decrying the "violence" of the "anarchists."[127] Few in the crowd shared the outrage of the RQIC at the assault on the fence or vandalism, reported journalist Lance Tapley. "The rather widespread acceptance of 'violence' was striking. ... 'Look at the violence of the police and globalization!' so many people told me when I brought up the subject of the Black Block's [sic] activities."[128] Indeed, a handful of anarchists were not the only ones engaged in "violence" at the wall:

Perhaps more surprising than the nearly 5000 tear gas canisters that police fired at demonstrators in Quebec was the willingness of the crowds to hold their ground. By the second day, it wasn't just black-clad anarchists and nihilist street kids dashing into the fray to hurl back the fuming, red-hot canisters, but ordinary college kids, angry locals, even a mother with a child on her back, incensed that the cops had fired into her group of peaceful demonstrators. The summit became a lesson in how indiscriminate force can radicalize a movement.[129]

On the Saturday, the RQIC held their own protest, the "March of the Americas" which drew over 60,000 protesters, overwhelmingly from the ranks of trade unions. In contrast to the radicals who protested at the fence and sought ways to breach or tear down the fence throughout the Summit, the RQIC and Common Frontiers scrupulously avoided challenging the state's right to wall off the city from dissent. With the radical groups and students maintaining a presence of thousands at the fence, and facing a

brutal police assault, the support of the huge labour contingent might have
decisively turned the clashes in favour of the protesters.

Unbeknownst to many participants, they were on a "March to Nowhere."
The "legal" protest route had been chosen by the People's Summit organizers
and their labour allies to avoid any possible confrontations at the fence:

> Rather than marching towards the perimeter fence and the Summit of
> the Americas meetings, march organizers chose a route that marched
> from the People's Summit away from the fence, through largely empty
> residential areas to the parking lot of a stadium in a vacant area several
> miles away. ... One thousand marshals from the FTQ kept very tight
> control over the march. When the march came to the point where
> some activists planned to split off and go up the hill to the fence, FTQ
> marshals signalled the Canadian Auto Workers (CAW) contingent
> walking behind CUPE to sit down and stop the march so that FTQ
> marshals could lock arms and prevent others from leaving the official
> march route.[130]

Many union members were incredulous and outraged that the People's
Summit organizers had led their protest away from the wall. Carol
Phillips, director of the international department of the CAW, explained,
"It's been very difficult for our members to keep them on this route [away
from the fence]." According to Phillips, many members of her union
were disappointed and embarrassed when they found out that they were
marching away from the perimeter fence.[131] One CAW member said
about the "legal" march: "Why was the 'legal protest' conducted miles
away from the security perimeter? Had I known I was marching towards
a parking lot, I would have stayed home and done that at the fucking
mall."[132] Another labour activist bitterly denounced the cowardice of the
leadership's "decision to avoid meaningful protest":

> The process of expedience and concession that came up with the plan
> to avoid the fence is beyond my understanding. It was as if the Second
> World War generals, who were preparing to drive the Nazis out of
> Europe, turned around and launched an attack in the direction of Baffin
> Island.[133]

Thousands of union protesters ultimately joined the protests at the fence,
and "the idea of marching on the perimeter was extremely popular with
the vast majority of rank-and-file union members and others who did not

break off the main march on Saturday." As the parking lot rally came to a close, a huge cheer went up through the crowd when it was announced that six points in the perimeter had been breached.[134]

Sporadic reinforcements from the labour march were not enough to turn the tide in favour of the protesters at the fence. A few trade meetings were delayed or cancelled, but police were able to contain the protests and the FTAA Summit went on as planned. Leaders nonetheless left Quebec City feeling rattled. Enrique Iglesias, the head of the Inter-American Development Bank, attended the FTAA meetings and told the press afterward: "We cannot ignore these kinds of things. The image demonstrators create can undermine the capacity of leaders to implant free trade."[135] Despite efforts by both government officials and development NGOs to isolate and demonize the "extremists," direct action protesters had clearly won the sympathy and respect of both local residents and the broader Canadian public. Opinion polls found that 74 percent of Canadians favoured a popular vote on any such trade agreement before the federal government signed on to it, and more than 1 in 5 Canadians over the age of 18 said they would have joined the protests in Quebec City if time and money permitted.[136] Even Prime Minister Chrétien was forced to admit: "Democracies face a crisis of legitimacy and relevancy."[137] Police may have won the battle, but the globalizers were losing the war.

What Could NGOs Have Done Differently?

Some argue that a productive division of labour between NGOs at the negotiating table and radicals in the street may have been possible, pointing to positive aspects of NGOs' involvement in the anti-globalization movement. Though NGOs did little to mobilize their members for the street protests and direct actions against the globalization agenda, NGO resources did trickle down to activists groups for campaigns not sanctioned by donors. NGOs also provided useful research and educational tools. Whatever limited contributions NGOs made to the movement, however, the ultimate impact of NGO activities was to further the globalizers' agenda.

When NGOs belatedly joined the anti-globalization movement, they devoted substantial resources to promoting reformist strategies while marginalizing radical goals and analyses. Much of the development NGOs literature on "globalization" was critical, but it tended at the same time to "studiously avoid confronting fundamental issues like imperialism, capitalism or colonisation in any substantive way," notes Aziz Choudry:

Cul-de-sacs of convenience and comfort are frequently constructed which exclude any focus on the issues of imperialism and colonialism, often couched in the language of "reality" and pragmatism. They invite people to question things up to a certain point, but fail to grapple with, and often obscure, the root causes of injustice.[138]

The intellectual output of many NGOs tilted the movement towards "reasonable" policy advocacy in collaboration with political and economic elites, and away from rejection of the entire neoliberal agenda.

Economist Michel Chossudovsky argues there is nothing wrong with representatives of a movement sitting down to negotiate with "the enemy" at certain times. But this strategy

must be applied vigorously in close liaison with constituent social movements. The underlying results and information of these negotiations, however, must be channelled with a view to reinforcing rather than weakening grass roots actions. In other words, we should not allow 'lobbying' to be conducted in an isolated and secretive fashion by organisations which are 'hand picked' by the governments and the WTO.[139]

No such accountability to the grassroots of the movement ever existed for NGOs. NGOs were in fact hand picked to represent the movement by the donors, to whom they are ultimately accountable. NGOs were accorded a seat at the table because their presence helped to weaken, rather than strengthen, the rejection of neoliberalism in the streets. The ease with which NGOs were co-opted by the World Bank and other neoliberal institutions demonstrates just how unfit these organizations were to take on a leadership role or lobby on the movement's behalf.

Critiques of the "betrayals" of NGOs within the anti-globalization movement have often attributed their actions to naïveté, poor political judgement or a lack of courage on the part of NGO leaders. But the hostility of NGOs to direct action and their seemingly irrational faith in lobbying were not the result of personality defects. The reason that NGOs acted as a drag on the movement's militancy and worked to water down its demands was not because they were *failing* as movement organizations, but because they were *successful* as agents of their government patrons. NGOs functioned as Trojan Horses within the movement, the friendly face of a "co-opt and clampdown" strategy pursued by Western elites.

9/11 and Anti-Globalization Denouement

The demise of the anti-globalization movement in North America was not ultimately caused by development NGOs, despite their well-funded and concerted efforts to disorient and de-radicalize protesters. As the summer of 2001 came to an end, many were confident that the movement could only get bigger and more militant. One trade unionist in Quebec City proclaimed: "This movement is going to keep growing, it's not just those few dressed in black who are at the barricades."[140] Though NGOs and the leadership of some trade unions and other mainstream organizations continued to try to hold back protests, the balance of forces within the movement was tilting towards the radicals. Protesters were hardening their stance against elites seeking to push through neoliberal trade agreements over popular opposition and direct action was gaining legitimacy. Mike Roselle, a founder of the Ruckus Society, one of the groups behind the Seattle blockades, observed: "People aren't that freaked out by someone breaking a Gap window anymore. … They know this is a serious grassroots uprising that spans leftists, environmentalists, labour, and students, and that people are not afraid to keep coming back for more."[141] The CAW's Phillips echoed this assessment: "A lot of our members who came to Quebec are now telling me they want to take part in the fight-back that takes place in the streets. A lot want training in direct action … Our activists are becoming more radical. This is what they're telling me."[142]

What ultimately did in the movement were the September 11, 2001 attacks. The globalizers immediately seized the opportunity to link their agenda to the emerging "War on Terror." U.S. Trade Representative Robert Zoellick called on the world to "fight terror with trade."[143] The attacks were also used by the authorities to ramp up the policing of protesters in the name of "anti-terrorism." Security concerns now trumped any questions about democratic freedoms and police were newly empowered to crack down on dissenters.

The media deemed public opposition to neoliberalism to be standing in sympathy with the anti- Americanism of fundamentalist jihadis. Though the authorities were trying to peg protesters as "domestic terrorists" before 9/11, after the attacks such demonization intensified. "After September 11th, politicians and pundits around the world instantly began spinning the terrorist attacks as part of a continuum of anti-American and anti-corporate violence," with the anti-globalization movement explicitly placed alongside Osama Bin Laden.[144] Less than a week after the attacks, the *National Post* equated protesting neoliberal globalization with terrorism: "Like terrorists, the anti-globalization movement is disdainful of democratic institutions. … Terrorism, if not so heinous as what we witnessed last week, has always been part of the protesters' game plan." [145] In trying to shut down the meetings of the IMF or the WTO, one British journalist reasoned, direct action protesters were "seeking to advance their political agenda through intimidation, which is a classic goal of terrorism."[146]

In the post-9/11 political climate of fear and patriotism, public sympathy for disruptive protests was greatly diminished. Organizers in Washington, DC cancelled demonstrations against the IMF and the World Bank that had been planned for late September 2001 after the attacks. Just weeks before, these same organizers had been anticipating as many as 100,000 demonstrators, predicting that the event would be a "second Seattle." Labour leaders called off anti-WTO protests slated for October 2001, destroying the fragile links between radical groups and the labour movement that had previously been built up. Though protests continued after September 11, 2001, the seemingly irresistible momentum of the movement was lost.

9

Hearts and Minds

Development and counterinsurgency warfare

In Canada, we understand our own middle-power role as one of bearing witness to the great evil that dwells in the South, an evil that traumatizes and overwhelms us. It is important to note that in the cultural story we tell about our international role, we always go to the South as innocent parties who are not implicated in the terrible histories we confront there.
—*Sherene Razack* [1]

In spite of the very common involvement of "development" with counterinsurgency throughout the post-war period, a surprising number of Western progressives have been drawn to "development" work by way of political commitments to and solidarity with Third World causes.
—*James Ferguson* [2]

On March 4, 2011, North Atlantic Treaty Organization (NATO) Secretary General Anders Fogh Rasmussen delivered a speech that left some corners of the NGO world scrambling to spin his message. Rasmussen reflected on the lessons of the last decade for military planners: "In today's world, we have to realise that the military is no longer the complete answer—now it is just part of the answer. Hard power is of little use if it cannot be combined with soft power." NATO's focus on soft power, Rasmussen emphasized, meant that development NGOs were now an essential element of the Western military alliance's strategies. To successfully defeat insurgencies, NATO needed "NGOs to spread their web of projects, from health care to promoting new approaches to agriculture."[3] Rasmussen pointed to NATO's experiences of working with NGOs in Afghanistan as a model to be emulated in future wars.

The Agency Co-ordinating Body for Afghan Relief (ACBAR), a coalition of 106 development and humanitarian NGOs active in the war-torn country, issued an indignant reply in a March 9 press release titled "NGOs are not a soft power." ACBAR objected to Rasmussen's comments because they implied partisanship in the way NGOs deliver aid. According to the NGO coalition, the Secretary General's remarks constituted "a denial of NGOs' identity and operational principles," which threatened to endanger the lives of NGO workers and beneficiaries alike.

> NGOs do not represent a "Soft Power" as incorrectly stated by Mr. Rasmussen. The true nature of a Non Governmental Organisation is independent, which is inherently incompatible with support to any military or political strategy. The core function of an NGO is to provide assistance regardless of any other socio-economic or political motivation.[4]

The incident reflected the sharp contradiction between the image of disinterested humanitarianism that NGOs project and the reality of the dominant trends within the aid system of the last decade. "Although the coupling of development with security is more pronounced in Afghanistan as a key battleground in the 'War on Terror' than in most other aid contexts," Jude Howell and Jeremy Lind of the London School of Economics write, "these trends are observed in development aid policy more generally."[5] If the 1990s were the age of globalization, the 2000s were the age of empire. The militarization of development aid—a trend that began in the 1990s—emerged full-blown in the post-9/11 period, with profound consequences for development NGOs. Western military planners increasingly looked to use aid as a tool to stabilize "post-conflict" countries and combat insurgencies. Poverty was re-conceptualized as a security threat, and development recast as a weapon in the fight against terrorism and "radical populism."

Operating in the shadow of the military, NGOs are deployed to win the "hearts and minds" of occupied populations. NGOs carry out small-scale development projects to improve living standards in areas under government control and to help build the legitimacy of newly-installed governments after a "regime change." NGOs work on "peace-building" or "conflict resolution" projects to discourage locals from joining or supporting any armed resistance or other disruptive activities. NGOs carry out "civic education" and "get out the vote" campaigns to encourage participation in elections that are typically organized following an invasion, though these are often tightly-controlled (and in some cases rigged) affairs of dubious democratic value.[6] NGO projects also provide on-the-ground intelligence about attitudes towards the occupation in particular regions. "In Kosovo, Sierra Leone, Afghanistan, East Timor and Iraq," political scientist Mark Duffield explains, "relief and development assistance has been given the job of remaking such countries into showcase examples of the benefits of Western involvement ... from the perspective of their prospective hosts and beneficiaries, NGOs are now indistinguishable from the occupying forces with which they have often arrived or on which they rely for protection."[7]

The incorporation of NGOs and their "techniques of 'soft power' resonate with the 'pacification' experiments implemented by the U.S. during the Vietnam War and serve a number of aims," explains social anthropologist Nosheen Ali:

> First, they achieve local goodwill and military intelligence, so that the efficacy of the war in the occupied territory may be enhanced. Second, the talk of protecting and serving civilians helps to silence critics, and cover up the devastation of lives and homes caused by military bombing. Third, these techniques serve to expand the military's already bloated existence. Finally, they give a positive image to the occupation at home, helping to justify and extend it.[8]

The objections of ACBAR and other NGOs notwithstanding, Rasmusssen's speech reflected a consensus among Western policy makers and military planners about the role of NGOs that developed in the wake of the U.S.-led invasions of Afghanistan and Iraq. Canada, an eager partner to U.S. military occupations, has been no exception to the trend. As aid flowed into war zones following on the heels of Western troops, Canadian NGOs increasingly found themselves riding shotgun in the Canadian military's armoured Humvee. Despite many attempts to distance themselves from their new role, development NGOs had become "implicated in a participatory militarism in which an ethnographically sensitive military strives to 'listen' and 'build relationships' to 'serve people'–in order to occupy better, and longer."[9]

Counterinsurgency: Win and Hold Popular Support

In 2007, the Canadian Forces released a counterinsurgency manual which laid out in detail the role of NGOs in the effort to win over "hearts and minds"–both on the battlefield and in Canada. Insurgency is as much a political struggle as a military one, the manual stresses, and it is an uphill fight. Insurgencies are most common in divided societies, driven by "the perception of oppression due to political, societal and economic grievances." "When these perceptions become sufficiently emotive, leaders may emerge who are able to organise protest or resistance, and influence people to risk imprisonment and even death in order to resist the established order." Groups may turn to armed resistance when the local authorities are "provoked" into using violence or adopting repressive measures to quell discontent. "Against such repression, the insurgent appears as the peoples' protector." Insurgents are motivated by "ideas for social change" and rooted in political and social movements that draw their support from those on the bottom of society. The aims of the insurgents–whether to "expel a foreign power," to overthrow a government perceived to be "under the control of foreigners," or to effect radical social transformation–must "appeal to as wide an audience as possible." Counterinsurgents, on the other hand, typically fight in support of "unpopular" governments that "fail to address or satisfy the basic needs of their populace."[10] Counterinsurgency is in effect war waged to preserve the status quo or to stabilize a foreign occupation.

Defeating an insurgency "involves much more than simply military action." "It is a multi-agency approach–military, paramilitary, political, economic, psychological and civic actions–that seeks to not only defeat the insurgents themselves, but the root causes of, and support for, the insurgency." To this end, the manual outlines the creation of operational and intelligence committees that include the "lead administrators from various non-governmental organisations (NGOs)" and other civilian agencies in the field "in order to co-ordinate all actions (kinetic and non-kinetic) to counter the insurgency." The NGOs' level of involvement is depicted in a table: top committees directing the counterinsurgency effort at the national level are comprised of military, UN and host country government representatives, but committees at the provincial level should include "administrators for major NGOs" and at the municipal level, "local NGO officers." "The multi-agency aspect of the [counterinsurgency] campaign demands close cross-agency planning and co-ordination down to the lowest levels."[11]

For the military, working with NGOs has a clear political purpose: to tilt public opinion away from the insurgency and towards the government in place. NGOs help to make living under occupation more attractive than living in insurgent-controlled areas where aid is withheld and populations subject to attack by occupying forces. Development activities are intended to make the population feel their grievances are being addressed, encouraging positive attitudes towards the government and the occupation. The manual describes a scenario in which troops defeat an insurgent stronghold, after which the military pays an NGO to move into the area and carry out a project with the population, which is in turn publicized in both the local and international media. Coordinating and liaising with NGOs in the field is important because it "leads to activities that support local authorities." The manual also recommends providing security to NGO convoys.[12]

Foreign occupation forces and local forces under their control possess superior firepower and resources, but insurgents often enjoy significant popular support. Foreign troops operate in an unfamiliar land amidst an unfamiliar culture, but NGOs can reduce this disadvantage for Canadian troops by providing information on "social, political, cultural, religious, economic, infrastructural and environmental factors in support of military operations and objectives." NGO personnel also serve as a set of eyes and ears on the ground for the military. Interactions with NGOs "should be a valuable source of information to intelligence staff in creating a knowledge base of the environment," though the manual warns that NGOs "cannot be perceived as intelligence gathering assets." The manual also suggests conducting reconnaissance patrols with NGOs.[13]

NGOs and their local partners also serve as useful channels for building support for the occupation, both among occupied populations and within Canada. "Because of their ability to inform, demonstrate and influence and even co-opt," NGOs have a key role to play in the war for hearts and minds. The manual recommends that "indigenous proxies such as social, religious, or political leaders who have credibility with target audiences and are sympathetic to the mission should be used to broadcast desired messages." How the Canadian public perceives the war is also considered integral to the success of the war effort itself, and NGOs can be recruited as credible, grassroots propagandists to alter perceptions among the Canadian public. According to the manual, "one constant regarding insurgency and [counterinsurgency] is the battle to win and hold popular support, in the theatre of operations and at home. ... [T]he populace of those nations contributing to the [counterinsurgency] must continue to support the mission that may well continue for years on end."[14] Elsewhere, Canadian military strategists discuss the need to wage what they call a "perception war" for Canadian hearts and minds, in order to foster "a strong national consensus behind [Canada's] foreign policy."[15]

Counterinsurgency warfare is not a popularity contest, but a struggle for power. In addition to fighting armed groups, counterinsurgents have to focus on neutralizing political threats to the government's legitimacy. In the manual, dissent tends to be classified as "insurgent activity" and peaceful political actions are described as threats to "order" and "stability." Any organization that "spreads propaganda unchecked" and "denies the government popular support," or any activity that "attempts to undermine the political, economic and military strength of a state," even if peaceful, is liable to be deemed "subversive." Targets of the counterinsurgent's suspicions include political parties and organizations that "have the appearance of challenging and defying the authority of government." According to the manual, suppression of these kinds of organizations and activities is legitimate and necessary.[16]

Current counterinsurgency doctrine has strong authoritarian tendencies. Strikes, sit-ins in public places, demonstrations and even absenteeism are described as forms of "passive resistance" that cause "disorder and disruption." Crowds, demonstrations, and "resulting riots" must be prevented or dispersed by police and military repression. Indeed, the Canadian Forces' manual suggests monitoring the "number and intensity of public demonstrations" as indicators of the security situation. The manual also recommends limiting freedom of the press to deny "subversives" access to the media, which can be used "to publicise real and contrived incidents," such as the torture of prisoners or other abuses by security forces, which "play upon the sensitivities of the populations of liberal democracies." These measures are considered legitimate under the doctrine, since protests can be "engineered," "stage managed" and "manipulated" by insurgents "with comparative ease" to cause "embarrassment to the security forces," to "weaken the government's control" and to "undermine the overall security situation." Similarly, local and international opinion can be "unduly and immediately influenced by enemy propaganda" and insurgent "media manipulation."[17] The manual notes that authoritarian regimes find it easier to "crush such open dissent" and complains of "the growing trend towards political groups using civil liberties and human rights to lower the tolerance of the public for harsher [counterinsurgency] measures." The broad definition of "subversion" and the paranoid mindset of counterinsurgents often lead to the targets of military action expanding beyond armed insurgents to any civilian groups perceived to be backing the insurgency's aims. "The security forces' operations must focus on eliminating the insurgents' subversive and support organizations." Elsewhere, the manual refers to the need to "root out" and "destroy" such organizations in areas under government control.[18]

Although the manual stresses that all military actions should minimize "collateral damage"–lest they provide grist for the "insurgent propaganda machine"–and that security forces should respect human rights and operate within the law, in practice militaries trying to suppress insurgencies have rarely played by these rules. With the difficulty in distinguishing between combatants and non-combatants, military forces fighting counterinsurgency wars have often resorted to political assassinations, massacres and other serious human rights abuses–not only against suspected insurgents, but against civilian "subversives" as well. Local security forces, trained and armed by the occupying military, have carried out the worst abuses.

Canada's counterinsurgency manual derives largely from U.S. practices, forged in the flames of previous imperial wars. Counterinsurgency warfare has been conducted against national liberation movements in Vietnam and Algeria in the 1960s, against guerrillas and social movements in South America in the 1970s, and against peasant-based rebels fighting for land reform during the near-genocidal civil wars of El Salvador and Guatemala in the 1980s. It has always been a bloody affair. With the rise of counterinsurgency warfare in the post-war period, "assassination, sabotage, kidnapping, torture, the overthrow of foreign governments, and other terroristic activities" became "intrinsic" parts of U.S. national security policy, according to historian Michael McClintock. In order to rationalize the ruthless methods of counterinsurgency warfare, resistance movements have had to be demonized. The resort to what amounted to state terrorism, McClintock explains, was "justified time and again as necessary to combat communist insurgency and, more recently, terrorism–as the only effective response to the barbarism ascribed to, or projected onto, our enemies–be they Sandinistas or the PLO."[19]

Afghanistan: Democracy at the Barrel of a Gun

Less than one month after the September 11 attacks, the U.S. invaded Afghanistan under the name Operation Enduring Freedom. (The name was originally "Operation Infinite Justice," but was changed after George W. Bush provoked international outrage by referring to it as a "crusade.") The U.S.-led invasion was accompanied by many promises to build democracy and protect women's rights. After sweeping aside the Taliban, however, fulfilling these promises was not the principal concern of the occupiers. After 9/11, U.S. foreign policy makers set in motion long-standing plans to consolidate their military presence and influence in West Asia and the Middle East. The U.S. sought to establish more pliant, pro-Western regimes in the region and expand its network of military bases, as part of a strategy to exert control over the region and its tremendous energy resources.[20]

Afghanistan was and is essential to these broader geopolitical designs. Before being named President of Afghanistan in December 2001, Hamid Karzai had been an executive with UNOCAL, an oil company seeking to build a pipeline across Afghanistan. President Karzai was placed in his position by the American envoy Zalmay Khalilzad, another figure with ties to UNOCAL. With a suitable regime in place, the U.S. was soon signing accords with the "democratic" Karzai administration for "enduring" U.S. bases in Afghanistan. Immediately after the invasion, the Karzai government took steps to resume work on the Turkmenistan-Afghanistan-Pakistan-India (TAPI) pipeline. The project aimed to bypass Iranian and Russian pipeline routes, delivering natural gas from the Caspian Sea to the world market via Afghanistan.[21]

While Afghans were generally relieved to see the end of the Taliban regime, public opinion surveys indicated a "deep distrust" of the new U.S.-backed administration. The Karzai government installed included warlords (the "Northern Alliance") who had committed numerous atrocities and destroyed much of the country during the 1992-1996 civil war. The chaos of this period was largely what led to the Taliban rising to power. The actual outcome of the invasion was to replace one group of fundamentalist warlords with another one: at least as fundamentalist and violent, but more willing to go along with the American agenda.

The first months of the Karzai government amply justified popular fears: Warlord-ministers and their armed thugs bulldozed houses and seized land from peasants, intimidated political rivals and skirmished with one another for control of territory. Their militias raped women and extorted small businesspersons with impunity, while others enforced Taliban-style "moral" restrictions. "We were happy after the collapse of the Taliban ... We thought there would be peace and stability. But nothing has changed ... [Afghan warlords] fight among themselves for their own goals. Their victims are innocent people. We are very angry," 25-year-old Tajik Rasood told journalists in July 2002, after he was wounded in the cross fire of a battle between local warlords.[22] In addition to the depredations of pro-

Karzai warlords, Afghans endured an abusive and corrupt Afghan police force, rigged elections, and graft, incompetence and nepotism within the state bureaucracy. These factors steadily turned Afghans against the new, "democratic" regime in Kabul.

What Karzai's government lacked in domestic legitimacy, it attempted to purchase through external funding. To build popular support for the warlord-dominated regime, occupation forces turned on the aid tap. CIDA pledged $1.2 billion from 2001 to 2011 to support the "transition to democracy" in Afghanistan. "In terms of numbers, starting in 2001 and for the next few years, Afghanistan will be the recipient of the biggest funding campaign ever approved by CIDA," the Montreal-based Development & Peace observed in a planning document. Most of the aid, the document noted, was bypassing the corrupt structures of the Karzai administration, so *"this new context opens up ... new possibilities for financial growth and dialogue with the [Canadian] government."*[23] (original emphasis) In the words of author Tariq Ali, NGOs "descended on the country like locusts after the occupation."[24] Only 46 international NGOs were operating in Afghanistan in 1999. By November 2002, the number had shot up to 350. By February 2007, there were some 1,100 registered NGOs, foreign and local, including many major Canadian NGOs.[25]

NGOs played a key role in implementing the Karzai government's development plans, including its "flagship" rural development program, the National Solidarity Program (NSP). Hastily created in 2003 by the World Bank, CIDA and other donors in anticipation of the following year's Presidential elections, the NSP was intended as a "participatory, grassroots" initiative serving to reach out and build political support among the rural population for the central government. CIDA contributed $13 million to the NSP, and 20 Afghan and international NGOs, including Oxfam, CARE and the Aga Khan Foundation, were selected as "facilitating partners" to help with the creation of Community Development Councils, through which small block grants for development projects of the community's choice would be distributed. The NGOs first assisted with the creation of councils in villages, and then with the design and implementation of projects.[26]

Despite the proliferation of NGO programs, the living conditions of ordinary Afghans failed to improve. "All development indicators show that poverty reduction efforts have had little impact on the daily life of most Afghans," the UN Office of the High Commissioner for Human Rights concluded in March 2010. "A key driver of poverty in Afghanistan is the abuse of power," the UN briefing explained, with the newly Afghan elites using "their influence to drive the public agenda for their own personal or vested interests." Canada's unflinching support for "mistrusted Afghan power-holders" had served to further entrench "abusive, dysfunctional, and corrupt political structures."[27] For Western-educated Afghans, however, the NGO boom that arrived with the occupation was quite lucrative. The influx of NGOs created a privileged, internationally-linked stratum within Afghan society, overwhelmingly located in Kabul, the capital:

> A reputed 10,000 NGO staff have turned Kabul into Klondike during the goldrush, building office blocks, driving up rents, cruising about in armoured jeeps and spending stupefying sums of other people's money, essentially on themselves. They take orders only from some distant agency, but then the same goes for the American army, NATO, the UN, the EU and the supposedly sovereign Afghan government.[28]

Night Raids and Development Aid

Remnants of the Taliban and other Islamist parties continued to sporadically attack government targets and clash with NATO troops in the South, but by 2003 many Western observers were confidently declaring Afghanistan to be a "post-conflict" country. Instead of dying down, however, fighting progressively intensified. As the foreign presence became more pervasive and the occupation dragged on, opposition to the foreign occupiers gained momentum and by 2005 had developed into full-blown insurgency. Taliban forces won the support of disaffected local communities, village leaders and local imams who felt excluded from power. The "neo-Taliban" reinvented themselves as a "liberation movement," tapping into widespread frustration with growing poverty and inequality, police and warlord abuses and the venality and corruption of the NATO-backed regime.[29] "[T]hough the Taliban have been entirely conflated with al-Qaeda in the Western media," Tariq Ali explains, "most of their supporters are driven by local concerns; their political evolution would be more likely to parallel that of Pakistan's domesticated Islamists if the invaders were to leave."[30]

In response to the deteriorating security situation, U.S. and NATO forces launched a counterinsurgency offensive. Initially, due to the shortage of troops on the ground, NATO forces had stepped up the frequency of air strikes, causing numerous civilian casualties.[31] Under pressure from the Karzai government, NATO strategy turned from aerial bombing to more targeted attacks with ground forces. The neo-Taliban did not hesitate to kill anyone working for the Karzai government or the occupation forces, and

NATO forces responded in kind. U.S. and Canadian Special Forces troops worked alongside elite Afghan commando units to hunt down suspected supporters of the insurgency. Operating with near total impunity, these units carried out frequent "night raids," breaking into houses to abduct or kill suspected insurgents. To gather intelligence, Afghan jailers and their foreign allies resorted to torturing detainees. Frustrated by an elusive enemy and an uncooperative population, foreign troops in some instances engaged in blind killing. Members of the U.S. 5th Stryker brigade, for example, dubbed themselves the "Kill Team" and hunted ordinary Afghans for sport, murdering farmers and taking parts of the victims' bodies as "trophies."[32]

In August 2005, 2,500 Canadian soldiers were deployed to the rural areas of Kandahar Province in the South, a hotbed of insurgency. Simultaneously, development aid was reconfigured towards winning the "hearts and minds" of Afghan villagers. The Canadian Forces created a Provincial Reconstruction Team (PRT) to put the government's 3-D concept into action. The purpose of the Kandahar PRT, which included CIDA personnel, was to align diplomatic and development efforts with the objectives of the counterinsurgency fight. Through Canada's PRT, the military engaged in reconstruction projects, and also financed NGO-implemented projects. "One unique aspect of the new [Canadian military] strategy is the way that development and humanitarian aid are being used specifically for the purpose of building loyalty towards coalition forces and democratic reforms," military historian Sean Maloney wrote in March 2006. "The strategic use of aid may offend some, but this approach is gaining credibility and has been adopted by CIDA and Foreign Affairs."[33]

Canadian NGOs integrated their activities into the war effort in Afghanistan. In 2004, Canadian NGOs were consulted by the military and CIDA officials about the creation of the Kandahar PRT.[34] According to a 2008 report on NGO-military relations commissioned by British and European NGOs entitled "Afghan Hearts, Afghan Minds," development NGOs are confronted by "politician-donors and NATO representatives who pressure them to operate in strategically prioritised provinces in order to align with 'hearts and minds' (WHAM) strategies."[35] With 50% of CIDA funding from 2008-2011 earmarked for Kandahar province, Canadian NGOs were pushed to move from the North and Central regions towards the rebellious South, despite massive security risks.[36] According to a 2007 Parliamentary report, NGOs often "work intimately with military support already in the field."[37]

NGOs became a vital source of intelligence for the military, functioning as eyes and ears for the occupation at the local level. U.S. Special Representative for Afghanistan and Pakistan Richard Holbrooke estimated that 90% of the coalition forces' intelligence in Afghanistan came from aid organizations on the ground.[38] A June 2008 Senate Committee report observed that Canadian troops regularly liaise with NGOs "to determine whether they need help with security," adding that "the degree of cooperation and intelligence sharing between different allied agencies in theatre is reaching unprecedented levels."[39]

Development aid was calibrated to improve the image of the Afghan government and the occupation forces, and Canadian military personnel openly boasted about deploying aid resources to defeat the insurgency. "It's a useful counterinsurgency tool," Lieutenant-Colonel Tom Doucette, commander of Canada's PRT, said of CIDA's work in Afghanistan.[40] By shifting the population's allegiances, development aid aimed to reduce the likelihood of Afghan villagers giving support or sanctuary to insurgent fighters. "The war will be won in the hinterland, with the people," said Colonel Steven Bowes, a Canadian PRT commander. "The enemy uses these areas as sanctuaries, and conventional military operations can only succeed up to a point. Projects that improve the basic living standard are a start, but we are not into development for development's sake."[41]

On the ground, NATO forces wielded aid coercively so as to extract greater cooperation from locals. U.S. troops distributing food and water made it clear to communities they were "helping" that further humanitarian and development aid would only be given as a reward for supporting the U.S. military.[42] In 2004, coalition forces distributed leaflets that threatened to cut off assistance unless the population provided information on al-Qaeda and Taliban leaders."[43] Canadian commanders also did not hesitate to use their control over development aid to pressure communities for support. After a roadside bomb attack hit his convoy near Deh-e-Bagh, a village in Kandahar province, Canadian General Jonathan Vance demanded an immediate meeting with the village elders. Vance spent over 50 minutes berating the elders for not preventing the attack, telling them: "If we keep blowing up on the roads I'm going to stop doing development."[44]

Control of development resources allowed NATO forces to exert considerable power over rural Afghans. Far from empowering the poor, development work controlled by the military served to manipulate the poverty of Afghan villagers. A March 2010 *Médecins sans frontières* (MSF) report noted that NGOs and other "integrated civilian agencies" were being used for counterinsurgency objectives:

In such a context, aid becomes "threat-based" rather than "needs-based"–that is, it is deployed according to military objectives not impartial assessments of humanitarian needs. Assistance thus becomes just another weapon at the service of the military, which can condition, deny or reward relief to those who fall in or out of line with its larger security agenda.[45]

Humanitarian Camouflage: Development and Warfare

NATO military officials described development projects–building schools, digging wells, providing medical help, establishing agricultural laboratories and drip-irrigation projects–as "security measures" that helped to "build a rapport with the villagers through education and employment." As Nosheen Ali notes:

> This new militarism–which the counterinsurgency doctrine calls "armed social work"–has blurred the lines between military warfare and civilian development. Because aid workers are increasingly seen as combatants, local and international NGO work has become extremely dangerous, aggravating civilian miseries caused by the war.[46]

By putting schools and hospitals on the frontlines, the counterinsurgency strategy effectively tied NGOs–both in practice and in locals' perceptions– ever closer to the military occupation. Attacks on aid personnel led to a 50% reduction in the areas covered by NGOs over the 2004-2008 period, limiting the operational space of development NGOs to those places where NATO forces were militarily dominant, reinforcing the association between aid workers and military forces.[47] Despite scrupulously maintaining its independence from NATO, MSF was forced to pull out of Afghanistan in 2004 after 5 staff members of the humanitarian organization were killed. According to MSF, ordinary Afghans are very sensitive to the politics of NGO funding. MSF teams working with Afghan refugees in Pakistan were asked repeatedly by displaced people: "Where do you get your funds?"[48]

With growing attacks on aid workers, many development NGOs discovered the downsides of the militarization of aid. NGO representatives issued statements denying that they were "force multipliers" or "soft power" instruments of the occupation forces and called for "urgent action" to preserve the operational distinction between NGOs and the military. Development NGOs working in Afghanistan began trying to make a distinction between "good" civilian development and "bad" military-led humanitarian and reconstruction initiatives like the PRTs. Some NGOs sought to avoid working directly with the military in the field. As one report on security issued by 11 organizations working in Afghanistan including CARE, Oxfam and Save the Children stressed, NGOs "rely on local acceptance to ensure their security, for which *their perceived identity as independent and impartial is critical.*"[49]

From an NGO perspective, the blurring of the line between development and warfare was caused by troops engaging directly in reconstruction and humanitarian projects through the PRTs. U.S. Special Forces were known to use a kind of "humanitarian camouflage," sending plainclothes troops into rural areas in the same kind of white 4x4 trucks as used by development NGOs. NGO lobbying eventually put a stop to this practice.[50] Moreover, attacks against aid workers did not come only from neo-Taliban insurgents. NGOs seeking to get out from under the wing of NATO military power faced the threat of violence from coalition troops as well. Attempts by NGOs to negotiate entry to insurgent-held areas have led to "targeting by and/or hostile behaviour" by coalition forces, according to the "Afghan Hearts, Afghan Minds" report. On some occasions, NGOs that hired staff members with relationships to insurgent groups in order to gain access found that NATO troops "target their staff assuming they are combatants."

> Most recently UNICEF and the International Committee of the Red Cross (ICRC) have been able to negotiate ceasefires with the Taliban to conduct vaccination days–which have been reportedly disrupted on two occasions by the activities of the international military rather than the Taliban.[51]

The distinction between warfare and development work was effectively erased by Western counterinsurgency operations in Afghanistan. But by placing blame for convergence of aid and warfare exclusively on the military, most NGO critiques conveniently concealed their own complicity in the process.

Given the key role military officers played in directing the development initiatives of both the Karzai government and CIDA, NGO efforts to distinguish between civilian- and military-led development were meaningless. According to Duane Bratt, the Canadian military leadership "not only linked the combat mission to the parallel goals of diplomacy and development," but also "made sure that the [Canadian Forces] was the lead agency in all three Ds."[52] Through the Strategic Advisory Team, a group of military officers were assigned to posts within various important departments of the Afghan government, which extended the Canadian military's reach to the top levels of the Karzai administration. Military officers reporting directly to Canadian Forces high command planned and executed the national government's development efforts alongside Afghan government officials. Lieutenant-Commander Rob Ferguson, one of the Team's members, explained: "No other country is as strategically placed as Canada with respect to influencing Afghanistan's development."[53]

Working alongside the Karzai government, NGOs and their CIDA-funded programs were firmly aligned with the military's counterinsurgency objectives. According to the Canadian Council for International Cooperation (CCIC), the Aga Khan Development Network "works closely with the Government of Afghanistan."Mennonite Economic Development Associates "enjoys the support of … the Ministry of Rehabilitation and Rural Development." And in 2002, World Vision Canada "began working in partnership with the Government of Afghanistan."[54] Development & Peace described its programs in Afghanistan as efforts to "help pacify" the country.[55] According to the "Afghan Hearts, Afghan Minds" report, development NGOs have had little choice but to collaborate with the Afghan government: "As a result of donor emphasis on state building and development approaches which channel funding through central government, NGOs have been gently coerced into joining national, government-aligned aid programmes"[56]

The National Solidarity Program (NSP) exemplified the integration of military aims and NGO projects. Though ostensibly a "national" development initiative of the Karzai government, the Canadian military worked intimately in the design and implementation of the NSP at every level. Canadian officers from the Strategic Advisory Team were "heavily involved" in planning the NSP and other rural development initiatives nominally headed by the Ministry of Rehabilitation and Rural Development.[57] Military forces also "played a critical role in the success of the National Solidarity Program" by providing security for its NGO and governmental implementing agencies, "an example of the military making development possible in areas where it could not otherwise proceed."[58]

The NSP helped the military to acquire a more solid foothold in participating rural villages. After community development councils were set up by the NSP, Provincial Reconstruction Teams channelled funding to these bodies, and NGO facilitating partners encouraged locals to apply for funding from the PRTs.[59] The "Afghan Hearts, Afghan Minds" report points to the NSP as an example of the tangled web of relationships between the military, the Afghan authorities and development NGOs:

> One example is the NSP, which provides small-scale project funding to local communities within a national framework. Just as NGOs were coerced into joining the NSP–and by extension, in the eyes of some, declaring solidarity with the government–[international] NGOs also feel under pressure from their respective governments and militaries to move into insecure areas where the different national PRTs operate. Indeed, several PRTs have sought to align themselves with and support the NSP and other national development programmes.[60]

Most accounts of the NSP argue that it was fairly effective at getting resources to the village level. Whatever its merits as a rural development program, the NGO-supported NSP was straight out of "orthodox counterinsurgency theory," according to John A. Nagl, one of the authors of the U.S. military's counterinsurgency manual. In a March 2009 policy briefing, Nagl emphasized that "a troop surge alone is not enough to win the war," and lauded the NSP as "one of the few initiatives from Kabul to have generated significant goodwill among rural communities." NGOs working through the "participatory" NSP were in effect "buttressing the Afghan government's legitimacy," wrote Nagl.[61]

One of the few voices to argue that NGOs were not innocent in this process was MSF. In its March 2010 report on the militarization of aid, MSF denounced in no uncertain terms "the co-optation of the aid system by the international coalition–at times *with the complicity of the aid community itself*–to the point where it is difficult to distinguish aid efforts from political and military action." Because many NGOs in Afghanistan had participated in the instrumentalization of development work for counterinsurgency ends, the report observed, "claims of neutrality, independence and impartiality can at times seem hypocritical or simply invocations aimed at reinforcing an organization's own illusions of purity."

> Neutrality is often abandoned for a so-called "pragmatic" approach by organizations hoping to participate in the integration of development and nation-building efforts. ... Independence is also compromised by the need for financial resources as many aid organizations rely on state-funding for survival. This gives donor countries undue leverage

for co-opting assistance in service of their political needs and leads beneficiaries to question the motives of aid workers.[62]

Blowback Against "NGO Warlords"

Counterinsurgency warfare appears to have poured fuel on the fire rather than quenching the flames of rebellion. Harsh military tactics steadily turned swaths of the Afghan population against the occupation. Indiscriminate by nature, air strikes produced regular civilian body counts, leading even President Karzai to plead with his foreign allies to change tactics. Poor intelligence produced many innocent victims of abductions or extra-judicial executions killed or arrested during night raids, while angering villagers. For the counterinsurgency planners, reliance on NGOs had perverse unintended consequences as well.

The parallel invasion of NGOs has not always endeared Afghans to the foreign presence. University-educated Afghans (less than 1% of the population has any university education) working for NGOs and other international agencies were one of the few social groups that strongly supported the occupation forces. While government civil servants were paid $60 per month on average, Afghans working for NGOs earned an average of $1,000 per month.[63] "Those with regular employment–whose children go to school, who can buy cars and kitchen appliances, who are fuelling the building boom in Afghanistan's largest city–do not want to go back to Taliban days."[64] While educated urbanites directly benefited from the NGO boom, those at the bottom of the social pyramid did not. According to a November 2007 Parliamentary report, the poor resented both the direct inequality heightened by NGO workers' inflated salaries and the indirect impact NGO spending had on the urban cost of living:

> At the local level, perceptions of development workers as receiving excessive wages, living in large homes, and generally living apart from the rest of society are not uncommon and result in local resentment and questions about the value derived from donor funding. Some of these views are reinforced by the inflationary effect of such a large, well-paid group on the local economy, making it that much more difficult for local residents to survive.[65]

The channelling of aid through NGOs was intended as a way to avoid the corruption of the Karzai government, but ordinary Afghans came to regard NGOs as just another layer of corrupt elites living off of the foreign occupation. "In an alarming sign of public perceptions," writes Lara Olson in the Journal of Military and Strategic Studies, "the term 'NGO warlords' has emerged to describe foreigners who rent expensive homes in Kabul, just like the warlords of the past."[66] According to Tariq Ali, Afghan politicians used denunciations of NGOs as a way of gaining popularity: "Even supporters of the occupation have lost patience with these bodies, and some of the most successful candidates in the 2005 National Assembly elections made an attack on them a centre-piece of their campaigns."[67] When an American military vehicle killed several pedestrians on the streets of Kabul in May 2006, the tragedy sparked mass protests against the foreign presence in the country. According to Jude Howell and Jeremy Lind, the protesters' anger was directed not only at the occupation forces but at NGOs as well:

> The protest quickly spiralled as hundreds of people rampaged through the streets. NGO offices were attacked and burned. The offices of CARE International were burned down, whereas others, such as Oxfam, saw their offices pillaged. In response, many international NGOs tightened their security arrangements, such as by removing signboards outside their offices, increasing the number of security guards, appointing security coordinators and relocating offices to less conspicuous locations.[68]

Afghanistan's ostentatious "NGO class" created by the occupation risked losing the "hearts and minds" of those supposed to benefit from their projects.

The Canadian Forces' combat mission in Afghanistan is officially over (though nearly 1,000 soldiers have stayed on in a "training" role), but military officials affirm that the enormous resources invested by the government in the transformation of Canada's armed forces will be used again in the near future. "Let's not kid ourselves," Gen. Andrew Leslie, author of Canada's counterinsurgency manual, told journalists. "It is logical to expect that we will go somewhere fairly similar to Afghanistan and do much the same sort of activity."[69] Putting development NGOs to work for military ends is not likely to end after Afghanistan. In April 2010, Bob Johnston, deputy head of CIDA's Afghan Task Force, described how five years of intense operations in Afghanistan strengthened the bond between the military and aid personnel. "After Afghanistan, we now have a fairly large pool of people who have gone through a very regimented form of training working with military." The Afghanistan experience changed CIDA and its associated NGOs working in the country, Johnston reported, creating "an expeditionary force ready to go somewhere else."[70]

Haiti: Terror and Celebration

"Terrorism" in the Middle East was not the only preoccupation of Western military officials in the post-9/11 world. Seen through the same dark lens of national security, popular resistance to neoliberalism in the Global South was also a growing concern for the military brass. In Latin America, for instance, General James Hill, head of Southern Command of the U.S. Army, identified "radical populism" (along with terrorism and drugs) as a danger to "hemispheric security." Speaking to the U.S. House of Representatives armed services committee meeting in March 2004, Gen. Hill explained the nature of the "emerging threat":

> Some leaders in the region are tapping into deep-seated frustrations of the failure of democratic reforms to deliver expected goods and services. By tapping into these frustrations, which run concurrently with frustrations caused by social and economic inequality, the leaders are at the same time able to reinforce their radical positions by inflaming anti-U.S. sentiment.[71]

Venezuela, Bolivia and Haiti were given as specific examples of this dangerous trend, but Gen. Hill also pointed to the general questioning of "the validity of neoliberal reforms" in the region. Increasingly, the dispossessed masses created by neoliberalism found themselves in the crosshairs of Western militaries.

If the Kandahar mission in Afghanistan is Canada's most prominent experience with counterinsurgency warfare, Canada's role in the occupation of Haiti is among the most obscure. In the counterinsurgency manual, Canadian Forces troops were described as fighting a "criminally-based insurgency" in Haiti. This was not a reference to the heavily armed force of former soldiers and ex-death squad members controlling much of the country following the coup. The "rebels," despite their well-known involvement in drug trafficking and other criminal activity, were allowed to retain their arms and continued to operate freely after the arrival of the U.S.-led Multinational Interim Force (MIF). Canadian troops, like their American counterparts, saw themselves engaged in a counterinsurgency war with organizations in the slums of Port-au-Prince. These slums were home to much of the country's poor majority and were strongly supportive of the Lavalas movement, the main political obstacle to neoliberalism in the country (see Chapter 6). Canada's military experience in Haiti provided the impetus, along with Afghanistan, for writing the counterinsurgency manual.

In the case of Haiti, development NGOs' most important contribution to winning "hearts and minds" was on the home front. Though larger NGOs such as Save the Children or World Vision generally avoided speaking out on the political situation in Haiti, "progressive" development NGOs such as Development & Peace and Alternatives were the most aggressive in accusing Lavalas of being behind criminal activity in the capital and calling for greater repression against the slums. Through press releases, contacts with journalists, testimony before Parliament, public conferences, newsletters, reports and other publications, Canadian NGOs denigrated the popular movement as "criminals" and "bandits." NGOs and their Haiti-based partners alike accused the UN mission of being too soft on the slums, denouncing its "pro-Lavalas" bias. With seemingly "progressive" institutions lined up behind the coup, domestic opposition to Canada's role in Haiti from the anti-war movement and other sectors on the Left was muted, especially in Quebec.

Haiti's Interim Years: "Non-governmental Government"

After President Aristide was removed from the country on a U.S. government plane on February 29, 2004, the occupying nations (U.S., Canada and France) installed an interim government headed by Gerard Latortue, a Florida businessman, on March 17, 2004. Officially hailed as a neutral caretaker administration, Latortue's government was dominated by representatives of the CIDA-funded civic opposition and was staunchly anti-Lavalas. Several leading figures in the Group of 184–an opposition umbrella group created by the U.S. government and funded by CIDA– joined the Latortue regime after the coup, including Justice Minister Bernard Gousse, Minister of Industry Danièle Saint-Lot and Minister of Education Pierre Buteau.[72] Social democratic NGO leaders also accepted posts in the interim government. Oxfam Quebec's in-country representative Philippe Mathieu became the Minister of Agriculture and Natural Resources; the *Mouvman Peyizan Papay's* (MPP) leader Chavannes Jean-Baptiste became one of the Prime Minister's consultants and was appointed to chair a Council for Peasant Affairs created by the interim government;[73] and Yves Andre Wainwright, a leading member of the *Plateforme haïtienne de plaidoyer pour un développement alternatif*

(PAPDA), was named Minister of the Environment. Both the MPP and PAPDA are groups supported by Alternatives and Development & Peace. Danielle Magloire, head of CONAP—a coalition of anti-Lavalas women's groups funded by CIDA and the Canadian Embassy—was nominated to the Council of the Wise, the 7-person body that appointed the Interim Government. Magloire later became the director of Rights & Democracy's Haiti office.[74] NGO personnel were so strongly represented in the interim regime that some dubbed Gerard Latortue's adminstration a "non-governmental government."[75]

The newly installed Latortue regime set about dismantling the modest social programs established during Aristide's second term and turned back the clock on the achievements of the democratic period. Subsidies for Haiti's impoverished farmers were slashed, the minimum wage was reduced and a successful adult literacy program was dismantled. Thousands of peasants in the Artibonite were evicted from their lands by local landlords and their hired thugs—in some cases supported by police—effectively reversing the limited land reform program that had been enacted in the last years of Preval's government (1999-2001).[76]

Neoliberal reforms got back on track, as the interim government began preparing the ground for the privatization of Haiti's state enterprises. The Interim Cooperation Framework, a document outlining the priorities of the Latortue government and the donor countries, touted "private sector participation" in state enterprises: "The transition period ... provide[s] a window of opportunity for implementing economic governance reforms ... that may be hard for a future government to undo." Canada helped draft the Interim Cooperation Framework and donated $147 million in support of it. The interim regime gave large businesses a three-year tax holiday. Former soldiers from Haiti's disbanded army—which had a long record of human rights abuses—were paid $30 million in "back wages."[77]

The dark days of state repression against the poor returned with a vengeance. The "rebels" took over Haiti's cities and towns including Port-au-Prince, casting a pall of terror over the country. Names of supporters of the overthrown government were read on the radio; many of the individuals named were subsequently hunted down. Bullet-riddled bodies piled up in the morgues or in mass graves at the *Piste d'Aviation*, which was used as a dumping ground for bodies during the first coup against Aristide. Former soldiers and death squad leaders established ad hoc courts and carried out public executions. Thousands became refugees in their own country, fleeing to Port-au-Prince and changing locations each night so as not to get caught, or hiding in the mountains and subsisting as best they could. "Today, in the streets of Port-au-Prince and in other cities and towns of Haiti, we have been seeing the kind of murder and mayhem that characterized the country between 1991 and 1994, following a violent coup d'etat carried out by Haiti's army, leading to three years of brutal de facto military rule," Haiti expert Robert Maguire told a U.S. congressional hearing three days into the coup d'état.[78]

An estimated 500-900 people were killed in Port-au-Prince in March 2004 alone, with hundreds more killed in other cities.[79] Numerous independent human rights investigations confirmed the political nature of the violence. After sending a delegation to the country one month after the coup, Amnesty International reported that "the persecution of those associated with the Fanmi Lavalas regime is widespread."

> Supporters of former President Aristide have suffered abuses ranging from threats to kidnapping and extrajudicial killings, especially in the poorer areas of Port-au-Prince where the former President garnered most support. Many of the victims were members of grassroots organizations who had been victims of human rights violations during the 1991-1994 military regime and who had been involved in actions seeking redress for these crimes, and who had also become politically involved in support of the Fanmi Lavalas regime.[80]

As former soldiers returned to public life in the country, politically motivated rapes increased massively. Rape was a common tactic of intimidation and humiliation used by the military against women involved in or associated with the popular movement during the first coup. Rapists convicted of crimes against women under Lavalas administrations were freed from jail by the rebels (along with the rest of the prison population) and returned to torment their female accusers and the judges who had put them behind bars.[81] The medical journal *The Lancet* published a study that estimated some 35,000 women were raped in the 2004-2006 coup period in Port-au-Prince alone.[82]

The campaign of terror waged by the rebels received the active support of the interim government. Three days after being appointed, Prime Minister Gerard Latortue openly embraced the rebels in a public appearance in Gonaives, hailing them as "freedom fighters." David Lee, a Canadian diplomat, endorsed Latortue's move, saying: "We're trying to encourage reconciliation." The Minister of Interior—himself a former member of the military—announced that the rebels who attacked Aristide's government would be integrated into the police force. A faction of the rebels declared the Haitian army to be re-established and with the support of residents set up a base in the upper-class neighborhood of Pétionville.[83] While U.S. Marines made a show of exerting their supremacy over the "rebels," occupying forces made little effort to disarm them, or to stop the killings. From the first days after the coup, the occupation forces joined in the repression, systematically targeting Haiti's popular movement as "subversive." In order to intimidate Lavalas supporters and stifle opposition to the coup, Multinational Interim Force (MIF) troops conducted "heavily armed patrols in the poorest areas," which included house-to-house searches and arrests. The patrols had the effect of "raising tensions" in the targeted neighbourhoods, according to the National Lawyers Guild.[84] Dozens of people were killed during "violent searches conducted by the MIF in particular in poorer neighbourhoods of Port-au-Prince," Amnesty International reported. On March 12, U.S. Marines killed as many as 12 people in Bel Air, a Lavalas stronghold. Residents claimed the victims were innocent bystanders, whose bodies were subsequently taken away by MIF troops. Though the MIF claimed to have killed only two people who had fired at their troops, no weapons were found on the scene.[85]

Ostensibly targeting "pro-Lavalas gangs," MIF raids rarely distinguished between armed Aristide supporters and unarmed Lavalas activists and political leaders. On the night of May 9, U.S. Marines violently broke into folk singer Annette "*So Ann*" Auguste's house and arrested the 60-year old folk singer and her entire family. According to an MIF spokesman, Auguste was targeted because she represented a threat to "MIF forces and stability and security in Haiti," although the raid found no weapons. Auguste, an outspoken opponent of the coup and a leading member of Fanmi Lavalas, remained in jail for over two years and was deemed a "prisoner of conscience" by Amnesty International. MIF troops also aggressively raided the offices of *Tet Kole*, a peasant organization, and *Anten Ouvriye*, a trade union.[86]

The 500 Canadian troops deployed as part of the 2,700-person MIF used similar tactics to intimidate pro-Lavalas neighbourhoods. Researcher Athena Kolbe interviewed victims of human rights abuses who described Canadian troops as having conducted house-to-house searches looking for "Lavalas *chimères*" and other Lavalas supporters. In one instance, Canadian troops uttered death threats to residents who refused to cooperate by naming Lavalas activists.[87] "Most disturbingly," noted Amnesty International, after the coup, escaped criminals released by the rebels during their rampage across the country began "working together with the Haitian police and the MIF to identify people associated with the Fanmi Lavalas regime, who are in some cases abducted or killed."[88]

The Politics of Human Rights

The prominent CIDA-funded Haitian human rights groups (NCHR-Haiti, CARLI, CEDH) that had relentlessly denounced human rights abuses under Aristide's government abruptly went silent with regard to the newly-installed interim government. "Six weeks after the February coup, as the morgues were overflowing with bodies, these same groups had failed to identify let alone investigate a single case in which a Lavalassian was the victim rather than the perpetrator of violence."[89]

Incredibly, a joint report on the first 45 days of the Latortue regime by NCHR-Haiti and the *Plateforme des organizations haïtiennes des droits humains* (POHDH) declared there had been "a decrease in the number of human rights abuses" and that such cases were "more isolated than before."[90] When challenged by members of a U.S. human rights delegation on why they were not investigating widespread reports of police killings in the slums, NCHR-Haiti explained that they "lacked access" to these areas because of their active role in the opposition movement. After the coup, the offices of NCHR-Haiti were adorned with "wanted" posters of Aristide and his ministers.[91] As late as July 2006, in the face of overwhelming evidence collected by less biased human rights observers, NCHR-Haiti still claimed that the Latortue government was "not directly implicated in political violence."[92]

NCHR-Haiti in particular helped to create the witch-hunt climate that existed after the coup. In March 2004, representatives of NCHR-Haiti regularly took to the airwaves of Haiti's radio stations, reading out the names of Lavalas supporters, whom they referred to as "criminals," and calling for their arrest. The interim government's police and the rebels relentlessly hunted down individuals named on these lists; many were arrested or killed, others disappeared, and many more were forced into hiding. On April 26, 2004 NCHR was joined by PAPDA, CONAP and other social democratic NGOs at a demonstration outside the national palace calling for the arrest of former Prime Minister Yvon Neptune and other leading members of Aristide's government.[93] Yvon Neptune was jailed for over 2 years on the basis of NCHR-Haiti's accusations and nearly died on hunger strike in prison. Neptune demanded that prosecutors either lay charges against him or release him. Thierry Fagart, head of the UN Human Rights Commission in Haiti, criticized NCHR-

Haiti's inability to produce any evidence implicating Neptune as "a real failure," demonstrating "a lack of responsibility." "I'm not comfortable with this kind of behaviour for this case. ... [T]he problem in this country ... is that most human rights NGOs are completely involved in politics."[94]

The blatant partisanship displayed by NCHR-Haiti was too much for Jocelyn McCalla, Executive Director of NCHR, its New York-based parent organization. McCalla called Neptune's treatment "a travesty of justice" and demanded his prompt release by the authorities. McCalla admonished NCHR-Haiti for being in "the dangerous position of defending a dysfunctional Haitian judicial system which delivers little other than injustice," and announced that the NCHR was severing all ties with its branch in Haiti. "Neither [Executive Director Pierre] Esperance, nor any member of the staff of NCHR-Haiti, speak for or on behalf of the National Coalition for Haitian Rights (NCHR), its board or its staff," McCalla declared in a March 11 press release. "We hope that in the near future NCHR-Haiti will adopt a new name that more accurately reflects its standing and mission in Haitian society."[95] Chastened, NCHR-Haiti renamed itself the *Réseau National pour la Défence des Droits Humains* (RNDDH–National Network for the Defence of Human Rights) shortly thereafter.

Partisanship on the question of human rights extended to CONAP, *Enfofamn*, *Famn Yo La*, *Solidarité Famn Ayisyen* (SOFA) and other elite-led women's rights NGOs. CIDA had spent millions on women's rights advocacy under Aristide, and under the interim government the Agency spent another $1.4 million for NGO projects dedicated to women's rights through its Kore Famn Fund alone. Yet in the wake of the coup, according to feminist activist Anne Sosin, "there was virtually no structure in place to respond to women who were victims of gender-specific abuses, particularly rape." The class divide between poor Haitian women and the elite-run, CIDA-funded women's groups that claimed to represent them was debilitating for the work of defending women's rights after the coup:

> There were very few women's organizations connected to women at the grassroots level. Groups that had been very vocal in denouncing abuses while Aristide was in power became silent after the coup. Moreover, there was a sense that certain women victims from poor neighborhoods were not welcome in these organizations–because of where they lived, because of their impoverished economic status and because they identified themselves with the Lavalas political party.[96]

Amnesty International remarked upon the flagrant partisanship of Haiti's foreign-funded human rights NGOs, which were "active in denouncing abuses committed under the Aristide period," but under the interim government "do not seem inclined to investigate abuses committed against pro-Aristide groups, dismissing them as mostly 'settlements of accounts'."[97] "When 20 to 30 people were killed a year, there was a cascade of condemnation pouring down on the Aristide government," human rights lawyer Brian Concannon Jr. observed. "Now that as many as 20 to 30 are getting killed a day, there is silence. ... It is an obvious double standard."[98]

CIDA and the Canadian NGOs, however, were glad to support the harmful and transparently partisan advocacy of these groups. CIDA gave NCHR/RNDDH $100,000 just days after the coup to fund the prosecution of Neptune. NCHR-Haiti was a partner organization of Development & Peace, Rights & Democracy and the Mennonite Central Committee, and was often cited as a reliable human rights organization by NGOs and the media.[99] In April 2005, shortly after NCHR-Haiti was forced to change its name to RNDDH, the *Concertation pour Haïti*, a coalition of the main development NGOs working in Haiti, invited NCHR-Haiti's Yolene Gilles to Canada for a speaking tour about the state of human rights in Haiti. In the weeks following the coup, Gilles had directly contributed to the climate of terror following the coup by reading out lists of "wanted" Lavalas supporters alleged to have committed abuses over the airwaves of elite-owned radio stations.[100]

Home Is Where the Hypocrisy Is

Canadian NGOs also worked to mobilize support for the occupation within Canada. On March 25, 2004, representatives of Oxfam Quebec, Development & Peace, International Centre for Legal Resources (ICLR) and Rights & Democracy appeared in Parliament before the Standing Committee on Foreign Affairs to testify on the situation in Haiti. Not once did any of the NGO representatives criticize the Canadian government's role in a violent coup d'état, nor did they mention the widespread repression against Lavalas supporters. Oxfam Quebec's Michel Verret told the Standing Committee: "Oxfam Quebec can only applaud the decision of the Security Council on February 29 to authorize the deployment of an international stabilization force to Haiti. ... the deployment of Canadian troops clearly demonstrates Canada's interest in Haiti." Rights & Democracy's Jean-Louis Roy endorsed the occupation of Haiti as a way of protecting Haitians' rights: "I think there has to be a strong international presence ... because there is a huge need in terms of political rights, social rights, and economic rights." Another Oxfam Quebec representative, Carlos Arancibia, told the Committee the coup offered an "opportunity to build peace and democracy." Marthe Lapierre of Development & Peace claimed the Latortue government was "creating hope among the Haitian population, based on what we've observed."[101]

These NGO representatives repeatedly denied that Aristide had been forcibly removed from power. Even when directly questioned about the legitimacy of Aristide's overthrow, Lapierre insisted that there had been no coup d'État: "We certainly can't prevent Mr. Aristide from now alleging that he was the victim of a coup d'État. But I ask you: if there really was a coup d'État, who seized power?" It was a strange question to ask while the country was occupied by 2,700 foreign troops and ruled by a hand-picked interim government. According to Richard Sanders of Coalition to Oppose the Arms Trade: "Instead of referring to Aristide's 'kidnapping,' 'forced removal' or 'exile,' the term used repeatedly by these quasi-government agencies was his 'departure.' This bland-sounding term was used 14 times during the hearing and on three occasions it was simply stated that Aristide had 'left' Haiti."[102]

The NGO representatives spent their time reminding the Standing Committee of the alleged crimes of Aristide and his supporters. The ICLR's Catherine Duhamel deplored the lack of RCMP resources going into investigations against Aristide's "cronies," which was "not only unacceptable," it was "absolutely ridiculous." Duhamel called on MPs to enact legislation retroactively criminalizing Aristide's elected government as a "terrorist" regime in the same class as the Duvalier dictatorships, the Taliban and Saddam Hussein's regime. Duhamel and others had little to say about the post-coup return to Haiti of convicted human rights abusers like ex-death squad leader Louis Jodel Chamblain. Development & Peace's Lapierre pointed repeatedly to the "serious human rights abuses" of Aristide and his supporters prior to the coup, but made no reference to the much more serious (and much more real) human rights abuses occurring in Haiti at that instant with the support of Canadian troops.[103] Such performances were commonplace. Not once throughout the 2004-2006 coup period did Canadian development NGOs speak out against human rights abuses against Lavalas supporters.

In the lead-up to the coup, development NGOs had called for a harder stance against Aristide's government. On December 15, 2003, on behalf of Quebec's development NGOs, the *Association québécoise des organismes de coopération internationale* (AQOCI) called for the Canadian government to "publicly denounce" President Aristide and his "regime," which was "rife with human rights abuses." Development & Peace went even further in a December 16, 2003 letter to Prime Minister Paul Martin, calling on Canada to demand that Aristide resign, and to help put in place an international force to disarm Aristide's supporters.[104] The NGOs were pushing on an open door.

Militarizing the HNP

After the initial shockwave of violence, Haiti's poor began to mobilize to voice their opposition to the coup d'état and the Latortue regime that had been imposed on them. As the Haiti Accompaniment Project reported in July 2004, "despite stepped up repression, many groups in Port-au-Prince and in other parts of the country were preparing for ongoing long-term mobilizations to call for the return of democracy to Haiti."[105] Over the summer and fall of 2004, Lavalas activists organized a series of large and growing protests to call for the end of repression and foreign occupation, the release of political prisoners and the restoration of the democratic government, including the exiled Aristide.

> As far as anyone could tell, support for Aristide and for Lavalas was as strong as ever in the Port-au-Prince slums, most obviously in neighbourhoods like Bel Air and Cité Soleil. Widespread public outrage over the February coup showed no sign of abating. A new round of democratic elections [without Lavalas] could never take place in such inappropriate circumstances.[106]

By this time, the new Haitian National Police (HNP) was ready to pick up where the rebels had left off. One of the first moves of the interim government was to create a new, reliable mechanism for repressing political resistance by the poor majority in the form of a highly militarized police force. This had been a major objective of the Haitian elite and the U.S. government ever since Aristide disbanded the Haitian Army in 1995. The interim government summarily fired any police officers suspected of loyalty to Lavalas. The top echelons of the police hierarchy were taken over by former Haitian Army officers and thousands of former soldiers were integrated into the HNP.[107] Canadian police led the UN police contingent sent to Haiti in June 2004 to train and vet police recruits and assist the HNP in day-to-day operations. Though its mission was to professionalize the HNP, the Canadian-led UN police contingent contributed to the militarization of the HNP and facilitated its abuses. According to security expert Robert Muggah, training conducted by RCMP officers for the new HNP encouraged the use of violent tactics: "Ongoing police training also appears to be employing military and police weapons in closequarter battle simulations, suggesting a worrying trend." The U.S. contributed to this worrying trend by supplying the HNP with $7 million worth of arms in 2004, including 5,435 "military style weapons."[108]

The interim government responded to the protests by launching another wave of repression in October 2004. Fanmi Lavalas party leaders were chased into exile, thrown in jail or forced underground. The repression was even harsher against the slums. Pro-Lavalas strongholds like Bel Air and Cité Soleil were targeted. Conducting near-daily raids in Port-au-Prince's *bidonvilles*, HNP officers terrorized the poor with massacres, summary executions, and arbitrary mass arrests. The country's prisons–emptied by the rebels during the lead-up to the coup–were soon overcrowded with poor people arrested in raids in pro-Lavalas neighbourhoods. The vast majority of those arrested were not charged with any crime.

The International Crisis Group reported that the HNP "have taken over old [Haitian Army] practices, including military-style operations in the capital's poor neighbourhoods with little regard for collateral damage to civilians. ... It is common to observe routine HNP patrols in Port-au-Prince carrying weapons that seem better adapted to war than police work (M16, Galil, M14, FAL, etc.)."[109] Unable to speak Creole and therefore understand what was going on around them, UN police officers often did little more than provide "back up" to HNP on their chaotic and brutal raids against poor neighbourhoods. A Canadian commander of the UN Civilian Police Unit declared that all he had done in Haiti was "engage in daily guerrilla warfare."[110]

On October 17, the capital city's general morgue received an additional 600 corpses and announced it had no more space. Gruesome reports from the morgue became so embarrassing for the interim government that it blocked journalists' access to the site.[111] The quantitative study of violence in the greater Port-au-Prince area published in *The Lancet* estimated that police, former soldiers and other anti-Lavalas forces had committed nearly 4,000 political murders in the two years following the coup.

After visiting the country in November 2004, human rights lawyer Tom Griffin wrote, "many Haitians, especially those living in poor neighborhoods, now struggle against inhuman horror."

Haiti's security and justice institutions fuel the cycle of violence. Summary executions are a police tactic. ... Haiti's brutal and disbanded army has returned to join the fray. Suspected dissidents fill the prisons, their constitutional rights ignored. As voices for non violent change are silenced by arrest, assassination or fear, violent defense becomes a credible option.[112]

In some instances Lavalas activists took up arms to fight back against the HNP attacks on their communities. In other cases, the onslaught of the police provoked a defensive alliance between the population and apolitical criminal gangs. "Many people in poorer areas have had negative experiences with agents of the State, especially those in neighbourhoods identified as strongholds of President Aristide's former government, and many have fallen victim to police violations. As a result, they have often identified more closely with armed gangs than with law enforcement officials."[113] Peaceful mass demonstrations, however, remained the principle form of popular resistance to the coup.

Criminalizing the Poor

To justify the repression, Haiti's grassroots were intensely demonized by the interim government, the local media and their foreign backers. Poor people, and Lavalas supporters in particular, were denounced as the source of all crime in the capital. Raids against pro-Lavalas slums were billed as "anti-gang" operations, rather than political repression. Police victims in the slums were posthumously labelled "bandits," "*chimères*," and "gang members."

> The HNP seems to be criminalising many of the urban poor through indiscriminate declarations by senior officers and indiscriminate repressive operations in the slums. This same pattern appears in the media, which systematically associates residents of poor neighbourhoods with "chimères" or, more commonly, "chimères Lavalas." Members of the business elite have fuelled this campaign, demanding a tougher stance towards "chimères Lavalas," ignoring the fact that many other gangs also are engaged in criminal, violent and destabilising acts. Repeated killings during pro-Lavalas demonstrations have been a consequence.[114]

Haitian NGOs, including the CIDA-funded human rights NGOs, contributed to the criminalization of the poor. Kidnappings for ransom—a new phenomenon in Port-au-Prince–were described by the interim regime as the result of a shadowy conspiracy of Aristide supporters, with the puppet master pulling the strings from exile in South Africa. Not a shred of evidence was ever produced to back up these claims. Nonetheless, Marc-Arthur Fils-Aimé, the head of *Institut Culturel Karl Lévêsque*, spoke for many in Haiti's NGO class when he declared that kidnappings and other crimes were part of "current Lavalassian practices" that, along with street demonstrations, were intended to "destabilize" the regime.[115] (*Institut Culturel Karl Lévêsque* is a member organization of PAPDA and a partner of Development & Peace.) Some sectors of Haitian society, Amnesty International remarked, "including some human rights organizations, equate being a member of a popular organization with being a member of the chimères."[116]

Canadian NGOs repeated the interim regime's claim that kidnappings and other violent crimes were part of a conspiracy of Aristide supporters to destabilize the country. On October 22, 2004, as government attacks on the slums were reaching a fever pitch, the *Concertation pour Haïti* (CPH) issued a press release denouncing the "armed partisans of former President Aristide" who had enacted "a systematic plan to make terror reign." The CPH lamented the lack of action by the HNP in the face of a wave of Lavalassian violence, going so far as to complain that police operations in the poor neighborhoods "regularly fail[ed] to produce results." Neither group mentioned the well-documented "results"–brutal killings and arbitrary arrests–produced by the ongoing police incursions into the pro-Lavalas slums. The CPH communiqué ended with a call for reinforcement and increased funding of the HNP.[117]

A few days earlier, Alternatives had produced a near identical analysis of the situation in Haiti. "A vast operation of terror has been set in motion in Port-au-Prince principally in the popular neighborhoods of Bel-Air and Cite Soleil. It is militants of Fanmi Lavalas who are behind this campaign," wrote Tania Vachon in the *Journal d'Alternatives*, published as a monthly insert in the French-language daily *Le Devoir*.[118] In a subsequent article, Alternatives Executive Director Pierre Beaudet claimed that Aristide was "joining hands with some of the hard-nose gangs in the capital to create havoc."[119] In their monthly paper, Alternatives published articles on Haiti featuring these same themes. Strongholds of Lavalas support in the slums were described as "pockets of destabilization" and Lavalas activists such as Samba Boukman and Ronald St. Jean were labelled "notorious criminals." The multitude of grassroots groups that continued to support Aristide after his overthrow was reduced to a handful of "Lavalas gangs." The thousands of poor Haitians, who time and again braved police repression to express their opposition to the coup, were denigrated as "armed partisans of Aristide." In several reports from Reuters and Associated Press journalists covering anti-coup demonstrations no mention was made of possession of arms among the crowds.[120]

With Lavalas blamed for violence, Latortue's international patrons were able to give their full backing to his campaign of repression. Despite a long-standing arms embargo on Haiti, the U.S. government authorized the shipment of thousands of new firearms to the Latortue government in November 2004, including military rifles and machine guns. Then-Prime Minister Paul Martin, visiting Haiti on November 14, promised Canada would stand "shoulder to shoulder" with the interim government in its effort to re-establish "security." "You're not going to have a democracy when people are afraid for their lives," said Martin.[121]

Port-au-Prince's poor understood the purpose of this campaign of vilification. "The police officers will say that this was an operation against gangs. But we are all innocent," said Eliphete Joseph, a young man from the Fort National district who spoke to journalists following a police massacre. "The worst thing is that Aristide is now in exile far from here in South Africa, but we are in Haiti, and they are persecuting us only because we live in a poor neighborhood."[122] "By saying we are 'gang members' or 'chimères,' the press are trying to discredit our demands for justice," a Bel-Air resident explained to the San Francisco Bay View. "Who cares about giving justice to those criminal gang members who just sell drugs and misbehave?"[123]

MINUSTAH Drags its Heels

One difficulty for the interim government was that the United Nations Stabilization Mission in Haiti (known by its French acronym, MINUSTAH) was sometimes ambivalent about prosecuting the war against the pro-Lavalas poor. MINUSTAH replaced the Multinational Interim Force in June 2004. On a few occasions, the Brazilian generals leading MINUSTAH's military contingent told the Haitian media that gangs couldn't be dealt with primarily through violence, since it was desperate socio-economic conditions–rather than a Lavalas conspiracy– that fuelled criminal activity in the slums.[124] Due to their reluctance, MINUSTAH came under heavy political pressure to crack down violently on pro-Lavalas areas. The U.S. and Canadian embassies also harassed the Brazilian generals to continue the counterinsurgency campaign.[125] The

Group of 184 staged demonstrations and organized "general strikes" where the owners shuttered their businesses as a way of pressuring MINUSTAH to continue the collective punishment of pro-Lavalas areas. Canadian NGOs joined the chorus demanding greater violence against Haiti's poor. In a June 29, 2005 article, Alternatives staffer François L'Écuyer accused MINUSTAH of pro-Lavalas bias, claiming MINUSTAH had provided protection to demonstrations of "Aristide's armed partisans" in February 2005. L'Écuyer criticized the mission for keeping police at bay and repeated Interim Justice Minister Bernard Gousse's claim that "escaped criminals" were among the crowds. In a different article, L'Écuyer compared Haitians opposed to the coup with al-Zarquawi in Iraq and the Taliban. The solution was for MINUSTAH to "stay out of politics" and to provide more arms to Haiti's police force, according to L'Écuyer.[126]

On February 8, 2005, journalists with the *Agence Haitienne de Presse* reported that a peaceful demonstration of thousands of Lavalas supporters "was interrupted by a police patrol accompanied by individuals in civilian dress, known as *attachés*, who reportedly began shooting at the demonstrators, injuring several of them," before UN troops intervened. Another Lavalas demonstration calling for the return of President Aristide and the release of hundreds of political prisoners occurred on February 28, 2005, where MINUSTAH troops stood by as police opened fire on unarmed demonstrators, killing five and wounding dozens. Journalists covering the protests uniformly described the participants as unarmed and peaceful.[127] Immediately following this last incident, demonstrators did receive a modicum of protection from the UN, due to the embarrassment caused by the February 28 killings. On March 4, MINUSTAH troops directly blocked HNP officers from supervising a follow-up protest in Bel Air, prompting an outraged response from the interim authorities and the elite.[128] It was a temporary lapse; MINUSTAH soon returned to its habit of allowing the HNP to terrorize peaceful protestors. On March 24, 2005 police opened fire on a demonstration in Cite Soleil, killing at least 3 demonstrators and on April 27, 2005 nine more protestors from Bel Air were killed despite UN supervision.[129] The UN's quick reversal was largely due to the badgering by the interim government and elite-owned Haitian media accusing the UN of defending Lavalas "gangsters."

Accusations of pro-Lavalas tendencies among UN forces were flatly contradicted by a detailed Harvard Law School human rights report published in March 2005. The Harvard report found that "MINUSTAH has effectively provided cover for the police to wage a campaign of terror ... Even more distressing than MINUSTAH's complicity in HNP abuses are credible allegations of human rights abuses perpetrated by MINUSTAH itself." The Harvard report noted that Bel-Air in particular was one of the neighbourhoods "pacified" by MINUSTAH while working hand in glove with the militarized HNP from October 2004 to January 2005. The reticence of the Brazilian commanders notwithstanding, the report described how "with the direct support of the UN's superior firepower and protection, including armored vehicles, bullet-proof vests and helmets, the HNP has been more aggressive in its neighborhood sweeps than before MINUSTAH's arrival." The targets of the UN's sweeps were "all too often, Aristide supporters, whether involved in illegal activity or not."[130]

Once Bel Air was "pacified," attention turned to Cité Soleil. The worst UN massacre was a raid on July 6, 2005 to kill a "gang" leader. According to Reuters, "about 400 UN troops with 41 armored vehicles and helicopters, and several dozen Haitian police officers," were involved in the raid. While the UN claimed only five "criminals" were killed "residents said the number of people killed... ranged from 25 to 40." Reuters quoted an MSF spokesperson in Haiti saying "27 people [were] wounded by gunshots on July 6. Three quarters were children and women."[131] The massacre drew widespread criticism from independent human rights observers. Just days earlier, the *Concertation pour Haïti* (CPH) had sent an open letter to the Canadian government calling for a reinforced MINUSTAH.[132]

In a January 27, 2006 open letter to UN Secretary General Kofi Annan and Canadian Ambassador to the UN Allan Rock, the CPH, joined by Rights & Democracy, again called for a tougher stance against the slums from the UN. Less than two weeks before the February 7, 2006 elections, the coalition of NGOs called for "drastic measures" to "end the passivity of the 'Blue Helmets'." The letter claimed Haitians had begun "to question the real motives of the presence of MINUSTAH and to wonder if the 'Blue Helmets' are there to protect the armed gangs rather than to establish order and put an end to violence."[133] On January 16, Haitian-American sweatshop magnate Andy Apaid and the Group of 184 had organized a poorly-attended demonstration to call for a renewed assault on Cité Soleil, and other business leaders threatened a private sector "strike" if the UN didn't act. But on the eve of elections, MINUSTAH's leadership decided to avoid a repeat of the July 6, 2005 scandal.[134]

The desired crackdown on Cité Soleil finally came in December 2006, and continued until February 2007. Tentative progress had been made by Préval's new adminstration in disarmament negotiations with armed groups in Cité Soleil, and a large demonstration in Cité Soleil had called for the return of Jean-Bertrand Aristide on December 16. These developments disturbed the U.S. and the Haitian elite, who were staunchly opposed to Aristide's return. When a wave of kidnappings swept the capital, gangs in Cité Soleil were blamed. With the necessary pretext in hand, the U.S. Embassy and the Haitian elite pressed recently-elected President Préval to give the UN a green light for military action against Cité Soleil.

Military analyst Walter Dorn described the UN operations as "guided by the principle of overwhelming force." The largest operation (Jauru Sudamericana, with 720 troops) expended 10,000 rounds of ammunition in 13 hours of fighting—an average of over 12 bullets fired per minute.[135] In the initial assault on December 22, 2006, 12 to 20 civilians were killed and several dozen more were wounded, including women and children. Residents told journalists that the victims' only crime was living in a targeted neighborhood. "They came here to terrorize the population," Cité Soleil resident Rose Martel told a Reuters journalist, referring to UN troops and police. "I don't think they really killed any bandits, unless they consider all of us as bandits." But UN spokespeople dismissed the victims as criminals, saying: "it's difficult for us to know for now how many bandits could have been killed or wounded." A dozen more civilians were killed in the fighting over the next two months.[136]

After these bloody and indiscriminate operations, many NGOs praised the UN occupation force for aiding their work. They displayed a similar nonchalance about the murder of innocents in a pro-Lavalas neighborhood. On January 31, 2007, for instance, the CECI's spokesperson told *Le Devoir* "the muscular interventions led by MINUSTAH in the hot zones of the capital have cooled down the passion of the armed groups. We can now circulate more freely in the capital."[137] Six days before these comments appeared, a UN raid on Cité Soleil left five dead and a dozen wounded, according to *Agence France Presse*. In a February 28, 2007 statement, the *Concertation pour Haïti* was "pleased to note that both the government and MINUSTAH are showing a firm commitment to arresting the key perpetrators of organized violence, dismantling the armed gangs and protecting the population."[138]

Containing Haiti Solidarity

Development NGOs also succeeded in silencing opposition to the coup in wider progressive circles, particularly in Quebec. Montreal's anti-war coalition, *Échec à la guerre*, passed a resolution on May 25, 2005 denouncing Canada's "direct participation in the overthrow of the Aristide government." Deploring the "hypocrisy" of the government's position, the resolution called for an "immediate end of any Canadian military or police presence in Haiti" and questioned the legitimacy of the UN occupation. "The problems of Haiti are not of a military or police order. Its problems are exploitation, domination and foreign interference, as much military as economic or political," the text read. Two member organizations, *Entraide Missionaire* and AQOCI, opposed the motion, but it was passed. However, the two NGOs threatened to withdraw from *Échec à la guerre* if the resolution wasn't retracted. Other members, not willing to split the organization over the question of Haiti, backed down and the statement was retracted. AQOCI, the umbrella group of Quebec's development NGOs, was particularly close to CIDA, holding regular meetings with CIDA representatives about funding opportunities for its members in Haiti. Maria-Luisa Monreal, AQOCI's director at the time, was invited as a guest to a banquet in honor of UN Secretary General Kofi Annan, held by the Canadian embassy in Haiti in March 2004, just after the coup.[140]

Alternatives also used its anti-globalization credentials to sway international audiences that might have otherwise opposed the coup. Alternatives brought PAPDA's executive director Camille Chalmers and other representatives of social democratic Haitian NGOs to the World Social Forum and other international gatherings during the coup. Alternatives also worked to counter incipient Brazilian opposition to the UN occupation of Haiti. In March 2005, Alternatives established a "trialogue" in Brazil between "the governments and organization of civil society of Brazil, Haiti and Canada" on how best to support the "transition." Alternatives initiated the trialogue "with the support of the Canadian government" and was assisted on its junket by "several ministers of the interim government of Haiti."[141]

Back to the Future? Empowerment and Empire

Speaking to journalists in 2009, former Canadian Forces brigadier-general Serge Labbé enthused about the "empowering" effects of the NSP and other participatory development projects in Afghanistan. "Empowered communities are where we see spontaneous human security developing," said Labbé, working at the time in the Afghan government's Ministry for Rural Rehabilitation and Development. "Empowered communities are communities where the people are willing to stand up against the Taliban and say 'this is a school that we built and we contributed to ... and, as a result, you are not going to touch it.'"[141] In the context of 21st century empire, "empowerment" is synonymous with obedience to an occupying force; "empowered" people are those willing to ally with the conquering power in exchange for the promise of aid. The deployment of emancipatory rhetoric for non-emancipatory ends is hardly novel. For instance, development consultant John Hailey suggests that there may be "a more sinister historical genesis" behind the enthusiasm of the donors for participation, rooted in the counterinsurgency campaigns of the Cold War:

> Researchers may find themselves examining how 'participative' or 'democratic' processes were used in the villagification strategies adopted by the British in Malaya in the early 1950s, and the 'pacification' campaigns used the USA in Vietnam in the late 1960s. In both these campaigns communities were relocated, and new 'democratic' decision-making processes and institutions were introduced. There is also some suspicion that US development agencies working in India in the 1970s encouraged the use of formal participative technologies in their efforts to break the stranglehold of Marxists over the community development process.[142]

There is an even longer history to inspirational words being used to advance awful ends. As Nosheen Ali reminds us: "Imperial power as the beacon of modernity, development, civilisation and women's empowerment is precisely the discourse used by British and French colonisers in Egypt, India and Algeria among other places to explain their occupations."[143] Like their missionary predecessors, NGOs now play the role of handmaidens to empire. With the instrumentalization of aid for military ends that counterinsurgency has brought about, NGOs have come full circle.

Writing in the *New York Times Magazine* in support of the U.S. occupation of Afghanistan in 2002, liberal luminary Michael Ignatieff connected the new development-based rhetoric of what he calls "Empire Lite" to the empire of old. In Afghanistan, he writes, the nation builders both military and civilian "all repeat the mantra that they are here to 'build capacity' and to 'empower local people.'"

> This is the authentic vocabulary of the new imperialism, only it isn't as new as it sounds. The British called it "indirect rule." Local agents ran the day-to-day administration; local potentates exercised some power, while real decisions were made back in imperial capitals. Indirect rule

is the pattern in Afghanistan: the illusion of self-government joined to the reality of imperial tutelage.[144]

The rhetoric and techniques of contemporary NGOs may be based on the latest trends, but the agenda behind them is much older.

10

Conclusion

Solidarity from the ground up

The NGO-ization of politics threatens to turn resistance into a well-mannered, reasonable, salaried, 9-to-5 job. With a few perks thrown in. Real resistance has real consequences. And no salary.
–Arundhati Roy [1]

When we become depressed at the thought of the enormous power that governments, multinational corporations, armies and police have to control minds, crush dissents, and destroy rebellions, we should consider a phenomenon that I have always found interesting: Those who possess enormous power are surprisingly nervous about their ability to hold on to their power. They react almost hysterically to what seem to be puny and unthreatening signs of opposition. ... Is it possible that the people in authority know something that we don't know?
–Howard Zinn [2]

The slow descent of development NGOs from idealism to imperialism has had no discernable impact on their public support. Overwhelmingly, Canadians remain optimistic about the ability of NGOs to effectively address the root causes of poverty. In a 2008 Environics poll, 91% of Canadians felt at least "some confidence" that Canadian NGOs operating abroad were making a positive difference in the world, while 47% expressed "a great deal of confidence."[3] These perceptions have supplied development NGOs with a steady stream of donations and volunteers from the Canadian public, which continues to invest aspirations for a better world in these organizations.

In reality, NGOs do more harm than good overall. While providing small, temporary benefits to poor recipients through their projects, NGOs are simultaneously an extension of the "development" apparatus used to subjugate and exploit the Global South. They have become a powerful and integral part of the neoliberal status quo, and have profited handsomely from this role, as Kenyan activist Firoze Manji explains:

> Far from helping to overturn the social relations that reproduced injustice and impoverishment, the main focus of development was to discover and implement solutions that would enable the victims to cope with, or find 'sustainable' solutions for living with, impoverishment. Over the last few decades development NGOs have played a critical role in that process. Their roles have gradually changed from an embryonic anti-imperialism to becoming an integral part of post-colonial social formations.[4]

Three decades since the onset of the NGO boom, many NGO insiders are suffering a crisis of faith. In 2008, leading NGO expert Michael Edwards observed that although "the NGO universe has been substantially transformed, with rates of growth in scale and profile that once would have been unthinkable," the impact of NGOs on poverty has been minimal. Despite unprecedented levels of NGO activity, nearly two decades worth of research showed that improvements in living conditions for the poor failed to go beyond the surface level and NGO initiatives remained unsustainable. "Does anyone believe that development NGOs still aim to 'work themselves out of a job,' that old NGO mantra?" asked Edwards. "Maybe it was never true, but there isn't much evidence to suggest that it is taken seriously today."[5]

Edwards did credit NGOs with one accomplishment: the "mainstreaming" of a host of words like "empowerment" and "participation" into the development vocabulary. Even with the change in language, however, NGOs could not deliver the far-reaching social transformations necessary to vanquish poverty:

> [D]evelopment NGOs have not changed power relations on anything like the necessary scale in the crucial areas of class, gender and race. … They have not been very innovative in finding ways to lever deep changes in the systems and structures that perpetuate poverty and the abuse of human rights, despite the recent boom in Corporate Social

Responsibility and public-private partnerships. ... They have not established strong connections with social movements that are more embedded in the political processes that are essential to sustained change.

"The rules of the international NGO world," Edwards concluded, "seem to stay pretty much the same."[6]

The staggering gulf between rhetoric and reality is an open secret within NGOs. Although seldom discussed in public, this awareness has left many organizations "scrambling for a new identity," according to NGO scholar Alison Van Rooy. Identity crises are not new to the NGO community. NGOs have gone through many cycles of reform in the past and constantly generate new internal critiques. Previous rounds of self-criticism have inspired shifts towards advocacy and participation, for instance, while current trends lean towards rights-based approaches and women's and girls' empowerment. But as Van Rooy explains, these reforms never fundamentally challenge how NGOs operate. "Most of this is only–but understandably–cosmetic," because of NGOs' "inability retroactively to grow roots" and escape the distorting influences of government grant-seeking and mass charity fundraising.[7]

Trapped in a monotonous cycle of technical fixes and development fads but unable to change its underlying nature, the NGO sector has become a graveyard for good intentions. Writing anonymously on the blog "Stuff Expatriate Aid Workers Like," one veteran NGO worker sardonically described how older NGO workers often engage in "a secondary and no less vital effort: destroying idealism in their own kind." Experienced NGO workers were once "naive college students" filled with great hopes of struggling against injustice and poverty, but upon entering the "real world" of the aid system "their idealism was destroyed by endless life-saving meetings, kill-joy bureaucracy [and] the cynicism (or alternately, the idiocy) of their superiors." The blogger therefore warns new recruits "not to seem too excited or hopeful about aid work and its impact" if they want to be accepted. In fact, senior NGO workers consider it a duty to pass on their world-weary cynicism to the younger generation:

> Great value is formally placed on idealism in the [international] NGO world, so it's rare to find open and straightforward efforts to destroy idealism. Instead, older [NGO workers] with the greatest amount of genuine field cred are forced to subversively attack idealism where it flourishes: in the hearts and minds of younger co-workers. ... Idealism

destruction and cynicism building take place via raised eyebrows and smirks, snide comments directly to or in earshot of young [NGO workers]. … The young [NGO worker] who challenges the older [NGO worker]'s cynicism will find his or her childish energy, enthusiasm and belief in "helping others," and ideas on how to do things differently quickly brushed off, derided or simply laughed at.[8]

A few insiders have been brave enough to break the ultimate taboo in the NGO world. In the 2008 article cited above, Michael Edwards referred to NGOs' dependence on government funding as "the elephant in the room," and unequivocally pointed to it as the source of the sector's malaise. Edwards, who has held senior management positions at Oxfam and Save the Children and worked as a Senior Civil Society Specialist of the World Bank's NGO Unit for several years, ended with a plea that "we need to break free from the foreign aid paradigm in order to liberate ourselves to achieve the impact that we so desperately want."[9] Coming from one of the most prominent, experienced researchers in the NGO community, Edwards's call cannot be dismissed lightly.

From Development to Solidarity

The reining pessimism and bitterness in the NGO world is indicative of the unconscious absorption of the ideology of the donors. Neoliberalism has always thrived on cynicism and hopelessness. Advocates of neoliberalism have defended their political choices not primarily by demonstrating the superiority of market-oriented policies, nor by offering any other coherent argument in favour of their view. From the beginning, neoliberals have tried to win popular consent—or at least acquiescence—by arguing that the rule of the market is natural and inevitable. The "end of history" has been reached. No other paths are possible. Resistance is futile. These are the defining ideas of the neoliberal age. British Prime Minister Margaret Thatcher's slogan, "There is no alternative," epitomized this counsel of despair.

This is obfuscation of the highest order. There have always existed many alternatives, many possible forms of social organization. "[I]n this era when there are mind-boggling technologies for bettering the human condition," journalist and communications scholar Robert McChesney argues, "[t]he notion that no superior alternative to the status quo exists is more farfetched today than ever."[10] There was nothing natural or inevitable about the rise of neoliberalism, nor is there any reason to suppose that the current sway it holds will last indefinitely. Neoliberalism is a man-made phenomenon, which can be unmade with a different balance of social and political forces.

Throughout the last three decades, there have been poor countries and regions defiantly pursuing egalitarian, and even socialist, development paths. Swimming against the tide of neoliberal globalization, Cuba has persevered in its commitment to equality and social justice. Despite a 60-year U.S. embargo against the island, Cuba has registered massive improvements in terms of literacy, health and education for its citizens. These social gains were maintained even after the economy suffered a massive blow in the early 1990s, when due to the collapse of the Soviet Union the country lost its main source of foreign support. Cuba's planned economy has allowed some degree of control over the impact of foreign investment and has not precluded significant innovation. In spite of–and in some cases in response to–formidable obstacles facing the Cuban revolution, the country has produced pioneering efforts in agro-ecological farming, social medicine and public health, adult education and pharmaceuticals.

Lest we assume that such advances towards equality are somehow incompatible with parliamentary democracy, the state of Kerala, a small, coastal strip of land on India's southwestern tip, proves otherwise. Since 1957, elected, Communist-led state governments have enacted sweeping land reforms, eliminating the most extreme forms of rural poverty. The state government has also conducted several successful mass literacy campaigns. Kerala is legendary for its frequent strikes, its strong, combative unions and its lively culture of political debate. "Even when the left has not held formal political power in Kerala," note sociologists Barbara H. Chasin and Richard W. Franke, "left organizations have demanded and won accessible health care, educational opportunities, real land reform, successful caste affirmative action, rural workers' pensions, and effective food distribution to all social classes."[11] Despite suffering the apparent disadvantages of a low per-capita GDP and one of the world's highest population densities (Kerala's population is comparable in size to Canada's–on a much smaller land mass), Keralites enjoy universal literacy and life expectancy rates that rival those of "developed" countries. Caste- and gender-based inequalities have also been significantly reduced, and the state has the lowest population growth rate in India. The "Kerala Model" stands as the exception to the polarizing rule of neoliberal capitalism in the rest of the country.

The most sustained challenge to neoliberalism has come from Latin America. Popular movements in Venezuela, Bolivia, Ecuador and other countries have elected a series of left-leaning governments that have banded together to take back control of their natural resources and kick the IMF and the World Bank out of the region. In Venezuela, the search for alternatives has been the most far-reaching. Venezuelan President Hugo Chavez, who has been elected to office three times, proclaims he is dedicated to building a "socialism for the 21st century." Proving that oil wealth needn't necessarily be a "curse" for poor countries, the Chavez government has funded extensive health and education programs (with the help of Cuban doctors and educators) in the country's long-neglected barrios. The Venezuelan government has also nationalized key industries and large landholdings and funded the creation of thousands of small, worker-owned cooperatives. But the most interesting elements of the Bolivarian Revolution are its experiments with radical new forms of democracy, represented by community councils and worker-managed state enterprises.

The revolt against neoliberalism has not been limited to the ballot box. In Argentina, there are currently 250 occupied factories operating under workers' control and employing more than 13,000. The South American nation was considered a neoliberal success story until its economy collapsed amidst a financial crisis in 2001-2002. In response to the crisis, workers took over bankrupted factories and began running them as cooperatives. Argentine journalist Marie Trigona argues that the workers in the occupied factories "have proven that they are capable of doing what bosses aren't interested in doing: creating jobs and work with dignity." Zanon, one of the most prominent occupied factories, changed its name to FaSinPat or *Fábrica Sin Patrones*, which means "Factory Without Bosses" in Spanish. Profiled in Naomi Klein's 2004 documentary *The Take*, the ceramic tile factory is still in operation today. At Zanon and other occupied factories, production is oriented to social needs, Trigona reports, and not just private profit:

> "At Zanon," workers constantly use the slogan: "*Zanon es del pueblo*" or Zanon belongs to the people. The workers have adopted the objective of producing not only to provide jobs and salaries for more than 470 people, but also to create new jobs, make donations in the community and to support other social movements. For many at the recuperated enterprises, the occupation of their workplace meant much more than safe-guarding their jobs, it also became part of a struggle for a world without exploitation.[12]

None of these places are paradises, but the material and social gains made as a result of political struggle are on a scale far beyond anything NGOs can claim to have accomplished. Given the power imbalances in the global system, any one of these attempts to break the neoliberal mold may ultimately come to naught. But attempts to forge more just and equitable societies in the South are not inevitably doomed to failure. The fate of such experiments are open questions, not foregone conclusions. Canadians have the opportunity–and the responsibility–to contribute to these struggles. To escape the dead-end of development NGOs, we need to revive the theory and practice of solidarity activism.

Solidarity begins with the realization that the poor of the Global South are not passive victims of global forces, but actors with agency of their own. Our task is not to impose what we think is the "right" way to do development or presume to speak on behalf of people in the South. Solidarity upholds self-determination as a first principle; our responsibility is to create the political space necessary for others to pursue their own paths. "Solidarity," writes Firoze Manji, "is not about fighting other people's battles."

> It is about establishing co-operation between different constituencies on the basis on mutual self-respect and concerns about the injustices suffered by each. It is about taking sides in the face of injustice or the processes that reproduce injustice. It is not built on sympathy or charity or the portrayal of others as objects of pity. It is not about fundraising to run your projects overseas, but raising funds that others can use to fight their own battles. It is about taking actions within one's own terrain that will enhance the capacity of others to succeed in their fight against injustice.[13]

Concretely, the three basic tasks of solidarity activism in Canada are: 1) to build ties of mutual support between Canadians and social movements in the South, 2) to raise awareness about the international role of Canada and mobilize opposition to the depredations of Canadian foreign policy and corporate interests, and 3) to connect "out there" issues with domestic struggles, as part of a broader effort to create a more just and ecologically sustainable world order. In seeking to reinvent an "ideology of solidarity" for the 21st century, there are many valuable lessons to be learned from the experience of the NGO radicals.

Points of Engagement in the South

One way solidarity activism can contribute to a more just world is by providing material or political support to social movements in the South. "'[D]evelopment' is far from being the only available form of engagement with the great questions of poverty, hunger, and oppression that rightly preoccupy us in thinking about the Third World," anthropologist James Ferguson argues in his book *The Anti-Politics Machine.* "The more interesting, and less explored, possibility is to seek out the typically non-state forces and organizations that challenge the existing dominant order and to see if links can be found between our expertise and their practical needs as they determine them." Ferguson suggests such kinds of alternative, "counter-hegemonic" points of engagement may exists in labour unions, peasant movements, opposition political parties, cooperatives, or churches and religious organizations of the Global South.[14]

In particular, priority should go to supporting organizations and individuals engaged in movements that directly challenge the neoliberal order or oppose malign aspects of Canada's international presence. Whether it is Haitians fighting against a Canadian-backed coup d'état or peasant communities in Central America facing expropriation and intimidation at the hands of Canadian mining corporations, these kinds of groups are far too politicized for development NGOs to be involved with–positively, at least.

Direct, human connections can fuel fundraising efforts at home. Shortly after the Sandinista revolution a delegation of B.C. trade unionists, fishermen, church and community activists visited Nicaragua in 1981 and witnessed the hope unleashed by the revolutionary process. One delegation member later recalled:

> The future looked so hopeful. There was a great burst of culture and songs and enthusiasm for literacy–and all these new health care programs. Everybody was "up." The enthusiasm! We got swept up in it. I remember us saying, "What are we going to do when we go home? There must be something we can do."[15]

Upon returning home, members of the solidarity tour founded Tools for Peace, an organization devoted to sending tools and other supplies to Nicaragua. By 1985, Tools for Peace had 126 chapters spread across the entire country and was sending over $1 million worth of aid each year to support the revolution and help the Nicaraguan people rebuild after years of civil war. Tools for Peace and other similar efforts show that in the right circumstances and despite considerable obstacles, the Canadian public can be moved to act in solidarity with popular struggles in the South.

Supporting social movements beyond our borders does not necessarily require Canadians to be directly involved in struggles in the South. Ferguson cautions that working on the ground in the Global South is "useful and appropriate" only "when a demand exists on the side of those working for their own empowerment" for the specific skills, knowledge or resources that groups from the North have to offer.[16] We have to be open to the possibility that our skills may not be relevant, or that our presence in the South may not be needed or wanted. Working for change at home is just as urgent, if not more so. "One of the most important forms of engagement," Ferguson stresses, "is simply the political participation in one's own society that is appropriate to any citizen."[17]

Fighting the "Shock Doctrine" on the Home Front

Speaking out and mobilizing against depredations of Canadian actors in the South–be they corporations, the state or NGOs–is often the greatest form of solidarity Canadians can offer. This may involve opposing Canadian support for abusive regimes, or pressuring Canadian corporations that attack workers' rights, damage the environment or commit human rights abuses. Campaigns of this sort can range from organizing letter writing to speaking out in the media against Canadian foreign policy, from lobbying and pressuring MPs to demonstrations and direct actions. A key priority of solidarity activism must be anti-war activism, and other efforts to build domestic political opposition to Canada's role in the necessary violence of neoliberalism.

The notion of the market as a peaceful, natural phenomenon that goes hand-in-hand with democracy is much older than neoliberalism itself. Writing in 1944, as the upheavals of two World Wars and the Great Depression were coming to a close, economic historian Karl Polanyi noted that it remained a widely shared belief among the economists of his day. Contrary to this view, Polanyi showed in his history of the rise of capitalism that in fact "the market has been the outcome of a conscious and often violent intervention on the part of government."[18]

Likewise, putting neoliberalism into practice required an incredible amount of state violence. To realize neoliberalism's "true vision," Naomi Klein writes in *The Shock Doctrine*, "authoritarian conditions are required." Since their implementation often provokes sharp resistance from the population, Klein argues, neoliberal policies have been accompanied by some sort of "major collective trauma ... one that either temporarily suspended democratic practices or blocked them entirely."[19] Neoliberalism was ultimately made possible by the monopoly of violence that the North exercises over the South.

In addition to opposing wars, invasions, and coups d'état, solidarity activists must also act as watchdogs over Canadian foreign policy more generally. Canada and other Western nations exert their power over the South through other, subtler forms of domination, not just episodic outbursts of violence. "It behooves us, therefore," political scientist Todd Gordon argues, "to keep a vigilant eye on the various actions taken by the Canadian government to advance Canada's interests in the world."[20] Given the powerful impact of Canada's international role on the rest of the world, our responsibility to act is that much greater.

The first barrier to mobilizing Canadians around these issues is ignorance. Providing alternative sources of information is imperative, by publishing articles and pamphlets, contacting (and often correcting) corporate journalists, and promoting independent media. Hosting talks, screening films, and putting on benefit events in support of groups in the South are other ways of reaching the public. People-to-people links are also important in this regard; fact-finding delegations or human rights observers can be useful for raising awareness within Canada, in addition to building stronger ties with groups in the South.

Popular education is the foundation of any successful international solidarity efforts. In general, educational work must provide Canadians with a deeper understanding of exploitative and unequal relations between North and South and counter the self-serving myths spun by the rich countries about their concern for global poverty. In this regard, fostering a better understanding of the motives behind violent Canadian interventions is vital. "The coups, wars and slaughters to install and maintain pro-corporate regimes," writes Klein, "have never been treated as capitalist crimes but have instead been written off as the excesses of overzealous dictators, as hot fronts of the Cold War, and now of the War on Terror."[21] Equally important is addressing wider issues of racism, sexism, and colonialism that often underpin North-South relations.

Particular energy should be focused on overcoming the tenacious idea that Canada is the exception to the rule in foreign policy. Canada's quiet diplomacy and tradition of peacekeeping are often contrasted with the U.S. and its aggressive, arrogant and self-interested foreign policy, and Canadians overwhelmingly embrace flattering characterizations of our international role. In June 2005, a Pew Global Attitudes Project survey of 16 Western nations confirmed the widespread belief in Canadian exceptionalism: "Canadians stand out for their nearly universal belief (94%) that other nations have a positive view of Canada."[22] Canadian foreign policy makers regularly reinforce these misconceptions, boasting that, unlike other Western powers, Canada has no colonial past that taints its dealings with the South. (This is merely one example of how the history of colonialism within Canada and the experience of Indigenous Peoples are erased from political discourse.) Unfortunately, even critics frequently chalk up foreign misdeeds to Canada's subordination to the reigning superpower. Yet as Sean Maloney argues, Canada is not simply a complacent ally of the empires of the day: "Canada projected power overseas for a wide variety of reasons, but many of them were in fact related to national self interest, and not always the manipulations of perfidious, imperial Brits or arrogant, messianic Yanks."[23]

Even with limited resources, educational work can have an important political influence. Although perpetually starved of funds by CIDA, development education and the solidarity activism it inspired made a tremendous impact. Brian K. Murphy argues that the development education efforts of the NGO radicals "may have been the most significant contribution of the NGOs, with more lasting effect than the millions of dollars NGOs used in programs in the Third World in the same period." Development education vastly increased the Canadian public's awareness of international issues, even though it was conducted by only a handful of organizations working on a shoestring budget.[24]

Beyond Neoliberalism

Oppositional protest can become an effective political force in Canada.[25] But frustrating the most aggressive designs of our political and corporate elites is not the same thing as advancing an alternative vision of the world. This alternate vision begins with the recognition of fundamental human equality. The Haitian-Canadian blogging team Joegodson Vilmond and Paul Jackson argue that important lessons for Canadians can be found in the egalitarian ethos of Haiti's popular movement, epitomized by the beautifully concise Kreyol saying, *tout moun se moun* (every person is a person).

Our task is to contribute to building a global society that recognizes the worth of every individual, in which people are free to fully develop their creativity and their personality, regardless of whether they are born in Montreal or Port-au-Prince. No one deserves to live a life of permanent emergency, to go hungry, to live on a toxic waste dump or a flood plain, to die of preventable diseases. No one deserves to be a slave to the plantation, to the assembly line, to the household chores for their whole lives. Everyone is worthy; *Tout moun se moun*. Solidarity activism is built around and motivated by this spirit.

This is perhaps the most important lesson Canadians can learn from social movements in the South. Unfortunately, outsiders too often visit Haiti or other places in the South with a closed mind, as Vilmond and Jackson note:

> From the North, Haiti is seen as a place to pity, to help, to manage, and to control, Northerners go to Haiti to teach, not to learn. ... We dare to suggest that those who want to lead instead follow the poor of Haiti. This requires much energy and courage. People from countries that profit from the global order are taught to look up the ladder, not down.[26]

Achieving a global society in which the worth of every member of the human family is respected would imply a sea change in how Canada currently relates to the South. Truly helping the poor, Gerald Caplan argues in *The Betrayal of Africa*, starts with reversing the multitude of Western practices that keep the South mired in poverty:

> If the West were serious about "helping" Africa, it would not use the World Trade Organization as a tool of the very richest against the very poorest. It would not insist on private sector solutions that don't benefit the poor or create employment. It would not dump its surplus food and clothing on African countries. It would not force down the price of African commodities sold on the world market. It would not tolerate tax havens and the massive tax evasion they facilitate. It would not strip Africa of its non-renewable resources without paying a fair price. It would not continue to drain away some of Africa's best brains. It would not charge prohibitive prices for medicines. In a word, there would be an end to the 101 ways in which rich countries systematically ensure that more wealth pours out of Africa into the West than the West transfers to Africa.[27]

In particular, dealing with the gathering ecological crises, which threaten to affect the poor countries most adversely of all, necessitates getting off the treadmill of economic growth and ending the North's monopolization of increasingly scarce resources. Former World Bank economist Herman E. Daly explains the growth obsession on the part of policymakers as a way of avoiding difficult questions related to environmental damage, unemployment and inequality: "It seems to me that the reason we have emphasised growth politically ... is that it would solve all these really crushing problems ... without being radical. It gives a win-win solution to all of these totally bone crushing problems. Take that away, and you have to go back to the really radical solutions and the politicians don't want to do that."[28] The ecological question makes all the more apparent the need for radical, egalitarian development paths not premised on endless growth.

The trouble is that no matter how necessary or just, "really radical solutions" will not be implemented unless the vested interests and power structures behind neoliberalism are uprooted. Canada's economic stake in the Global South has grown tremendously over the last 30 years under neoliberalism. Canadian banks and mining corporations have a particularly strong international presence, and Canadian companies in garment and textile manufacturing (usually in sweatshops), hydroelectric dam building and telecommunications are significant investors in the South as well. The share of Canadian corporate investments going to the South increased from just under 25% for the years 1973-79 to over 45% for 2000-07. Among the wealthy nations, Canada is a leading investor in the South and home to some of the world's largest multinational corporations.[29]

The necessary wholesale shift in Canada's orientation toward the rest of the world cannot be imagined without a similar shift in power relations within Canada. Neoliberalism is not simply a set of bad ideas or misguided policies; it is a political project of Canadian corporate elites. To advance this project, these elites and their allies in government act as willing partners of empire. "The one thing that a structural-cum-class analysis of Canadian policy-making should underscore," writes academic and anti-apartheid activist John S. Saul, "is just how limited in its impact a reformist approach (including the attempt to reform one particular aspect of Canada's foreign policy) must inevitably be without a far more fundamental transformation of Canadian society and polity."[30]

Beyond NGOs

Solidarity activism must be unabashedly political, not in the narrow sense of supporting a particular political party, but in the sense of fighting for a different social order. We need to take questions of power seriously and not content ourselves with the Sisyphean task of perpetual "resistance." Speaking with a clear, direct message to as wide an audience as possible was what made the NGO radicals threatening in the eyes of the Canadian government. These "fringe elements" unsettled the powers that be not because they were "preaching to the converted," but rather because their morally-charged stands on international issues often resonated with broad sections of Canadian society.

To go beyond straightforward pressure group or protest politics, enduring organizations that can consistently take up the larger political tasks of solidarity activism are required. If we are fighting to win, we need organizations or networks with the capacity to formulate a broader vision and articulate long-term strategy. A flowering of groups far removed from development NGOs is necessary, former Inter Pares policy analyst Brian K. Murphy suggests:

> We need new organizations, new forms, smaller and more political, value-driven organisations, new voices, new methods, moved by the ethics of common cause and social solidarity. We need diversity, dissent, debate—indeed, a breakdown in the self-interested and stale consensus about the role of NGOs, and a resurgent passion among truly citizen-led voluntary organizations to create the world, and transform it in the interest of everyone on the planet.[31]

Organizations and networks must guard their independence carefully, even if this means smaller budgets, fewer paid positions and lower salaries. Arundhati Roy points to what might be the greatest tragedy of the NGOs, namely that they draw in "people who might otherwise be activists in resistance movements, but now can feel they are doing some immediate, creative good (and earning a living while they're at it)." The promise of combining a commitment to social justice with a middle-class salary, professional status and the opportunity to travel throughout the world is understandably attractive—though ultimately false. "Real political resistance," Roy argues, "offers no such short cuts."[32]

Building up a diverse and reliable base of members and supporters who contribute to funding the organization or network is important. Solidarity activism involves tackling international issues that polarize opinion and will naturally attract the hostility of politicians, the corporate media, and even development NGOs. Solidarity activism is far too controversial for funding sources tied to the status quo – foundations, corporations or CIDA–to tolerate, and effective organizations must remain able to use confrontational tactics against political and corporate leaders when necessary. Obtaining charitable status may also be impossible for such overtly political organizations.

Limited funding may be a blessing in disguise. The top-heavy organizational structures of NGOs in many ways run counter to the needs of solidarity activism. Professional staff and hierarchical or bureaucratic structures not only require large amounts of funding, but also create a social and organizational divide (of knowledge, of experience and of status) between the staff on the one hand and the membership and the wider public on the other. These structures also tend to frustrate participation of volunteers and members, as we saw in the case of CUSO in Chapter 7.

In the absence of large budgets, organizations engaged in solidarity activism must strive to be truly voluntary: independent, democratic, non-hierarchical organizations with an active and engaged membership base. The activism of the NGO radicals of early 1970s, John Clark notes, was "poorly financed and run by highly committed but inexperienced volunteers" which were nonetheless "highly effective at capturing the public imagination."[33] Groups of passionate, politically-committed people are central to the success of solidarity activism; organizations should seek to nurture and support the enthusiasm, creativity and commitment of the widest possible portion of the membership.

When it comes to solidarity activism in Canada, we are not starting from scratch. There are countless groups all across Canada doing precisely this kind of activism, working on issues broadly related to the imperial thrust of Canada's foreign policy and the unjust global order it sustains. (For a list of solidarity groups in Canada, or to add your group to the list, visit *www.pavedwithgoodintentions.ca*.) But if NGOs have become too institutionalized, many solidarity groups in Canada suffer from the opposite problem: they are excessively informal or *ad hoc*. In addition, many of these groups are often focused on a particular region or counterpart group in the South and operate largely in isolation of one another. The question is how to bring these disparate opposition movements into communion with one another, and develop a coherent project for social change. What we are often missing is a shared outlook and a common language in which we express ourselves. Bringing these groups together into larger, multi-issue organizations or networks is key.

The greatest challenge for such organizations or networks is to reinvent an ideology of solidarity for the 21st century, which communicates a shared vision of a more just, egalitarian and sustainable global order and articulates a politics of common cause between ordinary people, both North and South. This involves seeing poverty and inequality not as consequences of "out there" forces affecting desperately poor people in far off lands, but as international manifestations of the same forces that confront us within Canada in workplaces, at schools, within homes and in communities. Solidarity activism requires organizations that are anchored in wider social and political struggles for social change at home.

Resistance to neoliberalism is perhaps the most promising rallying point for a dynamic, broad-based movement for social transformation within Canada. Domestically, Canada has not been unaffected by the rise of neoliberalism. Since the 1980s, with the exhaustion of the post-war economic boom, successive Conservative and Liberal governments have waged a war of attrition against Canada's welfare state while reducing taxes for corporations and the wealthiest. Indeed, Canada underwent its own form of "structural adjustment" in the mid-1990s, when Jean Chretien's Liberal government slashed federal funding for health care and social programs. Private sector employers have hardened their stance at the negotiating table against Canadian workers, demanding ever-larger concessions in the name of competitiveness. Federal and provincial governments, meanwhile, have made a habit of openly violating the trade union freedoms of public sector workers through the use of coercive "back-to-work" legislation. The result as elsewhere in the world has been spiralling wealth for a tiny minority combined with growing poverty, indebtedness and insecurity for the rest.[34]

Broken Ideological Pillars

No matter how urgent or necessary, overcoming neoliberalism—never mind capitalism—can seem like an impossible task. The slow, painstaking route of solidarity activism may appear too marginal for the crying needs that currently exist, too ineffectual given the small numbers of people aligned to such a perspective, too futile in the face of an unchanging and seemingly unchangeable status quo.

The current historical moment, however, demonstrates just how fragile the rule of neoliberalism actually is. Starting in January 2011, uprisings in

Tunisia, Egypt and throughout the Arab world sparked protests in Europe, notably in Spain where the *indignados* movement occupied town squares and demanded "real democracy." The spirit of revolt subsequently crossed the Atlantic, setting off the Occupy Wall Street (OWS) movement in New York City and across North America.

Once the Occupy protests began, mainstream media commentators were quick to disavow any relation between the political grievances of the Egyptians and Tunisians and the economically-motivated anger of Occupy. Yet in the Western "democracies," as wealth accumulates into fewer and fewer hands, the empty choices offered by the political system are starting to look hardly different from those of the Arab dictatorships. Democratic freedoms have been eroded by militarism abroad and neoliberalism at home, a process well underway before the War on Terror started, as we saw in Chapter 8. During the Arab Spring, the principle target of demonstrators' rage was the police and their abusive and suffocating grip on society, but political grievances intermingled freely with economic ones. In previous years, neoliberals hailed Tunisia and Egypt as "top reformers" in the region and the anti-regime protests were driven forward by popular frustrations and resentments aroused by these reforms: grinding unemployment, attacks on labour rights, crumbling social services and corrupt ruling cliques that enriched themselves while the people suffered.

The arc of protest demonstrated that neoliberalism has created the material and political basis for solidarity activism, drawing together the common grievances of ordinary people—the 99%—in rich and poor countries alike against the polarization of society to the benefit of an ultra-wealthy 1%. The fact that, in spite of years of Islamophobic propaganda peddled by politicians and the corporate media, protests in the Arab world could serve as political inspiration to large numbers of North Americans is as clear an indication as any of how shallow the mechanisms of ideological control are. In the wake of the 2008 financial crash, the legitimacy of neoliberalism and its market-*über-alles* rhetoric has never been so weak. Journalist Anthony Barnett reports that the rapid spread of the OWS movement has power holders worried the public in the North is beginning to see that the emperor has no clothes:

> Covering the G20 Summit for Newsnight in early November [2011], a few weeks after Occupy Wall Street began Paul Mason found it "was on everyone's lips ... OWS has, in just a few weeks, become global shorthand among policymakers for 'what can happen' if they don't regain control of the situation." ... The two fundamental ideological

pillars of the North Atlantic order, that it keeps the peace and that it delivers wealth for all, are clearly broken. Although not yet directly threatened, this makes what we can call the G20 elite distinctly anxious about their "control."[35]

There are grounds for guarded optimism, then, concerning the possibilities for a politics of common cause between North and South. Even if the current upsurge, represented by OWS and the Arab Spring, is temporarily beaten back, pessimism is still misplaced. In the historical frame of things, Robert McChesney argues, organized activism by ordinary people "is responsible for the degree of democracy we have today, for universal adult suffrage, for women's rights, for trade unions, for civil rights, for the freedoms we do enjoy."

It is true that it remains unclear how we might establish a viable, free, and humane post-capitalist order; the very notion has a utopian air about it. But every advance in history, from ending slavery and establishing democracy to ending formal colonialism, has at some point had to conquer the notion that it was impossible to do because it had never been done before.[36]

Notes

Preface

1 From the John Junkerman documentary film, "Power and Terror: Noam Chomsky in Our Times."
2 Peter Hallward, *Damming the Flood: Haiti, Aristide, and the Politics of Containment* (London: Verso, 2007), 182.
3 Barbara Briggs and Charles Kernaghan, "The US Economic Agenda: A Sweatshop Model of Development," *NACLA Report on the Americas* Vol. 27, No. 4 (January/February 1994), 37-40.
4 Interview by Brian Lamb on C-SPAN, June 1, 2003.
5 Dru Oja Jay, "What makes a scandal scandalous? The media and Pierre Pettigrew's apartment on rue Aristide Bruant," *The Dominion* No. 31, November 8, 2005.
6 Griffin, "Haiti Human Rights Investigation," 32.
7 Mark Schuller. "Haiti Is Finished! Haiti's 'End of History' meets Ends of Capitalism," in *Capitalizing on Catastrophe: Neoliberal Strategies in Disaster Reconstruction*, eds. Nandini Gunewardena and Mark Schuller (Lanham, MD: AltaMira Press, 2008), 194.
8 Cited in Jeb Sprague, "Invisible Violence: Ignoring murder in post-coup Haiti," *Extra!* July/August 2006. This was the Martissant Soccer Stadium massacre.
9 "Current Missions - Haiti, Kyrgyzstan and Lebanon," 2006-2008 Biennial Review, Royal Canadian Mounted Police, (http://www.rcmp-grc.gc.ca/po-mp/rev-revue/page10-eng.htm#1).
10 François L'Écuyer, "Haiti : Militarisation de la paix: La MINUSTAH complice ?" *Journal d'Alternatives*, June 29, 2005.
11 "Mission," Alternatives.ca, (http://www.alternatives.ca/en/about-us).

Chapter 1

1 Laura Macdonald, "A Mixed Blessing: The NGO Boom in Latin America," *NACLA Report on the Americas* Vol. 28, No. 5 (March/April 1995), 35.
2 David R. Morrison, *Aid and ebb tide: a history of CIDA and Canadian development assistance* (Waterloo, Ont.: Wilfrid Laurier University Press, 1998), 296.
3 Molly Kane, "Canada and Africa: Prospects for Internationalism and Common Cause," Keynote address at the Canadian Association of African Studies Annual Conference, May 3, 2008, University of Alberta, Edmonton, 5; "Poll findings: Canada and the world," *CBC News*, February 4, 2008, (http://www.cbc.ca/news/polls/canada-world/findings.html). War and the environment received 28% and 29% respectively, with the problem of world hunger (13%) a close third. All other problems received less than 5% of responses.
4 Cranford Pratt, "Middle Power Internationalism and Global Poverty," in *Middle Power Internationalism: The North South Dimension*, ed. Cranford Pratt (Kingston: McGill-Queen's University Press, 1990), 5.
5 We also recognize that NGOs draw on less positive attitudes towards the Global South held by the Canadian public, attitudes such as racism and condescending sense of pity, a.k.a. the so-called "white man's burden."

6   Since 1965, Canadian NGOs have sent over 65,000 volunteers to poor countries
     to work on all manner of projects. The ten largest volunteer-sending NGOs
     placed some 2,500 people in 2004 alone. The attraction of development work
     is evidenced by the large number of applications for postings overseas, with
     many agencies reporting that "the supply of interested volunteers is high and
     growing," and each year far outstrips the number of spaces available. "The Power
     of Volunteering: A Review of the Canadian Volunteer Cooperation Program,"
     Canadian International Development Agency, March 2005, 19.

7   William F. Fisher, "Doing Good? The Politics and Antipolitics of NGO
     Practices," *Annual Review of Anthropology* Vol. 26 (October 1997), 442.

8   Alison Van Rooy, "Good News! You May be Out of a Job: Reflections on the Past
     and Future 50 Years for Northern NGOs," in *Debating development: NGOs and the
     future*, eds. Deborah Eade and Ernst Ligteringen (Oxford, England: Oxfam GB
     for Oxfam International, 2001), 19.

9   Brian K. Murphy, "Canadian NGOs and the Politics of Participation," in *Conflicts
     of interest: Canada and the third world*, eds. Jamie Swift and Brian Tomlinson
     (Toronto: Between the Lines, 1991), 206.

10   Tina Wallace with Lisa Bornstein and Jennifer Chapman, *The Aid Chain: Coercion
     and Commitment in Development NGOs* (Warwickshire, UK: ITDG, 2006), 38.

11   On December 16, 2009, Minister of Immigration Jason Kenney boasted that
     his government had cancelled funding to KAIROS because of its support for
     Palestinian rights. Canadian diplomats had also complained to Ottawa that
     KAIROS's work in Mexico and Guatemala with "anti-mining" community
     groups could be inimical to Canadian mining investments in those countries. Les
     Whittington, "'Anti-Semitic' charge angers aid group," *Toronto Star*, December 18,
     2009; Lee Berthiaume, "Did KAIROS defunding come down to mining interests
     and one hand-written note?" *Embassy*, October 27, 2010.

12   Hélène Buzzetti, "Ottawa prive d'aide 12 groupes de femmes," *Le Devoir*, May 5,
     2010.

13   Lee Berthiaume, "Cutting out the development NGO 'heart'," *Embassy*, June 9,
     2010; Campbell Clark, "Canadian aid groups told to keep quiet on policy issues,"
     Globe and Mail, February 11, 2010.

14   Tim Groves, "Funding Axe Sharpened by Foreign Policy," *The Dominion* No. 67,
     March 8, 2010.

15   In February 2010, Keith Fountain, policy director for International Co-operation
     Minister Bev Oda, gave an official with a mainstream NGO a verbal warning that
     the organization's policy positions were under scrutiny: "Be careful about your
     advocacy." The NGO official did not want to be identified out of concern that it
     might jeopardize the group's CIDA funding. Clark, "Canadian aid groups told to
     keep quiet."

16   Berthiaume, "NGO 'heart'."

17   Brian Stewart, "Another critical group feels Ottawa's axe," *CBC News*, July 23,
     2010, (http://www.cbc.ca/news/canada/story/2010/07/23/f-vp-stewart.html).

18   Michel Lambert, "Avec ou sans Bev Oda, les organisations de coopération
     internationale réclament un dialogue!" Presse-toi à gauche, March 1, 2011,
     (http://www.pressegauche.org/spip.php?article6717), authors' trans.

19   Deborah Gyapong, "KAIROS' funding cut worries CCODP," *Canadian Catholic
     News*, March 14, 2011.

20   Gerald Caplan, "Stephen Harper's worst enemy," *Globe and Mail*, February 18,
     2011.

21 Tina Wallace, "NGO Dilemmas: Trojan Horses for Global Neoliberalism?" *Socialist Register 2004: The New Imperial Challenge* Vol. 40 (2003), 217.
22 Sean Maloney, "Helpful Fixer or Hired Gun? Why Canada Goes Overseas," *Policy Options* Vol. 22, No. 1 (January-February 2001), 59.
23 Mark Duffield, *Development, security and unending war: governing the world of peoples* (Cambridge, UK: Polity Press, 2007), 49.
24 Tim Brodhead and Brent Herbert-Copley, *Bridges of hope? Canadian voluntary agencies and the third world* (Ottawa: North-South Institute, 1988), 51.
25 Elizabeth Thompson, "Group loses funding over position on Middle East," Sun Media, December 17, 2009.
26 Lambert, "Avec ou sans Bev Oda," authors' trans.
27 Brodhead and Herbert-Copley, *Bridges of hope*, 52.
28 Maggie Black, *The no-nonsense guide to international development* (Toronto: Between the Lines, 2007), 112-113.
29 Jeffrey T. Jackson, *The Globalizers: Development Workers in Action* (Baltimore, Md.: Johns Hopkins University Press, 2005), 62.
30 Todd Gordon, "Canada's imperialist project: Capital and power in Canadian foreign policy," *Briarpatch*, May/June 2010.
31 Keith Spicer, *A Samaritan State? External aid in Canada's foreign policy* (Toronto: University of Toronto Press, 1966), 4.
32 Cranford Pratt, "Humane Internationalism and Canadian Development Assistance Policies," in *Canadian international development assistance policies: an appraisal*, ed. Cranford Pratt (Montreal: McGill-Queen's University Press, 1994), 334.
33 "Statistical Report on Official Development Assistance Fiscal Year 2007-2008," Statistical Analysis and Reporting Section, Chief Financial Officer Branch, Canadian International Development Agency, January 2010; Gordon, "Canada's imperialist project."
34 Pratt, "Humane Internationalism," 337.
35 Robert Carty and Virginia Smith, *Perpetuating poverty: the political economy of Canadian foreign aid* (Toronto: Between the Lines, 1981).
36 Fisher, "Doing Good," 446.
37 Murphy, "Politics of Participation," 193.
38 Gilbert Rist, *The history of development: From Western origins to global faith* (London: Zed Books, 2008), 11.
39 Michael Edwards, "Are NGOs Overrated? Why and How to Say 'No.'" *Current Issues in Comparative Education* Vol. 1, No. 1 (2002), 55, and Fisher, "Doing Good," 447.
40 Fisher, "Doing Good," 442.
41 Roger Riddell, *Does foreign aid really work?* (New York: Oxford University Press, 2007), 264.

Chapter 2

1 Arundhati Roy, "Help that hinders," *Le Monde diplomatique English edition*, November 2004.
2 Roger Riddell, *Does foreign aid really work?* (New York: Oxford University Press, 2007), 269.

3   David Lewis and Paul Opoku-Mensah, "Moving Forward Research Agendas
     on International NGOs: Theory, Agency and Context," *Journal of International
     Development* 18 (2006), 668-669.
4   Tina Wallace, "NGO Dilemmas: Trojan Horses for Global Neoliberalism?"
     Socialist Register 2004: The New Imperial Challenge Vol. 40 (2003), 204-205.
5   Maude Barlow and Tony Clarke, *Global Showdown* (Toronto: Stoddart, 2001), 2.
6   This was the "Volcker shock" of 1979, named after US Federal Reserve chairman
     Paul Volcker who massively increased the U.S. rate of interest in an effort to rein
     in persistent inflation. Since Third World debt was typically denominated in U.S.
     dollars, the cost of borrowing for most countries was influenced by U.S. monetary
     policy.
7   Jerome I. Levinson, a former official of the Inter-American Development Bank,
     cited in Doug Henwood, *Wall Street* (London: Verso, 1997), 294-295.
8   Graham Harrison, *Neoliberal Africa* (London: Zed Books, 2010), 79.
9   Judith Tendler, "Why social policy is condemned to a residual category of safety
     nets, and what to do about it," in *Social Policy in a Development Context*, ed.
     Thandika Mkandawire (New York: Palgrave Macmillan, 2004), 123.
10   Timothy Mitchell, "Dreamland: The Neoliberalism of Your Desires," *Middle East
     Report* Vol. 29, No. 210 (Spring 1999).
11   Noam Chomsky, "Jubilee 2000," Znet, May 15, 1998, (http://www.chomsky.info/
     articles/19980515.htm).
12   cf. Joseph E. Stiglitz, *Globalization and its discontents* (New York: W.W. Norton,
     2002); Susan George, *A fate worse than debt* (Harmondsworth, England: Penguin,
     1994).
13   John Walton and David Seddon, *Free markets & food riots: the politics of global
     adjustment* (Cambridge, Mass.: Blackwell, 1994), 42.
14   Firoze Manji, "Rights, Poverty and Development: NGOs and the Depoliticisation
     of Poverty," in *Development and Rights*, ed. Deborah Eade (Oxford: Oxfam UK,
     1998), 21.
15   Giovanni Andrea Cornia and Sanjay Reddy, "The Impact of Adjustment-Related
     Social Funds on Income Distribution and Poverty," WIDER Discussion Paper
     No. 2001/1, May 2001, 10-11.
16   David R. Morrison, *Aid and ebb tide: a history of CIDA and Canadian development
     assistance* (Waterloo, Ont.: Wilfrid Laurier University Press, 1998), 357.
17   Jean-Philippe Thérien, "Canadian Aid: A Comparative Perspective," in *Canadian
     international development assistance policies: an appraisal*, ed. Cranford Pratt
     (Montreal: McGill-Queen's University Press, 1994), 326. In 1987, UNICEF
     coined the term "adjustment with a human face" in a report arguing for the
     creation of compensatory funds to deal with these "social costs." This is one of
     many examples where NGO rhetoric has functioned to legitimize the neoliberal
     project while mildly criticizing it at the margins.
18   Morrison, *Aid and ebb tide*, 358. It fell back from this level briefly when the
     business community complained that it was not getting its fair share of CIDA
     contracts.
19   David R. Black and Peter McKenna, "Canada and Structural Adjustment in the
     South: The Significance of the Guyana Case," *Canadian Journal of Development
     Studies* Vol. VXI, No. 1 (1995), 72.
20   Manji, "Rights, Poverty and Development," 21.
21   Renate Pratt, "International Financial Institutions," in *Human rights in Canadian
     foreign policy*, eds. Robert Matthews and Cranford Pratt (Kingston, Ont.: McGill-
     Queen's University Press, 1988), 182.

22 Morrison, *Aid and ebb tide*, 260.
23 Eboe Hutchful, *Ghana's adjustment experience: the paradox of reform* (Geneva: UNRISD, 2002), 185.
24 Ian Gary, "Confrontation, Co-operation or Co-optation: NGOs and the Ghanaian State during Structural Adjustment," *Review of African Political Economy* Vol. 23, No. 68 (1996), 156-157.
25 Ibid., 157.
26 Ibid., 160; Hutchful, *Ghana's adjustment experience*, 185.
27 Gary, "Confrontation, Co-operation or Co-optation," 158.
28 As Hutchful stresses, "the NGO development should be seen as a new phenomenon by no means contiguous with the proliferation of 'peoples organizations' in the colonial and post-colonial periods." Hutchful, *Ghana's adjustment experience*, 184.
29 Frances Stewart, *Adjustment and poverty: options and choices* (New York: Routledge, 1995), 131.
30 Hutchful, *Ghana's adjustment experience*, 125.
31 Ibid., 91.
32 Rudolf Nsorwine Amenga-Etego and Sara Grusky, "The new face of conditionalities: the World Bank and water privatization in Ghana," in *The age of commodity: water privatization in Southern Africa*, eds. David A. McDonald and Greg Ruiters (London: Earthscan, 2005) 277.
33 Lynne Brydon and Karen Legge, *Adjusting society: the World Bank, the IMF, and Ghana* (New York: St. Martin's Press, 1996), 154.
34 Nii Kwaku Sowa, "Assessment of Poverty Reducing Policies and Programs in Ghana," paper presented at Assessment of Poverty Reduction Policies Conference, January 28-31, 2002, Rabat, Morocco, 25.
35 Hutchful, *Ghana's adjustment experience*, 91-92.
36 Gary, "Confrontation, Co-operation or Co-optation," 155.
37 Like many other development initiatives, PAMSCAD "engendered cynicism rather than enthusiasm." Brydon and Legge, *Adjusting society*, 155.
38 Cornia and Reddy, "The Impact of Adjustment-Related Social Funds," 11.
39 Tendler, "Why social policy is a residual category," 4-5.
40 Laura Macdonald, "A Mixed Blessing: The NGO Boom in Latin America," *NACLA Report on the Americas* Vol. 28, No. 5 (March/April 1995), 32.
41 Helena Ribe et al. "How Adjustment Programs Can Help the Poor: The World Bank's Experience," World Bank Discussion Papers No. 71, 1990, 18-19.
42 Beckmann cited in David Lewis, "Nongovernmentalism and the Reorganization of Public Action," in *The new development management: critiquing the dual modernization*, eds. Sadhvi Dar and Bill Cooke (London: Zed Books, 2008), 51.
43 Macdonald, "A Mixed Blessing," 32.
44 Cornia and Reddy, "The Impact of Adjustment-Related Social Funds," 11.
45 Judith Tendler, "Why Are Social Funds So Popular?" in *Local dynamics in an era of globalization: 21st century catalysts for development*, eds. Shahid Yusuf, Weiping Wu and Simon Evenett (New York: Oxford University Press, 2000), 121.
46 Michael Edwards and David Hulme, "Introduction: NGO performance and accountability," in *Beyond the magic bullet: NGO performance and accountability in the post-cold war world*, eds. Michael Edwards and David Hulme (West Hartford, Conn.: Kumarian Press, 1996), 16.
47 Macdonald, "A Mixed Blessing," 33.

48   James Petras, "Imperialism and NGOs in Latin America," *Monthly Review* Vol. 49, No. 7 (December 1997).
49   Ibid.
50   Marcia M. Burdette, "Structural Adjustment and Canadian Aid Policy," in *Canadian international development assistance policies: an appraisal*, ed. Cranford Pratt (Montreal: McGill-Queen's University Press, 1994), 229.

Chapter 3

1   Jennie M. Smith, *When the hands are many: community organization and social change in rural Haiti* (Ithica: Cornell University Press, 2001), 33.
2   Bill Quigley, "Anger and Hope," *Counterpunch*, November 10, 2008, (http://www.counterpunch.org/2008/11/10/anger-and-hope/).
3   Farmer heads medical NGO Partners in Health, which relies more on funds from universities and individual donors than on Western donor agencies. Tim Elfrink, "Paul Farmer at Barry: NGOs Aren't Doing Enough to Help Haitian People," Miami New Times Blogs, March 30, 2010, (http://blogs.miaminewtimes.com/riptide/2010/03/paul_farmer_at_barry_ngos_aren.php).
4   Jane Regan, "Resettlement Plan Excludes Almost 200,000 Families," *Inter Press Service*, February 14, 2011.
5   Mark Schuller, "Gluing Globalization: NGOs as Intermediaries in Haiti," *PoLAR: Political and Legal Anthropology Review* Vol. 32, No. 1 (May 2009), 91, 94.
6   Julie Hearn, "African NGOs: The New Compradors?" *Development and Change* Vol. 38, No. 6 (November 2007), 1095-1096.
7   Michael Edwards and David Hulme, "Introduction: NGO performance and accountability," in *Beyond the magic bullet: NGO performance and accountability in the post-cold war world*, eds. Michael Edwards and David Hulme (West Hartford, Conn.: Kumarian Press, 1996), 4.
8   Ian Smillie, "NGOs: Crisis and Opportunity in the New World Order," in *Transforming development: foreign aid for a changing world*, ed. Jim Freedman (Toronto: University of Toronto Press, 2000), 116.
9   Annie Kelly, "Growing discontent," *The Guardian*, February 20, 2008.
10 Thomas Dichter, "Hype and Hope: The Worrisome State of the Microcredit Movement," Microfinance Voices, CGAP, March 24, 2006, (http://www.microfinancegateway.org/p/site/m/template.rc/1.26.9051/).
11 Edwards and Hulme, "Introduction," 5.
12 Ibid., 7.
13 Andrew Clayton, Peter Oakley and Jon Taylor, "Civil Society Organizations and Service Provision," Civil Society and Social Movements Paper No. 2, United Nations Research Institute for Social Development, October 1, 2000, 7.
14 David Lewis and Nazneen Kanji, *Non-Governmental Organizations and Development* (New York: Routledge, 2009), 93.
15 David Lewis, *The management of non-governmental organizations: an introduction* (London: Routledge, 2001), 71. Certain studies showed that when NGO projects were more cost-effective than government, greater "efficiency" came at the expense of sustainability.
16 Ibid., 79.
17 NGOs tend to gloss over the dark side of success in the informal sector: alliances with corrupt politicians and police to control profitable market niches and Dickensian exploitation of workers. Divisions created by competition also

make collective action difficult to put into practice. See Mike Davis, *Planet of Slums* (London: Verso, 2006); Milford Bateman, *Why Doesn't Microfinance Work?* (London: Zed Books, 2010).

18 Trade liberalization, cuts to agricultural supports, layoffs in the public sector and privatization had greatly reduced the number of formal sector jobs available.

19 Dichter, "Hype and Hope."

20 Maren Duvendack et al., "What is the evidence of the impact of microfinance on the well-being of poor people?" EPPI-Centre, Social Science Research Unit, University of London, August 2011, 75.

21 Milford Bateman, "'Capitalism for the poor' no more?" *Red Pepper*, September 29, 2011.

22 John Gravois, "The De Soto Delusion," *Slate*, January 29, 2005, (http://www.slate.com/articles/news_and_politics/hey_wait_a_minute/2005/01/the_de_soto_delusion.html).

23 Davis, *Slums*, 80-81.

24 Roger Riddell, *Does Foreign Aid Really Work?* (New York: Oxford University Press, 2007), 272.

25 "It was suggested that many development projects would be more aptly called welfare projects, as they consisted predominantly of helping poor people gain access to goods and services that they were unable to pay for themselves." Ibid., 281.

26 Ibid.

27 Tina Wallace, "NGO Dilemmas: Trojan Horses for Global Neoliberalism?" *Socialist Register 2004: The New Imperial Challenge* Vol. 40 (2003), 210.

28 Judith Tendler, "Why social policy is condemned to a residual category of safety nets, and what to do about it," in *Social Policy in a Development Context*, ed. Thandika Mkandawire (New York: Palgrave Macmillan, 2004), 205-206.

29 Lewis, *The management of non-governmental development organizations*, 53.

30 Ibid., 79.

31 Edwards and Hulme, "Introduction," 5.

32 David Harvey, *A Brief History of Neoliberalism* (Oxford: Oxford University Press, 2005), 177.

33 Lewis and Kanji, *Non-Governmental Organizations and Development*, 93.

34 Shelley Feldman, "Paradoxes of Institutionalisation: The Depoliticisation of Bangladeshi NGOs," *Development in Practice* Vol. 13, No. 1 (February 2003), 23.

35 Erhard Berner and Benedict Phillips, "Left to their own devices? Community self-help between alternative development and neo-liberalism," paper presented at Beyond the Neoliberal Consensus on Urban Development: Other Voices from Europe and the South, N-Aerus Annual Seminar, May 15-17, 2003, Paris, France, 2.

36 Arundhati Roy, "Help that hinders," *Le Monde diplomatique English edition*, November 2004.

37 Riddell bases his numbers on an internal study done by the UK development NGO Christian Aid, and argued that this estimate is probably on the low end for NGOs. "It is likely that other industrialized-country NGOs would have fairly similar programme cost figures, some even higher." Riddell, *Does foreign aid really work*, 279.

38 David Mosse, *Cultivating development: an ethnography of aid policy and practice* (London: Pluto Press, 2005), 128.

39   Jeffrey T. Jackson, *The Globalizers: Development Workers in Action* (Baltimore, Md.: Johns Hopkins University Press, 2005), 93.
40   Daniel Jordan Smith, *A culture of corruption: everyday deception and popular discontent in Nigeria* (Princeton: Princeton University Press, 2007), 91.
41   Mandisi Majavu, "Saturday special: 'NGO night'," ZNet, June 9, 2008, (http://www.zcommunications.org/saturday-special-ngo-night-by-mandisi-majavu).
42   Peter Uvin, *Aiding violence: the development enterprise in Rwanda* (West Hartford, Conn.: Kumarian Press, 1998), 143, 146, 210-211.
43   Smith, *When the hands are many*, 31.
44   Schuller, "Gluing Globalization," 87.
45   Nazaire St. Fort and Jeb Sprague, "Haiti: Once-Vibrant Farming Sector in Dire Straits," *Inter Press Service*, March 4, 2008.
46   Smith, *When the hands are many*, 27.
47   Alice L. Morton, "Haiti: NGO Sector Study Vol. 1," World Bank, March 19, 1997, 5, 6.
48   Smith, *When the hands are many*, 36.
49   Mark Schuller, "Killing with Kindness? Impacts of International Development Aid on Participation and Autonomy Within Women's NGOs in Post-Coup Haiti" (PhD diss., University of California, Santa Barbara, December 2007), 243.
50   "Canadian Cooperation With Haiti: Reflecting on a Decade of 'Difficult Partnership,'" Canadian International Development Agency, December 2004, 12.
51   Alex Dupuy, "Globalization, the World Bank and the Haitian Economy," in *Contemporary Caribbean cultures and societies in a global context*, eds. Franklin W. Knight and Teresita Martinez Vergne (Chapel Hill: University of North Carolina Press, 2005), 46.
52   "Interim Cooperation Framework 2004-2006 Summary Report," Republic of Haiti, July 2004, 3.
53   Mark Schuller, "Haiti's food riots," *International Socialist Review* No. 59 (May/June 2008).
54   Dupuy, "World Bank and the Haitian Economy," 53-54.
55   Ibid., 54.
56   Peter Hallward, *Damming the Flood: Haiti, Aristide, and the Politics of Containment* (London: Verso, 2007), 349.
57   Noam Chomsky, "Humanitarian Imperialism: The New Doctrine of Imperial Right," *Monthly Review* Vol. 60, No. 4 (September 2008).
58   Cited in Lisa A. McGowan, "Democracy undermined, economic justice denied: structural adjustment and the aid juggernaut in Haiti," The Development Group for Alternative Policies, January 1997.
59   Dupuy, "World Bank and the Haitian Economy," 62-63.
60   Hallward, *Damming the Flood*, 6-7.
61   Dupuy, "World Bank and the Haitian Economy," 62-63.
62   Smith, *When the hands are many*, 36.
63   See Tim Schwartz, *Travesty in Haiti: a true account of Christian missions, orphanages, fraud, food aid and drug trafficking* (Lexington, KY: BookSurge Publishing, 2008); Laurie Richardson, "Feeding Dependency, Starving Democracy: USAID Policies in Haiti," Grassroots International, May 1997.
64   Patrick Cockburn, "The US is failing Haiti–again," *The Independent*, January 16, 2010, (http://www.independent.co.uk/opinion/commentators/patrick-cockburn-the-us-is-failing-haiti-ndash-again-1869539.html).
65   Schuller, "Killing with Kindness," 243.

66 Smith, *When the hands are many*, 37.
67 Ibid.
68 Ibid.
69 Ibid., 36.
70 "Canadian Cooperation with Haiti," 9.
71 Mark Schuller, "Fault Lines: Haiti's Earthquake and Reconstruction, Through the Eyes of Many," Huffington Post, March 3, 2010, (http://www.huffingtonpost.com/mark-schuller/fault-lines-haitis-earthq_b_483455.html).
72 "Haiti aid efforts criticized," *Associated Press*, March 7, 2010.
73 Ibid.
74 Beverley Bell, "'Miami Rice': The Business of Disaster in Haiti," Other Worlds, December 9, 2010, (http://www.otherworldsarepossible.org/another-haiti-possible/miami-rice-business-disaster-haiti).
75 Vivian cited in Edwards and Hulme, "Introduction," 5.
76 David Lewis, "Nongovernmentalism and the Reorganization of Public Action," in *The new development management: critiquing the dual modernization*, eds. Sadhvi Dar and Bill Cooke (London: Zed Books, 2008), 53.
77 Berner and Phillips, "Left to their own devices," 4, 8.
78 John Clark, *Democratizing development: the role of voluntary organizations* (West Hartford, Conn.: Kumarian Press, 1991), xi-xii.
79 Smillie, "Crisis and Opportunity," 131.
80 Evans cited in John Harriss, *Depoliticizing development: the World Bank and social capital* (London: Anthem, 2002), 73.

Chapter 4

1 William F. Fisher, "Doing Good? The Politics and Antipolitics of NGO Practices," *Annual Review of Anthropology* Vol. 26 (October 1997), 442.
2 Tim Brodhead and Brent Herbert-Copley, *Bridges of hope? Canadian voluntary agencies and the third world* (Ottawa: North-South Institute, 1988), 46.
3 "Charitable Status Question and Answer," Not-for-Profit and Charity Law, (http://www.law-nonprofit.org/charitable5.htm).
4 Ibid; Brodhead and Herbert-Copley, *Bridges of hope*, 51-52.
5 Linda Freeman, *The ambiguous champion: Canada and South Africa in the Trudeau and Mulroney years* (Toronto: University of Toronto Press, 1997), 187.
6 Ian Smillie, "NGOs: Crisis and Opportunity in the New World Order," in *Transforming development: foreign aid for a changing world*, ed. Jim Freedman (Toronto: University of Toronto Press, 2000), 120.
7 E.g. see Brodhead and Herbert-Copley, *Bridges of hope*, 52.
8 Murray Dobbin, "Harper's hitlist: The media and the Access to Information Act don't matter", Rabble.ca, March 24, 2010, (http://rabble.ca/news/2010/03/harpers-hitlist-media-and-access-information-act-dont-matter).
9 Ian Smillie, "Painting Canadian Roses Red," in *Beyond the magic bullet: NGO performance and accountability in the post-cold war world*, eds. Michael Edwards and David Hulme (West Hartford, Conn.: Kumarian Press, 1996), 189, 190.
10 Ibid., 188.
11 Allison Van Rooy, "Good news! You may be out of a job: reflections on the past and future 50 years for Northern NGOs" in Debating Development: NGOs and the future, eds. Deborah Eade and Ernst Ligteringen (Oxford, England: Oxfam GB for Oxfam International, 2001), 35.

12 Smillie, "Crisis and Opportunity," 121-123.
13 "A report on the CCIC-CIDA civil society dialogue on effective partnerships for development," Canadian Council for International Cooperation, May 2006, 18.
14 Brodhead and Herbert-Copley, *Bridges of hope*, 44.
15 Ibid., 57.
16 Brant Thompson, "A Profile of Canadian NGOs," Canadian Council for International Cooperation, January 1996, 2.
17 Michael Edwards and David Hulme, "Introduction: NGO performance and accountability," in *Beyond the magic bullet: NGO performance and accountability in the post-cold war world*, eds. Michael Edwards and David Hulme (West Hartford, Conn.: Kumarian Press, 1996), 5.
18 Authors' calculations based on "Statistical Report on Official Development Assistance Fiscal Year 2005-2006," Statistical Analysis and Reporting Section, Human Resources and Corporate Services Branch, Canadian International Development Agency, May 2008, Table C-1.
19 "A Guide to CIDA's Bilateral Responsive Mechanism (Unsolicited Proposals)," Canadian International Development Agency, 3-4.
20 Ian Smillie, *Non-governmental organisations and governments: stakeholders for development*, (OECD Publishing, 1993), 114.
21 Michelle Collins, "Foreign Affairs, CIDA Changes Leave NGOs 'Jittery'," *Embassy*, July 30, 2008.
22 "KAIROS & CIDA Funding FAQ," KAIROS, December 2010, (http://www.kairoscanada.org/get-involved/kairos-cida-funding/).
23 Lee Berthiaume, "New KAIROS proposal to test Oda's defunding explanation," *Embassy*, November 3, 2010.
24 Lee Berthiaume, "Cutting out the development NGO 'heart'," *Embassy*, June 9, 2010.
25 Guillaume Jacob, "Grossière ingérence: Coupures à KAIROS et Alternatives," *Montréal Campus*, March 11, 2010, (http://montrealcampus.ca/2010/03/grossiere-ingerence/).
26 Michel Lambert, "L'anguille sioniste?" Alternatives.ca, December 13, 2009, (http://journal.alternatives.ca/fra/journal-alternatives/blogues/michel-lambert/article/l-anguille-sioniste?lang=fr).
27 Tina Wallace with Lisa Bornstein and Jennifer Chapman, *The Aid Chain: Coercion and Commitment in Development NGOs* (Warwickshire, UK: ITDG, 2006), 48.
28 Barbara Pozzoni and Nalini Kumar, "A Review of the Literature on Participatory Approaches to Local Development for an Evaluation of the Effectiveness of World Bank Support for Community-Based and -Driven Development Approaches," Operations Evaluation Department, World Bank, 2005, vi.
29 Michael Edwards, "Have NGOs 'made a difference?' From Manchester to Birmingham with an elephant in the room," in *Can NGOs make a difference? The challenge of development alternatives*, eds. Anthony Bebbington, Sam Hickey and Diana Mitlin (London: Zed Books, 2008), 47.
30 Mosse cited in Glyn Williams, "Towards a repoliticization of participatory development: political capabilities and spaces of empowerment," in *Participation: from tyranny to transformation? Exploring new approaches to participation in development*, eds. Samuel Hickey and Giles Mohan (London: Zed Books, 2004), 98.

31 Waddington cited in Giles Mohan, "The disappointments of civil society: the politics of NGO intervention in northern Ghana," *Political Geography* Vol. 21, Issue 1 (January 2002), 144.
32 Tina Wallace, "NGO Dilemmas: Trojan Horses for Global Neoliberalism?" *Socialist Register 2004: The New Imperial Challenge* Vol. 40 (2003), 211.
33 Ibid., 214.
34 Cranford Pratt and Tim Brodhead, "Paying the Piper: CIDA and Canadian NGOs," in *Canadian international development assistance policies: an appraisal*, ed. Cranford Pratt (Montreal: McGill-Queen's University Press, 1994), 97.
35 Smillie, "Painting Canadian Roses Red," 190-91.
36 Pratt and Brodhead, "Paying the Piper," 111.
37 Authors' calculations based on "Statistical Report 2005-2006."
38 David R. Morrison, *Aid and ebb tide: a history of CIDA and Canadian development assistance* (Waterloo, Ont.: Wilfrid Laurier University Press, 1998), 524.
39 Collins, "Changes Leave NGOs 'Jittery'."
40 Wallace, "NGO Dilemmas," 10.
41 Brian K. Murphy, "Canadian NGOs and the Politics of Participation," in *Conflicts of interest: Canada and the third world*, eds. Jamie Swift and Brian Tomlinson (Toronto: Between the Lines, 1991), 184.
42 Edwards and Hulme, "Introduction," 9-10.
43 Wallace, "NGO Dilemmas," 10.
44 Murphy, "Politics of Participation," 184.
45 Michael Edwards "Are NGOs Overrated? Why and How to Say 'No.'" *Current Issues in Comparative Education* Vol.1, No. 1 (2002), 56.
46 Ian Smillie, *The land of lost content: a history of CUSO* (Toronto: Deneau, 1985), 357.
47 Smillie, "Crisis and Opportunity," 121.
48 Murphy cited in Issa G. Shivji, *Silences in NGO discourse: the role and future of NGOs in Africa* (Nairobi: Fahamu, 2007), 32-33.
49 Ibid., 33.
50 Brodhead and Herbert-Copley, *Bridges of hope*, 33.
51 David Lewis, "Nongovernmentalism and the Reorganization of Public Action," in *The new development management: critiquing the dual modernization*, eds. Sadhvi Dar and Bill Cooke (London: Zed Books, 2008), 54.
52 Mark Duffield, *Development, security and unending war: governing the world of peoples* (Cambridge, UK: Polity Press, 2007), 65.
53 Phillip Rawkins, "An Institutional Analysis of CIDA," in *Canadian international development assistance policies: an appraisal*, ed. Cranford Pratt (Montreal: McGill-Queen's University Press, 1994), 160.
54 Wallace, "NGO Dilemmas," 15.
55 Tom Lines, "Book Review: Ending Aid Dependence (Yash Tandon)," *South Bulletin* No. 2 (September 2008).
56 Pratt and Brodhead, "Paying the Piper," 113.
57 Morrison, *Aid and ebb tide*, 397.
58 Clarke cited Brodhead and Herbert-Copley, *Bridges of hope*, 51.
59 Noam Chomsky and Edward Herman, *Manufacturing consent: the political economy of the mass media* (New York: Pantheon Books, 1998), 2.
60 Murphy, "Politics of Participation," 197.
61 Chomsky and Herman, *Manufacturing consent*, lx.
62 Pratt and Brodhead, "Paying the Piper," 94.

63   Ibid., 87.
64   Wallace, "NGO Dilemmas," 2.
65   Murphy, "Politics of Participation," 196.
66   Brodhead and Herbert-Copley, *Bridges of hope*, 4.

Chapter 5

1   Gilbert Rist, *The history of development: From Western origins to global faith* (London: Zed Books, 2008), 230.
2   Roger Riddell, *Does Foreign Aid Really Work?* (New York: Oxford University Press, 2007), 266, 271.
3   Erhard Berner and Benedict Phillips, "Left to their own devices? Community self-help between alternative development and neo-liberalism," paper presented at Beyond the Neoliberal Consensus on Urban Development: Other Voices from Europe and the South, N-Aerus Annual Seminar, May 15-17, 2003, Paris, France, 9.
4   Jeremy Gould, "Conclusion: the politics of consultation," in *The new conditionality: the politics of poverty reduction strategies*, ed. Jeremy Gould (London: Zed Books, 2005), 135-36.
5   James Ferguson, *The anti-politics machine: "Development," depoliticization, and bureaucratic power in Lesotho* (Minneapolis: University of Minnesota Press, 1994), 225.
6   "Supporting organizations," Plan International, (http://plan-international.org/girls/campaign/supporting-organisations.php).
7   Giles Mohan, "The disappointments of civil society: the politics of NGO intervention in northern Ghana," *Political Geography* Vol. 21, No. 1 (January 2002), 148, 141.
8   Cranford Pratt, "Humane Internationalism and Canadian Development Assistance Policies," in *Canadian international development assistance policies: an appraisal*, ed. Cranford Pratt (Montreal: McGill-Queen's University Press, 1994), 107.
9   John Degnbol-Martinussen and Poul Engberg-Pedersen, *Aid: understanding international development cooperation* (London: Zed Books, 2003), 149.
10 David Lewis, "Nongovernmentalism and the Reorganization of Public Action" in *The new development management: critiquing the dual modernization*, eds. Sadhvi Dar and Bill Cooke (London: Zed Books, 2008), 50.
11 Tina Wallace with Lisa Bornstein and Jennifer Chapman, *The Aid Chain: Coercion and Commitment in Development NGOs* (Warwickshire, UK: ITDG, 2006), 38.
12 Degnbol-Martinussen and Engberg-Pedersen, *Aid*, 148.
13 Jeremy Gould, "Timing, Scale and Style: Capacity as Governmentality in Tanzania," in *The Aid Effect: Giving and Governing in International Development*, eds. David Mosse and David Lewis (London: Pluto Press, 2005), 79.
14 Alison Van Rooy, "Funding Civil Society: Fads, Fashions, Faith," CSO Accountability: Issues and Approaches e-discussion, United Nation Development Group, 2005, (http://www.undg.org/archive_docs/8903-__Funding_Civil_Society__Fads__Fashions__Faith__A__Van_Rooy__2005_.doc).
15 Tina Wallace, "NGO Dilemmas: Trojan Horses for Global Neoliberalism?" *Socialist Register 2004: The New Imperial Challenge* Vol. 40 (2003), 213.
16 Jeffrey T. Jackson, *The Globalizers: Development Workers in Action* (Baltimore, Md.: Johns Hopkins University Press, 2005), 101.

17   Riddell, *Does Foreign Aid Really Work*, 284-85.
18   Wallace, "NGO Dilemmas," 11.
19   Gould, "Timing, Scale and Style," 70.
20   Riddell, *Does Foreign Aid Really Work*, 279.
21   Gould, "Timing, Scale and Style," 79.
22   Maaria Seppänen, "Honduras: Transforming the concessional state," in *The new conditionality: the politics of poverty reduction strategies*, ed. Jeremy Gould (London: Zed Books, 2005), 116.
23   Eboe Hutchful, *Ghana's adjustment experience: the paradox of reform* (Geneva: UNRISD, 2002), 184-85.
24   Degnbol-Martinussen and Engberg-Pedersen, *Aid*, 149, 150.
25   Sarah Michael, *Undermining Development: The Absence of Power among Local NGOs in Africa* (Bloomington: Indiana University Press, 2004), 105.
26   Shelley Feldman, "Paradoxes of Institutionalisation: The Depoliticisation of Bangladeshi NGOs," *Development in Practice* Vol. 13, No. 1 (February 2003), 22.
27   Ibid., 14-15.
28   Degnbol-Martinussen and Engberg-Pedersen, *Aid*, 165.
29   Mohan, "The disappointments of civil society," 145, 143. Due to linguistic, cultural and political barriers their Northern partners often have little understanding of the intimate local dynamics of power and are thus in no position to second-guess their choice of beneficiaries or location of projects.
30   Mike Davis, *Planet of Slums* (London: Verso, 2006), 76.
31   Hutchful, *Ghana's adjustment experience*, 183-84.
32   James Petras and Henry Veltmeyer, *Globalization Unmasked: Imperialism in the 21st Century* (Halifax, N.S.: Fernwood, 2001), 133.
33   Laura Macdonald, "A Mixed Blessing: The NGO Boom in Latin America," *NACLA Report on the Americas* Vol. 28, No. 5 (March/April 1995), 35.
34   Arundhati Roy, "Help that hinders," *Le Monde diplomatique English edition*, November 2004.
35   Van Rooy, "Fads, Fashions, Faith."
36   Hutchful, *Ghana's adjustment experience*, 183-84.
37   Degnbol-Martinussen and Engberg-Pedersen, *Aid*, 153.
38   Wallace, *Aid Chain*, 138.
39   One exception might be Development & Peace's support for the Landless Workers Movement (MST) in Brazil, largely due to longstanding ties between the MST and radical priests in Brazilian Catholic Churches.
40   In the Philippines, a strong and organized Left has been able to exert some discipline over allied NGOs.
41   Feldman, "Paradoxes of Institutionalisation," 22.
42   Sangeeta Kamat, "NGOs and the New Democracy: The False Saviors of International Development," *Harvard International Review* Vol. 25, No. 1 (Spring 2003).
43   Mary Kaldor, *Global civil society: an answer to war* (Cambridge, UK: Blackwell Publishing, 2003), 100.
44   Davis, *Slums*, 76.
45   Hutchful, *Ghana's adjustment experience*, 183-84.
46   Roy, "Help that hinders."
47   Kamat, "False Saviors."
48   James Petras, "Imperialism and NGOs in Latin America," *Monthly Review* Vol. 49, No. 7 (December 1997).

49 Davis, *Slums*, 76.
50 Wallace, "NGO Dilemmas," 16.
51 Western Cape Anti-Eviction Campaign, "Fighting Foreclosure in South Africa," *The Nation*, April 7, 2009.
52 Noam Chomsky, *Fateful triangle: The United States, Israel, and the Palestinians* (Cambridge, MA: South End Press, 1999), 492.
53 Benoit Challand, *Palestinian civil society: foreign donors and the power to promote and exclude* (London: Routledge, 2009), 100-101.
54 Sari Hanafi and Linda Tabar, *The emergence of a Palestinian globalized elite: donors, international organizations, and local NGOs* (Jerusalem: Institute of Jerusalem Studies, 2005), 356.
55 Allam Jarrar, "The Palestinian NGO Sector: Development Perspectives," *Palestine-Israel Journal* Vol. 12, No. 1 (2005).
56 Rema Hammami cited in Asef Bayat, "Social Movements, Activism and Social Development in the Middle East," Civil Society and Social Movements Paper No. 3, United Nations Research Institute for Social Development, November 2000, 22-23.
57 See Rex Brynen, *A very political economy: Peacebuilding and foreign aid in the West Bank and Gaza* (Washington, D.C.: United States Institute of Peace Press, 2000).
58 Hanafi and Tabar, *Palestinian globalized elite*, 356.
59 Hammami cited in Bayat, "Social Movements," 22-23.
60 Hanafi and Tabar, *Palestinian globalized elite*, 354.
61 Sheila Carapico, "NGOs, INGOs, GO-NGOs and DO-NGOs: Making Sense of Non-Governmental Organizations," *Middle East Research and Information Project* Vol. 30, No. 214 (Spring 2000).
62 Cheryl Rubenberg, *Palestinian women: patriarchy and resistance in the West Bank* (Boulder, Co.: Lynne Rienner Publishers, 2001), 21.
63 Mufid Qassoum, "Aborting the Revolution: Imperial Agendas, 'Civil Society' and Global Manipulation," Between the Lines, July 8, 2003, (http://beirut.indymedia.org/ar/2003/07/348.shtml).
64 Julia Pitner, "NGOs' Dilemmas," *Middle East Research and Information Project* Vol. 30, No. 214 (Spring 2000).
65 Jarrar, "The Palestinian NGO Sector."
66 Hanafi and Tabar, *Palestinian globalized elite*, 18.
67 Ibid., 14.
68 Sara Roy, "De-development Revisited: Palestinian Economy and Society since Oslo," *Journal of Palestine Studies* Vol. 28, No. 3 (Spring 1999), 64.
69 Roni Ben Efrat, "Porcupine Tangos: The PA and the NGOs," *Challenge* No. 57 (September-October 1999).
70 Pitner, "NGOs' Dilemmas."
71 Michael Irving Jensen, "Peace, Aid and Renewed Anti-Colonial Resistance: The Development of Secular Palestinian NGOs in the post-Oslo Period," DIIS Working Paper No. 7, 2005, 16.
72 Hanafi and Tabar, *Palestinian globalized elite*, 30.
73 Jensen, "Anti-Colonial Resistance," 20.
74 Benoit Challand, "Civil Society, Autonomy and Donors: International Aid to Palestinian NGOs," EUI Working Paper No. 20, 2006, 17.
75 Sari Hanafi and Linda Tabar, "Palestinian NGOs and the Second Intifada," *Humanitarian Exchange* No. 28 (November 2004).

76 "This isolation is not necessarily only the responsibility of the NGOs, but can also be ascribed to the early militarization of the Intifada and Israel's reaction, both which marginalized individuals and institutions and robbed non-military action of its subversive potential." Hanafi and Tabar, *Palestinian globalized elite*, 16-17.

77 Hanafi and Tabar, "Second Intifada."

78 Hanafi and Tabar, *Palestinian globalized elite*, 18.

79 Thomas Tichar, "Education in the Struggle for Palestine: an interview with Rema Hammami," DevISSues: Politics and Conflict in the Middle East, ISS, December 2006, 14-17.

80 Ibid.

81 Seppänen, "Transforming the concessional state," 132.

82 Ibid., 134.

83 Ibid., 120.

84 Ibid., 121.

85 Ibid., 122.

86 Ibid., 132, 133.

87 Ibid., 122.

88 Ibid., 128, 129.

89 Ibid., 124.

90 Ibid., 124.

91 Manuel Torres Calderón, Thelma Mejia, Dan Alder and Paul Jeffrey, "Deciphering Honduras: Four Views of Post-Mitch Political Reality," Hemisphere Initiatives, September 2002, 22.

92 Seppänen, "Transforming the concessional state," 125.

93 Ibid., 126.

94 Calderón, Mejia, Alder and Jeffrey, "Deciphering Honduras," 23.

95 Seppänen, "Transforming the concessional state," 125, 126.

96 Jackson, *The Globalizers*, 100.

97 Seppänen, "Transforming the concessional state," 119.

98 Ibid., 123.

99 Ibid., 134.

100 R. F. Benitez Ramos, A. Barrance and H. Stewart, "Have the Lessons of Mitch Been Forgotten? The Critical Role of Sustainable Natural Resource Management for Poverty Reduction in Honduras," Poverty and Environment Partnership, January 2005, 35, 26, iv.

101 Ibid., 36-37.

102 Seppänen, "Transforming the concessional state," 133.

103 Adrienne Pine, *Working hard, drinking hard: on violence and survival in Honduras* (Berkeley: University of California Press, 2008), 175-176.

104 Sarah White, cited in Syed Hashemi, "NGO Accountability in Bangladesh: Beneficiaries, Donors and the State," in *Beyond the magic bullet: NGO performance and accountability in the post-cold war world*, eds. Michael Edwards and David Hulme (West Hartford, Conn.: Kumarian Press, 1996), 103.

105 Bode and Howes cited in David Lewis and Abul Hossain, "Beyond 'the Net'? Institutions, elites and the changing power structure in rural Bangladesh," in *Governance, Conflict, and Civic Action in South Asia*, eds. David N. Gellner and K. Hachhethu (New York: Sage, 2007).

106 Hashemi, "NGO Accountability in Bangladesh," 125.

107 Ibid., 105.

108 Ibid., 126.
109 Ibid., 124.
110 Ibid., 130, 127.
111 Ibid., 130.
112 Ibid., 129.
113 Kendall W. Stiles, "International Support for NGOs in Bangladesh: Some Unintended Consequences," *World Development* Vol. 30, No. 5 (May 2002), 837.
114 Hulme and Moore, cited in Ananya Roy, *Poverty capital: microfinance and the making of development* (New York: Routledge, 2010), 129. As this book goes to press, Yunus has been forced to step down as the head of the Grameen Bank under pressure from the government, amidst accusations of corruption. Yunus's attempts to form a political party have been cited as a motive for the government's moves.
115 "... moves among other NGOs to replicate this strategy stem[med] from the easy availability of donor support." Hashemi, "NGO Accountability in Bangladesh," 109.
116 S. M. Rahman, "A practitioner's view of the challenges facing NGO-based microfinance in Bangladesh" in *What's wrong with microfinance?* eds. Thomas Dichter and Malcolm Harper (Rugby: Practical Action Publishing, 2007), 193.
117 Stiles, "Unintended Consequences," 838-839.
118 Hashemi, "NGO Accountability in Bangladesh," 129.
119 Stiles, "Unintended Consequences," 838.
120 Feldman, "Paradoxes of Institutionalisation," 10.
121 David Lewis, *The management of non-governmental organizations: an introduction* (London: Routledge, 2001), 122.
122 Stiles, "Unintended Consequences," 843.
123 Ibid., 838-839.
124 Stuart Rutherford, *The pledge: ASA, peasant politics, and microfinance in the development of Bangladesh* (Oxford: Oxford University Press, 2009), 190.
125 Stiles, "Unintended Consequences," 838-39.
126 Sarah C. White, "NGOs, Civil Society, and the State in Bangladesh: The Politics of Representing the Poor," *Development and Change* Vol. 30, No. 2 (April 1999), 313.
127 Hashemi, "NGO Accountability in Bangladesh," 128.
128 Feldman, "Paradoxes of Institutionalisation," 22-23.
129 White, "Representing the Poor," 316.
130 Lewis and Hossain, "Beyond 'the Net'?"
131 Feldman, "Paradoxes of Institutionalisation," 22-23.
132 Hashemi, "NGO Accountability in Bangladesh," 128.
133 Rutherford, *The pledge*, 180.
134 Roy, *Poverty capital*, 129.
135 Stiles, "Unintended Consequences," 838-39.
136 Lewis and Hossain, "Beyond 'the Net'?"
137 Hashemi, "NGO Accountability in Bangladesh," 110.

Chapter 6

1   Cited in Robert I. Rotberg, *Haiti renewed: political and economic prospects* (Washington, D.C.: Brookings Institution Press, 1997), 22.

2   Mark Schuller, "Gluing Globalization: NGOs as Intermediaries in Haiti," *PoLAR: Political and Legal Anthropology Review* Vol. 32, No. 1 (May 2009), 91, 94.
3   Robert Maguire, "From Outsiders to Insiders: Emerging Leadership and Political Change in Haiti," in *Haiti renewed: political and economic prospects*, ed. Robert I. Rotberg (Washington, D.C.: Brookings Institution Press, 1997), 160.
4   Parliament of Canada, Testimony of Yasmine Shamsie, *Standing Committee on Foreign Affairs and International Development*, May 31, 2006.
5   Robert Maguire, "The Grassroots Movements," in *Haitian frustrations: Dilemmas for U.S. Policy*, ed. George Fauriol (Washington, D.C.: Center for Strategic and International Studies, 1995), 146. Maguire estimates there were 800-1,000 NGOs in Haiti in 1992.
6   Dewind and Kinley cited in Terry F. Buss, *Haiti in the balance: why foreign aid has failed and what we can do about it* (Washington, D.C.: Brookings Institution Press, 2008), 120.
7   Allan Nairn, "Haiti Under the Gun," *The Nation*, January 8/15, 1996.
8   Maguire, "The Grassroots Movements," 147.
9   The Haitian elite regarded the army as a vital instrument for preserving the "stability" craved by foreign investors, i.e. for controlling the population and putting down social unrest.
10   Jane Regan, "Aftermath of Invasion," *Covert Action Quarterly* (January 1995).
11   Buss, *Haiti in the balance*, 156.
12   Regan, "Aftermath of Invasion."
13   Laurie Richardson, "Feeding Dependency, Starving Democracy: USAID Policies in Haiti," Grassroots International, May 1997, 41.
14   Ibid., 24, 31.
15   Ibid., 24.
16   John Canham-Clyne and Worth Cooley-Prost, "U.S. AID go home!" *In These Times*, January 8, 1996.
17   Richardson, "Feeding Dependency," 23-24. For more on CDS, see also: M. Catherine Maternowska, *Reproducing inequities: poverty and the politics of population in Haiti* (New Brunswick, N.J.: Rutgers University Press, 2006); Deidre McFadyen, "FRAPH and CDS: Two faces of oppression in Haiti," in *Haiti: dangerous crossroads*, ed. North American Congress on Latin America (Boston: South End Press, 1995).
18   Jennie M. Smith, *When the hands are many: community organization and social change in rural Haiti* (Ithica: Cornell University Press, 2001), 30-31.
19   Peter Hallward, *Damming the Flood: Haiti, Aristide, and the Politics of Containment* (London: Verso, 2007), 380.
20   Schuller, "Gluing Globalization," 97.
21   Mark Schuller, "Killing with Kindness? Impacts of International Development Aid on Participation and Autonomy Within Women's NGOs in Post-Coup Haiti" (PhD diss., University of California, Santa Barbara, December 2007), 252.
22   Schuller, "Gluing Globalization," 94-95.
23   Ibid., 95.
24   Ibid., 90.
25   William Gillespie, "Goff, Stan. Hideous Dream. 2000." Spineless Books, May 11, 2003, (http://spinelessbooks.com/bookviews/GoffS_HD.html).
26   Gérard Pierre-Charles, "Lavalas: A Fork in the Road," Envio Digital No. 196, November 1997, (http://www.envio.org.ni/articulo/2053).

27 Schuller, "Gluing Globalization," 90. Keeping the state enterprises public was key for Fanmi Lavalas's political program, since the expansion of social programs depended on this source of revenue.

28 Sebastian von Einsiedel and David M. Malone, "Peace and Democracy for Haiti: A UN Mission Impossible?" *International Relations* Vol. 20, No. 2 (June 2006), 159.

29 Cited in Ben Dupuy, "The Attempted Character Assassination of Aristide," in *Censored 1999: The news that didn't make the news*, ed. Peter Phillips (New York: Seven Stories Press, 1999), 205.

30 Hallward, *Damming the Flood*, 182.

31 Ibid., 104.

32 Charles Arthur, *Haiti in Focus: A Guide to the People, Politics, and Culture* (New York: Interlink Publishing Group, 2002), 59-60. See, e.g. "Lavalas splits, violence increases," *Haiti Briefing* No. 23 (April 23, 1997): "Chavannes Jean-Baptiste, leader of the Peasant Movement of Papay, who supports Préval yet bizarrely still insists he is opposed to neo-liberalism ..." Many trace Jean-Baptiste's intense hostility to Aristide back to when he was passed over as Presidential successor in favour of Rene Préval.

33 Tom Reeves, "Haiti's Disappeared," ZNet, May 5, 2004, (http://www.zcommunications.org/haitis-disappeared-by-tom-reeves).

34 Hallward, *Damming the Flood*, 172.

35 Reeves, "Haiti's Disappeared."

36 Stan Goff, "A brief account of Haiti," Black Radical Congress, October 1999 (http://www.hartford-hwp.com/archives/43a/399.html).

37 Anne Sosin cited in Hallward, *Damming the Flood*, 184.

38 Peter Hallward, "Option Zero in Haiti," *New Left Review* No. 27 (May/June 2004).

39 Tom Reeves, "Still Up Against the Death Plan in Haiti," *Dollars and Sense*, No. 249, September/October 2003.

40 Anthony Fenton, "Declassified Documents: National Endowment for Democracy FY2005," The Narcosphere, February 15, 2006, (http://narcosphere.narconews.com/node/1156).

41 Anthony Fenton, "Haiti and the Danger of the Responsibility to Protect (R2P)," Upside Down World, December 22, 2008, (http://upsidedownworld.org/main/haiti-archives-51/1638-haiti-and-the-danger-of-the-responsibility-to-protect-r2p-).

42 Jeffrey D. Sachs, "From His First Day in Office, Bush Was Ousting Aristide," *Los Angeles Times*, March 4, 2004.

43 Hallward, "Option Zero in Haiti."

44 Walt Bogdanich and Jenny Nordberg, "Mixed U.S. Signals Helped Tilt Haiti Toward Chaos," *New York Times*, January 29, 2006.

45 "Canadian Cooperation With Haiti: Reflecting on a Decade of 'Difficult Partnership,'" Canadian International Development Agency, December 2004, 8.

46 One exception: The United Church's development programs worked with independent churches that supported Aristide, but its officers discounted these positions as ignorant. See Jim Hodgson, "Dissonant Voices: Northern NGO and Haitian Partner Perspectives on the Future of Haiti," in *Haiti: hope for a fragile state*, eds. Yasmine Shamsie and Andrew S. Thompson (Waterloo, Ont.: Wilfrid Laurier University Press, 2006).

47 "Support for the Processes of Democratization: Triennial Report on Results," Development & Peace, November 2003, 56-57.

48 Hallward, *Damming the Flood*, 82.
49 Reeves, "Haiti's Disappeared".
50 "Haiti's Civil Society: So much more than the 184," Haiti Support Group, July 6, 2004(http://www.haitisupportgroup.org/index.php?option=com_content&view=article&id=385%3Athe-group-of-184-is-dominated-by-private-sector-business-associations&catid=91&Itemid=231).
51 Thomas Griffin, cited in Richard Sanders, "The G184: Exposing the Haitian Elite's Enthusiasm for Violence," *Press for Conversion!* No. 61, September 2007, 34.
52 Ibid., 39.
53 Marie Kennedy and Chris Tilly, "Haiti in 2001: Political Deadlock, Economic Crisis," *Dollars and Sense*, No. 238, November/December 2001.
54 Hallward, *Damming the Flood*, 164-166.
55 Robert Fatton Jr., *Haiti's Predatory Republic: The Unending Transition To Democracy* (Boulder, Co.: Lynne Rienner Publishers, 2002), 181.
56 See Françoise Escarpit, "Haïti. Le pays n'est pas à reconstruire, mais à construire," *L'Humanité*, March 15, 2004; Hallward, *Damming the Flood*, 104-105, 160-161; Dupuy, "Character Assassination." Interim Prime Minister Gerard Latortue compares Aristide to Hitler in Nicolas Rossier's 2005 documentary film, "Aristide and the Endless Revolution."
57 Hallward, *Damming the Flood*, 105.
58 Darren Ell, "Haiti: the Damage Done: Part I of an Interview with Brian Concannon," *The Dominion* No. 44, March 14, 2007.
59 Hallward, *Damming the Flood*, 106.
60 Ibid., 105,
61 Reeves, "Haiti's Disappeared."
62 "Des institutions d'accompagnement se prononcent en faveur de la démission d'Aristide," AlterPresse, December 2, 2002, (http://www.alterpresse.org/spip.php?article308), authors' trans.
63 "'Aristide doit partir immédiatement,' selon la PAPDA," AlterPresse, January 28, 2004, (http://www.alterpresse.org/spip.php?article1091), authors' trans.
64 Danièle Magloire, Yolette Mengual, Yolette Jeanty, Olga Benoit, "Halte aux hordes lavalassiennes, pour que vive la vie !" AlterPresse, October 31, 2003, (http://www.alterpresse.org/spip.php?article845).
65 Brian Concannon Jr., "Letters: Who got rid of Aristide?" *London Review of Books* Vol. 26, No. 12, June 24, 2004.
66 "Canadian Cooperation With Haiti," 9, 12.
67 Cited in Tom Reeves, "Canada in Haiti," ZNet, June 7, 2004 (http://www.zcommunications.org/canada-in-haiti-by-tom-reeves-1).
68 Reeves, "Haiti's Disappeared."
69 Einsiedel and Malone, "Peace and Democracy for Haiti," 166.
70 Michel Vastel, "Haïti mise en tutelle par l'ONU ?" *l'Actualité*, March 15, 2003. This reportage led to Paradis being stripped of his position as Secretary of State for Latin America, and replaced as Minister of La Francophonie. See Anthony Fenton, "Canada's Growing Role In Haitian Affairs," *Haiti Progrès*, March 21, 2005.
71 Jeffrey Sachs, "U.S. Fingerprints," *Christian Science Monitor*, March 10, 2004.
72 Naomi Klein, "Aristide in Exile," *The Nation*, July 14, 2005.

Chapter 7

1   Brian K. Murphy, "Canadian NGOs and the Politics of Participation," in *Conflicts of interest: Canada and the third world*, eds. Jamie Swift and Brian Tomlinson (Toronto: Between the Lines, 1991), 197-198.

2   Matthew James Bunch, "All Roads Lead to Rome: Canada, the Freedom From Hunger Campaign, and the Rise of NGOs, 1960-1980" (PhD diss., University of Waterloo, 2007), 3.

3   Bunch, "All Roads Lead to Rome," 241.

4   Cranford Pratt, "Humane Internationalism and Canadian Development Assistance Policies," in *Canadian international development assistance policies: an appraisal*, ed. Cranford Pratt (Montreal: McGill-Queen's University Press, 1994), 337.

5   Bunch, "All Roads Lead to Rome," 241.

6   Cranford Pratt and Tim Brodhead, "Paying the Piper: CIDA and Canadian NGOs," in *Canadian international development assistance policies: an appraisal*, ed. Cranford Pratt (Montreal: McGill-Queen's University Press, 1994), 92.

7   Mark Duffield, *Development, security and unending war: governing the world of peoples* (Cambridge, UK: Polity Press, 2007), 49.

8   Firoze Manji and Carl O'Coill, "The missionary position: NGOs and development in Africa," *International Affairs* Vol. 78, No. 3 (2002), 567-83.

9   Brodhead and Herbert-Copley estimate that as late as 1985, over 10% of Canadians engaged in overseas development work were still missionaries. Tim Brodhead and Brent Herbert-Copley, *Bridges of hope? Canadian voluntary agencies and the third world* (Ottawa: North-South Institute, 1988).

10 Bunch, "All Roads Lead to Rome," 20, 88.

11 Ibid., 116-117.

12 David R. Morrison, *Aid and ebb tide: a history of CIDA and Canadian development assistance* (Waterloo, Ont.: Wilfrid Laurier University Press, 1998), 69.

13 Bunch, "All Roads Lead to Rome," 6.

14 Morrison, *Aid and ebb tide*, 69-70.

15 Ibid., 524.

16 Bunch, "All Roads Lead to Rome," 3-4.

17 Morrison, 219. While the strategy paper was cancelled after it was leaked, it revealed much about thinking on the uses of NGOs in government.

18 Brodhead and Herbert-Copley, *Bridges of hope*, 6.

19 Morrison, *Aid and ebb tide*, 68.

20 Manji and O'Coill, "The missionary position," 573, 575.

21 David Sogge, *Give and take: what's the matter with foreign aid?* (New York: Zed Books, 2002), 160.

22 Pratt and Brodhead, "Paying the Piper," 96.

23 Ian Smillie, *The land of lost content: a history of CUSO* (Toronto: Deneau, 1985), 129.

24 Judith Marshall, "Keeping pace: Solidarity work and the new globalism," *Southern Africa Report* Vol. 9, No. 4 (March 1994).

25 Smillie, *The land of lost content*, 132.

26 Bunch, "All Roads Lead to Rome," 17, 153.

27 Mark W. Charlton, *The making of Canadian food aid policy* (Montréal: McGill-Queen's University Press, 1992), 72.

28 Alison Van Rooy, "The frontiers of influence: NGO lobbying at the 1974 World Food Conference, the 1992 Earth Summit and beyond," *World Development* Vol. 25, No. 1 (1997), 94.

29 Bunch, "All Roads Lead to Rome," 162.

30 Van Rooy, "The frontiers of influence," 95.

31 Charlton, *Canadian food aid policy*, 27.

32 Bunch, "All Roads Lead to Rome," 110.

33 "The Canadian delegation feared that the NGOs were spying on them, bugging their meetings, and spreading rumours." Van Rooy, "The frontiers of influence," 95, 98, 111.

34 Morrison, *Aid and ebb tide*, 70.

35 Ibid., 129.

36 Cited in Brodhead and Herbert-Copley, *Bridges of hope*, 52.

37 Ibid., 115-116.

38 Smillie, *The land of lost content*, 17.

39 Emphasis added, ibid., 9.

40 Ibid., 35, and Morrison, *Aid and ebb tide*, 55.

41 Smillie, *The land of lost content*, 21.

42 Ibid., 262.

43 Ibid., 356.

44 Alison Van Rooy, "Good News! You May be Out of a Job: Reflections on the Past and Future 50 Years for Northern NGOs," in *Debating development: NGOs and the future*, eds. Deborah Eade and Ernst Ligteringen (Oxford, England: Oxfam GB for Oxfam International, 2001), 22.

45 Smillie, *The land of lost content*, 262.

46 Ibid., 111.

47 Ibid., 298.

48 The resolutions were nothing more than recommendations to the Board of Directors, which were frequently ignored and had little impact on how the organization was run. Nonetheless, the media often pounced on their radical content. Ibid., 270.

49 Canada's Export Development Corporation, however, quietly expanded its business with Chile, offering $89.5 million in concessional loans and $109.3 million in insurance to exporters over the period 1974-86. The exports financed by EDC loans included purchases of military aircraft by the Pinochet regime from Canadian manufacturers, items that were "potentially useful for counter-insurgency." Canada had immediately extended diplomatic recognition to Pinochet's regime and the Canadian ambassador to Chile hailed Pinochet's repression as a necessary step, derisively referring to the victims as "the riff raff of the Latin American Left." T.A. Keenleyside, "Development Assistance," in *Human rights in Canadian foreign policy*, eds. Robert Matthews and Cranford Pratt (Kingston, Ont.: McGill-Queen's University Press, 1988), 200.

50 Smillie, *The land of lost content*, 219-222.

51 Ibid., 113.

52 Ibid.

53 In fact, the decision to fire Wilson was made by a "liberally inclined" Board, according to Ian Smillie. Ibid., 117.

54 David Humphreys, "CIDA lifts financial ban on CUSO after management moves accepted," *Globe and Mail*, June 8, 1979, P9.

55 Smillie, *The land of lost content*, 268.

56 Brodhead and Herbert-Copley, *Bridges of hope*, 33, 74.

57 "While most NGOs are now secular, church-based organizations maintain a stronger financial footing through congregational support, and many have become politically prominent - perhaps demonstrating a relationship of cause and effect. ... The Ecumenical Council for Economic Justice has been a big player in the debate about debt-forgiveness, for example; and the churches were leading elements in solidarity work in Central America in the 1980s." Van Rooy, "Good News!," 20.

58 Murphy, "Politics of Participation," 161.

59 Ibid., 200.

60 Katharine Pearson and Timothy Draimin, "Public Policy Dialogue and Canadian Aid: The Case of Central America," in *Canadian international development assistance policies: an appraisal*, ed. Cranford Pratt (Montreal: McGill-Queen's University Press, 1994), 278.

61 Referring to the radical NGOs, rather than the CHF and its complicity with a blood-soaked death squad regime, from p. 93 of the Parliamentary Report "Independence and Internationalism," cited in Morrison, *Aid and ebb tide*, 532.

62 Murphy, "Politics of Participation," 181.

63 Pearson and Draimin, "Public Policy Dialogue," 286.

64 Pratt and Brodhead, "Paying the Piper," 107.

65 Linda Freeman, "Canada, Aid, and Peacemaking in Southern Africa," in *Aid as peacemaker: Canadian development assistance and Third World conflict*, ed. Robert Miller (Ottawa: Carleton University Press, 1992), 37.

66 Ibid.

67 Linda Freeman, *The ambiguous champion: Canada and South Africa in the Trudeau and Mulroney years* (Toronto: University of Toronto Press, 1997), 186.

68 Marshall, "Keeping pace."

69 Pratt and Brodhead, "Paying the Piper," 101.

70 Freeman, *The ambiguous champion*, 186.

71 Ibid., 187.

72 Marshall, "Keeping pace."

73 Freeman, *The ambiguous champion*, 187.

74 Renate Pratt, "International Financial Institutions," in *Human rights in Canadian foreign policy*, eds. Robert Matthews and Cranford Pratt (Kingston, Ont.: McGill-Queen's University Press, 1988), 182, 180.

75 Morrison, *Aid and ebb tide*, 108.

76 Ibid., 318.

77 Ibid.

78 Pratt and Brodhead, "Paying the Piper," 98.

79 Ian Smillie, "NGOs: Crisis and Opportunity in the New World Order," in *Transforming development: foreign aid for a changing world*, ed. Jim Freedman (Toronto: University of Toronto Press, 2000), 120.

80 Pratt and Brodhead, "Paying the Piper", 111.

81 Smillie, *The land of lost content*, 131.

82 Christopher Neal et al., "CUSO and Liberation Movements in Southern Africa: An Appeal for Solidarity," in *Aid as peacemaker: Canadian development assistance and Third World conflict*, ed. Robert Miller (Ottawa: Carleton University Press, 1992), 127.

83 Morrison, *Aid and ebb tide*, 70.

84 Brodhead and Herbert-Copley, *Bridges of hope*, 6.

85   Jean Christie cited in Morrison, *Aid and ebb tide*, 129.
86   "… the resonant 'solidarity' theme, which, in the 1980s, concentrated on
     revolutionary Grenada, Nicaragua and Cruise Missile testing, inevitably led to
     a decline in government support for development education. CIDA, watchful
     after the public controversies of the 1970s, gradually imposed tougher criteria
     on 'Public Participation' projects, requiring individual signed contracts for each,
     and refusing to finance those that CUSO had previously 'brokered' on behalf of
     learner centres and other organizations." Smillie, *The land of lost content*, 136.
87   Christopher Neal et al., "CUSO and Liberation Movements in Southern Africa,"
     127.
88   Morrison, *Aid and ebb tide*, 210.
89   Ibid., 289.
90   Parliament of Canada, Testimony of Stuart Wulff, *Foreign Affairs Committee*,
     April 18, 1996.
91   Morrison, *Aid and ebb tide*, 416.
92   "A Report on the CCIC-CIDA Civil Society Dialogue on Effective Partnerships
     for Development May 25-26, 2006," Canadian Council on International
     Cooperation, p. 18.
93   Morrison, *Aid and ebb tide*, 417-18.
94   Normand Tellier of CUSO, in Smillie, *The land of lost content*, 284.
95   Robert Pinkney, *NGOs, Africa and the global order* (Basingstoke: Palgrave
     Macmillan, 2009), 24.
96   John Clark, *Democratizing development: the role of voluntary organizations* (West
     Hartford, Conn.: Kumarian Press, 1991), xi-xii.
97   Ibid., 172.
98   Morrison, *Aid and ebb tide*, 264.
99   Michael Edwards, "Are NGOs Overrated? Why and How to Say 'No.'" *Current
     Issues in Comparative Education* Vol. 1, No. 1 (2002), 59.
100 Morrison, *Aid and ebb tide*, 264.
101 Brodhead and Herbert-Copley, *Bridges of hope*, 47.
102 Marcia M. Burdette, "Structural Adjustment and Canadian Aid Policy," in
     Canadian international development assistance policies: an appraisal, ed. Cranford
     Pratt (Montreal: McGill-Queen's University Press, 1994), 218.
103 Corey Robin, *Fear: the history of a political idea* (New York: Oxford University
     Press, 2004), 132.

Chapter 8

1   Cited in Noam Chomsky, "Hordes of Vigilantes and Popular Elements Defeat
     MAI, for Now," *Z Magazine*, August 1998.
2   In this chapter, the "anti-globalization movement" refers mainly to the
     mobilizations that took place in wealthy Northern countries.
3   Catherine Lalumière and Jean-Pierre Landau, "Report on the Multilateral
     Agreement on Investment," Ministry of the Economy, Finance and Industry,
     Republic of France, 1998, trans. Caroline Dumonteil.
4   "Citizens' groups: The non-governmental order," *The Economist*, December 9, 1999;
     Alison Van Rooy, "Good News! You May be Out of a Job: Reflections on the Past
     and Future 50 Years for Northern NGOs," in *Debating Development: NGOs and
     the future*, eds. Deborah Eade and Ernst Ligteringen (Oxford, England: Oxfam
     GB for Oxfam International, 2001), 28, 29; Naomi Klein, *Fences and windows:*

dispatches from the front lines of the globalization debate (Toronto: Vintage Canada, 2002), 20; Sebastian Mallaby, *The world's banker: a story of failed states, financial crises, and the wealth and poverty of nations* (New York: Penguin Press, 2004), 262. Mallaby called radical groups "NGO critics," though he also distinguished between "grown-up" NGOs like Oxfam and the more radical "NGO" groups who "always found things to hate," and "do not have an off switch."

5   Ian Smillie, "NGOs: Crisis and Opportunity in the New World Order," in *Transforming development: foreign aid for a changing world*, ed. Jim Freedman (Toronto: University of Toronto Press, 2000), 130.

6   "Angry and effective," *The Economist*, September 21, 2000.

7   Jim Davis, "This is what bureaucracy looks like," Infoshop.org, February 9, 2002, (http://www.infoshop.org/news6/bureaucracy.php).

8   Stephen McBride, *Paradigm shift: globalization and the Canadian state.* (Halifax, N.S.: Fernwood, 2001), 87-88.

9   David McNally, *Another world is possible: Globalization and anti-capitalism.* (Winnipeg: Arbeiter Ring Publishing, 2005), 276.

10 Ibid., 27.

11 Sam Gindin, "Capitalism and the Terrain of Social Justice," *Monthly Review* Vol. 53, No. 9 (February 2002).

12 McNally, *Another world is possible*, 274-75.

13 Alison Van Rooy, "The frontiers of influence: NGO lobbying at the 1974 World Food Conference, the 1992 Earth Summit and beyond," *World Development* Vol. 25, No. 1 (1997), 105.

14 Ibid., 104.

15 Tina Wallace, "NGO Dilemmas: Trojan Horses for Global Neoliberalism?" *Socialist Register 2004: The New Imperial Challenge* Vol. 40 (2003), 204.

16 Brian K. Murphy, "International NGOs and the challenge of modernity" in *Debating Development: NGOs and the future*, eds. Deborah Eade and Ernst Ligteringen (Oxford, England: Oxfam GB for Oxfam International, 2001), 81.

17 Ibid., 104.

18 Michael Edwards, "'Does the doormat influence the boot?': Critical thoughts on UK NGOs and international advocacy," *Development in practice* Vol. 3, No. 3 (October 1993), 163-175.

19 Maude Barlow and Tony Clarke, *Global showdown: how the new activists are fighting global corporate rule* (Toronto: Stoddart, 2001), 3.

20 Elizabeth Riddell-Dixon, "Democratizing Canadian Foreign Policy?: NGO Participation for the Copenhagen Summit for Social Development and the Beijing Conference on Women," *Canadian Foreign Policy* Vol. 11, No. 3 (2004), 116.

21 Kim Richard Nossal, "The democratization of Canadian foreign policy: the elusive ideal," in *Canada Among Nations, 1995: Democracy and Foreign Policy*, eds. Maxwell A. Cameron and Maureen Appel Molot (Ottawa: Carleton University Press, 1995), 29-43.

22 Cited in Riddell-Dixon, "Democratizing Canadian Foreign Policy," 102.

23 Barlow and Clarke, *Global showdown*, 27-28.

24 "Canada and APEC: Perspectives from Civil Society," Policy Working Group, Canadian Organizing Network for the 1997 People's Summit on APEC, April 22, 1997.

25 Abdul Aziz Choudry, "NGOs, social movements and anti-APEC activism: A study in power, knowledge and struggle" (PhD diss., Concordia University, 2008), 248.

26 "Canada and APEC."
27 Ibid.
28 Choudry, "NGOs, social movements and anti-APEC activism," 191.
29 Aziz Choudry, "Both Feet On the Ground Or a Seat At the Table: The Price of Being 'Civil'," paper presented at the Hemispheric Civil Society Conference, February 2003, Centre for Developing-Area Studies, McGill University, Montreal, Canada, 5-6.
30 Choudry, "NGOs, social movements and anti-APEC activism," 191.
31 Choudry, "Both Feet On the Ground Or a Seat At the Table," 5-6.
32 Choudry, "NGOs, social movements and anti-APEC activism," 253, 255.
33 "Within the coalition, there were those who were against APEC and opposed any involvement of the Canadian government in the APEC process. For others, APEC was here to stay and so every effort needed to be made to ensure that its agreements safeguarded human rights." "Canada and APEC."
34 Choudry, "NGOs, social movements and anti-APEC activism," 208.
35 "Canada and APEC."
36 Choudry, "NGOs, social movements and anti-APEC activism," 209-210, 230.
37 Ibid., 217, 203, 226.
38 "RCMP slammed in APEC report," *CBC News*, August 7, 2001, (http://www.cbc.ca/news/canada/story/2001/08/07/apec010807.html). The report came out four months after the 2001 Quebec City protests, where a new level of anti-protester violence had already been enshrined as the norm.
39 "1997 People's Summit on APEC," Canadian Organizing Network for the 1997 People's Summit on APEC, (http://web.archive.org/web/20010619204127/vcn.bc.ca/summit/popindex.htm).
40 Choudry, "NGOs, social movements and anti-APEC activism," 232.
41 Ibid., 248.
42 David Solnit, "The Battle for Reality," *Yes Magazine*, July 30, 2008.
43 Seth Ackerman, "Prattle in Seattle: WTO coverage misrepresented issues, protests," *Extra!* January/February 2000.
44 Noam Chomsky and Edward Herman, *Manufacturing consent: the political economy of the mass media* (New York: Pantheon Books, 1998), xliv.
45 Alexander Cockburn and Jeffrey St. Clair, *Five days that shook the world: Seattle and beyond* (London: Verso, 2000), 69.
46 Solnit, "Battle for Reality."
47 Barlow and Clarke, *Global showdown*, 44.
48 Robert Lenzner and Tomas Kellner, "Corporate Saboteurs," *Forbes*, November 27, 2000.
49 Klein, *Fences and windows*, 12.
50 Barlow and Clarke, *Global showdown*, 32.
51 Not included on this list are hundreds of demonstrations featuring similar demands in the Global South.
52 Davis, "This is what bureaucracy looks like."
53 Jeffrey St. Clair, "Seattle Diary: It's a Gas, Gas, Gas!" *Counterpunch*, December 16, 1999, (http://www.counterpunch.org/1999/12/16/seattle-diary/).
54 Tom Turner and Judith Barish, "Environmental, Labor Leaders Condemn Violence," *World Trade Observer* No. 4, (http://depts.washington.edu/wtohist/World_Trade_Obs/issue4/violence.htm).
55 Barlow and Clarke, *Global showdown*, 30.
56 Cockburn and St. Clair, *Five days that shook the world*, 67.
57 Davis, "This is what bureaucracy looks like."

58 "Report No. 2000/08: Anti-Globalization - A Spreading Phenomenon,"
    Canadian Security Intelligence Service, August 22, 2000.
59 Cockburn and St. Clair, *Five days that shook the world*, 10.
60 Barlow and Clarke, *Global showdown*, 48.
61 Klein, *Fences and windows*, 122.
62 "Citizens' groups," *The Economist.*
63 Aaron Bernstein, Lorraine Woellert and Paul Magnusson, "Time to Regroup,"
    BusinessWeek, August 6, 2001.
64 Jeff Ballinger, "How civil society can help: sweatshop workers as globalization's
    consequence," *Harvard International Review* Vol. XXXIII, No. 2 (Summer 2011),
    58. According to Ballinger's calculations based on a Lexis-Nexis database search,
    CSR was ubiquitous between 2003-2008, with 2,643 mentions. "[T]he vast
    majority of CSR press releases deal with environment-related issues and less than
    1 percent concern workplace issues."
65 Barlow and Clarke, *Global showdown*, 41.
66 Cockburn and St. Clair, *Five days that shook the world*, 1-2.
67 "Angry and effective," *The Economist.*
68 "Confronting Anti-Globalism," *BusinessWeek*, August 6, 2001.
69 Alison Van Rooy, "Funding Civil Society: Fads, Fashions, Faith," CSO
    Accountability: Issues and Approaches e-discussion, United Nation Development
    Group, 2005, (http://www.undg.org/archive_docs/8903-__Funding_Civil_
    Society__Fads__Fashions__Faith__A__Van_Rooy__2005_.doc).
70 Davis, "This is what bureaucracy looks like."
71 Oxfam Canada is here amalgamated with Oxfam International, the umbrella
    organization that since 1995 has directed the policy and advocacy work of the
    various national Oxfams. See Rex Fyles, "How Does Oxfam Canada Learn?
    Organizational Learning in a Real-life Voluntary Sector Organization," McGill-
    McConnell Papers, Centre for Voluntary Sector Research and Development,
    McGill University, February 2003.
72 Pascale Dufour, "L'espace canadien de protestation mondiale 1985 - 2006,"
    in *Espaces de protestation: Trois sociétés en comparaison* (Montreal: Presses de
    l'Université de Montréal, forthcoming), 12, authors' trans.
73 Tomas Kellner, "Power Without Firebombs," *Forbes*, November 27, 2000.
74 Ibid.
75 Fyles, "How Does Oxfam Canada Learn?" 55, 41, 54.
76 Tim Atwater, "New Faith in Free Trade: In Break With Allies, Oxfam Backs
    Globalization," *Washington Post*, April 11, 2002.
77 Kevin Watkins and Penny Fowler, "Rigged Rules and Double Standards: Trade,
    globalisation and the fight against poverty," Oxfam International, March 2002,
    Oxford, England, 5.
78 Walden Bello, "The Oxfam debate: From Controversy To Common
    Strategy," Focus on the Global South, May 2002, (http://www.focusweb.org/
    publications/2002/oxfam-debate-controversy-to-common-strategy.html).
79 Ibid.
80 Atwater, "New Faith in Free Trade."
81 "Oxfam trades up," *National Post*, April 20, 2002, page 8. The organization, which
    had "largely adhered to the protectionist, anti-corporatist view" of the anti-
    globalization protesters until recently, had finally come to its senses, according to
    the *Post*.

82 Patrick Bond, "Moderates wilt but radical South Africans struggle on," *Pambazuka News*, No. 60, April 18, 2002.
83 Mallaby, *The world's banker*, 379, 263.
84 "Citizens' groups," *The Economist*.
85 Patrick Bond, "Recalcitrant reformers require tougher tactics," *Pambazuka News*, No. 170, August 19, 2004.
86 Mallaby, *The world's banker*, 145.
87 Ibid., 115.
88 Nick Buxton, "Debt Cancellation and Civil Society: A Case Study of Jubilee 2000" in *Fighting for Human Rights*, ed. Paul Gready (New York: Routledge, 2004), 67-68.
89 Pettifor in Romilly Greenhill, Henry Northover, Ashok Sinha and Ann Pettifor, "Did the G8 Drop the Debt?" Jubilee Debt Campaign, CAFOD and Jubilee Research, May 2003, 8.
90 Ibid., 12.
91 Mallaby, *The world's banker*, 248.
92 Andrew Bauck, "International Financial Institutions: The Campaign for Debt Relief," in *Advocacy for social justice: a global action and reflection guide*, eds. David Cohen, Rosa de la Vega and Gabrielle Watson (Bloomfield, Ct.: Kumarian Press, 2001).
93 Buxton, "Debt Cancellation and Civil Society," 56.
94 "How to Blunt the Anti-Globalization Backlash," *BusinessWeek*, August 6, 2001.
95 Mallaby, *The world's banker*, 252.
96 Buxton, "Debt Cancellation and Civil Society."
97 Mallaby, *The world's banker*, 409.
98 Eric Toussaint, "Exposing the G7 lies," *Green Left Weekly*, July 7, 1999, (http://www.greenleft.org.au/node/19285).
99 Bond, "Recalcitrant reformers."
100 Jie Yang and Dan Nyberg, "External Debt Sustainability in HIPC Completion Point Countries: An Update," IMF Working Paper No. 09/128, June 2009.
101 Bill Cooke, "Rules of thumb for participatory change agents," in *Participation: from tyranny to transformation? Exploring new approaches to participation in development*, eds. Samuel Hickey and Giles Mohan (London: Zed Books, 2004), 44.
102 Cited in David Lewis and Nazneen Kanji, *Non-Governmental Organizations and Development* (New York: Routledge, 2009), 86.
103 John Dillon, "Lessons from the First Year and Challenges for the Jubilee Debt Campaign," Coalition for Global Solidarity, February 11, 2000, (http://www.globalsolidarity.org/articles/dillon.html).
104 Buxton, "Debt Cancellation and Civil Society," 62-63.
105 Bond, "Recalcitrant reformers."
106 Mallaby, *The world's banker*, 265-66.
107 Ibid., 264.
108 Jeremy Gould and Julia Ojanen, "Tanzania: merging in the circle," in *The new conditionality: the politics of poverty reduction strategies*, ed. Jeremy Gould (London: Zed Books, 2005), 17-65.
109 Buxton, "Debt Cancellation and Civil Society," 68.
110 Ibid.
111 "Citizens' groups," *The Economist*.

112 Marc Lortie and Sylvie Bédard, "Citizen involvement in Canadian foreign policy; The Summit of the Americas experience 2001," *International Journal* Vol. 57, No. 3 (Summer 2002), 7-8.

113 Jennifer Lew, "We don't even know what they're trading away: Protesters promise to take hard line against secretive summit," *Capital News*, January 19, 2001, (http://carleton.ca/Capital_News/19012001/n7.htm).

114 Lortie and Bédard, "Citizen involvement in Canadian foreign policy," 2, 8.

115 Marc Bonhomme, "Québec, avril 2001, le début d'un temps nouveau?" *Inprecor* No. 459-460 (June/July 2001), authors' trans.

116 Lortie and Bédard, "Citizen involvement in Canadian foreign policy," 7.

117 Kevin MacKay, "Solidarity and symbolic protest: lessons for labour from the Quebec City Summit of the Americas," *Labour/Le Travail* Vol. 50, (Fall 2002).

118 MaRK, "Breaking The Barricades: Quebec's Carnival Of Resistance Against Capitalism," *The Northeastern Anarchist*, November 2002, http://nefac.net/node/118.

119 Katherine Dwyer, "Lessons of Quebec City," *International Socialist Review* No. 18 (June/July 2001).

120 Pascale Dufour and Janet Conway, "Emerging Visions of Another World? Tensions and Collaboration at the Quebec Social Forum," *Journal of World-Systems Research* Vol. XVI, No. 1 (2010), 34-35.

121 Shawn Ewald, "Solidarité: A Quebec Diary," Archives of Global Protests, (http://www.nadir.org/nadir/initiativ/agp/a20/diary.htm).

122 Bonhomme, "Québec, avril 2001."

123 Mona Josée Gagnon, "The labour movement and civil society: Reflections on the people's summit from quebec," *Just Labour* Vol. 1 (2002), 63. "The final debate with roving mikes at the People's Summit was also rather far from the positions of the labour organizations and of RQIC."

124 "NO FTAA! Another Americas Is Possible!" People's Summit of the Americas, Common Frontiers and RQIC, (http://www.web.net/comfront/teachin.htm).

125 Maude Barlow, "Summing up the Summit," Council of Canadians, April 25, 2001, (http://www.canadians.org/trade/issues/FTAA/Quebec/index.html).

126 MaRK, "Breaking The Barricades."

127 Dufour and Conway, "Emerging Visions," 35.

128 Cited in Dwyer, "Lessons of Quebec City."

129 Sarah Ferguson, "First Tear Gas, Now Bullets: Activists Weigh the Cost of Confrontation," *Village Voice*, July 17, 2001.

130 Dwyer, "Lessons of Quebec City." Ironically, the organizers who sought to avoid confrontation with police and politicians were employing nonviolent direct action tactics against participants to keep them from straying from the appointed route.

131 Ibid.

132 Ewald, "Solidarité: A Quebec Diary."

133 P. Jones, cited in MacKay, "Solidarity and symbolic protest."

134 Dwyer, "Lessons of Quebec City."

135 Roger Burbach, "Spotlight: Popular upheaval hits free trade meetings in Quebec City," Redress Information & Analysis, April 24, 2001, (http://www.redress.btinternet.co.uk/quebec.htm).

136 Dwyer, "Lessons of Quebec City."

137 Burbach, "Spotlight."

138 Aziz Choudry, "Finding Voice: Telling Our Own Stories," ZNet, December 20, 2002, (http://www.zcommunications.org/finding-voice-telling-our-own-stories-by-aziz-choudry).

139 Cited in ibid.
140 Burbach, "Spotlight."
141 Ferguson, "First Tear Gas, Now Bullets."
142 Dwyer, "Lessons of Quebec City."
143 Klein, *Fences and windows*, 239.
144 Klein, *Fences and windows*, 238.
145 Leo Panitch, "Violence as a Tool of Order and Change: The War on Terrorism and the Antiglobalization Movement," *Monthly Review* Vol. 54, No. 2 (June 2002).
146 Klein, *Fences and windows*, 238.

Chapter 9

1   Sherene Razack, *Dark threats and white knights: the Somalia Affair, peacekeeping, and the new imperialism* (Toronto: University of Toronto Press, 2004), 156.
2   James Ferguson, *The anti-politics machine: "Development," depoliticization, and bureaucratic power in Lesotho* (Minneapolis: University of Minnesota Press, 1994), 284.
3   Anders Fogh Rasmussen, "Speech," NATO Strategic Concept Seminar, March 4, 2010, Helsinki, Finland, (http://www.nato.int/cps/en/natolive/opinions_61891. htm).
4   "NGO's are not a soft power," Agency Co-ordinating Body for Afghan Relief, March 9, 2010, (http://www.afghanaid.org.uk/news.php/16/acbar_press_release_ ngos_are_not_a_soft_power_).
5   Jude Howell and Jeremy Lind, "Manufacturing Civil Society and the Limits of Legitimacy: Aid, Security and Civil Society after 9/11 in Afghanistan," *European Journal of Development Research* Vol. 21 (2009).
6   On 2004 elections, see Sonali Kolhatkar, "Elections in Afghanistan," *Z Magazine*, November 2004; On 2010 elections, see Alissa J. Rubin and Carlotta Gall, "Widespread Fraud Seen in Latest Afghan Elections," *New York Times*, September 24, 2010.
7   Mark Duffield, *Development, security and unending war: governing the world of peoples* (Cambridge, UK: Polity Press, 2007), 130-131.
8   Nosheen Ali, "Books vs bombs? Humanitarian development and the narrative of terror in Northern Pakistan," *Third World Quarterly* Vol. 31, No. 4 (2010), 553, 556.
9   Ibid.
10 "Counter-Insurgency Operations Manual (draft)," Canadian Forces, 2007, 17, 14, 21, 12, 129, 12.
11 Ibid., 43, 72, 50, 89.
12 Ibid., 140, 153, 78.
13 Ibid., 154, 81.
14 Ibid., 153, 144.
15 Anthony Fenton, "Propafghanda," ZNet, June 1, 2007, (http://www.zmag.org/ znet/viewArticle/15283).
16 "Counter-Insurgency Operations Manual," 26.
17 Ibid., 31. "...a modern military seeking to defend its parent or foster society, must be prepared to exploit modern media and deny its use to an opponent."
18 Ibid., 91, 82, 30, 149, 142, 26-27, 48.
19 Michael McClintock, *Instruments of statecraft: U.S. guerrilla warfare, counterinsurgency, and counter-terrorism, 1940-1990* (New York: Pantheon Books, 1992).

20   Noam Chomsky, *Hegemony or Survival: America's Quest for Global Dominance* (New York: Metropolitan Books, 2003), 173-186.

21   John Foster, "The disconnect between pipelines and transparency," *Globe and Mail*, September 3, 2010.

22   Sonali Kolhatkar, "Replacing one terrorist state with another," ZNet, October 6, 2003, (http://www.zcommunications.org/replacing-one-terrorist-state-with-another-by-sonali-kolhatkar).

23   "Program Framework for the Middle East (2007-2011)," Development & Peace, June 2007, 4-5.

24   "From 2001 donor countries put most of their money into the country through the UN and NGOs." Omar Zakhilwal and Jane Murphy Thomas, "Afghanistan: What kind of peace? The role of rural development in peacebuilding," in *The paradoxes of peacebuilding post-9/11*, ed. Stephen Baranyi (Vancouver: UBC Press, 2008); Tariq Ali, "Afghanistan: Mirage of the good war," *New Left Review* No. 50 (March/April 2008).

25   Howell and Lind, "Manufacturing Civil Society."

26   Zakhilwal and Murphy Thomas, "Afghanistan: What kind of peace?"

27   "Human Rights Dimension of Poverty in Afghanistan," United Nations Office of the High Commissioner for Human Rights, March 2010, 4.

28   Simon Jenkins, "It takes inane optimism to see victory in Afghanistan," *The Guardian*, August 8, 2007.

29   Antonio Giustozzi, "Afghanistan: transition without end: an analytical narrative on state-making," Crisis States Research Centre Working Paper No. 40, November 2008, 35, 42, 40.

30   Ali, "Mirage of the good war."

31   "The rise in the use of combat airpower in Afghanistan was driven both by a major increase in Taliban activity after 2005 and the lack of adequate NATO/ISAF and Afghan ground forces." Anthony H. Cordesman, "US Airpower in Iraq and Afghanistan: 2004-2007," Center for Strategic and International Studies, December 13, 2007, 1.

32   The soldiers were brought before military tribunals only when the magazines *Rolling Stone* and *Der Spiegel* published photos of the Kill Team's grim exploits. According to *Rolling Stone*, military investigators had refused to pursue information from one of the soldiers' family members about the killings. Mark Boal, "The Kill Team: How U.S. Soldiers in Afghanistan Murdered Innocent Civilians," *Rolling Stone*, March 11, 2011; See also Jerome Starkey, "Afghan death squads 'acting on foreign orders'," *The Independent*, May 16, 2008; "Getting away with murder? The impunity of international forces in Afghanistan," Amnesty International, February 26, 2009; Marc W. Herold, "Afghanistan: Terror, U.S. style," *Frontline*, March 11, 2009.

33   Sean Maloney, "Soldiers Not Peacekeepers: We are at war. Will Canada admit it?" *The Walrus*, March 2006.

34   Ian Smillie and Larry Minear, *The Charity of Nations: Humanitarian Action in a Calculating World* (Bloomfield, Conn.: Kumarian Press, 2004), 104.

35   Sippi Azarbaijani-Moghaddam, Mirwais Wardak, Idrees Zaman and Annabel Taylor, "Afghan Hearts, Afghan Minds: Exploring Afghan perceptions of civil-military relations," European Network of NGOs in Afghanistan (ENNA) and the British and Irish Agencies Afghanistan Group (BAAG), June 2008, 12.

36   "Aid in the Crosshairs: Civil-Military Relations in Afghanistan," CCIC Briefing Note, Canadian Council for International Cooperation, April 2009, 9.

37 Natalie Mychajlyszyn, "Afghanistan: Reconstruction and Development," Parliament of Canada, Political and Social Affairs Division, November 20, 2007.
38 Robert Burns, "Envoy laments weak US knowledge about Taliban," *Associated Press*, April 7, 2009.
39 "How Are We Doing in Afghanistan? Canadians Need to Know," Parliament of Canada, Standing Senate Committee on National Security and Defence, June 2008.
40 "Afghan leaders work with Cdn. development agency," CTV.ca News, May 3, 2006, (http://www.ctvbc.ctv.ca/servlet/an/plocal/CTVNews/20060503/afghanistan_meeting_060521/20060521/)
41 Maloney, "Soldiers Not Peacekeepers."
42 Meghann McNiff Lindholm, "Winning the Peace: In service of Afghanistan's most Vulnerable population," International and Maternal and Child Health Departments, Boston University School of Public Health, March 2008, 13.
43 Michiel Hofman, "Afghanistan: A Return to Humanitarian Action," Médecins sans frontières, March 11, 2010, 4.
44 Brian Hutchinson, "Part 1: The Long Road," *National Post*, June 24, 2011.
45 Hofman, "Return to Humanitarian Action," 4.
46 Ali, "Books vs bombs," 553-4.
47 Nipa Banerjee, "Too soon forgotten," *Ottawa Citizen*, August 15, 2008.
48 Hofman, "Return to Humanitarian Action," 6.
49 Matt Waldman, "Caught in the Conflict: Civilians and the international security strategy in Afghanistan," ActionAid, Afghanaid, CARE Afghanistan, Christian Aid, Cordaid, DACAAR, Interchurch Organisation for Development Cooperation, International Rescue Committee, Marie Stopes International, Oxfam International, Save the Children UK, April 2009, 17. Indicative of their actual neutrality, the report declined to comment critically on NATO's actions, but denounced the insurgents for their "unjustifiable" violations of international law.
50 Taylor Owen and Patrick Travers, "3D Vision: Can Canada reconcile its defence, diplomacy, and development objectives in Afghanistan?" *The Walrus*, July/August 2007.
51 Azarbaijani-Moghaddam, Wardak, Zaman and Taylor, "Afghan Hearts, Afghan Minds," 24-25, 35, 32.
52 Duane Bratt, "Canada's Role in Afghanistan: Dilemmas of the 3D's Approach: Is Defense, Diplomacy and Development Working?" *Development Forum* Vol. 1, No. 1 (Spring 2008), 5.
53 Lieutenant-Colonel Michel-Henri St-Louis, "The Strategic Advisory Team in Afghanistan - Part of the Canadian comprehensive approach to stability operations," *Canadian Military Journal* Vol. 9, No. 3 (2009).
54 "Canadian NGO's in Afghanistan," Canadian Council for International Cooperation, 1-2.
55 Development & Peace's objectives for the region are virtually indistinguishable from those of the Harper government: to "help pacify Iraq and Afghanistan"; to "help combat the rise of various forms of terrorism in the Middle East"; to "counter Iranian hegemonic tendencies in the Levant"; and to "help consolidate Lebanese political unity." "Program Framework (2007-2011)," 12.
56 Azarbaijani-Moghaddam, Wardak, Zaman and Taylor, "Afghan Hearts, Afghan Minds," 29.
57 St-Louis, "The Strategic Advisory Team in Afghanistan."
58 Lindholm, "Winning the Peace," 8.

59   Azarbaijani-Moghaddam, Wardak, Zaman and Taylor, "Afghan Hearts, Afghan Minds," 22.

60   Ibid., 29.

61   John A. Nagl, Dr. Andrew M. Exum and Ahmed A. Humayun, "A Pathway to Success in Afghanistan: The National Solidarity Program," Center for a New American Security, March 16, 2009, 1,4.

62   Hofman, "Return to Humanitarian Action," 6.

63   Zakhilwal and Murphy Thomas, "Afghanistan: What kind of peace?"

64   Gloria Galloway, "Economic growth, jobs are secret to Afghan win," *Globe and Mail*, October 6, 2009.

65   Mychajlyszyn, "Afghanistan: Reconstruction and Development."

66   Lara Olson, "Fighting for Humanitarian Space: NGOs in Afghanistan," *Journal of Military and Strategic Studies* Vol. 9, No. 1 (Fall 2006), 18.

67   Ali, "Mirage of the good war."

68   Howell and Lind, "Manufacturing Civil Society."

69   Jon Elmer, "Counterinsurgency Manual Shows Military's New Face," *Inter Press Service*, March 22, 2007.

70   Jeff Davis, "Feds' go-to team in Afghanistan part of new whole-of-government strategy," *Hill Times*, April 19, 2010.

71   Cited in Adolfo Gilly, "The Emerging 'Threat' of Radical Populism," *NACLA Report on the Americas* Vol. 39, No. 2 (September/October 2005).

72   Peter Hallward, *Damming the Flood: Haiti, Aristide, and the Politics of Containment* (London: Verso, 2007), 260.

73   "Chavannes Jean-Baptiste, Haiti, Sustainable Development," Goldman Environmental Prize, Islands and Island Nations 2005, (http://www.goldmanprize.org/node/112); Charles Arthur, "Latortue calls on UNIDO to come and help Haiti," AlterPresse, November 28, 2005, (http://www.alterpresse.org/spip.php?article3665).

74   Yves Engler, "The Politics of Money: Haiti and the Left," *Canadian Dimension*, November/December 2005.

75   Mark Schuller, "Killing with Kindness? Impacts of International Development Aid on Participation and Autonomy Within Women's NGOs in Post-Coup Haiti" (PhD diss., University of California, Santa Barbara, December 2007), 245.

76   "Haiti: Forcible eviction of peasant families, Artibonite," FIAN, May 18, 2008, (http://www.fian.org/cases/letter-campaigns/haiti-forcible-eviction-of-peasant-families-artibonite); Beverly Bell, "In Haiti, Land Reform as a Pillar of Reconstruction," Other Worlds, March 3, 2011, (http://www.otherworldsarepossible.org/another-haiti-possible/haiti-land-reform-pillar-reconstruction).

77   By 2010, Téléco the state-owned telephone company had been sold off. Nikolas Barry-Shaw, "Malign Neglect or Imperialism?" ZNet, October 24, 2005, (http://www.zcommunications.org/malign-neglect-or-imperialism-by-nik-barry-shaw).

78   "Haitians Displaced by Political Reprisals," Refugees International, August 4, 2004.

79   Repression reigned in Gonaives, Petit Goave and Cap Haitien as well as the countryside, but estimates for the number of victims in these cities and towns do not exist.

80   "Haiti: Breaking the cycle of violence: A last chance for Haiti?" Amnesty International, June 20, 2004, 19, 18.

81   "Haiti: Obliterating justice, overturning of sentences for Raboteau massacre by Supreme Court is a huge step backwards," Amnesty International, May 26, 2005.

82 Not all the rapes recorded by the study were politically motivated.
83 "South Africa to Become Permanent Home for Aristide," *Washington Post*, March 25, 2004; "Convicts Rule Haiti Town, Executions Plague Another," *Reuters*, March 24, 2004; Thomas M. Griffin, Esq., "Haiti Human Rights Investigation: November 11-21," Center for the Study of Human Rights, University of Miami Law School, 18-24.
84 "Summary Report of Phase II of National Lawyers Guild Delegation to Haiti: April 12-19 2004," National Lawyers Guild, 2.
85 "Breaking the cycle of violence," 31, 29.
86 Ibid., 25, 29.
87 Jeff Heinrich, "Canadian troops in Haiti accused of making death, rape threats," *Montreal Gazette*, September 2, 2006.
88 "Breaking the cycle of violence," 17.
89 Hallward, *Damming the Flood*, 154.
90 Cited in Richard Sanders, "NCHR-Haiti Reviews Coup Regime's 'First 45 Days': 'Blame-the-Victims' Approach Betrays Democracy and Human Rights," *Press For Conversion!* No. 61, September 2007.
91 Tom Reeves, "Haiti's Disappeared," ZNet, May 5, 2004, (http://www.zcommunications.org/haitis-disappeared-by-tom-reeves).
92 "Rapport: Regard sur la situation générale des droits humains en Haïti sous le gouvernement intérimaire, Février 2004-Juin 2006," Réseau national de defense des droits humains (RNDDH), July 2006, 2, authors' trans.
93 Reeves, "Haiti's Disappeared"; Sanders, "NCHR-Haiti Reviews Coup Regime's 'First 45 Days'."
94 Christian Heyne, Stuart Neatby and John Dimond-Gibson, "Theirry Fagart on La Scierie," HaitiAnalysis.com, February 22, 2007, (http://www.haitianalysis.com/2007/2/22/theirry-fagart-on-the-la-scierie-massacre).
95 "NCHR-Haiti Does Not Speak for the National Coalition for Haitian Rights (NCHR)," National Coalition for Haitian Rights, March 11, 2005.
96 Freddie Schrider, "Haiti Interview: with Anne Sosin, of Vidwa - Vizyon dwa Ayisyen," Rights Action, May 12, 2006, (http://www.rightsaction.org/articles/HAIT_Interview%20_with%20_VIDWA.htm).
97 "Breaking the cycle of violence," 19.
98 Reed Lindsay, "Haiti's government accused of brutal reign of terror: Aristide supporters say killings, prison used to repress them," *San Francisco Chronicle*, October 31, 2004.
99 Richard Sanders, "Lies without Borders: How CIDA-funded 'NGOs' waged a propaganda war to justify Haiti's 2004 coup," *Press for Conversion!* No. 63, November 2008.
100 Engler, "Politics of Money."
101 Sanders, "Lies Without Borders"; Parliament of Canada, Testimony of Marthe Lapierre, *Standing Committee on Foreign Affairs and International Trade*, March 25, 2004.
102 Richard Sanders, "CIDA-funded 'NGOs' Herald Aristide's 'Departure'," *Press for Conversion!* No. 63, November 2008.
103 Testimony of Marthe Lapierre, *Standing Committee*.
104 Development & Peace sweepingly declared all persons involved in the thousands of *organizations populaires* supporting Aristide to be, by definition, members of "armed gangs" and violent government-sponsored "militias." Robert Letendre, "Développement et Paix demande au gouvernement canadien de réclamer la

démission d'Aristide," December 16, 2003, (http://www.alterpresse.org/spip.
php?article954); "Le Gouvernement canadien doit cesser d'appuyer un président
contesté par son propre people," AQOCI, December 15, 2003, (http://www.aqoci.
qc.ca/media/commPress/comPress_2003-12-15.html), authors' trans.

105 Laura Flynn, Robert Roth and Leslie Fleming, "Report of the Haiti
     Accompaniment Project," Haiti Accompaniment Project, June 29-July 9, 2004.

106 Hallward, *Damming the Flood,* 277.

107 Robert Muggah, "Securing Haiti's Transition: Reviewing Human Insecurity and
     the Prospects for Disarmament, Demobilization, and Reintegration," Occasional
     Paper No. 14, Small Arms Survey, October 2005, 17; Griffin, "Haiti Human
     Rights Investigation," 34.

108 Muggah, "Securing Haiti's Transition," 17.

109 "Spoiling Security in Haiti," Latin America/Caribbean Report No. 13,
     International Crisis Group, May 31, 2005, 13-14.

110 Griffin, "Haiti Human Rights Investigation," 40.

111 Ibid., 53.

112 Ibid., 1.

113 Eirin Mobekk and Anne M. Street, "Disarmament, demobilisation and
     reintegration: What role should the EU play in Haiti?" ActionAid International,
     October 4, 2006, 3.

114 "Unfortunately, most Haitian human rights NGOs have not been [sic] spoken out
     about these abuses." "Spoiling Security in Haiti," 11.

115 Marc-Arthur Fils-Aimé, "Haiti - Pourquoi Aristide est-il parti à ce moment-là ?"
     Alterinfos, September 1, 2004, (http://www.alterinfos.org/spip.php?article1030).
     Fils-Aimé accused Noam Chomsky and other anti-imperialist critics of
     "encouraging" these violent practices through their criticism of the coup.

116 "Breaking the cycle of violence," 18.

117 Marthe Lapierre and Marie Marsolais, "Haïti : de l'insécurité à la terreur,"
     Concertation pour Haiti, October 22, 2004, (http://www.alterpresse.org/spip.
     php?article1834).

118 Tania Vachon, "Les victimes politiques de Jeanne," *Journal d'Alternatives,* October
     19, 2004.

119 Pierre Beaudet, "Haiti, the struggle continues," ZNet, October 2, 2005, (http://
     www.zcommunications.org/haiti-the-struggle-continues-by-pierre-beaudet).
     When challenged, Beaudet could not produce any evidence for this claim.

120 François L'Écuyer, "Haiti : Militarisation de la paix: La MINUSTAH complice ?"
     Journal d'Alternatives, June 29, 2005, authors' trans.

121 Muggah, "Securing Haiti's Transition," 12; "Martin says violence preventing
     democracy from taking hold in Haiti," *CBC News,* November 14, 2004, (http://
     www.cbc.ca/world/story/2004/11/14/haiti041114.html).

122 Lapierre and Marsolais, "Haïti : de l'insécurité à la terreur."

123 Lyn Duff, "'We won't be peaceful and let them kill us any longer': Bel Air
     interview with Roaean Baptiste," *San Francisco Bay View,* February 8, 2006.

124 "Many fear the HNP is increasingly a source of criminal violence, rather than
     an effective institution to reduce crime and guarantee public security." "Spoiling
     Security in Haiti," 10.

125 "We are under extreme pressure from the international community to use
     violence," General Augusto Heleno Ribeiro, MINUSTAH's military commander,
     told a congressional commission in Brazil. Tim Pelzer, "Canada plays big

role in propping up Haiti regime," ZNet, January 10, 2005, (http://www.zcommunications.org/canada-plays-big-role-in-propping-up-haiti-regime-by-tim-pelzer).

126 L'Écuyer, "Militarisation de la paix"; Beaudet, "Haiti, the struggle continues."

127 "Keeping the Peace in Haiti? An Assessment of the United Nations Stabilization Mission in Haiti Using Compliance with its Prescribed Mandate as a Barometer for Success," Harvard Law Student Advocates for Human Rights and Centro de Justiça Global, March 2005, 40.

128 Hallward, *Damming the Flood,* 299.

129 "Pettigrew's Painter speaks about Haitian Blood on the hands of the Canadian Government," HaitiAction.Net, June 17, 2005, (http://www.haitiaction.net/News/YE/6_17_5.html).

130 "Keeping the Peace in Haiti," 38.

131 Joseph Guyler Delva, "U.N. troops accused in deaths of Haiti residents," *Reuters,* July 15, 2005.

132 Marthe Lapierre and Suzanne Loiselle, "Haiti : Des ONGs canadiens craignent 'le pire'," Concertation pour Haïti, June 28, 2005, (http://www.alterpresse.org/spip.php?article2732).

133 Jean-Louis Roy and Marthe Lapierre, "An open letter concerning the climate of insecurity in Haiti and the mandate of MINUSTAH," Rights & Democracy and Concertation pour Haïti, January 27, 2006.

134 Hallward, *Damming the Flood,* 300.

135 A. Walter Dorn, "Intelligence-Led Peacekeeping: The United Nations Stabilization Mission in Haiti (MINUSTAH), 2006-07," *Intelligence and National Security* Vol. 24, No. 6 (December 2009).

136 Joseph Guyler Delva, "At least nine killed in Haitian slum raid," *Reuters,* December 22, 2006.

137 Estelle Zehler, "Le CECI en Haïti - Rendre possible un développement durable," *Le Devoir,* January 31, 2007.

138 "Haiti: Canada Can and Must Do More," Concertation pour Haïti, February 28, 2007, (http://www.dd-rd.ca/site/what_we_do/index.php?id=2107&subsection=themes&subsubsection=theme_documents).

139 Échec documents obtained from Kevin Skerrett, e-mail to the authors, March 24, 2008; "Rapport Annuel 2003-2004," AQOCI, June 2004, 16.

140 François L'Écuyer "Alternatives en Haïti," Alternatives.ca, February 6, 2006, (http://journal.alternatives.ca/fra/organisation/archives-419/projets-internationaux/article/alternatives-en-haiti).

141 Galloway, "Economic growth, jobs are secret to Afghan win."

142 John Hailey "Beyond the Formulaic: Process and Practice in South Asian NGOs," in *Participation: The New Tyranny?* eds. Bill Cooke and Uma Kothari (London: Zed Books, 2001), 99-100.

143 Ali, "Books vs bombs," 555.

144 Michael Ignatieff, "Nation-Building Lite," *New York Times Magazine,* July 28, 2002.

Chapter 10

1 Arundhati Roy, "Help that hinders," *Le Monde diplomatique English edition,* November 2004.

2   Zinn cited in Harvey J. Kaye, *Why do ruling classes fear history? and other questions* (New York: St. Martin's Press, 1996), 10.

3   "Poll findings: Canada and the world," *CBC News*, February 4, 2008, (http://www. cbc.ca/news/polls/canada-world/findings.html).

4   Firoze Manji, "Rights, Poverty and Development: NGOs and the Depoliticisation of Poverty," in *Development and Rights*, ed. Deborah Eade (Oxford: Oxfam UK, 1998), 1-2.

5   Michael Edwards, "Have NGOs 'made a difference?' From Manchester to Birmingham with an elephant in the room," *in Can NGOs make a difference? The challenge of development alternatives*, eds. Anthony Bebbington, Sam Hickey and Diana Mitlin (London: Zed Books, 2008), 47.

6   Ibid., 46. Of course, the whole point of CSR was to short-circuit pressures for deep changes to the systems and structures that perpetuate poverty, because these structures are also profitable for corporations.

7   Allison Van Rooy, "Good news! You may be out of a job: reflections on the past and future 50 years for Northern NGOs" in *Debating Development: NGOs and the future*, eds. Deborah Eade and Ernst Ligteringen (Oxford, England: Oxfam GB for Oxfam International, 2001), 38. The attempt to associate themselves with the anti-globalization movement and christen their organizations as the apostles of "global civil society" exemplifies such superficial efforts by development NGOs to adopt a new identity without changing their underlying nature.

8   Shotgun shack (pseudonym), "#29 Destroying Idealism," Stuff Expat Aid Workers Like, February 28, 2011, (http://stuffexpataidworkerslike.com/2011/02/28/29-destroying-idealism/).

9   Edwards, "Have NGOs 'made a difference'," 50.

10   Robert W. McChesney "Noam Chomsky and the Struggle Against Neoliberalism," *Monthly Review* Vol. 50, No. 11 (April 1999).

11   Barbara H. Chasin and Richard W. Franke, "Letters: The Kerala Difference," *New York Review of Books*, October 24, 1991.

12   Marie Trigona, "Argentine Factory Wins Legal Battle: FASINPAT Zanon Belongs to the People," Upside Down World, August 14, 2009, (http://upsidedownworld.org/main/content/view/2052/32/).

13   Manji, "Rights, Poverty and Development," 14.

14   James Ferguson, *The anti-politics machine: "Development," depoliticization, and bureaucratic power in Lesotho* (Minneapolis: University of Minnesota Press, 1994), 279, 285-86.

15   "Tools for Peace, a 'Made in Canada' Peace Movement," Peace and War in the 20th Century Web Project, McMaster University, (http://pw20c.mcmaster.ca/case-study/tools-peace-made-canada-peace-movement).

16   Ferguson, *The anti-politics machine*, 286.

17   Ibid., 285-86.

18   Karl Polanyi, *The great transformation: The political and economic origins of our time* (Boston: Beacon Press, 2001), 258.

19   Naomi Klein, *The shock doctrine: the rise of disaster capitalism* (Toronto: A.A. Knopf Canada, 2007), 29.

20   Todd Gordon, "Canadian Imperialism Stumbles Onward," The Bullet No. 433, November 29, 2010, (http://www.socialistproject.ca/bullet/433.php).

21   Klein, *The shock doctrine*, 29.

22   "U.S. Image Up Slightly, But Still Negative," Pew Global Attitudes Project, June 23, 2005, (http://www.pewglobal.org/2005/06/23/us-image-up-slightly-but-still-negative/).

23 Sean Maloney, "Helpful Fixer or Hired Gun? Why Canada Goes Overseas," *Policy Options* Vol. 22, No. 1 (January-February 2001), 59. Maloney here is speaking of military engagements.

24 Brian K. Murphy, "Canadian NGOs and the Politics of Participation," in *Conflicts of interest: Canada and the third world*, eds. Jamie Swift and Brian Tomlinson (Toronto: Between the Lines, 1991), 171-72.

25 We learned this first hand, through our experience in the anti-war movement and the anti-globalization movement. It is almost certain that Canada would have joined the "Coalition of the Willing" that invaded Iraq in 2003, if not for the hundreds of thousands of Canadians who marched against war and occupation. And if the Free Trade Agreement of the Americas (FTAA) is today a dead letter, it is in part due to the efforts of the anti-globalization movement in Canada.

26 Joegodson Vilmond and Paul Jackson, "Tout Moun Se Moun," Heart of Haiti, May 6, 2010, (http://heartofhaiti.wordpress.com/2010/05/06/).

27 Cited in Molly Kane, "Canada and Africa: Prospects for Internationalism and Common Cause," Keynote address at the Canadian Association of African Studies Annual Conference, May 3, 2008, University of Alberta, Edmonton, 6.

28 Herman E. Daly, "Uneconomic growth in theory and in fact," First Annual Feasta Lecture, April 26, 1999, Trinity College, Dublin, 13.

29 Todd Gordon, "Canada's imperialist project: Capital and power in Canadian foreign policy," *Briarpatch*, May/June 2010.

30 John S. Saul, *The next liberation struggle: Capitalism, Socialism and Democracy in Southern Africa* (Toronto: Between the Lines, 2005), 276.

31 Brian K. Murphy, "International NGOs and the challenge of modernity" in *Debating Development: NGOs and the future*, eds. Deborah Eade and Ernst Ligteringen (Oxford, England: Oxfam GB for Oxfam International, 2001), 81.

32 Roy, "Help that hinders." Roy is speaking here of activists in the South, but her point applies equally to the North.

33 Cited in Ian Anderson, "Northern NGO Advocacy: Perceptions, Reality, and the Challenge," in *Debating Development: NGOs and the future*, eds. Deborah Eade and Ernst Ligteringen (Oxford, England: Oxfam GB for Oxfam International, 2001), 222.

34 See Stephen McBride and Heather Whiteside, *Private affluence, public austerity: economic crisis and democratic malaise in Canada* (Halifax: Fernwood Publishing, 2011).

35 Anthony Barnett, "The Long and the Quick of Revolution," Open Democracy, December 16, 2011, (http://www.opendemocracy.net/anthony-barnett/long-and-quick-of-revolution).

36 McChesney, "Noam Chomsky."

Index

Nikolas Barry-Shaw is an independent researcher living in Montreal. He is a member of Haiti Action Montreal and the Canada-Haiti Action Network, but is better known for his stellar defensive play on the basketball court. He is working on his jumpshot.

Dru Oja Jay is a Montreal-based writer, organizer, and web developer. He is co-founder of the Media Co-op and a founding editor of the *Dominion*. Dru is a co-author of Offsetting Resistance (offsettingresistance.ca), a report about the effects of foundation funding on Environmental NGOs.

For the index, bibliography, listing of
solidarity groups across Canada and
other resources, visit:

www.pavedwithgoodintentions.ca